The
Princeton
Review®

LSAT®

DISCARDED

PREMIUM PREP

28th Edition

The Staff of The Princeton Review

PrincetonReview.com

| Penguin |

The Princeton Review
110 East 42nd Street, 7th Floor
New York, NY 10017
Email: editorialsupport@review.com

ISBN: 978-0-525-56922-0
ISSN: 2687-8747

Editor: Selena Coppock
Production Editors: Sarah Litt, Liz Dacey
Production Artist: Jennifer Chapman

Printed in the United States of America.

10 9 8 7 6 5 4 3 2 1

28th Edition

Editorial
Rob Franek, Editor-in-Chief
David Soto, Director of Content Development
Stephen Koch, Survey Manager
Deborah Weber, Director of Production
Gabriel Berlin, Production Design Manager
Selena Coppock, Managing Editor
Aaron Riccio, Senior Editor
Meave Shelton, Senior Editor
Chris Chimera, Editor
Eleanor Green, Editor
Orion McBean, Editor
Brian Saladino, Editor
Patricia Murphy, Editorial Assistant

Penguin Random House Publishing Team
Tom Russell, VP, Publisher
Alison Stoltzfus, Publishing Director
Amanda Yee, Associate Managing Editor
Ellen Reed, Production Manager
Suzanne Lee, Designer

Acknowledgments

A successful LSAT program is a collaborative effort. We'd like to thank Spencer LeDoux, Karen Hoover, and Jennifer Wooddell for their expertise, and most especially Chad Chasteen, the National Content Director of LSAT Programs for The Princeton Review. A special thank you to Shadna Wise for her persistence in making this improved version of LSAT Premium Prep a reality.

Special thanks to Adam Robinson, who conceived of and perfected the Joe Bloggs approach to standardized tests and many of the other successful techniques used by The Princeton Review.

Contents

Get More (Free) Content

at **PrincetonReview.com/prep**

As easy as 1·2·3

1 In addition to the 105 licensed LSAT questions in your book, your purchase of LSAT Premium Prep entitles you to 3 official LSAT practice tests which are stored online. Go to PrincetonReview.com/prep

2 You'll see a welcome page where you can register this book using the unique code that is printed on the inside, front cover of this book. That number starts with "321" and is your unique, single-use* code that will unlock REAL LSAT exams for you to practice on.

3 After placing this free order, you'll either be asked to log in or to answer a few simple questions in order to set up a new Princeton Review account.

4 Finally, click on the "Home" button, also found under "My Account" from the top toolbar. You're all set to access your valuable online content!

* Unique code cannot be resold and reused, so products purchased from secondhand market may not have access to 3 online, official, LSAT practice tests.

Once you've registered, you can...

- Access 3 real LSAT practice tests, plus detailed answers and explanations for every question and online score reports

- Plan your review sessions with study guides based on your schedule—4 weeks, 8 weeks, 12 weeks

- Read important opinions and advice about the LSAT and law school

- Access detailed profiles for hundreds of law schools to help you find the school that is right for you

- Find out more information about financial aid and scholarships to help you pay for law school

- Check out top 10 rankings including Best Professors, Most Competitive Students, Best Career Prospects, and tons more

Need to report a potential **content** issue?

Contact **EditorialSupport@review.com** and include:

- full title of the book
- ISBN
- page number

Need to report a **technical** issue?

Contact **TPRStudentTech@review.com** and provide:

- your full name
- email address used to register the book
- full book title and ISBN
- Operating system (Mac/PC) and browser (Firefox, Safari, etc.)

Look For These Icons Throughout The Book

 PREMIUM CONTENT

 ONLINE ARTICLES

 PROVEN TECHNIQUES

 APPLIED STRATEGIES

 DIGITAL TABLET

Chapter 1
General Information and Strategies

In this chapter, we're going to give you an overall preparation plan for the LSAT. Before we hit you with some test-taking techniques, we want to make sure that you know all that we know about the LSAT itself. We'll start with a few pages' worth of information on the test. Make sure you read all this information carefully so you'll know exactly what you're up against.

"CRACKING" THE LAW SCHOOL ADMISSION TEST

We hope you've bought this book at least a few months before the date of the LSAT you plan to take, so you'll have time to (a) actually follow the suggestions we make, including working on actual LSAT tests released by the Law School Admission Council (LSAC); (b) work through the specific problems in Chapters 2, 3, and 4 (at least twice); and (c) complete all three practice tests online.

If you've bought this book only a few weeks before the LSAT, read through this chapter and absorb the test-taking tips that we give you; then work through Chapters 2, 3, and 4. Finally, try to take at least one of the tests that you can find online in your Student Tools.

If you've bought (or are merely opening) this book for the first time only a few *days* before the LSAT, well, we admire your bravado. Take a complete test to see approximately what you would score on a real LSAT. If it's more than five or six points below where you want to be, consider skipping the test and taking it at a later date. The best way to improve your score dramatically is to work steadily on hundreds of problems throughout the course of a few months.

WHAT IS THE LSAT?

The LSAT is a tightly timed, multiple-choice test that almost always consists of 99 to 102 questions. By *tightly timed*, we mean that the test is designed so that the "average" test-taker (someone scoring around the fiftieth percentile) should not be able to comfortably complete all the questions in the time allotted. The LSAT also includes a 35-minute essay. The LSAT is required by every American Bar Association (ABA)-certified law school in the United States—if you want to go to a U.S. law school, you not only have to take the LSAT, but you must do pretty well on it to boot. (The ABA recently added a small asterisk to this policy and will now allow some schools to admit up to 10% of a class without the LSAT. Two schools have taken them up on the policy change as of the printing of this book. So, the LSAT is still king.)

The LSAC Website

You should go to **www.lsac.org** as soon as you decide to take the test. Spend some time exploring the website. On the site, you can sign up for the LSAT and for the Credential Assembly Service (CAS), you can order previously released LSATs, and you can obtain information about law schools and the application process. Some testing sites fill up very quickly, so you should register for a location as soon as possible.

WHEN IS THE LSAT GIVEN?

The LSAT is administered multiple times per year. In 2020, it will be administered in January, February, March, April, June, July, September, October, and November. Visit https://www.lsac.org/lsat/lsat-dates-deadlines-score-release-dates for information about specific dates. Some law schools will continue accepting applications until July for fall admission that same year. See Chapter 7 on Law School Admissions for more information about when and how to apply to law school.

HOW IMPORTANT IS THE LSAT?

The LSAT is not only required by every single ABA-approved U.S. law school, but also weighted very heavily in the admissions process. For many schools, it is weighted just as heavily as (or even more heavily than) your undergraduate grade point average (GPA). That's the number that you worked very hard on in college, remember? The fact that a four-hour, multiple-choice test—one that is a questionable indicator of how well you'll do in law school—is considered as important as your undergraduate performance over the course of four *years* seems unjust. If you feel this way, you are not alone, but there isn't anything you can do about it. Instead, you need to focus on reaching your highest potential score.

HOW IS THE LSAT SCORED?

The LSAT is scored on a scale of 120 to 180, with the median score being approximately 152. You need to get about 60 questions right (out of 99–102) to get that median score of 152, which means you need to bat about 60 percent. Very few people get a perfect score, mainly because the test is designed so that very few people can correctly answer all the questions, let alone do so in the time allotted.

Along with your LSAT score, you will receive a percentile ranking. This ranking compares your performance with that of everyone else who has taken the LSAT for the previous three years. Because a 152 is the median LSAT score, it would give you a percentile ranking of approximately 50. A score of 156 moves you up to a ranking of about 70. A 164 pulls you up to a ranking of 90. And any score over 167 puts you above 95 percent of all the LSAT takers.

As you can see, small numerical jumps (five points or so) can lead to a huge difference in percentile points. That means you're jumping over 20 percent of all test-takers if, on your first practice test, you score a 150, but on the real test, you score a 155. Small gains can net big results.

The following table summarizes the number of questions you can skip or miss and still reach your LSAT goal. Notice that 93 percent of those taking the test make *more* than 15 errors. Take this into consideration as you develop your strategy of exactly how many questions you intend to answer or skip.

Approximate Number of Errors (Out of 102)	LSAT Score	Percentile Rank
1	180	approx. 99+
4	175	approx. 99+
8	170	approx. 98+
15	165	approx. 93+
22	160	approx. 82+
32	155	approx. 66+
43	150	approx. 46+
52	145	approx. 27+
62	140	approx. 14+
69	135	approx. 5+

What Is a Good Score?

A good score on the LSAT is one that gets you into the law school you want to attend. Many people feel that they have to score at least a 160 to get into a "good" law school. That's pure myth. Remember, any ABA-approved law school has to meet very strict standards in terms of its teaching staff, library, and facilities. Most schools use the Socratic method to teach students basic law. Therefore, a student's fundamental law school experience can be very similar no matter where he or she goes to school—be it NYU or Quinnipiac Law School. Read through Chapter 7 for a much more comprehensive discussion of "good" scores and where to go to law school.

WHO'S RESPONSIBLE FOR THIS, ANYWAY?

The LSAT is brought to you by the wonderful folks at LSAC, based in Newtown, Pennsylvania. They work with the law schools and the ABA on many facets of the admissions process. You will register for the Credential Assembly Service (CAS), and that too is run by LSAC. See Chapter 7 for a full discussion of this alphabet soup.

WHAT EXACTLY IS ON THE LSAT?

The LSAT is made up of five 35-minute multiple-choice sections. Two of the five multiple-choice sections will be Logical Reasoning (Arguments), one will be Analytical Reasoning (Games), and one will be Reading Comprehension. The remaining section (which is usually one of the first three to be administered) will be an experimental section that will not count toward your score. During this section you will do 35 minutes of unpaid work for LSAC, allowing them to test out new types of questions on a representative audience. This experimental section can be Arguments, Games, or Reading Comprehension. The LSAT Writing Test is administered separately through the LSAC website and will not count toward your score, though the schools you apply to will receive a copy of it.

For instance, your LSAT could look as follows:

Section 1:   Games (35 minutes)

Section 2:   Experimental Reading Comprehension (35 minutes)

Section 3:   Arguments (35 minutes)

10-minute break

Section 4:   Reading Comprehension (35 minutes)

Section 5:   Arguments (35 minutes)

LSAT Writing Test—Administered online separately

As you can see, it's just over three hours of focused work. And because administrators check your ID and admissions ticket before the test begins, you can add another hour's worth of administrative mumbo-jumbo to that number. That's why we say that you should prepare very well for this test—so you have to take it only once.

The Structure of an Arguments Section

There will be two scored Arguments sections, each lasting 35 minutes, on your LSAT. Each section has between 24 and 26 questions. Tests in the past frequently attached two questions to one argument, but LSAC has more or less phased out this style of question; you will almost certainly see one question per argument. Typically, the argument passages are no more than three or four sentences in length, but they can still be very dense and every word is potentially important, making critical reading the key skill on this section. The arguments are not arranged in strict order of difficulty, although the questions near the beginning of a section are generally easier than those at the end.

The Structure of a Games Section

You will be given four "logic games" in a 35-minute section. Each game will have a setup and a set of conditions or clues that are attached to it. Then five to seven questions will ask you about various possible arrangements of the elements in the game. The four games are not arranged in order of difficulty.

The Structure of a Reading Comprehension Section

In this 35-minute section, you will be given four reading comprehension passages, of about 60 to 80 lines each. Three of the passages will be written by one author; the fourth will be a combination of two shorter passages from two different sources discussing the same general subject. In each case, between five and eight questions will be attached to each passage. This is probably something you're familiar with from the SAT, the ACT, or any of the other myriad standardized tests you might have taken over the years. These passages are not arranged in any order of difficulty.

WHAT DOES ALL THIS TEST?

According to the LSAC, "The LSAT is designed to measure skills that are considered essential for success in law school: the reading and comprehension of complex texts with accuracy and insight; the organization and management of information and the ability to draw reasonable inferences from it; the ability to think critically; and the analysis and evaluation of the reasoning and arguments of others." This means that the LSAT tests a few different things in order to measure your ability to think like a lawyer. The most important is your ability to read a passage or argument very closely and figure out what the author is and is not saying. On some questions, you'll have to figure out what the author is *implying*, and on others, what the author is *assuming to be true*. You'll find that the ability to read efficiently and identify the salient parts of a passage will be very useful on the test. Games test your ability to work with certain types of analytical reasoning, including conditional logic and logical deduction.

Online Articles
Go online for more opinions and advice on the LSAT.

The schools all have access to your complete undergraduate transcript, your academic and professional recommendations, and your essays. They could also ask for some of your undergraduate papers if they wanted to. However, all this reading would take too much time and cost admissions offices too much money—hence, they've got a neat little shortcut in the form of the LSAT. When they combine this with your undergraduate GPA, they generate your index, a number that allows them to quickly sort your application into one of a few preliminary piles to make the process of evaluating the increasing number of applications more efficient.

The overriding point is that whatever it's testing, your goal is to do as well as possible on the LSAT and take it only once. That's exactly what we're going to show you how to do.

GENERAL STRATEGIES

The following are several key things you should do when taking any multiple-choice test, especially the LSAT. Make sure you follow all of these mantras—they are the sum of more than 20 years' worth of our experience in researching and preparing hundreds of thousands of test-takers to take the LSAT.

Proven Techniques
Let's dive in!

Technique #1: Don't Rush

Most test-takers believe that the key to success on the LSAT is to go faster. Realize, though, that your *accuracy*—your likelihood of getting a question right when you work it—is also a key factor in how well you perform. Generally speaking, the faster you work, the lower your accuracy will be. What this means is that there's a pacing "sweet spot" somewhere between working as fast as you can and working as carefully as you can. Practice on real LSAT sections is important, because you need to find the proper balance for yourself on each of the three section types.

Don't let the tight timing of the LSAT scare you into rushing. Most test-takers do their best when they don't try to answer every question on every section.

On most LSAT questions, you'll find that you can eliminate two or three answer choices relatively easily. Some test-takers simply pick the best-looking answer from the remaining ones and move on; this is poor strategy. It's only once you're down to two or three remaining choices that the real work on this test begins. Don't let the clock force you into bad decisions.

Your mantra: *I will fight the urge to rush and will work more deliberately, making choices about where to concentrate my energies so I can answer questions more accurately and end up with a higher score.*

Technique #2: Select an Answer for Every Question

Unlike some tests, the LSAT has no penalty for guessing, meaning that no points are subtracted for wrong answers. Therefore, even if you don't get to work on every question in a section, you want to make sure to answer every question before time is called. Even if you do only 75 percent of the test, you'll get an average of five more questions correct by picking a "letter of the day" and selecting it for the remaining 25 percent of the questions. Make sure you watch the time carefully. Just to be safe, assume you'll need the last minute to guess on any unanswered questions. If you still have time remaining, you can change your answers on any questions you have time to work through.

Unanswered questions will display white ovals so you can easily spot which questions still need an answer.

This is a key concept that you should remember when you're taking the practice tests online and when you're taking previously administered LSATs for practice. Some people want to wait until test day to answer the questions they don't get to, thinking that they should see what their "real" score will be on practice tests. However, if you answer every question you didn't get to on your practice tests, you *are* finding out what your real score would be. And this will ensure that you won't forget to do it on test day—guessing could be the difference between a 159 and a 161, for instance.

Your mantra: *I will always remember to select an answer for every question, even the ones I don't get to, thereby getting a higher score.*

Technique #3: Use Process of Elimination

One solace (perhaps) on multiple-choice tests is the fact that all of the correct answers will be in front of you. Naturally, each will be camouflaged by four incorrect answers, some of which will look just as good as, and often better than, the credited response. But the fact remains that if you can clear away some of that distraction, you'll be left staring at the credited response. Don't expect that the correct answers will just leap off the page at you. They won't. In fact, those choices that leap off the page at you are often very attractive *wrong* answers. Remember that the test-writers have to be sure that they end up with a normal curve when they administer the test. Making a wrong answer look very appealing (with a small, camouflaged flaw) is a great way to make sure that not everyone gets all the questions right.

Process of Elimination (POE) may be a very different test-taking strategy from what you are used to. If you look first at the answer choices critically, with an eye toward trying to see what's wrong with them, you'll do better on almost any standardized test than by always trying to find the right answer. This is because, given enough time and creativity, you can justify the correctness of any answer choice that you find appealing. That skill may be useful in certain situations, but on the LSAT, creativity of that sort is dangerous.

Your mantra: *I will always try to eliminate answer choices using Process of Elimination, thereby increasing my chances on each question and getting a higher score.*

Technique #4: Be Prepared for Anything

You will be. Honest. You might not always feel that way, but you will be. True, you'll be nervous on test day, but a little nervousness is good because it can keep you focused. Just don't let this test psych you out. Remember that when you go into the test, you'll have worked through reams of LSAT problems and will be a lot more prepared than all the other people who didn't put in the same amount of work you did. You'll have absorbed all the techniques we've given you, and you'll be wise to all the tricks and traps that the LSAT can throw at you.

Therefore, don't let anything get to you. If the room is too cold for you, you've brought along a sweater. If the room gets too warm, you've layered your clothing and can get comfortable. If the people sitting next to you are scratching away loudly or coughing nervously, you've practiced working in an environment with similar distractions and know how to tune them out and stay focused on the task at hand. Relax and stay focused; you're prepared for anything.

No matter how prepared you are, it may happen that you lose focus temporarily. If you find yourself getting distracted or anxious, take a moment to focus and move on with confidence.

Your mantra: *I'm fully prepared to succeed. Nothing will distract me on test day. Nothing.*

Technique #5: Practice Consistently, on Real LSATs

This book gives you access to three real LSATs and about 105 practice questions licensed from the Law School Admission Council. The best way to prepare for the LSAT is by practicing on actual LSAT questions, and that is exactly what you will be doing throughout this book. Unfortunately, that's just the tip of the iceberg. You should order *at least* six additional recent, real tests from LSAC (**www.lsac.org** or 215-968-1001), if not more. Here's a rough study plan for you, over a two-month period.

Week 1:   Order at least six real LSATs (the most recent ones) from LSAC. Take one of the LSATs timed. Have a friend proctor the test for you so it's as legitimate as possible.

Week 2:   Work through the Arguments chapter in this book; redo the Arguments questions from the test you took in week 1. Take the first of the three practice LSATs available through your online Student Tools.

Week 3:   Work through the Games chapter in this book; redo the games from the test you took in week 1. Take the second of the three practice LSATs available through your online Student Tools.

> **Practice Material**
> If possible, order the 10 most recent real LSATs from LSAC—5 to take as full-length practice tests and 5 to use for timed section practice. If you're beginning the preparation process more than two months in advance, order more than 10 tests.

Week 4:   Work through the Reading Comprehension chapter in this book; redo the reading comprehension passages from the test you took in week 1 and from the practice LSAT you took in week 3.

Week 5: Read through Chapter 6 in this book for pacing tips. Work untimed through one of the real LSATs you've ordered from LSAC; time yourself on another one.

Week 6: Review your mistakes in the work you did in week 5 and review the Arguments, Games, and Reading Comprehension chapters in this book. Work the specific problems again. Take the third practice test available in your online Student Tools.

Week 7: Work untimed through another real LSAT you've ordered from LSAC; time yourself on another one (this should be the fifth real LSAT you've looked at).

Week 8: Review all the general techniques in this book, and review any specific problems you might be having in Arguments, Games, and Reading Comprehension. Read the Writing Sample chapter in this book (Chapter 5). Take one more real LSAT timed (using a friend as a proctor again) and analyze your performance thoroughly.

If you follow this plan, you'll be well prepared for the LSAT when it comes around. Don't worry too much about your scores on any of these practice tests. Your performance on the real LSAT should be a bit higher than any of your practice tests if you've been working steadily; you should be taking the LSAT at the culmination of your studies, and if you follow the plan above, you will be. Never let more than one or two days pass without looking at LSAT problems once you've started this workout. You'll waste valuable study time relearning techniques that you would have remembered if you had been practicing steadily. The best athletes and musicians are the ones who practice all the time—follow their example and you'll be totally prepared for the LSAT on test day.

Your mantra: *I will work steadily and consistently to master the techniques in this manual by practicing them on real LSATs found online in my Student Tools and additional, real LSATs that I've ordered from LSAC.*

Technique #6: Choose Your Battles

Not all questions on the LSAT are created equal, yet each is worth the same one raw point. Also, most test-takers won't have enough time to finish all the questions and still maintain a high level of accuracy. Clearly, it is in your best interest to choose carefully which questions to work through and, even more important, which questions to skip if you don't have time for them all. By knowing the test and by knowing yourself, you will be able to make good *predictions* about which questions are your friends and which are your enemies before you start working on them; this will save you time, prevent frustration, and ultimately get you more points.

Your mantra: *I will fight my urge to work aimlessly through all of the questions in the order they are presented. Instead, I will make good decisions based on sound reasoning that will ultimately get me the most points.*

Technique #7: Keep Your Stylus Moving

During almost any standardized test, you can find people who have just completely lost their concentration. Losing concentration can take different forms, but we've all experienced it—staring at the same question for too long, reading and rereading without really having anything sink in. Needless to say, you don't want to join this group of test zombies.

Using your stylus is a surprisingly easy way to stay focused and on task, and it can help to ensure that you're sticking with the method and visualizing information.

You should constantly be eliminating incorrect answers, highlighting, underlining, and then on scratch paper, using a pen to jot down key pieces of information, take notes, draw diagrams, and so on. Don't let the test take *you*—take the test on your own terms; attack the test. Keeping your stylus and pen involved in the process prevents you from getting passive and losing touch. Stay engaged, stay aggressive, and stay confident.

Your mantra: *I will use my stylus and pen to stay engaged with the test and maximize my performance.*

Summary:
General Strategies

Take the mantras from this chapter, learn them well, and—most important—use them. They are the distilled wisdom of much test-taking expertise. Here they are again.

- I will fight the urge to rush and will work more deliberately, making choices about where to concentrate my energies so I can answer questions more accurately and end up with a higher score.

- I will always remember to select an answer for every question, even the ones I don't get to, thereby getting a higher score.

- I will always try to eliminate answer choices using Process of Elimination, thereby increasing my chances on each question and getting a higher score.

- I'm fully prepared to succeed. Nothing will distract me on test day. Nothing.

- I will work steadily and consistently to master the techniques in this manual by practicing them on real LSAT questions found in this book and real, full LSATs found online.

- I will fight my urge to work aimlessly through all of the questions in the order they are presented. Instead, I will make good decisions based on sound reasoning that will ultimately get me the most points.

- I will use my stylus to stay engaged with the test and maximize my performance.

Got 'em? Good. Now let's break the test down section by section.

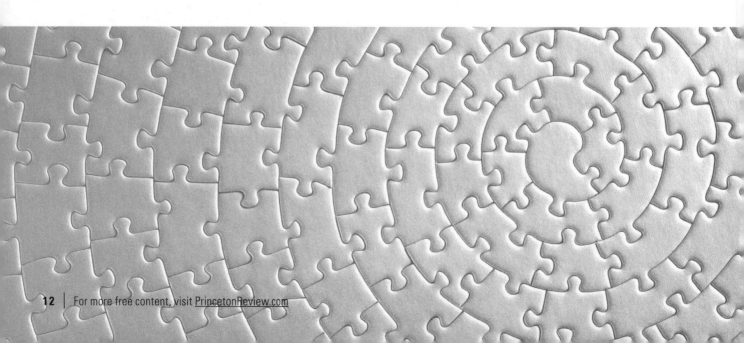

Chapter 2
Arguments

For better or for worse, Arguments (logical reasoning, in LSAT-speak) questions make up half of the LSAT. For the past six years, there have been between 50 and 52 Arguments questions on the LSAT. The good news is that if you can substantially increase your Arguments performance, you will take a major step toward achieving the LSAT score you need. How do you go about improving your Arguments score? Well, let's get right to it.

WHAT DOES THIS SECTION TEST?

The Arguments section of the LSAT tests a very useful skill: the ability to read closely and critically. It also tests your ability to break down an argument into parts, to identify flaws and methods of reasoning, and to find assumptions. Many arguments contain flaws that you have to identify to be able to get the correct answer. It's a minefield.

WHY IS THIS SECTION ON THE LSAT?

Of all the sections on the test, this section relates the most to your future career as a lawyer. Evaluating an argument for its completeness, identifying assumptions, and making sound inferences are skills that will be useful to you in law school and beyond.

Memorize the Instructions

If you took the advice in Chapter 1, you've already completed a real LSAT (preferably one from the last year or two), and you're familiar with the directions that appear at the start of each Arguments section. Here they are again.

> Directions: Each question in this section is based on reasoning presented in a brief passage. In answering questions, you should not make as-sumptions that are by common sense standards implausible, superfluous, or incompatible with the passage. For some questions, more than one of the choices could conceivably answer the question. However, you are to choose the **best** answer; that is, choose the response that most accurately and completely answers the question.

When you're ready to take the real LSAT, you'll no longer need to read these directions—in fact, doing so would be a waste of time—but you can learn something from them. First, they tell you that the tasks you will be asked to perform will revolve around the reasoning used in each argument. They also indirectly tell you how important it is to stick only to the information presented on the page and not to consider any outside information. As for the part about picking the best answer, we'll get to that a little later on—first you'll learn how to simply and efficiently understand the reasoning of an LSAT argument.

THE SECTION ITSELF

There are two scored Arguments sections on the LSAT. Each one will have between 24 and 26 questions, for a total of 48 to 52 Arguments questions. Some Arguments passages may be followed by two questions, although most Arguments passages, especially on recent tests, are followed by a single question. The fact that you are presented with 25 or so arguments to do in a 35-minute period indicates that the Arguments section is just as time intensive as the Games or Reading Comprehension sections.

ARGUMENTS: STRATEGIES

The next few pages cover the general strategies you need to use during the Arguments sections of the LSAT. These pages contain a few simple rules that you must take to heart. We've taught hundreds of thousands of students how to work through arguments, and these strategies reflect some of the wisdom we have gained in the process.

Always Read the Question First

Why should you read the question first? Because often the question will tell you what you should be looking for when you read the argument—whether it be the conclusion of the argument, a weak spot in the argument, how to diagram the argument, or something else. If you don't read the question until after you've read the argument, you'll often find that you need to read the argument *again*—wasting valuable time—after you learn what your task is. The question is a tip-off, so use it.

Your mantra: *I will always read the question first.*

Pay Close Attention

Reading arguments too quickly is a recipe for disaster, even though they appear short and simple. Usually the arguments are merely three sentences, and the answer choices are just a sentence each. But their brevity can be deceptive because very often complex ideas are presented in these sentences. The answers often hinge on whether you've read each word correctly, especially words like *not*, *but*, or *some*. You should be reading as closely as if you were deconstructing Shakespeare, not as if you were reading the latest thriller on the beach. Most arguments also follow predictable patterns of reasoning that can help you deconstruct the argument. Slow down, and pay attention!

Your mantra: *I will slow down and read the arguments and answer choices carefully the first time.*

Choose Your Battles

What should you do if you read the first sentence of the argument and you don't understand what it's saying? Should you read sentence two? The answer is NO. Sentence two is not there to help you understand sentence one. Neither is sentence three. Neither are the answer choices—the answer choices exist to generate a bell curve, not to get you a 180. If you start reading an argument and you are confused, make sure you're focused and read the first sentence again more slowly. If this still doesn't help, skip that question. There are 24 to 26 arguments in the section—do another one! It doesn't matter which Arguments questions you work on, just that you do good work on those that you choose to do. Focus your time first on the questions you know you can get right. The LSAT rewards confidence, so it's important to maintain a confident mindset. Working through difficult questions when there are other, more manageable ones still available is not good form. Yes, you will feel as if you should finish the argument once you've invested the time to read part of it. But trust us; you'll benefit by leaving it. Remember, you can always come back to it later when there are no better opportunities to get points. Just mark the argument so you can find it if you have time later. Come back to it when it won't affect other questions that are more likely to yield points. After all, that's what you're after—points.

Your mantra: *If I don't understand the first sentence of an argument and I don't see a common purpose or pattern of reasoning, I will skip to another argument that I do understand.*

Strategy
Each question is worth the same number of points, so focus first on questions you can do without struggling.

Answer Each Question as You Go

Each question will appear on screen individually. When you're confident you've found the credited response, select your answer and move to the next screen. If you aren't sure of an answer, be sure to flag the question so you can return to answer it later. If you don't think you'll have time to return to the question, POE as many choices as you can and select one from the remaining choices. Flag it so you can return if you have time and move on to the next screen.

Your mantra: *I will select answers to every question as I go and flag questions that I'm skipping for the time being.*

Here Are Your Arguments Mantras
I will always read the question first.

I will slow down and read the arguments and answer choices carefully the first time.

If I don't understand the first sentence of an argument and I don't see a common purpose or pattern of reasoning, I will skip to another argument that I do understand.

I will select answers to every question as I go and flag questions that I'm skipping for the time being.

I will take a 10-second break after every five or six arguments.

Breathe

Please remember to do this! You will of course feel some anxiety, but this energy can actually be helpful, because it keeps your adrenaline pumping and can help keep you focused. So, don't get so stressed out that you lose the thread of reality. After finishing five or six questions, take 10 seconds, close your eyes, and inhale deeply three times. You'll invest only about a minute over the course of the entire section for these short breaks, but the payback will be enormous because they will help you to stay focused and to avoid careless errors. Trust us on this one.

Your mantra: *I will take a 10-second break after every five or six arguments.*

ARGUMENTS: HOW TO READ THEM

The first step in tackling LSAT arguments is to make sure you're thinking critically when you read. Maybe you've had a lot of practice reading critically (philosophy and literature majors, please stand up) or maybe you haven't. Perhaps you haven't been in an academic environment for a while and you're out of practice. The next few pages show you on what level you need to be reading arguments to be able to answer questions correctly.

Argument Basics

So, what is an argument? When people hear the term *argument,* they often think of a debate between two people, with each party trying to advance his or her own view. People often are emotionally invested in an argument, and thus arguments can become heated quickly. On the LSAT, it's crucial that you don't develop such an emotional response to the information.

Here's a definition of arguments that applies to the LSAT: "An argument is the *reasoned presentation* of *an idea* that is *supported by evidence* that is *assumed to be true.*" Notice that we've italicized certain words for emphasis. We explain these phrases in detail below.

Reasoned presentation: The author of an LSAT argument has organized the information presented according to a predictable, logical structure, however flawed the end result may be.

An idea: The conclusion of the author's argument is really nothing more than an idea. Just because it's on the LSAT doesn't mean it's valid. In fact, the only way to evaluate the validity of an author's conclusion is to examine the evidence in support of it and decide whether the author makes any leaps of logic between the evidence and his or her conclusion.

Supported by evidence: All of the arguments on the test in which an author is advancing a conclusion—there are a few exceptions to this, which we'll refer to as "passages" rather than "arguments"—have some kind of evidence presented in support of the author's conclusion.

> ## Arguments and Flaws
>
> Keep in mind that it is generally difficult to make an airtight case for a point of view if you have only three or four sentences in which to get that point across. Yet that's exactly the format of an argument on the LSAT. What can you take from that? The vast majority of the arguments you run across on this test are flawed in some way. That's a valuable thing to know because it reminds you to maintain a critical stance when evaluating these arguments. As you read an argument, always pay attention to *what* the author is trying to persuade you of, what evidence the author is using to make the case, and where the author has lapsed in making a solid connection. Developing an eye for the common purpose and reasoning patterns will also help you evaluate arguments more quickly and efficiently.

Assumed to be true: On the LSAT, you are not allowed to question the validity of the *evidence* presented in support of a claim. In other words, you have to assume that whatever information the author presents as evidence is, in fact, true, even when the evidence includes arguable statements. You can question the validity of the *argument* by evaluating whether the evidence alone is able to support the conclusion without making a large leap.

Your Goal: Conclusions and Premises

Remember that arguments are constructed to persuade you of the author's idea. Thus, you should always get a firm grasp on the argument's conclusion (whether or not you think it's valid) and how the arguer structured the evidence to reach that conclusion. If you understand the conclusion and the reasoning behind it, you've won half the battle because most of the questions in Arguments revolve around the hows and whys of the arguer's reasoning.

Sample Argument #1

Let's start with something fairly simple. Although this argument is simple, its structure is similar to that of many real LSAT arguments that you will see. Here it is.

> Serena has to move to Kentucky. She lost the lease on her New York apartment, and her company is moving to Kentucky.

Okay, now what? You've got to make sure you understand the following things about this argument:

- the point that the author is trying to make (we'll call this the author's conclusion)
- the evidence or reasons the author presents in support of his or her argument (we'll refer to these as the author's premises)

If you are able to identify the conclusion and premises, you are well on your way to being able to tackle an LSAT question about the argument. After reading the argument again, try to identify the following elements:

- author's conclusion
- author's premises

Careful!
Though a great starting point, signal words can sometimes be a trap. Not all signal words introduce a conclusion.

What's the author's conclusion?   When looking for the author's conclusion, try to figure out what the author is attempting to persuade us of. Ultimately, the author is trying to persuade you that Serena has to move to Kentucky. The rest of the information (about the lease and her company's move) is given in support of that conclusion. Often, the author's conclusion is signaled by words such as *thus*, *therefore*, or *so*, or is a recommendation, a prediction, or an explanation of the evidence presented.

What if I didn't properly identify the author's conclusion?   Getting the author's conclusion and understanding the reasoning behind it is crucial to tackling an argument effectively and performing whatever task the question demands of you. But let's face it, not every argument will be as simplistic as this one. It would be a good idea to have a technique to use when you aren't sure of an argument's conclusion. This technique is called the Why Test.

The Why Test

The Why Test should be applied to verify that you have found the author's conclusion. Let's take the previous example and see how it works. If you had said that the author's conclusion was that she had lost her lease, the next step is to ask *Why did the author lose her lease?* There is absolutely no evidence in the argument to answer that question. Therefore, that statement can't be the author's actual conclusion.

Now, let's say that you had chosen the fact that the author's company was moving to Kentucky as the proper conclusion. You would ask *Why is the author's company moving to Kentucky?* Once again, the argument does not answer that question. But notice what happens when you use the Why Test on the author's actual conclusion: that she has to move to Kentucky. *Why does she have to move to Kentucky?* Now you have some answers: because she lost the lease on her New York apartment, and because her company is moving to Kentucky. In this case, the Why Test works perfectly. You have identified the author's conclusion.

What are the author's premises?   So, why does the author think that Serena has to move to Kentucky? (1) She lost the lease on her apartment in New York, and (2) her company is relocating to Kentucky. Each of these is a premise in support of the conclusion. Now you know the author's conclusion and the premises behind it. This should be the first step you take in analyzing almost every argument on the LSAT. After taking a look at this argument, however, you might be thinking that Serena may not have thought this whole thing through. After all, couldn't she get another apartment in New York? And does she really have to stick with this company even though it's moving halfway across the country? If you're asking these kinds of questions, good! Hold onto those thoughts for another few minutes—we'll come back to these questions soon.

> Use the Why Test to determine whether you've properly identified the conclusion of the argument.

Sample Argument #2

Now let's take a look at another argument that deals with a slightly more complicated subject, one that's closer to what you'll see on the LSAT.

> The mayor of the town of Shasta sent a letter to the townspeople instructing them to burn less wood. A few weeks after the letter was delivered, there was a noticeable decrease in the amount of wood the townspeople of Shasta were burning on a daily basis. Therefore, it is obvious that the letter was successful in helping the mayor achieve his goal.

Now, let's identify the conclusion and premises in this argument.

Later we'll see that this is an argument with a "causal" flaw.

What's the author's conclusion?   The author is trying to persuade you that the letter was, in fact, the only cause of the townspeople's burning less wood. Notice the phrase "it is obvious that," which indicates that a point is being made and that the point is debatable. Is there enough information preceding this statement to completely back it up? Can two short sentences persuade us that there is an "obvious" conclusion that you should come to when evaluating this information? Not if you're thinking about the issue critically and thinking about some of the other possible causes for this effect.

What are the author's premises?   Use the Why Test here. If you've identified the right conclusion, asking "why" will provide the author's premises. *Why did the author conclude that the letter was successful in getting the townspeople of Shasta to burn less wood?* The author's premises are that the mayor sent a letter, and that the townspeople started burning less wood a few weeks later.

What's missing?   Remember when we said that you need to be critical and ask questions? Well, here's your chance. Arguments on the LSAT are full of holes, so be skeptical and poke holes in this author's reasoning.

What do you think about the author's conclusion that the letter was responsible for helping the mayor achieve his or her goal? In evaluating the author's argument, you should start with his or her premises—they're the only facts that you have to go on. The purpose of this argument is to simply interpret the one piece of evidence given. The mayor sends a letter to the townspeople, urging them to burn less wood, and a few weeks later, the townspeople start to burn less wood. (Remember that you have to accept these facts at face value. You have to accept that, for instance, there was in fact a noticeable decrease in the amount of wood being burned in Shasta.) Now, do you know *for certain* that the mayor's letter is what caused the decline in burning? Couldn't it have been something else? This author evidently doesn't think so—he or she thinks that there couldn't be any other factors involved and this is the only way to interpret the evidence. You could probably come up with a hundred possible reasons that might explain why the residents of Shasta started to burn less wood, other than the mayor's letter. (For example, the price of firewood could have doubled right before the decline in burning.) But by asking these questions, you know the important thing—that this author *assumes* that there wasn't any other cause.

What is an assumption?   An assumption, both in life and on the LSAT, is a leap of logic that we make to get from one piece of information to another. For instance, if you see a friend of yours wearing a yellow shirt and you conclude that your friend likes yellow, you would be making the following assumptions:

- Your friend isn't wearing the yellow shirt only as his or her work uniform.
- Your friend was not threatened by a madman who said that, unless he or she wore a yellow shirt for one month straight, his or her house would be burned to the ground.
- Your friend was not down to his or her last clean shirt, the one that he or she wears only when everything else needs to be washed.
- Your friend…

You get the point. You make these assumptions because you've seen a particular effect (in this case, your friend wearing a yellow shirt), and you think you've identified the proper cause (in this case, that your friend likes yellow and not that he or she is wearing a uniform or needs to do some laundry). Then, whether or not it's true, you *assume a connection* between the cause and the effect. You've made a leap of logic.

Assumptions on the LSAT

The assumptions made in the arguments on the LSAT are also leaps of logic. Sometimes, the logic is so simple that it looks as if the author has actually stated it but really hasn't. The author's assumption is never explicitly stated in the passage. By definition, it is always unstated.

> In LSAT terms, an assumption is an unstated premise that is required in order to make an argument's conclusion valid.

Go back to the wood-burning argument. Here, you have an observed effect: the townspeople of Shasta burning less wood. You have a possible cause: the mayor's letter. On the LSAT, the arguer will often try to make a direct connection between these two pieces of information—in this case, that the letter *caused* the wood-burning decrease.

However, as you've seen from the above example, you're also assuming the following:

- that the decrease in the burning of wood was not because of an increase in the price of wood
- that the town didn't experience unexpectedly warm temperatures, lessening the demand for wood as a heat source
- that the townspeople actually received and read the letter the mayor sent out
- that…

Once again, you get the point. The author actually made many assumptions when she made the leap of logic from the letter being sent and people burning less wood on one hand, and the conclusion that the letter was successful on the other hand. They all revolve around two basic assumptions: that the letter could have caused the decline in firewood use, and that no other factor was the cause of the decline.

This Is All Really Exciting, But…

You want to get to the answer choices, don't you? Well, we will—soon. But what has been the point of the last several pages? To show you how to read the argument itself in a critical way. This will help you immensely in evaluating the answer choices because you will already understand the author's conclusion and the premises on which it is based, and you'll also have spotted any potential problems with the argument. This means that many times you'll have the answer to the question in mind before you read any answer choices, and you can simply eliminate any that don't match.

The reason we want you to stop and think before going to the answer choices is that the answer choices are not there to help you get a good score on the LSAT. Four of the answer choices are going to be wrong, and their purpose is to distract you from the "best" answer choice. True, many times this "best" choice will merely be the least sketchy of five sketchy answer choices. Nonetheless, the more work you put into analyzing the argument before reading the choices, the better your chance of eliminating the four distractors and choosing the "credited response."

Why do we hammer this into you, anyway? Because you may or may not have had a lot of practice reading critically. You're not simply reading for pleasure, or reading the newspaper or a menu at a restaurant—here, you've got to focus your attention on these short paragraphs. Read LSAT arguments critically, as if you're reading a contract you're about to sign. Don't just casually glance over them so you can quickly get to the answer choices. You'll end up spending more time with the answer choices trying to determine the credited response if you don't have a solid understanding of the author's conclusion and how she got there. The single most important thing to read extremely carefully is the author's conclusion, whenever it is explicitly stated. Take the time to think critically about the argument, to break it down, and to be sure that you can paraphrase what the author is saying and articulate any flaws in his or her reasoning. Doing this will actually save you time by enabling you to evaluate the answer choices more quickly and efficiently.

WORKING ARGUMENTS: A STEP-BY-STEP PROCESS

We have developed a four-step process for working LSAT arguments. It is a very simple process that will keep you on task and increase your odds of success if you follow it for every argument that you do. Here are the steps.

> Step 1: Assess the question
> Step 2: Analyze the argument
> Step 3: Act
> Step 4: Answer using Process of Elimination

Now let's look at these steps in more detail.

Step 1: Assess the question   Sound familiar? This is one of your mantras. Reading the question first will tip you off about what you need to look for in the argument. Don't waste time reading the argument before you know how you will need to evaluate it for that particular question. If you don't know what your task is, you are unlikely to perform it effectively.

Step 2: Analyze the argument   This is what we've been practicing for the last few pages. You've got to read the argument *critically*, looking for the author's conclusion and the evidence used to support it. When the author's conclusion is explicitly stated, use the underline tool to make a note of it. If necessary, jot down short, simple paraphrases of the premises and any flaws you found in the argument on your scratch paper.

Analyze
Some question types don't require you to find the conclusion, premises, and flaws. We'll cover these types later in the chapter.

To find flaws, you should keep your eyes open for any shifts in the author's language or gaps in the argument. Look for common purpose and reasoning patterns. Remember that the author's conclusion is reached using *only* the information on the page in front of you, so any gaps in the language or in the evidence indicate problems with the argument. You'll always want to be sure that you're reading critically and articulating the parts of the argument (both stated and unstated) in your own words. This will take a few extra seconds, but the investment will more than pay off by saving you loads of time in dealing with the answer choices.

Step 3: Act The particular strategy you'll use to answer a given question will be determined by the type of question being asked (one more reason to start by focusing on the question task). Each question task will have different criteria for what constitutes an acceptable answer. You'll want to think about that before going to the choices.

The test-writers rely on the fact that the people who are taking the LSAT feel pressured to get through all the questions quickly. Many answer choices will seem appealing if you don't have a clear idea of what you're looking for before you start reading through them. The best way to keep yourself from falling into this trap is to predict what the right answer will say or do before you even look at the choices, and write that prediction down on your scratch paper!

Step 4: Answer using Process of Elimination

We first mentioned Process of Elimination (POE) in Chapter 1. It's a key to success on every section of the LSAT, especially Arguments and Reading Comprehension.

THE ELEVEN TYPES OF ARGUMENTS QUESTIONS

Almost every question in the Arguments section of the exam will fit into one of the following eleven categories: Main Point, Necessary Assumption, Sufficient Assumption, Weaken, Strengthen, Resolve/Explain, Inference, Reasoning, Flaw, Principle, and Parallel-the-Reasoning. Each of these types of questions has its own unique characteristics, which we'll cover in the following pages. At the end of each question type, you'll find a chart summarizing the most important things to remember. The chart will be repeated in full at the end of the chapter for all eleven categories.

Process of Elimination

Most people look for the best answer and, in the process, end up falling for answer choices that are designed to look appealing but actually contain artfully concealed flaws. The part that looks good looks *really* good, and the little bit that's wrong blends right into the background if you're not reading carefully and critically. The "best" answer on a tricky question won't necessarily sound very good at all. That's why the question is difficult. But if you're keenly attuned to getting rid of those choices with identifiable flaws, you'll be left with one that wasn't appealing, but *didn't have anything wrong with it*. And that's the winner because it's the "best" one of a group of flawed answers. If you can find a reason to eliminate a choice, you've just improved your chances of getting the question right. So be aggressive about finding the flaws in answer choices that will allow you to eliminate them. At the same time, don't eliminate choices that you don't understand or that don't have a distinct problem.

So, Are You Ready?

We're finally going to give you an entire LSAT argument. First, we'll give you the whole argument, and you can approach it by using the process we just outlined. Then, you can compare your results against ours. Finally, after each Argument "lesson," we'll explain some extra techniques that you'll want to absorb. That way, by the end of Lesson 11, you'll know everything you need to answer any Argument question the LSAT might throw at you. This first lesson is about Main Point questions. Good luck!

LESSON 1: MAIN POINT QUESTIONS

These questions are relatively rare, but because finding the main point is essential to answering most other Arguments questions correctly, it's a good place to start.

The Argument

1. Mayor McKinney's policies have often been criticized on the grounds that they benefit only wealthy city residents, but that is not a fair evaluation. Some of McKinney's policies have clearly benefited the city's less affluent residents. McKinney actively supported last year's proposal to lower the city's high property taxes. Because of this tax decrease, more development is taking place in the city, helping to end the housing shortage and stabilize the rents in the city.

    Which one of the following most accurately expresses the main conclusion of the argument?

    (A) It is impossible to tell whether McKinney is more committed to the interests of the wealthy than to those of the poor.

    (B) McKinney's policies have often been criticized for benefiting only wealthy city residents.

    (C) The decrease in property taxes that McKinney supported caused more development to take place in the city.

    (D) The criticism that McKinney's policies benefit only the wealthy is unjustified.

    (E) McKinney's efforts helped end the housing shortage and stabilize the rents in the city.

PrepTest 45, Section 4, Question 1

Here's How to Crack It

Step 1: Assess the question

Did you remember to read the question before you started reading the argument? Here it is again.

> Which one of the following most accurately expresses the main conclusion of the argument?

This question asks for the main conclusion of the argument, so analyze the argument with the goal of identifying the author's conclusion.

Step 2: Analyze the argument

Read the argument. Read it slowly enough that you maintain a critical stance and identify the author's conclusion and premises. Here it is again.

> Mayor McKinney's policies have often been criticized on the grounds that they benefit only wealthy city residents, but that is not a fair evaluation. Some of McKinney's policies have clearly benefited the city's less affluent residents. McKinney actively supported last year's proposal to lower the city's high property taxes. Because of this tax decrease, more development is taking place in the city, helping to end the housing shortage and stabilize the rents in the city.

Keep in mind that you need to find only the conclusion and premises when you're working on a Main Point question. Finding assumptions won't help you, so don't waste precious time trying to figure them out. Here's what we found for the author's conclusion and premises.

- Author's conclusion: *Mayor McKinney's policies have often been criticized on the grounds that they benefit only wealthy city residents, but that is not a fair evaluation.*
- Author's premises: *The mayor's policies have lowered property taxes which have in turn increased development and decreased the housing shortage, which have stabilized rents.*

If you had trouble identifying the conclusion, try thinking about why the author wrote this argument. The purpose of the argument is to disagree with someone else's conclusion—those criticizing the mayor's policies as benefiting only the wealthy. Therefore, the conclusion is the opposite of the criticism. The purpose of an argument—whether it is intended to interpret facts, solve a problem, or disagree with a position—is intimately connected to the main point.

Remember to use the Why Test to check the author's conclusion if you're not sure. Let's go to Step 3.

Step 3: Act

Now that you've broken down the argument and have all the pieces clear in your mind, it's time to make sure that you approach the answer choices knowing what it is that you've been asked to find. If you're not sure about exactly what you're supposed to be looking for, you will be much more likely to fall for one of the appealing trap answer choices designed to distract you from the credited

Assess
Always read
the question first.

Hint:
Always underline
conclusion of an argument
so that you can
quickly refer back to it.

response. Just to be sure you're ready for the next step, we said that the author's conclusion was that it's not fair to evaluate the mayor's policies on the grounds that they benefit the wealthy.

> The credited response to a Main Point question will articulate the author's conclusion.

Step 4: Answer using Process of Elimination   Okay, now let's look at each of the answer choices. Your goal is to eliminate four of the choices by removing anything that doesn't match the paraphrase of the author's main point. If any part of it doesn't fit, the whole thing is wrong and you need to get rid of it.

(A)   It is impossible to tell whether McKinney is more committed to the interests of the wealthy than to those of the poor.

Does this sound like the author's conclusion? No, the conclusion is that the criticism is not fair, not that it's impossible to tell whose interests the mayor is more committed to. Eliminate it.

(B)   McKinney's policies have often been criticized for benefiting only wealthy city residents.

Is this the author's conclusion? No, this is a paraphrase of the position that the author is disagreeing with. Eliminate it.

(C)   The decrease in property taxes that McKinney supported caused more development to take place in the city.

This may look pretty good if you expect the conclusion to be the last sentence of the argument—a common trap answer. This is actually evidence for why the criticism is unfair. Eliminate it.

(D)   The criticism that McKinney's policies benefit only the wealthy is unjustified.

Does this sound like the author's conclusion? Yes. Keep it.

(E)   McKinney's efforts helped end the housing shortage and stabilize the rents in the city.

This choice has the same problem as (C). This answer is another paraphrase of a premise in the argument, not the conclusion. Eliminate it. Well, it looks like you've got (D), the right answer here. Nice job!

Arguments Technique: Use Process of Elimination

Let's go into a bit more depth with Process of Elimination. Choices (A), (B), (C), and (E) above all presented you with specific reasons for eliminating them. Following are ways in which you can analyze answer choices to see if you can eliminate them.

Make Sure the Answer Is Relevant

LSAT arguments have very specific limits; the author of an argument stays within the argument's scope in reaching his conclusion. Anything else is not relevant. When you read an argument, you must pretend that you know only what is written on the page in front of you. Never assume anything else. Thus, any answer choice that is outside the scope of the argument can be eliminated. You did this for (A) in the last example. Many times, answer choices will be so general that they are no longer relevant. Arguments are usually about specific things—such as Mayor McKinney's policies benefiting the wealthy—as opposed to "being more committed." The ultimate deciding factor about what is or is not within the scope of the argument is the *exact wording* of the conclusion.

Watch Out for Extreme Language

Pay attention to the wording of the answer choices. For some question types (most notably Main Point and Inference), extreme, absolute language (*never, must, exactly, cannot, always, only*) tends to be wrong, and choices with extreme language can often be eliminated. Keep in mind, however, that an argument that uses strong language can support an *equally* strong answer choice. You should always note extreme language anywhere—in the passage, the question, or the answer choices—as it will frequently play an important role.

Careful!
Think of extreme language as a red flag. You should always check it against what was specified in the passage before using it to eliminate an answer choice.

Beware of Premises

Make sure that you have clearly identified the conclusion using the Why Test so you don't mistakenly choose an answer choice that is a paraphrase of a premise. You saw this in (B), (C), and (E) in the last example.

> Arguments Technique:
> Watch Out for the Word *Conclusion*
> You'll notice that we've labeled these first questions "Main Point" questions. Your task on these questions is to determine the author's conclusion. You might be wondering why we don't just call them *conclusion* questions. Well, there is a method to our madness. You'll find that words such as "conclusion" or "concluded" may appear in other types of questions as well. You'll see this when we get to Lesson 7 on Inference questions.

Summary: Cracking Main Point Questions

Check out the chart below for some quick tips on Main Point questions. The left column of the chart shows some of the ways in which the LSAT folks will ask you to find the conclusion. The right column is a brief summary of the techniques you should use when approaching Main Point questions.

Sample Question Phrasings	Act
What is the author's main point? *The main conclusion drawn in the author's argument is that…* *The argument is structured to lead to which one of the following conclusions?*	• Identify the conclusion and premises. • Use the Why Test, and then match your conclusion against the five answer choices. • Be careful not to fall for a premise in the answer choices. • When down to two choices, look for extreme wording and relevance to eliminate one choice and be left with the credited response.

LESSON 2: NECESSARY ASSUMPTION QUESTIONS

Assumption questions ask you to pick the choice that fills a gap in the author's reasoning. A *necessary* assumption is something that the argument relies on but doesn't state—something that *needs* to be true in order for the argument to work.

The Argument

2. In addition to the labor and materials used to make wine, the reputation of the vineyard where the grapes originate plays a role in determining the price of the finished wine. Therefore, an expensive wine is not always a good wine.

   Which one of the following is an assumption on which the argument depends?

   (A) The price of a bottle of wine should be a reflection of the wine's quality.

   (B) Price is never an accurate indication of the quality of a bottle of wine.

   (C) The reputation of a vineyard does not always indicate the quality of its wines.

   (D) The reputation of a vineyard generally plays a greater role than the quality of its grapes in determining its wines' prices.

   (E) Wines produced by lesser-known vineyards generally are priced to reflect accurately the wines' quality.

   (A)

   (C)

   (D)

   (E)

   PrepTest 44, Section 2, Question 9

Here's How to Crack It

Step 1: Assess the question   Here's the question again.

   Which one of the following is an assumption on which the argument depends?

It includes not only the word *assumption*, but also the word *depend*. This sort of language—*relies on*, *depends on*, *requires*—is a sure sign of a Necessary Assumption question.

Step 2: Analyze the argument   On a Necessary Assumption question, you analyze the argument by finding its conclusion and premises, as before. But there's something else you need to do. If possible, you need to find what's wrong with the argument before you go to the answer choices. Do this by maintaining a skeptical attitude and looking for differences in wording in the conclusion and premises.

If Assumed
Sometimes a question will ask you, "Which of the following, if assumed, allows the conclusion to be properly drawn?" This is a Sufficient Assumption question, not a Necessary Assumption question. We'll discuss Sufficient Assumption questions in the next lesson.

Here's the argument again.

> In addition to the labor and materials used to make wine, the reputation of the vineyard where the grapes originate plays a role in determining the price of the finished wine. Therefore, an expensive wine is not always a good wine.

One thing to look for in any argument like this is a new idea or a judgment call in the conclusion. On the LSAT, you're always looking for a gap in the reasoning between the premises and the conclusion. If an important idea is missing from the premises, or a new idea is introduced in the conclusion, then that's a serious problem with the argument. Here's what we came up with.

- Author's conclusion: *Therefore, an expensive wine is not always a good wine.*
- Author's premises: *In addition to the labor and materials used to make wine, the reputation of the vineyard where the grapes originate also plays a role in the price of the finished wine.*
- Author's assumption: *Labor, materials, and reputation of a vineyard do not guarantee the quality of the wine.*

Answer Choice Wording

We've written assumptions in language that matches the tone of the LSAT for the purposes of this book, but you don't have to come up with anything that fancy while you're working under timed conditions. Just locate the potential problems with an argument and leave writing the answer choices to the LSAC.

Where did we get our assumptions? By noticing that the premise discusses the factors that determine the price of a bottle of wine, but the conclusion introduces the idea of a "good" wine.

You may be looking at the assumption we found and asking, "Didn't the argument basically say that?" In the premises, we're told that several things determine the price of a finished wine. That may explain why a wine might be expensive, but does it explain why the expensive wine might not always be a good wine?

Not really. In fact, when you look at it closely, it is a pretty big jump. The connection between price and quality is never explained.

When you're looking for the problems in an argument, it's important not to give the argument the benefit of the doubt because it seems to make sense or seems reasonable. Be skeptical and examine the language of the conclusion very closely.

Step 3: Act Once you've found one or more problems with the argument, you're almost ready to go. Realize that an assumption will not only *help* the argument, usually by fixing one of the problems you've identified, but it will also be essential to the argument. Here, you want something that supplies the idea that the factors that determine the price of a wine do not guarantee its quality.

> The credited response to a Necessary Assumption question will be a statement that is essential for the argument's conclusion to be valid.

Step 4: Answer using Process of Elimination   Let's take the choices one at a time.

> (A)   The price of a bottle of wine should be a reflection of the wine's quality.   (A)

Look carefully at the wording of this answer: it is actually the opposite of the assumption you are looking for. The author's position is that price is NOT a reflection of quality. Eliminate it.

> (B)   Price is never an accurate indication of the quality of a bottle of wine.   (B)

This one seems to go along with the argument more or less, but notice how demanding this choice is. It says that price is *never* an accurate indication of quality. That language is too strong. An assumption is something the argument *needs*, but we don't want to pick a choice that's *more* than what the argument needs. This falls in that category; eliminate it.

> (C)   The reputation of a vineyard does not always indicate the quality of its wines.

Notice how careful the language here is. This choice uses the phrase "does not always" rather than "never." It also connects a part of the premise—reputation of the vineyard—with the conclusion—quality of the wine. Keep this one for now.

> (D)   The reputation of a vineyard generally plays a greater role than the quality of its grapes in determining its wines' prices.   (D)

Initially this one may look tempting, since the reputation of the vineyard may very well play a greater role than the quality of its grapes in determining its wines' prices. After all, isn't it reasonable to think that could be why an expensive bottle of wine might not be as good as a cheap one? If the argument's primary concern were to point out the factor that plays a greater role in determining the price of a wine, then this answer choice would be relevant. But the relevance of the choice is determined by what the argument is trying to do—its *scope*.

To determine the exact scope of the argument, look at the conclusion. Is the argument primarily concerned with identifying which factor plays a greater role in price? No. You can now be certain that this choice isn't relevant and eliminate it.

> (E)   Wines produced by lesser-known vineyards generally are priced to reflect accurately the wines' quality.

Even if this is true, that the price of wines from vineyards reflects their quality is not relevant to either the premise or the conclusion. Eliminate it.

To check out the "Toughest Law Schools to Get Into," visit PrincetonReview.com

You're left with (C), which is the credited response. Notice that (C) isn't exactly what we came up with when we analyzed the argument; this is quite common on the LSAT. But we recognized that it related to a part of the conclusion that was problematic (introducing the new idea of "good"), that it connected this idea back to the factors of pricing discussed in the premises, and that it had the proper strength for this argument. Noting that an important idea is missing from the premises, or a new idea is introduced in the conclusion, and recognizing that it's a serious problem with the argument will help you recognize assumptions, even when they don't exactly match the assumptions you expected to find.

Arguments Technique: How to Spot an Assumption

Finding an assumption can be one of the most difficult things to do on the LSAT. But as we said before, sometimes looking for a language shift between the conclusion and the premises will help you spot it. Let's look at an example of how this works. Consider the following argument.

> Ronald Reagan ate too many jelly beans. Therefore, he was a bad president.

All right. You probably already think you know the assumption here; it's pretty obvious. After all, how do you get from "too many jelly beans" to "bad president"? This argument just doesn't make any sense, and the reason it doesn't make sense is that there's no connection between eating a lot of jelly beans and being a bad president.

But now consider this argument.

> Ronald Reagan was responsible for creating a huge national debt. Therefore, he was a bad president.

Suppose you were a staunch Reagan supporter, and someone came up to you and made this argument. How would you respond? You'd probably say that the debt wasn't his fault, that it was caused by Congress, Jimmy Carter, or the policies of a previous administration. You would attack the premise of the argument rather than its assumption. But why? Well, because the assumption here might seem reasonable to you. Consider the following parts of the argument:

- Conclusion: *Ronald Reagan was a bad president.*
- Premise: *Ronald Reagan was responsible for creating a huge debt.*

As far as the LSAT is concerned, the assumption of this argument works in basically the same way as the assumption of the first version. Initially, we saw that the link from "ate too many jelly beans" to "bad president" was what the argument was missing. Here, what's missing is the link from "huge national debt" to "bad president." In the first case, the assumption stands out more because it seems ridiculous. It's important to understand, though, that your real-world beliefs about whether or not an assumption is plausible play no role in analyzing arguments on the LSAT. Even if you consider it reasonable to associate huge national debt with being a bad president, this is still the connection the argument needs to establish in order for its conclusion to be properly drawn. Of course, assumptions that you consider reasonable are more difficult to spot, because unless you pay very close attention, you may not even realize they're there.

It's also important to understand, as you analyze arguments, that there is a *big difference* between an assumption of the argument and its conclusion. The conclusions of the two arguments above are the same: "[Ronald Reagan] was a bad president." The conclusion of an argument is the single, well-defined thing that the author wants us to believe. Once you start thinking about *why* we should believe it, you're moving past the conclusion into the reasoning of the argument. Also consider the purpose of these arguments. In both cases, you are given a fact (premise) and then a conclusion. The purpose for both of these is the same—to interpret the evidence. Once you recognize the purpose structure of the argument, it becomes easier to find the assumptions even if you didn't see them initially.

Finally, don't make your life too difficult when you're analyzing an argument to find its assumptions. You don't need to write LSAT answer choices in order to have a good sense of what's wrong with an argument. In the national debt argument above, for example, it's enough to know what the argument does wrong: that it's missing the connection from "huge debt" to "bad president." Knowing that this is the link your answer will need to supply is plenty to get you ready to evaluate the answer choices.

Arguments Technique: The Negation Test

We said before that a necessary assumption is something the argument *needs* in order for its conclusion to follow from the premises. We've described a number of ways to find necessary assumptions for yourself, but when you're doing Process of Elimination on Necessary Assumption questions, there is something you can do that will tell you for certain whether a particular fact is essential to an argument.

We call it the Negation Test.

Careful!
The Negation Test works only for Necessary Assumption questions. Sufficient Assumption questions, which we'll look at next, must be cracked differently.

> Negate the answer choice to see whether the conclusion remains intact. If the conclusion falls apart, then the choice is a valid assumption and thus the credited response.

Think of an argument as a canyon that you need to get across. On one side of the gap is the premise, and on the other side is the conclusion. You need a bridge—the assumption—to get from one side to the other. What happens if you take out the bridge? You can no longer get from the premises to the conclusion. Because a necessary assumption is required by the argument, all you have to do is suppose the choice you're looking at is *untrue*. If the choice is essential to the argument, then the conclusion and premises should no longer be connected without it. It takes a bit of practice, but it's the strongest elimination technique there is for Necessary Assumption questions.

Try it with two choices from the first example in this lesson—the one about the price of wine on page 29. If you need to, flip back to review the conclusion and premises of the argument. Then take a look at your answer.

 The reputation of a vineyard does not always indicate the quality of its wines.

To negate a choice, often all you have to do is negate the main verb. In this case, here's how it looks.

> The reputation of the vineyard DOES always indicate the quality of its wines.

What does this mean? That the reputation of the vineyard guarantees the quality of the wine. Supposing that this is true, how much sense does the argument make? Not much. After all, the whole point was that the factors that determine price, including the reputation of the vineyard, do not determine the quality of a wine.

Notice that the same method can be used to eliminate answers as well as confirm them. Take this other choice from the same question.

 The price of a bottle of wine should be a reflection of the wine's quality.

Negated, it looks like this.

> The price of a bottle of wine should NOT be a reflection of the wine's quality.

If this is true, it doesn't destroy the bridge (assumption) that the author is using to connect the premises with the conclusion. Remember the author's assumption— *Labor, materials, and reputation of a vineyard do not guarantee the quality of the wine.* Negated, this answer choice *agrees* with the assumption! This is the opposite of what you need it to do.

Certainly, the Negation Test can be confusing to do in some cases, especially if the answer is long and convoluted to start with. For this reason, the Negation Test shouldn't be a first-line elimination method for you. The best time to use negation is when you're down to two choices, or to confirm your final choice. If you make the effort to practice using the Negation Test on Necessary Assumption questions, you'll find it gets easier to do.

Now let's try another Necessary Assumption question.

Hint:
If it's hard to tell where to throw in a NOT, simply say, "It's not true that…" followed by the answer choice.

The Argument

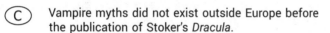

3. Bram Stoker's 1897 novel *Dracula* portrayed vampires—the "undead" who roam at night to suck the blood of living people—as able to turn into bats. As a result of the pervasive influence of this novel, many people now assume that a vampire's being able to turn into a bat is an essential part of vampire myths. However, this assumption is false, for vampire myths existed in Europe long before Stoker's book.

Which one of the following is an assumption on which the argument depends?

(A) At least one of the European vampire myths that predated Stoker's book did not portray vampires as strictly nocturnal.

(B) Vampire myths in Central and South America, where real vampire bats are found, portray vampires as able to turn into bats.

(C) Vampire myths did not exist outside Europe before the publication of Stoker's *Dracula*.

(D) At least one of the European vampire myths that predated Stoker's book did not portray vampires as able to turn into bats.

(E) At the time he wrote *Dracula*, Stoker was familiar with earlier European vampire myths.

PrepTest 44, Section 2, Question 18

Here's How to Crack It

Step 1: Assess the question As always, read the question first. Here it is again.

Which one of the following is an assumption on which the argument depends?

The words *assumption* and *depends* tell you that this is a Necessary Assumption question. You know that you'll need to identify the conclusion and the premises and that you'll need to think about the gap in the author's logic.

Step 2: Analyze the argument Read the argument. Identify the important parts. Here it is again.

Bram Stoker's 1897 novel *Dracula* portrayed vampires—the "undead" who roam at night to suck the blood of living people—as able to turn into bats. As a result of the pervasive influence of this novel, many people now assume that a vampire's being able to turn into a bat is an essential part of vampire myths. However, this assumption is false, for vampire myths existed in Europe long before Stoker's book.

Don't Forget!
Always mark the conclusion on all Necessary Assumption questions.

One common purpose structure you will see on the LSAT is when the author disagrees with something. The conclusion will be phrased as the opposite of someone else's opinion. (You saw this on the Mayor McKinney question in the previous section.) You're told that many people now assume that a vampire's being able to turn into a bat is an essential part of vampire myths. Notice the word *however* at the beginning of the last sentence. This tells you that the author is about to disagree with the previous statement, and you can quickly identify the conclusion as the last line of the argument: "this assumption is false…."

What information is given to support this? That vampire myths existed in Europe long before Stoker's book. If you notice that this premise never mentions whether vampires were able to turn into bats, you're on your way to finding the assumption.

- Author's conclusion: …*this assumption (a vampire being able to turn into a bat is essential to vampire myths) is false…*
- Author's premises: …*for vampire myths existed in Europe long before Stoker's book.*
- Author's assumption: *When the purpose of the argument is to disagree, the author makes an assumption that both points of view cannot be valid at the same time. In this case, since we know the author disagrees with the portrayal of vampires turning into bats, then he assumes that the earlier myths did not portray vampires as able to turn into bats.*

Step 3: Act Remember that the right answer will have to link the conclusion and the premise together somehow. Use that as your first POE criterion and move to the answer choices.

Step 4: Answer using Process of Elimination Here we go.

(A) At least one of the European vampire myths that predated Stoker's book did not portray vampires as strictly nocturnal.

Does this suggest a link between the pre-existing myths and Stoker's portrayal that vampires could turn into bats? No, so eliminate it.

(B) Vampire myths in Central and South America, where real vampire bats are found, portray vampires as able to turn into bats.

Does this suggest a link between the pre-existing myths and Stoker's portrayal that vampires could turn into bats? Well, it does mention myths and bats, so it's okay to hold onto this for your first pass.

(C) Vampire myths did not exist outside Europe before the publication of Stoker's *Dracula*.

Does this suggest a link between the pre-existing myths and Stoker's portrayal that vampires could turn into bats? It does mention both the book and the myths, so hold on to it.

(D)   At least one of the European vampire myths that predated Stoker's book did not portray vampires as able to turn into bats.   (D)

Does this suggest a link between the pre-existing myths and Stoker's portrayal that vampires could turn into bats? It mentions both the premise and the conclusion. Hold on to it.

(E)   At the time he wrote *Dracula,* Stoker was familiar with earlier European vampire myths.   (E)

Does this suggest a link between the pre-existing myths and Stoker's portrayal that vampires could turn into bats? No. It is not necessary that Stoker knew anything about the earlier myths, and there is no mention of bats, so eliminate it.

You're Down to Three This Time—Now What?

This will happen from time to time. You'll have to do some more thinking. Always reread the conclusion and the question before you compare the answer choices. Here they are again.

> Author's conclusion: *…this assumption (a vampire being able to turn into a bat is essential to vampire myths) is false…*
> Question: *Which one of the following is an assumption on which the argument depends?*

Let's start with (B). If you negate (B), it will read, "Vampire myths in Central and South America, where real vampire bats are found, DO NOT portray vampires as able to turn into bats." Remember that when you negate the correct answer, you should no longer be able to connect the premises and the conclusion. Negated, this answer choice does nothing to stop a connection between European myths and whether vampires can turn into bats. It becomes clear that myths in other countries aren't relevant. Eliminate it.

So, if myths in other countries aren't relevant to this argument, then what about (C)? Negated, it will read, "Vampire myths DID exist outside Europe before the publication of Stoker's *Dracula.*" Again, this doesn't prevent a connection between the European myths and whether vampires could turn into bats. Get rid of it.

That leaves you with (D).

(D)   At least one of the European vampire myths that predated Stoker's book did not portray vampires as able to turn into bats.   (D)

Try negation. What if at least one of the European vampire myths that predated Stoker's book did not portray vampires as able to turn into bats? That would mean that NONE of the myths did not portray vampires as able to turn into bats, and if none of them did not, that means they ALL DID portray vampires as able to turn

Tip:
The negation of "at least one" is "none."

into bats. Wait—if they all said vampires could turn into bats then the conclusion doesn't follow. The negated version of (D) destroys the argument and is therefore the credited response to the argument.

Negating (D) was trickier because it had the quantity "at least one" in it. When an answer has a quantity, negate that rather than the verb. If you get confused, remember to fall back on saying, "It's not true that..." followed by the answer choice.

Summary: Cracking Necessary Assumption Questions

We've just covered a ton of information regarding Necessary Assumption questions. Remember that a necessary assumption is something that the argument *needs* in order for its conclusion to be correctly reached. For that reason, any answer you pick on a Necessary Assumption question should, at a bare minimum, help the author's argument. If you negate the right answer on a Necessary Assumption question, what you'll find is that the argument either disintegrates entirely, or the connection between the premises and the conclusion is severed. Finally, watch out for choices that are too strongly worded or overly specific; these types of choices may seem right to you at first, but they frequently go too far or insist upon too much.

Below is a chart that summarizes Necessary Assumption questions.

Sample Question Phrasings	Act
Which of the following is an assumption on which the argument relies? *The argument above assumes which of the following?* *The writer's argument depends on which of the following?*	• Identify the conclusion, premises, and assumptions of the author. • If you are having trouble finding an assumption, look for a gap between two different ideas in the argument. • The assumption will always at least mildly strengthen the author's conclusion and is NECESSARY for the conclusion to follow from the information provided. • When down to two choices, negate each statement to see if the argument falls apart. If it does, that's your answer.

LESSON 3: SUFFICIENT ASSUMPTION QUESTIONS

Sufficient Assumption questions have a lot in common with the Necessary Assumption questions you just looked at it. Both ask you to identify the missing gap in the author's reasoning.

Sufficient Assumption questions, however, differ in that they aren't asking you for an assumption that is *required* by the argument; rather, they simply are asking you for an assumption, that, if true, would allow for the conclusion to follow. In other words, they are asking you for information that would *prove* the conclusion is true.

Because of this, Sufficient Assumption questions will often have credited answers that are stronger, broader, or more far-reaching than credited responses on Necessary Assumption questions. Let's revisit Ronald Reagan to see why.

> Ronald Reagan ate too many jelly beans. Therefore, he was a bad president.

Now, when we originally analyzed this argument, we identified the huge assumption that the argument makes: namely, that eating a certain quantity of jelly beans reflects in some way upon one's skill at being leader of the free world.

This is a necessary assumption; if eating jelly beans didn't reflect at least *somewhat* upon Reagan's ability to be president, then this argument has no hope of proving its conclusion.

But what if the LSAT was willing to grant to you a premise that said that the number of jelly beans one eats is the *only* indicator of one's ability to preside? Would that do it for the argument? We don't *need* jelly beans to be the only factor, but if they were, would the conclusion follow logically? You bet it would.

Try the Negation Test though. If eating jelly beans wasn't the only indicator of Ronald Reagan's presidential prowess, would the argument fall to pieces? Not necessarily—you needed to know only that jelly beans have something to do with his abilities as a president.

This is what separates Sufficient Assumption questions from Necessary Assumption questions. The credited responses can be more extreme, and the Negation Test can't help us.

Let's look at an example from a real, past LSAT.

The Argument

4. The only preexisting recordings that are transferred onto compact disc are those that record companies believe will sell well enough on compact disc to be profitable. So, most classic jazz recordings will not be transferred onto compact disc, because few classic jazz recordings are played on the radio.

   The conclusion above follows logically if which one of the following is assumed?

   (A) Few of the preexisting recordings that record companies believe can be profitably transferred to compact disc are classic jazz recordings.

   (B) Few compact discs featuring classic jazz recordings are played on the radio.

   (C) The only recordings that are played on the radio are ones that record companies believe can be profitably sold as compact discs.

   (D) Most record companies are less interested in preserving classic jazz recordings than in making a profit.

   (E) No recording that is not played on the radio is one that record companies believe would be profitable if transferred to compact disc.

PrepTest 45, Section 4, Question 22

Here's How to Crack It

Step 1: Assess the question   What makes this a Sufficient Assumption question? Here it is.

   The conclusion above follows logically if which one of the following is assumed?

The word *assumed* can reliably tell you that you're looking at an assumption question of some sort. Notice, however, that the test-writers aren't asking you for an assumption on which the argument relies or depends, as they did with Necessary Assumption questions. Rather, they're giving you a hypothetical: If you plug this answer choice into the argument as a missing premise, would it be enough to prove the conclusion is true?

Step 2: Analyze the argument   Just as you did with Necessary Assumption questions, you'll start off by looking for the argument's conclusion and premises. Here's the argument one more time.

> The only preexisting recordings that are transferred onto compact disc are those that record companies believe will sell well enough on compact disc to be profitable. So, most classic jazz recordings will not be transferred onto compact disc, because few classic jazz recordings are played on the radio.

And here's what our analysis reveals.

- Author's conclusion: *So, most classic jazz recordings will not be transferred onto compact disc.*
- Author's premises: *The only preexisting recordings that are transferred are those that record companies believe will sell well enough to be profitable. And…because few classical jazz recordings are played on the radio.*
- Author's assumption: *The purpose of this argument is to interpret evidence. Notice that the premises are facts—not problems or another opinion—and the conclusion is not disagreeing or offering a solution. So, the assumption is that there are no other factors that determine why record companies might transfer a recording to a CD.*

Step 3: Act   The good thing about Sufficient Assumption questions is that the correct responses don't introduce new information. Instead, they make the connection between the premises and the conclusion as strong as possible. Go ahead; make a wish for the answer choice that would do the best job of sealing the deal on the conclusion, and you're likely to find something similar in the answer choices.

In this case, there is a language shift between sales of CD's being profitable and recordings played on the radio and which recordings record companies will transfer to CD. You'd love to see an answer choice telling you that the only recordings that would be profitable are ones that are played on the radio. Keep your wish in mind as you go to the answer choices.

> The credited response to a Sufficient Assumption question will make an explicit connection between the premises and the conclusion—strong enough to prove the conclusion.

Step 4: Answer using Process of Elimination   Now go to the answer choices, keeping in mind that your correct answer choice must prove the conclusion and will not bring in new information. Let's take a look.

(A)   Few of the preexisting recordings that record companies believe can be profitably transferred to compact disc are classic jazz recordings.

This may seem helpful at first, but how does this link to the recordings being played on the radio? If anything, it's more a rehash of the conclusion. This doesn't create a link between the premises and the conclusion that *proves* the conclusion is true. Get rid of it.

(B)   Few compact discs featuring classic jazz recordings are played on the radio.

Here's our missing radio link, but now where is the link to profitability? This answer looks like an existing premise, which certainly helps the conclusion but doesn't prove the conclusion is true. Eliminate it.

(C)   The only recordings that are played on the radio are ones that record companies believe can be profitably sold as compact discs.

Be careful here! You may decide to keep this on the first pass since it links radio play with profitability. Read this choice again and notice the direction of this answer—that profitability proves radio play. We need to prove that radio play guarantees profitability. So close, but it has to go!

(D)   Most record companies are less interested in preserving classic jazz recordings than in making a profit.

This choice is bringing in new information that doesn't tie the idea of profitability with radio play. It is out of scope, so eliminate it.

(E)   No recording that is not played on the radio is one that record companies believe would be profitable if transferred to compact disc.

Wait, what did that say? The double negative makes the answer difficult to decipher, but you should keep it on the first pass through the answers because it includes both radio play and profitability. On the second pass, get rid of the double negative—"No recording that is not" becomes "A recording that is." So now the answer reads, "A recording that is played on the radio is one that record companies believe will be profitable if transferred to compact disc." Aha! This is exactly what you wanted in an answer choice! If you add this to the premises, the conclusion clearly follows directly from the premises. It is the missing link, shoring up the gap between the language of the premises and the language of the conclusion.

Summary: Cracking Sufficient Assumption Questions

Sufficient Assumption questions always bring up ideas in the conclusion that are not discussed in the premises. The credited response will make an explicit connection between the two, positively sealing the deal on the conclusion. On more difficult Sufficient Assumption questions, you may see conditional statements or answer choices that seem very similar. Focus on proving the conclusion and making sure the answer choice goes in the right direction, eliminating answer choices that bring in new information that doesn't get you any closer to the conclusion. Look for the strongest answer.

Sample Question Phrasings	Act
Which one of the following, if assumed, would enable the conclusion to be properly drawn? *The conclusion follows logically if which one of the following is assumed?*	• Identify the conclusion, premises, and assumptions of the author. • Look for language in the conclusion that is not accounted for in the premise. • Paraphrase an answer that would strongly connect the premises to the conclusion and shore up the language gap. • Eliminate answer choices that bring in new information.

LESSON 4: WEAKEN QUESTIONS

Weaken questions ask you to identify a fact that would work against the argument. Sometimes the answer you pick will directly contradict the conclusion; at other times, it will merely sever the connection between the premises and the conclusion, destroying the argument's reasoning. Either way, the right answer will exploit a gap in the argument.

The Argument

5. The top 50 centimeters of soil on Tiliga Island contain bones from the native birds eaten by the islanders since the first human immigration to the island 3,000 years ago. A comparison of this top layer with the underlying 150 centimeters of soil—accumulated over 80,000 years—reveals that before humans arrived on Tiliga, a much larger and more diverse population of birds lived there. Thus, the arrival of humans dramatically decreased the population and diversity of birds on Tiliga.

Which one of the following statements, if true, most seriously weakens the argument?

 (A) The bird species known to have been eaten by the islanders had few natural predators on Tiliga.

 (B) Many of the bird species that disappeared from Tiliga did not disappear from other, similar, uninhabited islands until much later.

 (C) The arrival of a species of microbe, carried by some birds but deadly to many others, immediately preceded the first human immigration to Tiliga.

 (D) Bones from bird species known to have been eaten by the islanders were found in the underlying 150 centimeters of soil.

 (E) The birds that lived on Tiliga prior to the first human immigration generally did not fly well.

PrepTest 44, Section 2, Question 4

Here's How to Crack It

Step 1: Assess the question   Always go to the question first. Here it is.

Which one of the following, if true, most seriously weakens the argument?

The word *weaken* or one of its synonyms—*undermine, call into question, cast doubt upon*—is a clear indication of the kind of question you're facing here. You want to find a way to hurt the argument's conclusion.

Step 2: Analyze the argument   As usual, start by finding and marking the conclusion and the premises. And because the right answer on a Weaken question will often attack a conspicuous problem with the argument's reasoning, you also need to look for the purpose and common patterns of reasoning before you proceed. Here's the argument again.

> The top 50 centimeters of soil on Tiliga Island contain bones from the native birds eaten by the islanders since the first human immigration to the island 3,000 years ago. A comparison of this top layer with the underlying 150 centimeters of soil—accumulated over 80,000 years—reveals that before humans arrived on Tiliga, a much larger and more diverse population of birds lived there. Thus, the arrival of humans dramatically decreased the population and diversity of birds on Tiliga.

And here's what we came up with from our analysis.

- Author's conclusion: *The arrival of humans dramatically decreased the number and diversity of birds on Tiliga.*
- Author's premises: *The archaeological record shows the bones of birds eaten by the islanders after humans arrived on Tiliga, and that the bird population was larger and more diverse before the arrival of humans.*
- Author's assumption: *Humans, and no other factors, are responsible for the birds' decline.*

This assumption falls under one of the common patterns of reasoning. The author sees that two events occurred at roughly the same time and assumes that one must have caused the other, and that nothing else could have been a factor—that there is no other cause.

Step 3: Act   On a Weaken question, you don't have to predict the exact content of the right answer. You know what's wrong with the argument, and the chances are that the right answer will exploit that flaw somehow. In this case, you anticipate that the answer choice you want will describe something else that could have caused the drop in bird population and diversity.

> Remember that the premises must be accepted as true. The credited response to a Weaken question will give a reason why the author's conclusion might not be true, despite the true premises offered in support of the conclusion.

Step 4: Answer using Process of Elimination   Keep your eyes on the prize; remember that what you want is something that hurts the conclusion that humans are responsible for the birds' decline.

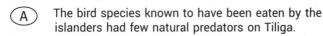

(A)   The bird species known to have been eaten by the islanders had few natural predators on Tiliga.

Does this hurt the conclusion? If the birds had few natural predators other than humans, then this choice doesn't hurt the conclusion. If anything, it could strengthen the conclusion by showing humans were the biggest predators of the birds. This choice goes in the wrong direction, so eliminate it.

(B)   Many of the bird species that disappeared from Tiliga did not disappear from other, similar, uninhabited islands until much later.

Does this hurt the conclusion? If the same birds that disappeared from Tiliga after the humans arrived did not disappear from other islands, then it is more likely that humans caused the decline on Tiliga. This choice also goes in the wrong direction, so eliminate it.

(C)   The arrival of a species of microbe, carried by some birds but deadly to many others, immediately preceded the first human immigration to Tiliga.

Does this hurt the conclusion? You might initially be turned off by the mention of a microbe, but remember that you are looking for another reason for the birds' decline. If a microbe that kills many birds was introduced to the island just before the humans arrived, then the microbe could be responsible for the decline. If so, that would hurt the conclusion, so keep it.

(D)   Bones from bird species known to have been eaten by the islanders were found in the underlying 150 centimeters of soil.

Does this hurt the conclusion? Not really. So the same birds eaten by the islanders were there before the humans were. Nice to know, but this isn't a potential reason for the decline of the other birds. Eliminate it.

(E)   The birds that lived on Tiliga prior to the first human immigration generally did not fly well.

Does this hurt the conclusion? Well, it depends how not flying well impacted the birds' ability to survive. You may want to keep this on the first pass.

You have two choices left, a circumstance you'll frequently encounter on the LSAT. How do you make up your mind?

POE Hint:
Answer choices for question types that contain the words "if true" in the question stem sometimes bring in new information. If the new information is relevant, the fact that it's "new" is not a reason to eliminate it.

Arguments Technique: Look for Direct Impact

On Weaken questions, your task is to find the strongest attack on the conclusion. There might be more than one answer that seems to be working against the overall reasoning, so you need to go back, make sure you understand the conclusion fully, and then look for the one that has the most direct impact on it.

Things that can be important here are quantity words and the overall strength of language involved. Generally speaking, because you want a clear attack, you'll often see strong wording in the right answer. More important, you want to make sure that the answer you pick hits the conclusion squarely. Try comparing the impact of your two remaining choices in the previous example.

As a reminder, here's the argument's conclusion.

> The arrival of humans dramatically decreased the number and diversity of birds on Tiliga.

And here's (C).

> The arrival of a species of microbe, carried by some birds but deadly to many others, immediately preceded the first human immigration to Tiliga.

Does this really hurt the conclusion? Since the reasoning of this argument assumes a causal link between the arrival of the humans and the decline of the birds, then by offering another possible cause—say, a microbe—this answer makes a direct attack on the conclusion. Keep it.

By contrast, here's (E).

> The birds that lived on Tiliga prior to the first human immigration generally did not fly well.

Does this really hurt the conclusion? While this choice may seem to have potential, it lacks the detail needed to tell definitively if this was a problem that could have caused the birds to decline. You don't know if the birds never flew well—like penguins or ostriches—even when they were thriving, or if this was a new development that made them easier prey for predators. Remember that if you have to justify an answer, or you find yourself saying, "It could be true if…", then the answer is wrong. This is not as strong as (C), so eliminate it.

When more than one answer choice seems to do the job, make sure you go back to the conclusion and look for the choice that attacks it most directly.

Arguments Technique: Common Patterns of Reasoning

There are a few classic flawed patterns of reasoning that show up repeatedly on the LSAT. It's helpful to become familiar with these so that you can more easily recognize the assumptions that are built into them.

Causal Arguments

"Causal" is shorthand for cause and effect. A causal argument links an observed effect with a possible cause for that effect. A causal argument also assumes that there was no other cause for the observed effect. The argument on the page 45 is an example of a causal argument.

Take a look at this simple causal argument.

> Every time I walk my dog, it rains. Therefore, walking my dog
> must be the cause of the rain.

Absurd, right? However, this is classic causality. You see the observed effect (it's raining), you see a concurrent event (walking the dog), and then the author connects the two by saying that walking his dog caused the rain, thereby implying that nothing else caused it. So why are causal assumptions so popular on the LSAT? Because people often confuse *correlation* with *causality*. Let's call the possible cause (A) and the effect (B); then let's map out what the common assumptions are when working with a causal argument.

> 1. Something caused B—that is, B didn't occur by chance.
> 2. Nothing other than A could have caused B.
> 3. B did not cause A.

Of course, causal arguments on the LSAT won't be that absurd, but they'll have the same basic structure. The great thing about being able to identify causal arguments is that once you know where their potential weaknesses are, it becomes much easier to identify the credited response for Assumption, Weaken, and Strengthen questions.

- On Necessary and Sufficient Assumption questions, the credited response will be a paraphrase of the causal assumption you've identified.
- For Weaken questions, the credited response will suggest an alternate cause for the observed effect.
- For Strengthen questions, the credited response will eliminate a possible alternate cause or give more evidence linking the stated possible cause with the stated effect.

Sampling Arguments

Another popular type of Argument on the LSAT is the *sampling* or *statistical* argument. These arguments have a conclusion that is based on a survey of a selected group or a statistic from a study. This assumes that a given statistic or sample is sufficient to justify a given conclusion or that an individual or small group is representative of a large group.

Sampling Assumptions

- A given statistic or sample is representative of the whole.

- The sampling was conducted correctly.

Whenever you see something about a group used as evidence to conclude something about a larger population, remember that the argument's potential weakness is that the sample is skewed because the small sample is unrepresentative.

Arguments by Analogy

A third type of common flawed reasoning on the LSAT is argument *by analogy*. These arguments use a comparison to draw a conclusion about a certain group. In this case, the author assumes that a given group, idea, or action is logically similar to another group, idea, or action without providing evidence that the items are similar.

Analogy Assumption

One group, idea, or action is the same as another, with respect to the terms of the argument.

To strengthen arguments that have faulty analogies, provide evidence that the groups, ideas, or actions are comparable. To weaken such an argument, you would need to find a relevant way in which the two things being compared are dissimilar.

The Argument

6. Barr: The National Tea Association cites tea's recent visibility in advertising and magazine articles as evidence of tea's increasing popularity. However, a neutral polling company, the Survey Group, has tracked tea sales at numerous stores for the last 20 years and has found no change in the amount of tea sold. We can thus conclude that tea is no more popular now than it ever was.

Which one of the following, if true, most seriously weakens Barr's argument?

(A) The National Tea Association has announced that it plans to carry out its own retail survey in the next year.

(B) A survey by an unrelated polling organization shows that the public is generally receptive to the idea of trying new types of tea.

(C) The Survey Group is funded by a consortium of consumer advocacy groups.

(D) The stores from which the Survey Group collected information about tea sales are all located in the same small region of the country.

(E) Tea has been the subject of an expensive and efficient advertising campaign funded, in part, by the National Tea Association.

PrepTest 44, Section 4, Question 5

To check out law schools with the "Most Liberal Students," visit Princeton-Review.com/ law-school-rankings.

Here's How to Crack It

Step 1: Assess the question This question might be familiar. Here it is again.

Which of the following, if true, most seriously weakens Barr's argument?

Clearly, you're out to weaken the argument.

Step 2: Analyze the argument   Read the argument carefully. Identify the conclusion, the premises the author offers as evidence, and any assumptions he or she makes. Here's the body of the argument.

> Barr: The National Tea Association cites tea's recent visibility in advertising and magazine articles as evidence of tea's increasing popularity. However, a neutral polling company, the Survey Group, has tracked tea sales at numerous stores for the last 20 years and has found no change in the amount of tea sold. We can thus conclude that tea is no more popular now than it ever was.

Did you recognize this as a sampling argument? The conclusion suggests that tea has not gained in popularity over the last 20 years. What is the author's evidence? A survey/study. Whenever the argument uses a survey or poll or study as its premises, be on the lookout for flawed sampling reasoning.

What are the automatic assumptions that an author makes in a sampling argument? That the sample represents the larger group and that the sampling was conducted correctly. Here, the disagree purpose structure helps you as well. The author is disagreeing with the National Tea Association's position and using the study as evidence. He assumes that the data from the tracked stores applies to all tea sales everywhere.

Let's summarize:

- Author's conclusion: *Tea is no more popular now than it ever was.*
- Author's premises: *The Survey Group has found no change in the amount of tea sold at numerous stores over the last 20 years.*
- Author's assumption: *That the Survey Group data is representative of the tea market everywhere.*

Step 3: Act   You're looking for evidence that the sample in the Survey Group's data is not representative, or that there is some problem with the way the Survey Group collected its information.

Step 4: Answer using Process of Elimination   Be careful here. Because you're looking for a potential problem with the data, the right answer might seem out of scope because it introduces new information that doesn't necessarily refer to something in the body of the argument. Let's look at them one by one.

   The National Tea Association has announced that it plans to carry out its own retail survey in the next year.

Does this show a potential problem with the data collected by the Survey Group? Even if the National Tea Association does plan to do its own survey, that doesn't invalidate the Survey Group's information. Eliminate it.

(B)   A survey by an unrelated polling organization shows that the public is generally receptive to the idea of trying new types of tea.

Does this show a potential problem with the data collected by the Survey Group? Well, different results from a different source could potentially weaken the initial data. Keep this one for now.

(C)   The Survey Group is funded by a consortium of consumer advocacy groups.

Does this show a potential problem with the data collected by the Survey Group? There is not enough information here to connect how the group is funded with the findings of the group. This is out of scope of the argument. Get rid of it.

(D)   The stores from which the Survey Group collected information about tea sales are all located in the same small region of the country.

You can also find law schools with the "Most Conservative Students," at PrincetonReview.com/law-school-rankings.

Does this show a potential problem with the data collected by the Survey Group? This is what you need to be careful of. The choice may seem irrelevant at first glance, but if all the stores were in the same region, it is possible that tea sales have increased in other regions. Weakening an argument doesn't require destroying it; casting doubt by pointing out how the data might not be representative of the larger group is all that's required of the credited response. This effectively weakens the argument.

(E)   Tea has been the subject of an expensive and efficient advertising campaign funded, in part, by the National Tea Association.

Does this show a potential problem with the data collected by the Survey Group? Even if tea has been the subject of an advertising campaign, you don't know if the campaign worked or that tea has become more popular. Eliminate it.

You did keep (B) at first, but compared with (D), it's not as good. Just because people are more receptive to the idea of trying new types of tea does not prove that tea is more popular. Choice (D) does not require additional justification to make it weaken the argument, so it is the better choice.

Summary:
Cracking Weaken Questions

Remember these two key ideas when answering Weaken questions: the correct answer will probably attack one of the author's assumptions, and you should treat each answer choice as hypothetically true, looking for its direct negative impact on the conclusion. On more difficult Weaken questions, there will often be an appealing answer that, with just a little interpretation, looks right. The key is to avoid making any new assumptions when you try to determine the impact of an answer. Look to eliminate, not justify.

Sample Question Phrasings	Act
Which one of the following, if true, would most undermine the author's conclusion? *Which of the following statements, if true, would most call into question the results achieved by the scientists?*	• Identify the conclusion, premises, and assumptions of the author. • Read critically, looking for instances in which the author made large leaps in logic. • Then, when you go to the answer choices, look for a choice that has the most negative impact on that leap in logic. • Assume all choices to be hypothetically true.

LESSON 5: STRENGTHEN QUESTIONS

Strengthen questions are the flipside of Weaken questions. Now what you're asked to do is pick a new fact that confirms the conclusion, or at the very least, helps the conclusion seem more likely. If there are problems with the argument, the answer here will most often address them.

The Argument

7. Increases in the occurrence of hearing loss among teenagers are due in part to their listening to loud music through stereo headphones. So a group of concerned parents is recommending that headphone manufacturers include in their product lines stereo headphones that automatically turn off when a dangerous level of loudness is reached. It is clear that adoption of this recommendation would not significantly reduce the occurrence of hearing loss in teenagers, however, since almost all stereo headphones that teenagers use are bought by the teenagers themselves.

Which one of the following, if true, provides the most support for the argument?

(A) Loud music is most dangerous to hearing when it is played through stereo headphones.

(B) No other cause of hearing loss in teenagers is as damaging as their listening to loud music through stereo headphones.

(C) Parents of teenagers generally do not themselves listen to loud music through stereo headphones.

(D) Teenagers who now listen to music at dangerously loud levels choose to do so despite their awareness of the risks involved.

(E) A few headphone manufacturers already plan to market stereo headphones that automatically turn off when a dangerous level of loudness is reached.

PrepTest 44, Section 2, Question 7

To check out law schools with the "Most Diverse Faculty," take a look at your online student tools. If you haven't registered yet, go to PrincetonReview.com/prep.

Here's How to Crack It

Step 1: Assess the question As always, begin with the task at hand. Here it is.

Which of the following, if true, provides the most support for the argument?

Note the use of the word *support* here. This word and the word *strengthen* are the two most frequently seen clues that you're looking at in a Strengthen question. As you'll see later, however, it's important to make sure what's supporting what on a question like this. You're asked to pick the *answer* that supports the *argument*. This is the pattern you see in Strengthen questions.

Step 2: Analyze the argument   Once you've identified the question, you know how much analysis you need to do. As with Weaken and Assumption questions, start by finding the conclusion and the premises. Then look for the purpose or any patterns of reasoning. Here's the argument for this question.

> Increases in the occurrence of hearing loss among teenagers are due in part to their listening to loud music through stereo headphones. So a group of concerned parents is recommending that headphone manufacturers include in their product lines stereo headphones that automatically turn off when a dangerous level of loudness is reached. It is clear that adoption of this recommendation would not significantly reduce the occurrence of hearing loss in teenagers, however, since almost all stereo headphones that teenagers use are bought by the teenagers themselves.

And here's a quick analysis.

- Author's conclusion: *It is clear that adoption of this recommendation would not significantly reduce the occurrence of hearing loss in teenagers.*
- Author's premises: *Teenagers buy their own headphones.*
- Author's assumption: *Since the purpose of this argument is to reject a proposed solution, it is assuming that teenagers will not buy the headphones that shut off when dangerous levels of loudness are reached.*

Step 3: Act   Since the author does not come right out and say that teens won't buy the headphones, chances are that you'll find an answer that makes this connection. Failing that, you'll need to keep in mind that you're broadly looking for choices that agree with the author's conclusion. In this case, that the parents' headphone solution will not work.

> The credited response to a Strengthen question will provide information in support of the conclusion, or it will weaken an alternate interpretation of the premises.

Step 4: Answer using Process of Elimination   Remember that you want something that helps the conclusion here.

 (A) Loud music is most dangerous to hearing when it is played through stereo headphones.

Does this show that the parents' solution won't work? This is not relevant because it doesn't matter whether listening through headphones is the most dangerous. The argument does not compare different methods of listening to music. Eliminate this one.

 (B) No other cause of hearing loss in teenagers is as damaging as their listening to loud music through stereo headphones.

Does this show that the parents' solution won't work? This choice would strengthen a causal argument (no other cause) but since that reasoning isn't in play in this argument this choice doesn't work. Eliminate it.

 (C) Parents of teenagers generally do not themselves listen to loud music through stereo headphones.

Does this show that the parents' solution won't work? Be careful not to fall into the trap of thinking that if the parents don't listen to their own advice then neither will their teenagers. This isn't about common sense; it's about what you can prove from the information in the argument. This does not work without a lot of justification, so get rid of it.

 (D) Teenagers who now listen to music at dangerously loud levels choose to do so despite their awareness of the risks involved.

Does this show that the parents' solution won't work? If the teenagers are aware of the risk and want to listen to dangerously loud music anyway, then this shows that they are unlikely to buy the new headphones. This rules out the possibility that perhaps the teens were unaware of the danger. Keep this choice for now.

Careful!
Watch out for Weaken answers on Strengthen questions, and vice versa.

 (E) A few headphone manufacturers already plan to market stereo headphones that automatically turn off when a dangerous level of loudness is reached.

Does this show that the parents' solution won't work? The author thinks that teenagers won't buy the headphones. If the manufacturers already plan to sell the safe headphones, then they think people will buy them. If anything, this strengthens the parents' position and weakens the author's. The problem is that there still isn't any direct link between making the headphones and getting teens to use them, or show the teens won't use them.

Principle Strengthen

Another type of Strengthen question asks you to find a "principle" to "justify" the argument. This time, instead of a specific fact or piece of evidence, the correct answer will be a general rule that will strengthen the argument as a whole. These tend to prove the conclusion is true very much like sufficient assumption questions. The answer may help the conclusion in an unexpected or rather extreme way, so don't shy away from answers that are strongly worded.

The Argument

8. Pacifist: It is immoral to do anything that causes harm to another person. But, since using force causes harm to another person, it is also immoral to threaten to use force, even when such a threat is made in self-defense.

    Which one of the following principles, if valid, would most help to justify the pacifist's reasoning?

    (A) Given the potential harm caused by the use of force, the line between use of force in self-defense and the aggressive use of force is always vague.

    (B) It is immoral to threaten to do what it is immoral to do.

    (C) It is immoral to do anything that causes more harm than good.

    (D) Whether a threat made in self-defense is immoral depends on the circumstances.

    (E) It is immoral to carry out a threat if making the threat is itself immoral.

    PrepTest 44, Section 4, Question 2

Here's How to Crack It

Step 1: Assess the question As always, look at the question first.

> Which one of the following principles, if valid, would most help to justify the pacifist's reasoning?

Now you're looking to "justify"—basically, to strengthen—the pacifist's conclusion. Notice how the question also includes the proviso "if valid," just as a Strengthen question would include "if true." Remember that your choices are going to be generally worded rules rather than specific facts.

Step 2: Analyze the argument   Just as you would on a Strengthen question, analyze the argument by finding the conclusion (the judgment we're looking to justify) and the premises (the circumstances involved). You'll also want to see if you can find a conspicuous gap in the reasoning. Take a look at the argument.

> Pacifist: It is immoral to do anything that causes harm to another person. But, since using force causes harm to another person, it is also immoral to threaten to use force, even when such a threat is made in self-defense.

Here's how to break it down:

- Author's conclusion: *…it is immoral to threaten to use force…*
- Author's premises: *It is immoral to do anything that causes harm to another person. But since using force causes harm to another person…*
- Author's assumption: *What is the purpose of this argument? Since the author is not disagreeing or solving a problem, the purpose is to interpret the statement that it is immoral to DO anything that causes harm. He interprets this to mean that it is also immoral to THREATEN to do anything that causes harm. He assumes that threatening to do harm is just as bad as doing harm.*

To check out the "Schools with the Best Quality of Life," take a look at your online student tools. If you haven't registered yet, go to PrincetonReview.com/prep.

Step 3: Act   You're looking for an answer that supports the pacifist's position that it is immoral to threaten to use force. The credited response will probably do this by somehow connecting the *threat* of doing harm to the *act* of doing harm.

Step 4: Answer using Process of Elimination   Make sure you take each answer choice back to the argument and see whether it supports the pacifist's conclusion. Since you're looking for an answer that justifies, or proves, the conclusion, the stronger the answer choice, the better.

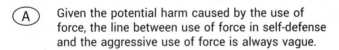

(A) Given the potential harm caused by the use of force, the line between use of force in self-defense and the aggressive use of force is always vague.

Does this prove that threatening to use force is as bad as using force? There is no discussion of vagueness. The line in the argument is very clear. Eliminate this answer.

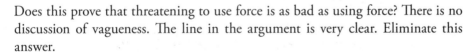

(B) It is immoral to threaten to do what it is immoral to do.

Does this prove that threatening to use force is as bad as using force? If this is valid, then since you know from the premise that it is immoral to do harm to others, that would mean that it is immoral to threaten to do harm to others as well. This choice justifies the pacifist's conclusion. Keep it.

(C) It is immoral to do anything that causes more harm than good.

Does this prove that threatening to use force is as bad as using force? Does the pacifist make any exception in his argument for a situation that does more good than harm? No, so eliminate this answer.

(D) Whether a threat made in self-defense is immoral depends on the circumstances.

Does this prove that threatening to use force is as bad as using force? Since the author includes threats made in self-defense as immoral, this answer doesn't work. It goes against the argument, so get rid of it.

(E) It is immoral to carry out a threat if making the threat is itself immoral.

Does this prove that threatening to use force is as bad as using force? Be careful here! This is saying that an action is immoral if the threat is immoral, which is the opposite of what we need the answer to say. This is one way that Principle Strengthen questions can be tricky.

> **Understanding Principle Strengthen Questions**
> In Principle Strengthen questions, a principle that "justifies" the conclusion may legitimately help the conclusion using a method that's a little different from the one in the original argument. Make sure you know what kind of Principle question you are dealing with: Principle Strengthen question or Principle Match, which requires a somewhat different method.

What If I Can't Find an Assumption?

We've been talking quite a bit about what an important role the assumptions play in weakening or strengthening arguments on the LSAT. You may be asking yourself, "What am I supposed to do if I can't find an assumption?" Well, there's still hope. Finding assumptions is one of the trickier skills for many students to develop. In addition to identifying the purpose structure and looking for the common flawed patterns of reasoning, here are two ideas to keep in mind.

First, look for any shifts in the author's language. Anytime the author makes a conclusion, evaluate that conclusion *only* on the basis of the evidence we're given in support of that conclusion. If there are any changes in language between the premises and the conclusion, these changes clue you into assumptions. This shift can be blatant, as when something that was never mentioned before suddenly shows up in the conclusion. Or it can be more subtle, such as if the author makes a statement that is more strongly qualified than the evidence. For instance, if you had evidence about what "almost always" is the case and concluded something that "will" happen, that would require a leap in logic.

Remember also that arguments can have multiple assumptions. Even if you identify an assumption correctly, it might not be the "right" one (meaning it might not be the one the credited response hinges on).

What if you can't articulate an assumption, or you find the "wrong" one? Don't worry; there's *still* hope. As we've been saying, you should approach the answer choices armed with an assumption or at least an understanding of the gap between the conclusion and premises. This is because it's not necessary for you to be able to *generate* the assumption to find the best answer. You can also be prepared to *recognize* an assumption (or an answer that will impact it, in the case of Weaken and Strengthen questions). Sure, you might find that you can get through POE more quickly if you have a neatly paraphrased assumption jotted down, but if you've at least identified any gaps in the argument, you'll be able to evaluate the answer choices and recognize the ones that don't have the proper impact.

Arguments Technique: What to Do When You're Down to Two

As you do more LSAT arguments, you may find yourself falling into a predictable pattern in which you find it easy to eliminate three of the answer choices but then have no clear idea of which one of the two remaining choices is correct. There's the first problem. You should know that it isn't your job to determine which is the *correct* answer. The trickiest incorrect answers on LSAT arguments are usually mostly right—they contain just a word or two that makes them wrong.

Very often these wrong answers will even sound better than the "credited response." The writers of the LSAT are experts at writing answers that are *almost* all correct, so if you spot anything that makes the choice wrong, even one word, eliminate it.

Now, what do you do when you get down to two choices? Well, you focus on finding something that makes one of them incorrect. There must be something appealing about each of them, or you would have eliminated one of them by now.

Here are a few steps to follow when you are down to two choices.

1. Identify how the answer choices are different.
2. Go back to the argument and reread, keeping the difference in mind. Use the difference that you've spotted to help you read the argument from a new, critical perspective. Try to find something in the language of the argument that points out a problem with one of the remaining two choices. Focus on the statement of the conclusion; this is very often what makes the final decision, especially if you didn't read it closely enough the first time.
3. Eliminate the choice with the flaw. Now that you've found the problem, eliminate that choice and move on.

This process will work on any type of Argument question—and, for that matter, on Games and Reading Comprehension. Be critical and methodical, and you'll get results.

Summary: Cracking Strengthen Questions

With Strengthen questions, you once again looked for what impact each of the answer choices had on the argument—only this time, a favorable impact. Focus on finding the flaws that allow you to eliminate the attractive wrong answers and leave you with the only choice that has a direct impact on the argument. Look at the chart below.

Careful!

Not all questions that use the word support are Strengthen questions. Strengthen questions ask you to support the argument's conclusion, but Inference questions ask you to use the passage to support an answer choice.

Sample Question Phrasings	Act
Which one of the following statements, if true, would most support the author's conclusion? *Which of the following statements, if true, would strengthen the author's argument?* *Which of the following principles, if established, justifies the actions taken by Mia in the argument above?*	• Identify the conclusion, premises, and assumptions of the author. • Read critically, looking for where the author made large leaps in logic. • Then, when you go to the answer choices, look for a choice that has the most positive impact on that gap. • Assume all choices to be hypothetically true.

LESSON 6: RESOLVE/EXPLAIN QUESTIONS

So far, you've been working with arguments in which the author has presented evidence to support a conclusion. And with the exception of Main Point questions, you've been paying attention to any gaps in the argument that might help you to pinpoint the assumptions the author has made. The process for analyzing the argument (Step 2) has been almost identical for Main Point, Assumption, Weaken, and Strengthen question types.

Step 2 is a bit different in answering Resolve/Explain questions. That's because the "argument" attached to these questions is more like a passage. With these types of questions, the author will present a couple of pieces of information that don't seem to fit together. Your task will be to find the answer choice that will do the best job of *resolving* the apparent discrepancy between these two pieces of information and that will *explain* how both pieces of information could be true at once. The other steps remain the same; you just don't have the same pieces to break down that you've seen so far.

Look at a typical passage that would be used in asking a Resolve/Explain question.

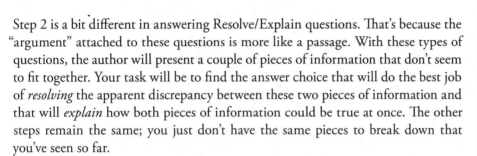

The ancient Dirdirs used water power for various purposes in the outlying cities and towns in their empire. However, they did not use this technology in their capital city of Avallone.

Notice that there's no evidence provided to support a particular claim, just two pieces of information that don't really seem to fit with each other. Here you've got this ancient culture that has this certain type of technology but doesn't use it in the capital city. That's the discrepancy or paradox, right? Good. Your goal then will be to spot an answer choice that in some way resolves or explains that discrepancy or paradox. You might be able to think up a few reasons the Dirdirs had this technology and didn't use it, such as the following:

- There were no rivers or other bodies of water in or near Avallone.
- It was cheaper or more efficient to use another source of power in the capital, such as abundant labor.
- There was not enough space for the equipment in Avallone.

That's good for a start. You could actually come up with a multitude of theoretical reasons they didn't use this technology (the actual historical reason has something to do with the fact that it would have caused social unrest because this technology would have put too many people out of work), but the nice thing is that you don't have to! All you have to do is identify the discrepancy and be able to recognize the answer choice that allows both parts of the discrepancy to be true. That'll save you a lot of work and keep you from generating ideas that are far away from what the test-writers were thinking when they wrote the question. Now you will put this idea to work on a full question.

> Your goal will be to spot an answer choice that resolves or explains the discrepancy or paradox.

The Argument

9. In the past, combining children of different ages in one classroom was usually a failure; it resulted in confused younger children, who were given inadequate attention and instruction, and bored older ones, who had to sit through previously learned lessons. Recently, however, the practice has been revived with excellent results. Mixed-age classrooms today are stimulating to older children and enable younger children to learn much more efficiently than in standard classrooms.

Which one of the following, if true, most helps to resolve the apparent discrepancy in the passage?

(A) On average, mixed-age classrooms today are somewhat larger in enrollment than were the ones of the past.

(B) Mixed-age classrooms of the past were better equipped than are those of today.

(C) Today's mixed-age classrooms, unlike those of the past, emphasize group projects that are engaging to students of different ages.

(D) Today's mixed-age classrooms have students of a greater range of ages than did those of the past.

(E) Few of the teachers who are reviving mixed-age classrooms today were students in mixed-age classrooms when they were young.

PrepTest 44, Section 2, Question 3

Here's How to Crack It

Step 1: Assess the question   Here it is again.

Which one of the following, if true, most helps to resolve the apparent discrepancy in the passage?

This question is tipping your hand—it's telling you that there is something you need to *resolve* in the *passage*. When the question stem doesn't use the word "argument," you are not looking for any gaps in the reasoning. The information in the passage contains a *discrepancy* or *paradox*, and you're going to have to find an answer choice that resolves these seemingly opposing facts.

Step 2: Analyze the argument Read through the argument, looking for any situations or facts that seem contrary to one another. Here it is again.

> In the past, combining children of different ages in one classroom was usually a failure; it resulted in confused younger children, who were given inadequate attention and instruction, and bored older ones, who had to sit through previously learned lessons. Recently, however, the practice has been revived with excellent results. Mixed-age classrooms today are stimulating to older children and enable younger children to learn much more efficiently than in standard classrooms.

Analyze
There's no need to find the conclusion and premises on Resolve/ Explain questions.

What is the apparent discrepancy? In the past, mixed-age classrooms were not successful, but now they are.

Step 3: Act Remember that there are probably a number of specific theories we could come up with to explain this discrepancy, and if one possible explanation jumps into your head, that's fine—it may turn out to be an answer choice. But fundamentally, you just need to be aware of the *discrepancy* and see what impact, if any, each of the answer choices will have on it.

> The credited response to a Resolve/Explain question will be a hypothetically true statement that explains how all aspects of the paradox or discrepancy can be true.

Step 4: Answer using Process of Elimination Just as with Weaken and Strengthen answer choices, you first have to accept each of the answer choices here as facts, and then apply them to the argument. One of these facts, when added to the argument, will resolve the apparent paradox, or explain the supposed discrepancy.

Let's see which one of the following choices does this.

 On average, mixed-age classrooms today are somewhat larger in enrollment than were the ones of the past.

Does this explain why mixed-age classrooms were not successful but now are? No. A larger class size does not resolve the discrepancy in success. Eliminate it.

B   Mixed-age classrooms of the past were better equipped than are those of today.

Does this explain why mixed-age classrooms were not successful but now are? If mixed-age classrooms of the past were better equipped, then why would the new mixed-age classrooms be more successful? This makes the discrepancy worse. Get rid of it.

 C   Today's mixed-age classrooms, unlike those of the past, emphasize group projects that are engaging to students of different ages.

Does this explain why mixed-age classrooms were not successful but now are? Notice how this answer sets up a contrast between the student activities in today's mixed-age classrooms and those of the past. If the projects are engaging to students of different ages, then this could explain why today's classrooms are more successful. Keep this one.

 D   Today's mixed-age classrooms have students of a greater range of ages than did those of the past.

Does this explain why mixed-age classrooms were not successful but now are? A wider age range does not clear up the difference in the success of the new classrooms versus the old ones. Eliminate it.

 E   Few of the teachers who are reviving mixed-age classrooms today were students in mixed-age classrooms when they were young.

Does this explain why mixed-age classrooms were not successful but now are? Whether the teachers attended mixed-age classes is not relevant to the change in success. Eliminate it.

Some people can find this type of question challenging because they can see how more than one of the answers could work. If this sounds like something you do, remember to follow the process and be crystal clear what you need the credited response to do. Asking yourself the same question as you do POE—in this case, "Does this explain why mixed-age classrooms were not successful but now are?"— will help you stay focused on the task at hand. If you find yourself wanting to justify any of the answers by supplying additional information to make them work, they are wrong and you need to eliminate them.

Arguments Technique: Using Process of Elimination with Resolve/Explain Questions

In using Process of Elimination (POE) with Resolve/Explain questions, it is important to remember that the correct answer will be some explanation that will allow *both* of the facts from the passage to be true. In the Dirdir question, the two facts were (a) they had water power, and (b) they did not use this technology in their capital city. In the mixed-age classrooms passage, the facts were (a) mixed-age classrooms in the past were usually a failure, and (b) mixed-age classrooms today are successful. The correct answer in each case allowed each of these facts to be true independently of the other and allowed both to make sense together.

Additionally, note that the phrasing of most Resolve/Explain questions contains the clause "if true." Your methodology should be exactly the same here as it is with Weaken and Strengthen questions—you assume each of the five answer choices to be hypothetically true and look for the impact of each one on the discrepancy. In the case of Resolve/Explain questions, the impact will relate to whether or not or how well the choice resolves an apparent discrepancy.

Summary: Cracking Resolve/Explain Questions

With Resolve/Explain questions, the only thing you must find before going to the answer choices is the apparent discrepancy or paradox. Remember that you have to work under the belief that the answers are true, regardless of how unreasonable they may seem. Evaluate what impact the answer choice would have on the discrepancy *if it were true*. Finally, look to see which one of the answer choices allows both of the facts or sides in the passage to be true at the same time. Only one of them will do this.

Sample Question Phrasings	Act
Which one of the following provides the best resolution to the apparent paradox described by the committee member? *Which of the following statements, if true, would explain the discrepancy found by the scientists?*	• Identify the apparent discrepancy or paradox. • Go to the answer choices and look for a piece of information that, when added to the information given, allows both facts from the passage to be true. • Assume all choices to be hypothetically true.

LESSON 7: INFERENCE QUESTIONS

Like the arguments attached to Resolve/Explain questions, most Inference arguments are not written in the familiar *conclusion supported by premises* format. Instead, they will be passages that may or may not seem to be headed somewhere. And the test-writers will ask you to find a piece of information that either must be true, based on the information provided in the argument, or will be best supported by the argument. That something can come from anywhere in the passage and doesn't have to come from anything important.

Here are a few tips right off the bat. You can't use any information that is not included in the passage, you don't have to find the main conclusion, and you have to pay very close attention to any qualifying language (*most, always, each, few, might*) that is used. Ready to put this information to work? Then let's get to it.

The Argument

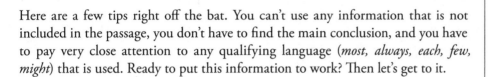

10. Artists have different ways of producing contours and hatching, and analysis of these stylistic features can help to distinguish works by a famous artist both from forgeries and from works genuinely by other artists. Indeed, this analysis has shown that many of the drawings formerly attributed to Michelangelo are actually by the artist Giulio Clovio, Michelangelo's contemporary.

   If the statements above are true, then which one of the following must also be true?

   (A) Contours and hatching are the main features that distinguish the drawing styles of different artists.

   (B) Many of the drawings formerly attributed to Michelangelo are actually forgeries.

   (C) No forgery can perfectly duplicate the contour and hatching styles of a famous artist.

   (D) The contour and hatching styles used to identify the drawings of Clovio cited can be shown to be features of all Clovio's works.

   (E) There is an analyzable difference between Clovio's contour and hatching styles and those of Michelangelo.

   PrepTest 44, Section 4, Question 15

Here's How to Crack It

Step 1: Assess the question Inference questions can be worded in several ways. Here's a common one.

> If the statements above are true, then which one of the following must also be true?

You're looking for something that's an absolutely 100 percent airtight logical consequence of the material presented in the argument, which as you can see in this case is more like a short descriptive passage.

Step 2: Analyze the argument Sometimes on Inference questions there isn't a lot of analysis you can do. In those cases, just read the passage and do a quick paraphrase of the information given. Most often, these passages are not arguments, though when they are you still have to treat all the parts as true and not look for gaps in the reasoning. Sometimes there are a series of statements that appear to be begging to be put together. Look at the passage again.

Analyze
Do not look for the conclusion and premises on Inference questions.

> Artists have different ways of producing contours and hatching, and analysis of these stylistic features can help to distinguish works by a famous artist both from forgeries and from works genuinely by other artists. Indeed, this analysis has shown that many of the drawings formerly attributed to Michelangelo are actually by the artist Giulio Clovio, Michelangelo's contemporary.

Focus on the facts in this passage, and paraphrase them so you can more readily recognize any connections.

- Fact 1: *Analysis of certain stylistic features can help distinguish who the artist is.*
- Fact 2: *This analysis helped to show that some art is Clovio's instead of Michelangelo's.*

An inference is something you can prove from the information given. It is not to be confused with an assumption, which doesn't need proof. Once you have paraphrased the facts, look to see what you know to be true on the basis of them. If you notice a logical progression leading to a particular conclusion, it always pays to go ahead and combine the facts for yourself before you do POE. So, what do you know for sure from the facts above?

- *Artists stylistic features are different enough that they can be used to help identify who made the art.*
- *Since the analysis was used to differentiate between Clovio's work and Michelangelo's, there must be some differences between Clovio's style and Michelangelo's style.*

Step 3: Act   These conclusions are very likely to figure into the right answer somehow, which is why you should bother to paraphrase the passage and look for them in the first place.

> The credited response to an Inference question is the statement best supported by the passage.

Step 4: Answer using Process of Elimination   When using POE on Inference question answers, look at the choices with an open mind. It is sometimes hard to predict exactly what inference will be in the answers. Combining facts is one way to make inferences on the LSAT, or sometimes the test-writers will make an inference by just taking a small logical step away from something said in the passage. Take each choice on its own merits and always go back to the passage for *proof!*

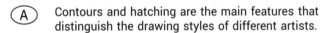   (A)   Contours and hatching are the main features that distinguish the drawing styles of different artists.

The passage mentions contours and hatching as examples of stylistic features, but it does not claim that these are the *main* features that distinguish artists' works. This choice is more specific and more demanding than our original, so eliminate the choice.

(B)   Many of the drawings formerly attributed to Michelangelo are actually forgeries.   (B̶)

A forgery is a fake meant to be passed off as an original work of art. Many Michelangelo works have now been attributed to Clovio, but there is no proof in the passage that those works were forgeries. You should eliminate this choice.

(C)   No forgery can perfectly duplicate the contour and hatching styles of a famous artist.

The passage states that stylistic differences "help to distinguish" works, which is not the same as claiming that no forgery can perfectly duplicate an artist's style. This goes too far, so eliminate it.

(D)   The contour and hatching styles used to identify the drawings of Clovio cited can be shown to be features of all Clovio's works.   (D̶)

There is no evidence in the passage that all of Clovio's works had the same style features. Be careful not to make an assumption here! All you know for sure is that the stylistic features are unique and that the styles of Clovio and Michelangelo are different. If you can't prove it, you can't choose it! Since you don't have enough information to prove this, eliminate it.

(E) There is an analyzable difference between Clovio's contour and hatching styles and those of Michelangelo.

Here, at last, is the inference we came up with in the first place. Because some of Michelangelo's works have been reattributed to Clovio using analysis of contour and hatching styles, there must be a discernible difference. This is the choice you want.

Arguments Technique: Look for Extreme Language

Do you remember the Process of Elimination techniques used to get rid of wrong answer choices in Main Point questions in Lesson 1? They included relevance, opposites, and extreme language. Relevance is still certainly an issue with Inference questions because if there is something in an answer choice that wasn't mentioned in the argument, there's no way you could have inferred it from the information presented. However, when it comes to Inference questions, extreme wording (as you saw in some of the answers in the previous examples) plays a key role. It is much easier to say that something is *usually* true than to say that something is *always* true. It is much more difficult to back up the second phrase. Take a look at another example.

1. Most literature professors are skilled readers.
2. All literature professors are skilled readers.

It's much easier to prove that something is usually true than it is to prove that something is always true.

There's only one difference between these two sentences: one has the word *most*; the other has the word *all*. Yet there is a vast difference between these two statements. Certainly, anyone who has reached such a high position has done more than her fair share of reading. Very rigorous standards must be met and outstanding academic performance must be demonstrated. This requires a ton of reading. It's reasonable to think that if someone's doing that much reading, he or she is probably a skilled reader. But if you were asked which of those statements *must be true*, you would have to eliminate the second statement. It would be incredibly difficult to prove that *all* literature professors are skilled readers. It would take only *one* person who never really liked to read, but was driven to this level of success for other reasons, to disprove the second statement. It would be much easier to prove the first statement because it leaves a lot more room for a few exceptions to the general rule. Both statements involve strong wording, but the second is *too* strong.

Take a look at the following chart.

Safely Vague		Dangerously Extreme	
might	possible	always	not
could	usually	never	positively
may	sometimes	at no time	absolutely
can	at least once	must	unequivocally
some	frequently	will	every
		all	

The sample Inference question you just worked through asked you to find the answer choice that could be "properly inferred," in other words, the one that *must be true* based on the information in the argument. Other Inference questions will require a slightly different task. Rather than finding the answer that must be true, you will be asked to find the one that would be best supported by the information in the argument. This may seem like a subtle difference, but it is important to pay attention to nuances in language such as this on the LSAT. Let's take a look at how these work.

The Argument

---

11. Coffee and tea contain methylxanthines, which cause temporary increases in the natural production of vasopressin, a hormone produced by the pituitary gland. Vasopressin causes clumping of blood cells, and the clumping is more pronounced in women than in men. This is probably the explanation of the fact that women face as much as a tenfold higher risk than men do of complications following angioplasty, a technique used to clear clogged arteries.

    Which one of the following statements is most strongly supported by the information above?

(A) Men, but not women, should be given methylxanthines prior to undergoing angioplasty.

(B) In spite of the risks, angioplasty is the only effective treatment for clogged arteries.

(C) Women probably drink more coffee and tea, on average, than do men.

(D) Prior to undergoing angioplasty, women should avoid coffee and tea.

(E) Angioplasty should not be used to treat clogged arteries.

PrepTest 44, Section 4, Question 12

Here's How to Crack It

Step 1: Assess the question   Make sure that you're clear about your task. Notice that the question stem makes no mention of an argument—that's a classic sign that this is an Inference question. This question asks us to find the answer that is "most strongly supported" by the information in the passage. You don't have to be able to show that the answer *must be true* according to the information we have from the author. You still need evidence from the author's language, but it doesn't *have to be* true.

Step 2: Analyze the argument   You still need to read the passage carefully. This step will be the same as it was with your first Inference question. Pay close attention to qualifying language, underlining key words and jotting down any notes you need to keep things straight. Here's the passage again.

> Coffee and tea contain methylxanthines, which cause temporary increases in the natural production of vasopressin, a hormone produced by the pituitary gland. Vasopressin causes clumping of blood cells, and the clumping is more pronounced in women than in men. This is probably the explanation of the fact that women face as much as a tenfold higher risk than men do of complications following angioplasty, a technique used to clear clogged arteries.

To summarize, a substance in coffee and tea increases vasopressin, which, in turn, causes clumping of blood cells. This clumping is more pronounced in women than in men, and may explain why women face a higher risk of complications after angioplasty.

Step 3: Act   Remember that on Inference questions, you can't predict with any assurance what the test-writers will look for. Head right to the answer choices and start Step 4. Just be sure to go back to the passage for proof.

Step 4: Answer using Process of Elimination   Check out each answer choice in turn and see which ones you can eliminate. Be on the lookout for answers that fall outside of the scope of the information that you've been given or are inconsistent with what you were told, answers that include extreme language, and answers that make unwarranted comparisons. If any part of an answer choice isn't supported, get rid of it. Here we go.

(A)   Men, but not women, should be given methylxanthines prior to undergoing angioplasty.   Ⓐ

What do you know from the passage? Methylxanthines increase vasopressin, which causes blood cell clumping. Clumping can lead to complications, so it would be bad to give men methylxanthines. Eliminate this choice.

(B)   In spite of the risks, angioplasty is the only effective treatment for clogged arteries.   Ⓑ

The passage doesn't provide enough information to say that angioplasty is the only effective treatment for clogged arteries. "Only" makes this choice extreme and unsupported. Eliminate it.

(C)   Women probably drink more coffee and tea, on average, than do men.   Ⓒ

You may be tempted by this at first, since women are at a greater risk for complications than men, but there is no support in the passage that the reason is that women drink more coffee and tea. All you know for sure is that the clumping is more pronounced for women than for men, but not why. Get rid of this one.

(D)   Prior to undergoing angioplasty, women should avoid coffee and tea.   Ⓓ

What do you know from the passage? Because consuming methylxanthines increases the risk of blood cell clumping, which in turn increases the risk of complications after angioplasty, women would be well advised to avoid coffee and tea before undergoing angioplasty. Keep this one for now.

(E)   Angioplasty should not be used to treat clogged arteries.   Ⓔ

This goes too far. Though the passage mentions complications of angioplasty, that's not enough to claim that the treatment should not be used. This one should be eliminated too.

There you have it. You found (D), which is the credited response. Notice that you can't say *for sure* that women should avoid coffee and tea before angioplasty, but this is a reasonable inference from the given facts.

In summary, when you have this kind of weaker inference, you have a little bit more latitude. You still need evidence from the passage to support the choice, but you don't have to be able to show that an answer *must be true*.

Arguments Technique: Watch Out for the Word *Support*

The word *support* shows up in two different types of Arguments questions, and you'll need to be able to keep them straight if you hope to approach the questions effectively. Take a look at a couple of sample questions.

> Which one of the following, if true, provides the most support for the argument?

> The passage provides the most support for which one of the following?

If you're not careful, you might mistakenly think that these two questions ask you to perform the same task. After all, they both talk about support, right? Actually, you have two different tasks here, and if you get them mixed up, you're going to have a difficult time with POE. Examine the first question more closely. Here it is again.

> Which one of the following, if true, provides the most support for the argument?

Read Carefully!
"The statements above, if true, provide the most support for which one of the following?" Notice that "if true" refers to "the statements above." Because these statements are being used to support one of the answer choices, this is an *Inference* question, not a *Strengthen* question.

This should look familiar. Care to guess what your task is here? If you identified this as a Strengthen question, bravo! There are two indicators that will help you to properly identify it. First, notice the phrase "if true," referring to "the following," and recall that it is the answers on Strengthen questions that are hypothetically true. Second, notice that you are being asked to find the answer choice that *provides the most support for* the argument. In other words, you're being asked to evaluate the impact that each answer choice has on the author's conclusion. Sound familiar? We hope so.

Here's the second question again.

> The passage provides the most support for which one of the following?

Notice the difference here. Aside from the obvious lack of the words *if true*, this question also asks for the support to happen, but *in the other direction*. Here you are asked to find the answer choice that *is best supported by* the passage. That's what you were just doing in the question you worked on a minute ago, so this is an Inference question.

Here, eliminate answers that aren't relevant because the passage doesn't offer enough evidence to support them, a pretty different mode of elimination from that used with Strengthen questions. The words *if true*, when referring to the choices, indicate hypotheticals in the answers, so it won't be an Inference question.

> Two things to look for: If the *answer choices* are being used to support the *argument*, you have a Strengthen question. If the *passage* is being used to support one of the *answer choices*, you have an Inference question.

Arguments Technique: Look for Conditional Statements and Find the Contrapositive

Do you know what an "if…then" statement is? If you've taken any classes in logic, you might know it as a "conditional statement." Actually, it's very simple. Read this sentence.

If you hit a glass with a hammer, the glass will break.

When you run across a statement such as this, you can diagram it. A common way to diagram conditional statements is to use a symbol for each element in the statement—here we'll use "H" for hitting the glass with a hammer and "B" for breaking—and use an arrow to connect them, showing that the action leads directly to the effect. So H → B would represent the original statement.

This statement would seem reasonable to most people because it's what you would expect to happen in the real world. On the LSAT, you have to take this statement as true if it were part of an argument because, as we stated earlier, you have to accept all of the evidence presented in arguments at face value. This is true even when they aren't things that necessarily make reasonable sense.

With Inference questions, you are often asked to identify another statement—in the form of an answer choice—that also *must be true* if the statements in the argument are accepted as true.

Conditional Statements: Sufficient and Necessary

Once you diagram a conditional statement, use the terms *sufficient* and *necessary* to describe the function of each side of the diagram.

The left side is the sufficient side because it is enough, on its own, to know something else (the right side).

The right side is the necessary side because it is a requirement of something else (the left side).

You can use these terms to take apart and diagram difficult sentences containing conditional language by asking yourself, "Which factor is enough to know something else?" or "Which factor seems to be a requirement of something else?"

Here's the original statement.

If you hit a glass with a hammer, the glass will break.

You can come up with a few other statements that you think would also have to be true.

For example, you could say

If the glass is broken, it was hit with a hammer.

You would symbolize this as B ➔ H. That seems like a reasonable outcome, but can you say that it *must be true* given our original statement?

Not *necessarily*. The glass could have been thrown out the window, stepped on by a giraffe, shot up with a Red Rider BB gun, and so on. If this were an answer choice on an Inference question in which the argument contained our original statement, what would you do? Hopefully, you would eliminate it because it doesn't have to be true. You could also suppose that

If you don't hit a glass with a hammer, the glass won't break.

In this case, your symbolization would become ~H ➔ ~B. Once again this seems reasonable in many cases, but does it *have to be true*? Again, not necessarily. It could have been thrown out the window, run over by a car, shattered by an opera singer's high C note, and so on. If this were an answer choice on an Inference question in which the argument contained our original statement, what would you do? Hopefully, you would eliminate it too because just like the last one, it doesn't have to be true.

How about this statement.

If the glass isn't broken, it wasn't hit with a hammer.

This would be symbolized as ~B ➔ ~H. This *must* be true. It makes sense if you think about it because you know for sure that if you hit the glass with a hammer, you're definitely going to break the glass. So if you come across an unbroken glass, there's no way it could have been hit with a hammer, at least not if you accept the truth of the original statement the way we have to on the LSAT. The only way that you could argue the truth of the above statement is by arguing the truth of the original. And while you can do that in real life, you can't do it on the LSAT.

This statement, which must always be true given that the original statement is true, is known as the *contrapositive*.

> To create the contrapositive of a statement, take the original statement (or its symbolization, which is easier to work with) and perform the following two steps: Flip the order of the statements and then negate each of them.

Here's how it works with our original.

$$H \rightarrow B$$

Flip the order of the statements and negate each of them to get the contrapositive.

$$\sim B \rightarrow \sim H$$

Now, what do you do if you have to negate something that's already negative? Let's take a look at an example.

If Pablo attends the dance, Christina won't attend the dance.

You can symbolize this as follows:

$$P \rightarrow \sim C$$

How do you negate ~C? Well, two negatives make a positive. When you negate a statement like "Christina won't attend the dance," it becomes "Christina will attend the dance." The contrapositive of your original statement is

$$C \rightarrow \sim P$$

With these examples, which are tied to real life and make reasonable sense, it might seem as if it's more work to learn how to apply this process than it would be to just reason out what the only other true statement would be. And it would be pretty reasonable to do that if you understand the way conditionals and contrapositives work and if the original statement makes sense. If only the LSAT were always that straightforward.

Instead, what will often happen is the original statement will be some abstract and complicated notion that's hard to get a handle on. For instance, you might see a conditional statement such as "Copper will not be added to the alloy only if aluminum is also not added to the alloy." Not nearly as intuitive, is it? Add to that the pressure of taking a timed, standardized exam and you'll wish you had memorized the simple symbols above.

These steps always work so it's worth having them at your disposal. We're telling you all this because sometimes arguments contain "if…then" statements like the ones above. Usually the LSAT writers then ask an Inference question that requires you to find the answer that *must be true*. A couple of the answer choices will seem like reasonable things to believe. Another one or two may be variations on the original conditional statement, but won't be valid contrapositives.

It's possible that the credited response may just actually be the contrapositive—that depends on how complicated the argument is and how many pieces of information the passage contains—but regardless, knowing how to derive the contrapositive will help you eliminate wrong choices. Having both the original and contrapositive statements makes it easier to see the difference between what is *definitely* true and what merely *could* be true.

Arguments Technique: Look for Little Things That Mean a Lot

Another key to cracking Inference questions is to pay close attention to detail. Inferences are often made around seemingly innocuous words or phrases. For instance, anytime you see a term of quantity, comparison, or frequency, odds are it contains an inference.

> Statement: *Most people like Picasso.*
> Inference: *Some people may not like Picasso.*

> Statement: *Unlike her jacket, mine is real leather.*
> Inference: *Her jacket is not real leather.*

> Statement: *Russ almost never shows up on time.*
> Inference: *Russ rarely (or occasionally) does show up on time.*

Keep an eye out for details, and you'll stand a better chance of getting Inference questions right.

Summary: Cracking Inference Questions

With Inference questions, read the argument carefully and pay close attention to details such as qualifying language. Once you're at the answer choices, your goal is to eliminate the four answer choices that *don't have to be true* or are not *wholly supported* by evidence provided in the argument. You're also going to look out for relevance and, especially, issues of extreme language.

The way that Inference questions are phrased can be very tricky. See the "Sample Question Phrasings" column in the chart below for some examples.

Sample Question Phrasings	Act
Which one of the following statements can be validly inferred from the information above? *If the statements above are true, then which of the following must also be true?* *Which one of the following conclusions can be validly drawn from the passage above?** *Which one of the following conclusions is best supported by the passage above?**	• Read carefully, paying close attention to qualifying language, and then go to the answer choices. • Once there, eliminate any answer choices that are not *directly* supported by evidence in the passage. • Look for relevance and extreme language to eliminate answer choices. • Use the contrapositive if there are "if...then" statements contained in the passage and in the answer choices.

*Even though the stems in these questions contain the term "conclusions," they are not Main Point questions. Main Point questions ask you to find the conclusion, whereas Inference questions ask you for a conclusion, one of many that could possibly be derived from the passage. They are *Inference* questions, not *Main Point* questions. For contrast, review the sample Main Point question phrasings on page 28.

LESSON 8: REASONING QUESTIONS

So far, the questions you've seen in the Arguments section have been concerned with the literal contents: what's the conclusion, how do you attack or support it, or what does it assume? What piece of information will resolve two seemingly inconsistent pieces of information, or what else do you know to be true if the statements in the argument are true? Now you're going to look at some questions that deal with the arguments on a more abstract or descriptive level.

The first of these is the Reasoning question task, which asks you to determine not what the argument is about, but how the argument is made. This sounds quite straightforward, doesn't it? Well, sometimes it will be, but sometimes it will be rather difficult because of very attractive incorrect answers and deliberately impenetrable vocabulary. The answers to Reasoning questions will fall into one of two categories: general answers that don't actually mention the subject matter of the argument, and specific answers that do address the subject matter of the argument. Occasionally, the answer choices will be a mix of both.

So how do you approach questions such as these? Well, first you have to be able to identify the task. Then your goal is to describe what's happening in the argument—in other words, how the author arrived at his or her conclusion. Give one a try.

The Argument

12. An artificial hormone has recently been developed that increases milk production in cows. Its development has prompted some lawmakers to propose that milk labels should be required to provide information to consumers about what artificial substances were used in milk production. This proposal should not be implemented: just imagine trying to list every synthetic fertilizer used to grow the grass and grain the cows ate, or every fungicide used to keep the grain from spoiling!

The argument proceeds by

(A) proposing an alternative course of action for achieving the objectives of the proposal being argued against

(B) raising considerations in order to show that the proposal being argued against, if strictly implemented, would lead to absurd consequences

(C) using specific examples in order to show that an alternative to the proposal being argued against would better achieve the ends to which the original proposal was directed

(D) introducing a case analogous to the one under consideration to show that a general implementation of the proposal being argued against would be impossible

(E) questioning the motivation of those who made the proposal being argued against

Here's How to Crack It

Step 1: Assess the question   You've read the question, but here it is again.

> The argument proceeds by

This asks you to describe the author's method of reasoning. Read the argument and look at the purpose structure of the argument to see how he or she gets from the evidence to his main point.

Step 2: Analyze the argument   Read the argument closely, paying attention to the author's reasoning. To do this, you'll have to identify the conclusion and the premises because this will allow you to understand the structure of the argument—in other words, how the author used the evidence to support his or her conclusion. You don't need to identify any gaps in the reasoning. Here it is again.

Analyze
Find the conclusion
and premises on
Reasoning questions.

> An artificial hormone has recently been developed that increases milk production in cows. Its development has prompted some lawmakers to propose that milk labels should be required to provide information to consumers about what artificial substances were used in milk production. This proposal should not be implemented: just imagine trying to list every synthetic fertilizer used to grow the grass and grain the cows ate, or every fungicide used to keep the grain from spoiling!

What is the purpose of this argument? To disagree—you can tell because the argument presents a proposal and then the author does not want the proposal implemented.

- Author's conclusion: *This proposal (that milk labels should be required to list artificial substances used in milk production) should not be implemented.*
- Author's premises: *Such labels would have to list so many synthetic products as to be impossible to implement.*

Step 3: Act   Your goal here is simply to describe how the author made his argument. In this case, the author disagrees with implementing a proposal by presenting reasons that make the proposal too difficult to implement.

> The credited response to a Reasoning question will describe how the author constructed the argument.

Step 4: Answer using Process of Elimination Now you're going to approach the answer choices. The credited response will be a paraphrase of the author's reasoning: the proposal shouldn't be implemented because it will be unreasonable to do so. Check them out.

(A) proposing an alternative course of action for achieving the objectives of the proposal being argued against (Ⱥ)

The author doesn't propose an alternative course of action, so eliminate it.

(B) raising considerations in order to show that the proposal being argued against, if strictly implemented, would lead to absurd consequences (B)

While the wording is different, it does line up with the disagree purpose structure and the author's position since he points out that there are too many ingredients to reasonably list. Keep it.

(C) using specific examples in order to show that an alternative to the proposal being argued against would better achieve the ends to which the original proposal was directed (Ȼ)

What alternative proposal? The author isn't trying to solve the problem, just point out that the current proposal shouldn't be implemented.

(D) introducing a case analogous to the one under consideration to show that a general implementation of the proposal being argued against would be impossible (Ð)

Although the author implies that the proposal would be impossible, he does not offer an analogous case to the one described in the argument. Eliminate it.

(E) questioning the motivation of those who made the proposal being argued against

There is no mention of the motivation of those making the label proposal. Get rid of it.

That one was pretty straightforward. You were able to recognize the credited response pretty easily because you understood the author's reasoning and purpose structure before you approached the answer choices. Note how abstract the answers were. They didn't mention any of the specific details from the argument but took a much broader view.

Arguments Technique: Using Process of Elimination with Reasoning Questions

You may have noticed that when we discussed some of the answer choices, we took each word or phrase from the answer choice and asked, "Does this correspond to anything that actually occurred in the argument?" Most of the time, the answer to this question was no. The answer choices might sound abstract and technical, but unless you can go back to the argument and say, "Ah, yes, this is where the author gives the example and this is where he or she gives the counterexample," then an answer choice that mentions "examples" and "counterexamples" will be wrong. This technique is the key to dealing with Reasoning questions; it should allow you to eliminate two or three answer choices every time. One other nice advantage of this technique is that it works even if you can't articulate the author's reasoning in your own words.

Look through the answers on Reasoning questions slowly and make sure to match each piece of the answer choice to a piece of the argument. When you come across something in an answer choice that doesn't correspond to anything in the argument, get rid of that choice. If it's even a little wrong, it's all wrong.

Hint:
On Reasoning questions, try to match each piece of the answer choice to a piece of the argument.

Summary: Cracking Reasoning Questions

In Reasoning questions, you should come up with your own description of how the argument unfolds. If you're able to come up with a terse, exact description of the argument, you can usually match it with one of the answer choices. Even if you can't come up with a good description, you can eliminate any answers that have elements that don't correspond with what actually happens in the author's argument. The vocabulary in the answer choices will probably be more esoteric than that which you used, but as long as the meaning is the same, you're fine.

Sample Question Phrasings	Act
The argument proceeds by… *Leah responds to Kevin by doing which of the following?* *The method the activist uses to object to the developer's argument is to…* *Dr. Jacobs does which of the following?* *Which one of the following most accurately describes the role played in the argument by the claim that…*	• Read the argument carefully and then describe what is happening in your own words, focusing on the purpose structure and the author's conclusion and premises. • Take this description and rigorously apply it to all the answer choices. • Once you're at the answer choices, use the technique of comparing the actions described in the answer choices against those that actually occur in the argument. • Eliminate anything that doesn't appear in the argument.

LESSON 9: FLAW QUESTIONS

Flaw questions are similar to Reasoning questions, but they're dissimilar enough that they call for a slightly different approach. On recent LSATs, Flaw questions have been far more common than have Reasoning questions. So what's the difference? Well, while a Reasoning question asks you to identify what the argument does or how it's argued, a Flaw question asks you what the argument does *wrong*. And as we mentioned before, if you find a problematic assumption in an argument, you've probably found its flaw. The approach to Flaw and Reasoning questions is the same, but with one important distinction: during Step 2, you should break down the argument into its parts and locate the assumption. After you've spotted the assumption, you just need to state what's wrong with the argument. Look at the following argument.

The Argument

13. According to some astronomers, Earth is struck by a meteorite large enough to cause an ice age on an average of once every 100 million years. The last such incident occurred nearly 100 million years ago, so we can expect that Earth will be struck by such a meteorite in the near future. This clearly warrants funding to determine whether there is a means to protect our planet from such meteorite strikes.

The reasoning in the argument is most subject to criticism on the grounds that the argument

(A) makes a bold prescription on the basis of evidence that establishes only a high probability for a disastrous event

(B) presumes, without providing justification, that the probability of a chance event's occurring is not affected by whether the event has occurred during a period in which it would be expected to occur

(C) moves from evidence about the average frequency of an event to a specific prediction about when the next such event will occur

(D) fails to specify the likelihood that, if such a meteorite should strike Earth, the meteorite would indeed cause an ice age

(E) presumes, without providing justification, that some feasible means can be found to deter large meteorite strikes

PrepTest 45, Section 4, Question 19

Here's How to Crack It

Step 1: Assess the question   You've already read the question, but here it is again.

> The reasoning in the argument is most subject to criticism on the grounds that the argument

Now, you're expected to describe why the above argument is bad. Remember that this is different from "weakening" an argument, in which you'd hypothesize that the five answer choices were true. All you're looking for here is to describe the way in which the argument is bad, not add something that would make it worse.

Step 2: Analyze the argument   Okay, so start by breaking it down into its parts.

- Author's conclusion: *This (likelihood of a large meteorite strike) clearly warrants funding to determine whether there is a means to protect our planet from such meteorite strikes.*
- Author's premises: *Earth is struck by a meteorite large enough to cause an ice age on an average of once every 100 million years. The last such incident occurred nearly 100 million years ago, so we can expect that Earth will be struck by such a meteorite in the near future.*
- Author's assumption: *How did the author get from an average time between meteor strikes to needing to prepare for an imminent meteor strike? He is interpreting the statistic incorrectly to assume that an average amount of time is an actual, predictable amount of time.*

Step 3: Act   The correct answer to a Flaw question often draws attention to an assumption. If the assumption is that an average amount of time can be used to reliably predict the next meteorite strike, then the flaw is that the author fails to consider that the statistic might not be an accurate predictor. The credited response should draw attention to this weak link between the average and the prediction.

> The credited response to a Flaw question will describe how the premises don't necessarily lead to the conclusion, often drawing attention to a key assumption.

Step 4: Answer using Process of Elimination   Now you're going to attack the answer choices. Let's see if you can find an answer choice that has something to do with the author making an analogy.

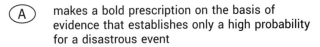

(A)   makes a bold prescription on the basis of evidence that establishes only a high probability for a disastrous event

This answer describes the progression of the argument, but this isn't what makes the argument's logic problematic. This describes the argument's conclusion and premises, but not the assumption, and the assumption is where the argument is flawed. Eliminate it.

(B)   presumes, without providing justification, that the probability of a chance event's occurring is not affected by whether the event has occurred during a period in which it would be expected to occur

Does this match the assumption that average time can be a reliable predictor? Let's match this to the specific details in the argument. The probability of a chance event (meteorite strike) is not affected by whether the event (meteorite strike) has occurred during a period of time (100 million years) it was expected to. This is the opposite of what we are looking for. Get rid of it.

(C)   moves from evidence about the average frequency of an event to a specific prediction about when the next such event will occur

Does this match the assumption that average time can be a reliable predictor? Well, it addresses the shift from average frequency (average time) to a specific prediction (the next meteorite strike), which lines up with the assumption. Keep this one for now.

(D)   fails to specify the likelihood that, if such a meteorite should strike Earth, the meteorite would indeed cause an ice age

This answer doesn't match the assumption because the argument is centered on the asteroid strike itself, not the results of such a strike. Eliminate it.

(E)   presumes, without providing justification, that some feasible means can be found to deter large meteorite strikes

Be careful here! You may think that the author believes this based on his conclusion that the possible meteorite strike warrants funding, but if you look carefully at this conclusion, the author wants funding to determine if there *is* a way to protect the planet, which may or may not involve deterring the meteor. This choice is not nearly as strong as (C), so get rid of it.

You know that Flaw questions deal with gaps or assumptions in an argument. You also know that they're pretty similar to Reasoning questions and that they can exhibit similar "traps" (such as overly wordy or confusing answers). Finally, you can use similar POE techniques on Flaw questions, such as trying to match each word or phrase in the answer choices with something in the argument.

Arguments Technique: Using Process of Elimination with Flaw Questions

One thing you might have noticed that we did when discussing some of the answer choices was again to take each word or phrase from the answer choice and ask, "Does this correspond to anything that actually occurred in the argument?" Most of the time, the answer is no. The answer choices might sound impressive ("the author assumes what he sets out to prove," "the author appeals to authority," and so on), but unless you can go back to the argument and say, "Ah, yes, *this* is where the author gives evidence" or "*this* is where the author makes a prediction," then an answer choice that mentions "examples" or "predictions" will be wrong. This technique is HUGE. It will eliminate two or three answer choices every time.

Therefore, take answer choices on Flaw questions very slowly, and make sure to match each piece of the answer choice to a piece of the argument. Once you come across something in an answer choice that doesn't correspond to anything in the argument, you can get rid of that answer choice. Once it's a little wrong, it's all wrong.

This process will allow you to eliminate two or three answer choices in most cases, but what about the ones that remain? You'll find that some of the answer choices on Flaw questions will be consistent with the argument but won't represent a flaw in the author's reasoning. Once you've eliminated any answer choices on Flaw questions that are not consistent with what actually happened in the argument, then go back to check the rest to see if they represent a logical flaw in the structure of the author's argument.

The Argument

14. Advertisement: Each of the Economic Merit Prize winners from the past 25 years is covered by the Acme retirement plan. Since the winners of the nation's most prestigious award for economists have thus clearly recognized that the Acme plan offers them a financially secure future, it is probably a good plan for anyone with retirement needs similar to theirs.

The advertisement's argumentation is most vulnerable to criticism on which one of the following grounds?

(A) It ignores the possibility that the majority of Economic Merit Prize winners from previous years used a retirement plan other than the Acme plan.

(B) It fails to address adequately the possibility that any of several retirement plans would be good enough for, and offer a financially secure future to, Economic Merit Prize winners.

(C) It appeals to the fact that supposed experts have endorsed the argument's main conclusion, rather than appealing to direct evidence for that conclusion.

(D) It takes for granted that some winners of the Economic Merit Prize have deliberately selected the Acme retirement plan, rather than having had it chosen for them by their employers.

(E) It presumes, without providing justification, that each of the Economic Merit Prize winners has retirement plan needs that are identical to the advertisement's intended audience's retirement plan needs.

PrepTest 44, Section 4, Question 20

Here's How to Crack It

Step 1: Assess the question   Here's the question again.

The advertisement's argumentation is most vulnerable to criticism on which one of the following grounds?

This is a classic Flaw question. You're asked to describe what's wrong with the author's reasoning.

Step 2: Analyze the argument   Again, you're reading for the conclusion and the premises, and you should think about the purpose structure and the assumptions the author makes. Here's the argument again.

> Advertisement: Each of the Economic Merit Prize winners from the past 25 years is covered by the Acme retirement plan. Since the winners of the nation's most prestigious award for economists have thus clearly recognized that the Acme plan offers them a financially secure future, it is probably a good plan for anyone with retirement needs similar to theirs.

What is the purpose structure of this argument? The author is interpreting the fact that all Economic Merit Prize winners have an Acme retirement plan to mean that they must recognize the plan provides a secure future, and thus the Acme plan is good for anyone with similar retirement needs.

Think about this for a moment. Remember that the conclusion for an argument with an Interpret purpose structure is often unwarranted by the evidence, and that the general assumption is that there is no other way to interpret the data. The author goes from a premise that all the winners *have* a particular retirement plan to the winners *clearly recognize* the benefits of the plan. The author believes that the winners chose the plan for its benefits.

But, what if the winners didn't choose the plan? The plan could have been the prize, or could just be a popular plan, or the only plan available. The author doesn't consider this possibility. Let's summarize.

- Author's conclusion: *Acme retirement plan is probably a good plan for anyone with retirement needs similar to those of Economic Merit Prize winners.*
- Author's premises: *The winners are covered by the plan and have recognized that it provides them a secure future.*
- Author's assumption: *The winners chose the plan.*

Step 3: Act   Remember to jot a note about what you need the credited response to do. In this case, you need the answer that matches how the winners might not have chosen the retirement plan.

Step 4: Answer using Process of Elimination

 (A)   It ignores the possibility that the majority of Economic Merit Prize winners from previous years used a retirement plan other than the Acme plan.

This doesn't seem to match what you're looking for. The ad concerns people whose needs are similar to winners from the past 25 years, so previous winners are not relevant. Eliminate it.

 (B)   It fails to address adequately the possibility that any of several retirement plans would be good enough for, and offer a financially secure future to, Economic Merit Prize winners.

The issue is whether the plan is good for people whose needs are similar to those of the winners, not what's good for the winners themselves. Eliminate it.

(C) It appeals to the fact that supposed experts have endorsed the argument's main conclusion, rather than appealing to direct evidence for that conclusion.

This one is confusing, so be sure to match it to the parts of the argument. Who would the supposed experts be? The winners? Maybe, but did the winners endorse (approve) the argument's main conclusion (the Acme retirement plan is probably good for anyone with retirement needs similar to those of the winners)? Not in the argument. The winners' supposed choice of plan is used to support the conclusion, so this choice doesn't match and you should get rid of it.

(D) It takes for granted that some winners of the Economic Merit Prize have deliberately selected the Acme retirement plan, rather than having had it chosen for them by their employers.

This looks like a good match. The argument states that the winners recognize the plan's benefits, but it does not provide evidence that the winners had the opportunity to choose this plan for themselves. If the plan was chosen for them by their employers, it might not be the best plan for the winners or for people with needs similar to theirs. Keep this one for now.

(E) It presumes, without providing justification, that each of the Economic Merit Prize winners has retirement plan needs that are identical to the advertisement's intended audience's retirement plan needs.

Watch the language on this one. The conclusion refers to people with similar, not identical, needs. Remember that one word can break an answer choice. That leaves (D) as the credited response.

Summary: Cracking Flaw Questions

The key to cracking Flaw questions is finding what's wrong with the argument before you go to the answer choices. Just remember that these questions are different from Weaken questions, in which new information is brought in to attack the argument, and are different from Reasoning questions, in which finding the key assumption won't be nearly as useful.

Sample Question Phrasings	Act
Which of the following indicates a flaw in the author's reasoning? *The reasoning in the argument is most vulnerable to criticism on the grounds that the argument…* *The argument above relies on which of the following questionable techniques?*	• Break down the argument into its parts; the flaw is usually related to the assumption. • State in your own words what the problem with the argument is. • With each answer, try to match the actions described in the answer choices with those of the argument itself. Look for the choice that has the same problem you found. • Eliminate the answers that don't match; look for the answer that addresses the assumption.

LESSON 10: PRINCIPLE MATCH QUESTIONS

You're nearing the home stretch. The last two question types we will cover are Principle Match and Parallel-the-Reasoning.

We've already covered questions that ask you to find a Principle that strengthens or justifies the conclusion. Principle Match questions, on the other hand, ask for a generalization or rule that "conforms," or is consistent with the argument's method. The analysis you need to do will be similar to Reasoning questions, but the answers may be broader than you might expect.

While many Principle questions are reasonable, some can get nasty, and it's hard to tell which is which until you're in the middle of them. Therefore, you might consider holding off on Principle Match questions until you've worked most other types.

Let's look at how one works.

The Argument

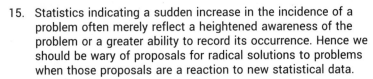

15. Statistics indicating a sudden increase in the incidence of a problem often merely reflect a heightened awareness of the problem or a greater ability to record its occurrence. Hence we should be wary of proposals for radical solutions to problems when those proposals are a reaction to new statistical data.

    The argumentation conforms most closely to which one of the following principles?

    (A) A better cognizance of a problem does not warrant the undertaking of a radical solution to the problem.

    (B) Attempts to stop the occurrence of a problem should be preceded by a determination that the problem actually exists.

    (C) Proposals for radical solutions to problems should be based on statistical data alone.

    (D) Statistical data should not be manipulated to make a radical solution to a problem seem more justified than it actually is.

    (E) Radical solutions to problems can cause other problems and end up doing more harm than good.

    PrepTest 44, Section 4, Question 4

Here's How to Crack It

Step 1: Assess the question   First, as always, you have to identify your task. Here it is again.

> The argumentation conforms most closely to which one of the following principles?

You are asked to find a principle among the answers with which the argument would be consistent. The choices will be generally worded statements—like a moral to a story that could apply to multiple situations—and what you need to do is pick the one to which the argument "conforms," or fits. If this reminds you of how you work a Reasoning question, then you're on the right track.

Step 2: Analyze the argument   You need to have a clear understanding of what's happening in the argument. Not all Principle Match questions will be true arguments. Some are more like stories that simply describe a certain situation. If that is the case, be sure to paraphrase the situation. Since this argument has a conclusion and premise, start by noting them.

- Author's conclusion: *We should be wary of proposals for radical solutions to problems when those proposals are a reaction to new statistical data.*
- Author's premises: *Statistics that indicate increased incidence of a problem may actually reflect increased awareness of the problem or increased ability to measure it.*

Step 3: Act   Because you're going to be asked to identify the principle with which the argument would fit best, you should be able to state in basic terms what's going on. For this example, you might come up with something like "Greater awareness or better measurements alone are not a good reason for radical solutions to problems."

Step 4: Answer using Process of Elimination   As you evaluate the answer choices, match the general descriptions in the answers to the specifics in the argument. Eliminate any that are not consistent with your paraphrase or that don't match the information presented in the argument.

 A better cognizance of a problem does not warrant the undertaking of a radical solution to the problem.

This sounds like a pretty close match to what you are looking for; it says that the statistics may reflect greater awareness (cognizance) of a problem rather than an actual increase in its incidence. Thus, taking radical action might not be warranted. Hold on to it.

(B) Attempts to stop the occurrence of a problem should be preceded by a determination that the problem actually exists.

This does not match the argument. Radical solutions are not necessarily the same as stopping a problem. In addition, the author accepts that problems exist but questions whether their apparent increase in frequency is real. Get rid of it.

(C) Proposals for radical solutions to problems should be based on statistical data alone.

Be sure to read this one carefully. It says that radical solutions *should* be based on data alone. This goes against your paraphrase and the author's suggestion. Eliminate it.

(D) Statistical data should not be manipulated to make a radical solution to a problem seem more justified than it actually is.

This statement may seem reasonable, but does it match the argument? While the author might even agree with this statement, the passage made no mention of manipulating data and this doesn't match your paraphrase. Get rid of it.

(E) Radical solutions to problems can cause other problems and end up doing more harm than good.

Again, this statement may be true, or at least seem reasonable, but it doesn't match the argument or your paraphrase. Eliminate it.

Now you're left with (A), the correct answer. Notice that once you understood that the author was suggesting that statistics alone are not a good reason for radical solutions, you were able to eliminate any answer that didn't match up with your paraphrase.

———————————○———————————

This question illustrates how there can be a pretty big difference between a Principle Match question that asks you to find a principle that conforms to the reasoning and a Principle Strengthen question that asks you to justify the reasoning. (See page 58 for Principle Strengthen questions.) Of course, the answer on both will go along with the conclusion of the argument. But a principle to which the argument "conforms" must also match the argument's method.

Sometimes, the question will ask you to find an answer choice that would conform to a principle contained in the argument. Your approach should stay the same. In this case, paraphrase the principle and then find the answer choice that matches it best piece by piece.

Try one.

The Argument

16. Etiquette firmly opposes both obscene and malicious talk, but this does not imply that speech needs to be restricted by law. Etiquette does not necessarily even oppose the expression of offensive ideas. Rather, it dictates that there are situations in which the expression of potentially offensive, disturbing, or controversial ideas is inappropriate and that, where appropriate, the expression and discussion of such ideas is to be done in a civil manner.

Which one of the following judgments most closely corresponds to the principles of etiquette stated above?

(A) Neighbors should not be gruff or unfriendly to one another when they meet on the street.

(B) When prosecutors elicit testimony from a cooperative witness, they should do so without intensive questioning.

(C) There should be restrictions on speech only if a large majority of the population finds the speech offensive and hateful.

(D) The journalists at a news conference should not ask a politician potentially embarrassing questions about a controversial policy issue.

(E) The moderator of a panel discussion of a divisive moral issue should not allow participants to engage in name-calling.

PrepTest 45, Section 4, Question 21

Here's How to Crack It

Step 1: Assess the question First, as always, you have to identify your task. Here it is again.

Which one of the following judgments most closely corresponds to the principles of etiquette stated above?

You are asked to find a situation among the answers that is consistent with the general rule in the argument. This time, the choices will be specific situations and you need to pick the one that fits most accurately and completely with the principle in the argument.

Step 2: Analyze the argument Again, you need to have a clear understanding of what's happening in the argument. This one does not have a clear conclusion and premise, so just start by reading the rule carefully. First, you are told that etiquette opposes obscene and malicious talk, but not the expression of offensive ideas as long as they are discussed when appropriate and in a civil (polite) manner.

Step 3: Act You need to identify the situation in the answers that best matches the argument, so start with a paraphrase of the principle. Here, you might come up with something like this: etiquette allows for polite discussion even if the topics being discussed are offensive or controversial.

Step 4: Answer using Process of Elimination As you evaluate the answer choices, match the specific descriptions in the answers to the general rule in the argument. Eliminate any that are not consistent with your paraphrase or that don't match the principle presented in the argument.

 Neighbors should not be gruff or unfriendly to one another when they meet on the street.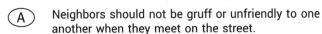

Does this match your paraphrase? There is no mention of discussing offensive or controversial material, so this doesn't match. Get rid of it.

 When prosecutors elicit testimony from a cooperative witness, they should do so without intensive questioning. B

This does not match the argument. This addresses being polite, but not politely discussing something controversial. Eliminate it.

 There should be restrictions on speech only if a large majority of the population finds the speech offensive and hateful. C

So, the only reason for restricting speech is what the majority finds offensive? The principle is about how to discuss offensive material, not when to restrict it. This one has to go.

 The journalists at a news conference should not ask a politician potentially embarrassing questions about a controversial policy issue. D

This almost matches, but it is about being polite and not embarrassing a politician, not about how to discuss controversial topics. Get rid of it.

(E) The moderator of a panel discussion of a divisive moral issue should not allow participants to engage in name-calling.

This sounds like a pretty close match to what you are looking for; a moderator not allowing name-calling during discussion of a divisive issue lines up with polite discussion of controversial topics. This is your best answer.

This may have felt like it was trickier or involved more work. These can often be time-consuming questions, which is one of the reasons they are best saved for later. Your best approach is to have a solid paraphrase of the principle in the argument and then to match each answer choice to your paraphrase and the argument very carefully.

Arguments Technique: Using Process of Elimination with Principle Match Questions

As we saw from these examples, you are looking for a principle among the answer choices that will match the conditions in the argument, or you might be asked to find an answer choice that would conform to a principle in the argument. Either way your task stays the same: eliminate any answers that don't match up with your paraphrase.

The important thing to remember: you're looking for an answer choice that matches the decision or action in the principle. The principle will be more general, but will match all the parts in the situation.

Summary: Cracking Principle Match Questions

Refer to the chart below on how to approach Principle Match questions.

Sample Question Phrasings	Act
The reasoning above most closely conforms to which of the following principles? *Which of the following examples conforms most closely to the principle given in the argument above?*	• Make sure you know in which direction the argument flows. Are you being asked to find a principle that conforms to a situation, or a situation that conforms to a principle? • Once you're sure, look for an answer that most closely matches the general principle underlying the argument.

LESSON 11: PARALLEL-THE-REASONING QUESTIONS

We're finally at the end. And there is a reason we saved Parallel-the-Reasoning questions for last—because you should probably avoid them until you've worked all the other questions you can tackle. These questions are not necessarily more difficult, but they are certainly more time-consuming on average than most other question types. Don't forget that all of the questions are worth one point each; why spend more time for the same reward?

The reason that these take so long is that you have to perform Step 2 (Analyze the argument) for six arguments rather than just one! Each answer choice is another argument. Many arguments attached to Parallel-the-Reasoning questions can be diagrammed in some fashion. Your job is then to find the answer choice that has the same diagram.

There are two major types of Parallel-the-Reasoning questions. One type asks you to simply parallel (match) the reasoning, which means the argument and the credited response are not logically flawed. The other type asks you to parallel the "flaw" or "error," which means the argument and the answer will contain the same reasoning error. Use this to guide your Process of Elimination: eliminate flawed answers on a Parallel-the-Reasoning, and get rid of logically correct answers on a Parallel-the-Flaw.

Let's do a more diagrammable Parallel-the-Flaw first.

The Argument

17. Political scientist: All governments worthy of respect allow their citizens to dissent from governmental policies. No government worthy of respect leaves minorities unprotected. Thus any government that protects minorities permits criticism of its policies.

The flawed pattern of reasoning in which one of the following most closely parallels that in the political scientist's argument?

(A) Politicians are admirable if they put the interests of those they serve above their own interests. So politicians who sometimes ignore the interests of their own constituents in favor of the nation as a whole deserve admiration, for they are putting the interests of those they serve above their own.

(B) All jazz musicians are capable of improvising and no jazz musician is incapable of reading music. Therefore all musicians who can read music can improvise.

(C) Ecosystems with cool, dry climates are populated by large mammals. No ecosystems populated by large mammals have abundant and varied plant life. Thus ecosystems that do not have cool, dry climates have abundant and varied plant life.

(D) Some intellectuals are not socially active, and no intellectual is a professional athlete. Therefore any professional athlete is socially active.

(E) First-person narratives reveal the thoughts of the narrator but conceal those of the other characters. Some third-person narratives reveal the motives of every character. Thus books that rely on making all characters' motives apparent should be written in the third person.

PrepTest 44, Section 4, Question 19

Here's How to Crack It

Step 1: Assess the question   Good, you've read the question. Here it is again.

The flawed pattern of reasoning in which one of the following most closely parallels that in the political scientist's argument?

Okay, so it's a Parallel-the-Reasoning argument, and you know that you have to try to diagram the argument, if possible, and match that diagram against the diagrams for each of the answer choices. You also know that the reasoning itself is bad because the question asks for the "flawed" pattern of reasoning.

Careful!
Some Parallel-the-Reasoning questions are not about flawed arguments. Read the question carefully.

Step 2: Analyze the argument
As always, read it through carefully, looking for conclusions and premises as well as any of the common flawed patterns of reasoning. Here it is again.

> Political scientist: All governments worthy of respect allow their citizens to dissent from governmental policies. No government worthy of respect leaves minorities unprotected. Thus any government that protects minorities permits criticism of its policies.

This looks eminently diagrammable. When you see quantities like "all" or "none," you can turn these statements into conditionals and diagram them. Don't forget to note the conclusion and premises, and since you're looking for a flaw, the assumption.

- Author's conclusion: *Any government that protects minorities permits criticism of its policies.*
- Author's premises: *All governments worthy of respect allow their citizens to dissent from government policies and no government worthy of respect leaves minorities unprotected.*
- Author's assumption: *The author takes two separate facts and concludes that if you have one, you must also have the other.*

Step 3: Act
Here's what we get when we diagram.

All governments worthy of respect allow their citizens to dissent (A → B); no government worthy of respect leaves minorities unprotected (A → C). So, any government that protects minorities permits criticism of its policies (C → B).

The arguer didn't properly connect C (not protecting minorities) with B (allow dissent). Just because a government worthy of respect has these two traits does not guarantee that these two traits are always together. Now all we have to do is eliminate any answer choice that doesn't exhibit the same flawed logic

> The credited response to a Parallel-the-Reasoning question will be a new argument that matches the key features and structure of the original argument.

Step 4: Answer using Process of Elimination   Now you're going to carry your diagram to the answer choices and eliminate anything that doesn't match.

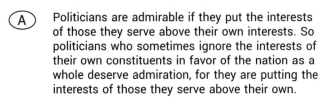

Diagram it: politicians who put others' interests above their own are admirable (A → B). Politicians who put national interests above their own constituents' interests are admirable (A → B again). This doesn't match the argument, so it isn't the answer. Eliminate it.

(B)   All jazz musicians are capable of improvising and no jazz musician is incapable of reading music. Therefore all musicians who can read music can improvise.

Diagram it: jazz musicians can improvise (A → B) and jazz musicians can read music (A → C), so musicians who can read music can improvise (C → B). Bingo! This is the same type of flawed reasoning as that above since this argument fails to consider that some jazz musicians might be able to do one but not the other. Hold on to it.

(C)   Ecosystems with cool, dry climates are populated by large mammals. No ecosystems populated by large mammals have abundant and varied plant life. Thus ecosystems that do not have cool, dry climates have abundant and varied plant life.

Diagram it: a place with a cool, dry climate has large mammals (A → B). A place with large mammals has lots of plants (B → C). A place without a cool, dry climate has lots of plants (~A → C). This doesn't match the argument, so it isn't the answer. Get rid of it.

(D)   Some intellectuals are not socially active, and no intellectual is a professional athlete. Therefore any professional athlete is socially active.

This one works out to A → B for the first part, A → ~C for the middle, and C → B for the last sentence. This can be appealing because it is really close, and if you miss translating the middle as, "if one is an intellectual, one is not an athlete," you can fall for it. Get rid of this one.

(E)   First-person narratives reveal the thoughts of the narrator but conceal those of the other characters. Some third-person narratives reveal the motives of every character. Thus books that rely on making all characters' motives apparent should be written in the third person.

You have (A → B but ~C) in the first sentence, and then (D → B and C) in the second sentence. The final sentence becomes (B and C → D). It's not even close to the original. It's out.

This leaves you with (B) because it's the only one that matches the structure of the original.

———————————————————

Nice job! You got the right answer simply by diagramming the statement in the argument, and then diagramming each of the answer choices until you found the one that matched the original diagram. However, you probably noticed that it took a long time to do this question. Many times, Parallel-the-Reasoning questions are even longer than this one and could take you three minutes to do. If you spend your time doing these questions, you might get through only half of an Arguments section! Therefore, be sure to save these for the end.

The Argument

18. A small car offers less protection in an accident than a large car does, but since a smaller car is more maneuverable, it is better to drive a small car because then accidents will be less likely.

    Which one of the following arguments employs reasoning most similar to that employed by the argument above?

    (A) An artist's best work is generally that done in the time before the artist becomes very well known. When artists grow famous and are diverted from artistic creation by demands for public appearances, their artistic work suffers. So artists' achieving great fame can diminish their artistic reputations.

    (B) It is best to insist that a child spend at least some time every day reading indoors. Even though it may cause the child some unhappiness to have to stay indoors when others are outside playing, the child can benefit from the time by learning to enjoy books and becoming prepared for lifelong learning.

    (C) For this work, vehicles built of lightweight materials are more practical than vehicles built of heavy materials. This is so because while lighter vehicles do not last as long as heavier vehicles, they are cheaper to replace.

    (D) Although it is important to limit the amount of sugar and fat in one's diet, it would be a mistake to try to follow a diet totally lacking in sugar and fat. It is better to consume sugar and fat in moderation, for then the cravings that lead to uncontrolled binges will be prevented.

    (E) A person who exercises vigorously every day has less body fat than an average person to draw upon in the event of a wasting illness. But one should still endeavor to exercise vigorously every day, because doing so significantly decreases the chances of contracting a wasting illness.

    PrepTest 44, Section 4, Question 21

Here's How to Crack It

Step 1: Assess the question   Read the question first, as always. Here it is.

> Which one of the following arguments employs reasoning most similar to that employed by the argument above?

This question is asking us to parallel the reasoning, with no mention of any flaws. You'll have to diagram or summarize the argument as best you can, diagram each answer, and see if they match.

Step 2: Analyze the argument   Read it carefully, keeping a sharp eye out for "all," "only," "some," or "most" wording, as well as conditional statements.

> A small car offers less protection in an accident than a large car does, but since a smaller car is more maneuverable, it is better to drive a small car because then accidents will be less likely.

This doesn't contain conditional statements, but it still has a clear argument structure that you can work with and map out. You are asked to match the reasoning, not the flaw, so don't worry about finding flaws or assumptions.

- Author's conclusion: *Driving a small car is better because of the lower likelihood of accidents.*
- Author's premises: *Even though small cars offer less protection than large cars, they are more maneuverable.*

Step 3: Act   Summarize the argument in general terms to make it easier to match the answers to it. In general terms, the author chooses one option over another because the disadvantage (less protection) of the chosen option is outweighed by an advantage (maneuverability) that makes the disadvantage a non-issue (accidents less likely). Now we need to find an answer that has similar features.

Step 4: Answer using Process of Elimination   Now analyze your answers and eliminate answers that don't match.

 An artist's best work is generally that done in the time before the artist becomes very well known. When artists grow famous and are diverted from artistic creation by demands for public appearances, their artistic work suffers. So artists' achieving great fame can diminish their artistic reputations.

Does this match your summary? There is no choice of a better option in this argument, so it doesn't match. Eliminate it!

It is best to insist that a child spend at least some time every day reading indoors. Even though it may cause the child some unhappiness to have to stay indoors when others are outside playing, the child can benefit from the time by learning to enjoy books and becoming prepared for lifelong learning.

Does this match your summary? One option (read inside) is chosen over another (playing outside) because the disadvantage (unhappy) is outweighed by an advantage (lifelong learning), but where is the advantage making the disadvantage a non-issue? It's not. Get rid of it!

 For this work, vehicles built of lightweight materials are more practical than vehicles built of heavy materials. This is so because while lighter vehicles do not last as long as heavier vehicles, they are cheaper to replace.

In mapping this one out, you have one option (lightweight materials) chosen over another (heavy materials) because the advantage (cheaper) outweighs the disadvantage (not last as long). It doesn't imply that the advantage of being cheaper to replace makes the disadvantage of not lasting as long a non-issue, but this choice is the closest to the original so far, so keep it.

 Although it is important to limit the amount of sugar and fat in one's diet, it would be a mistake to try to follow a diet totally lacking in sugar and fat. It is better to consume sugar and fat in moderation, for then the cravings that lead to uncontrolled binges will be prevented.

How well does this one hold up? Here, the choice is not between two entirely different options each with an advantage or disadvantage. It is about limiting the only option presented to prevent one negative consequence. It doesn't match, so this one is out.

 A person who exercises vigorously every day has less body fat than an average person to draw upon in the event of a wasting illness. But one should still endeavor to exercise vigorously every day, because doing so significantly decreases the chances of contracting a wasting illness.

Does this match your summary? One option (exercise) is better than another (not exercise) because the advantage (not getting sick) is outweighed by the disadvantage (less body fat) by making the disadvantage a non-issue (getting sick less likely). So far so good! Let's keep it.

Now compare (C) and (E). Choice (C) arrives at the conclusion that lightweight vehicles are better not because they make replacement a non-issue—that's still going to happen—but because they are cheaper to replace. The heavier vehicles are a better option if you want to avoid having to replace the vehicle. Both the original argument and (E) endorse the option that reduces the likelihood of the disadvantage, while (C) does not. That makes (E) the credited response.

Wow. Good work! But notice again how long it took to map out each and every answer choice, which means you might want to skip this one altogether, or save it for the very end. Notice, also, how similar the answers were. You can save a little time and headache by eliminating an answer as soon as you find a part that doesn't match.

Hint:
Whenever possible, diagram Parallel-the-Reasoning on scratch paper then diagram the answer choices and compare the diagrams.

Arguments Technique: Using Process of Elimination with Parallel-the-Reasoning Questions

It's pretty straightforward—if you are able to diagram the argument, then you must go to the answer choices and diagram those as well. Write it out and then you've got proof that the choice either matches or doesn't match the argument.

Sometimes you can't diagram Parallel-the-Reasoning questions. In these instances, try to describe the reasoning in the argument in general terms. Look for patterns that can be easily summed up (for example, we have two things that appear to be similar and then we note a difference, or one thing is attributed to be the cause of another). Try to find an answer that could be summed up in the same way. Start by matching up conclusions; then work backward through the argument to match up each piece. If you find any part of an answer choice that you can't match up with part of the original argument, eliminate it.

Summary: Cracking Parallel-the-Reasoning Questions

Refer to the chart below on how to approach Parallel-the-Reasoning questions.

Sample Question Phrasings	Act
Which one of the following is most similar in reasoning to the argument above? *The flawed pattern of reasoning exhibited by the argument above is most similar to that in which of the following?*	• Parallel-the-Reasoning questions will either contain flawed or valid reasoning, and the question will tip you off. • Try to diagram the argument and then diagram each of the answer choices, comparing each one to the diagram you came up with for the argument itself. • If the argument is flawed, be careful not to choose an answer that fixes it. • Save Parallel-the-Reasoning questions for LAST.

CRACKING ARGUMENTS: PUTTING IT ALL TOGETHER

Now you've learned how to approach every type of question they will throw at you in an Arguments section.

How do you integrate this knowledge into working a whole Arguments section?

Pace Yourself

Hint
Check out the pacing chart on page 358.

You know that you have only 35 minutes to tackle an entire Arguments section. But you're also faced with the fact that to get the credited response, you have to invest a significant amount of time in each argument. Hopefully, you've seen that these questions are doable—with the right approach—but that you might fall for traps or miss key words if you rush through them too quickly.

The bottom line on effective pacing is this: *don't rush!* There are questions in which you'll be able to analyze the argument easily, predict the answer accurately, and find the answer you predicted quickly. Keep moving through these questions. But there will be others in which the argument takes a little extra time to analyze, or in which two or more of the answer choices seem as if they have a shot—or, alternatively, in which none of the answer choices is what you were hoping for. In these cases, it's important to slow down. Take more time to understand the question, the argument, and the answer choices when you're struggling. This isn't wasted time; it's the real work of LSAT Arguments.

Of course, along with spending time where you need to spend it, you should also keep an overall sense of what target you need to hit. You can arrive at a rough pacing target for Arguments by looking at the percentage you get right on the section and dividing that number by 3; round up to get a sense of what number of questions you're aiming for. For example, if you're getting 60 percent right on Arguments sections, then you'll want to shoot for 20 questions on each Arguments section. You might not hit this number exactly, but if you're significantly short of that number, then chances are you'll need to work faster to improve; if, on the other hand, you're getting 60 percent right but more or less finishing the section, then the only way you're going to be able to improve is to work on your accuracy; that will most likely necessitate slowing down.

Choose Wisely

You know that you have to invest a certain amount of time into each type of Arguments question to get the credited response. But you also know that some types of Arguments take less time than others. For instance, compare the amount of time that a Main Point question takes to the amount of time that a Parallel-the-Reasoning question takes. You have a choice in how to spend your time with each question. Does it make sense to tackle a bunch of time-consuming questions when there are others that take much less time to do but give you the same number of points? As you do more practice problems and evaluate your performance on them, you should get a pretty clear sense of where your strengths and weaknesses lie. You'll benefit by making charts of your performance on each section, broken down by question type, so that you can see your progress. (See Chapter 6 for additional study tips and information on evaluating your progress.) To help you plan your approach, here's a chart of the proportion of questions of each type that have shown up on recently administered LSATs.

	Approximate Number Per Section	Approximate % of Total Arguments
Main Point	2	7%
Necessary Assumption	3	7%
Sufficient Assumption	3	7%
Weaken	3–4	13%
Strengthen	2	8%
Resolve/Explain	1–2	5%
Inference	4	14%
Reasoning	2	6%
Flaw	3–4	13%
Principle	2–3	10%
Parallel-the-Reasoning	2	7%
Other	1	3%

The bottom line is this: do the questions that take you the least amount of time and that you're most comfortable with first. Open your test booklet, and just take a look at what's on the page. Go after the ones that look short, sweet, and to the point, and leave the longer ones for later. Give priority to the tasks that you know play to your strengths. Likewise, if you come to an argument that really stumps you, don't worry about it—just put a mark next to it and move on. You can always come back once you've gone through all of the other arguments in the section.

Finally...

Practice, practice, practice. There are a number of different tasks that you'll be asked to perform in the Arguments section. As we've seen, each task will vary slightly in how you approach the argument and what you need to get out of it. There's no substitute for experience here. Use those previously administered LSATs that you've ordered from LSAC to get plenty of practice.

And remember that it's not enough to just work all the Arguments questions under the Sun. You'll have to go back and carefully evaluate your work. Figure out *why* you missed a question rather than simply looking at the right answer to learn why that one works. Did you miss the question because you didn't understand the argument? Did you miss a key word? Did you fall for an attractive distractor? Was the credited response one that didn't look very good but didn't have any flaw? Did you misinterpret the task presented by the question?

This kind of detailed evaluation will take time, but it is well worth it. Do it for Arguments. Do it for Games. Do it for Reading Comprehension. There are many places where errors can creep into the process. You'll be able to improve only if you know what your tendencies are and how you can go about changing those tendencies that negatively impact your performance.

Now you know what you need to do, so keep up the effort and you'll see the results.

YOU AND YOUR CHART

The chart on the following pages will help you on the Arguments section. Lucky for you, we have posted a PDF of this chart in your online Student Tools—you can print it from there, then you should become intimately familiar with this chart. Put it in a prominent place. Make another copy and carry it along with you so you can refer to it while you're working practice problems. You should know this chart like the back of your hand by the time you take the real LSAT.

Question Type	Sample Question Phrasings	Act
Main Point	*What is the author's main point?* *The main conclusion drawn in the author's argument is that...* *The argument is structured to lead to which one of the following conclusions?*	• Identify the conclusion and premises. • Use the Why Test and then match your conclusion against the five answer choices. • Be careful not to fall for the opposite. • When down to two choices, look for extreme wording and relevance to eliminate one choice.
Necessary Assumption	*Which of the following is an assumption on which the argument relies?* *The argument above assumes which of the following?* *The writer's argument depends upon assuming which of the following?*	• Identify the conclusion, premises, and assumptions of the author. • If you're having trouble finding the assumption, look for a gap between two different ideas in the argument. • The assumption will always at least mildly strengthen the author's conclusion and is NECESSARY for the conclusion to follow from the information provided. • When down to two choices, negate each statement to see if the argument falls apart. If it does, that's your answer.

Question Type	Sample Question Phrasings	Act
Sufficient Assumption	*Which one of the following, if assumed, would enable the conclusion to be properly drawn?* *The conclusion follows logically if which one of the following is assumed?*	• Identify the conclusion, premises, and assumptions of the author. • Look for language in the conclusion that is not accounted for in the premise. • Paraphrase an answer that would strongly connect the premises to the conclusion and shore up the language gap. • Eliminate answer choices that bring in new information.
Weaken	*Which one of the following, if true, would most undermine the author's conclusion?* *Which of the following statements, if true, would most call into question the results achieved by the scientists?*	• Identify the conclusion, premises, and assumptions of the author. • Read critically, looking for instances in which the author made large leaps in logic. • Then, when you go to the answer choices, look for a choice that has the most negative impact on that leap in logic. • Assume all choices to be hypothetically true.

Question Type	Sample Question Phrasings	Act
Strengthen	*Which one of the following statements, if true, would most support the author's conclusion?* *Which one of the following statements, if true, would strengthen the author's argument?* *Which of the following principles, if established, justifies the conclusion drawn in the argument above?*	• Identify the conclusion, premises, and assumptions of the author. • Read critically, looking for where the author made large leaps in logic. • Then, when you go to the answer choices, look for a choice that has the most positive impact on that gap. • Assume all choices to be hypothetically true.
Resolve/ Explain	*Which one of the following provides the best resolution to the apparent paradox described by the committee member?* *Which one of the following statements, if true, would explain the discrepancy found by the scientists?*	• Identify the apparent discrepancy or paradox. • Go to the answer choices and look for a piece of information that, when added to the argument, allows both facts from the argument to be true. • Assume all choices to be hypothetically true.
Inference	*Which one of the following statements can be validly inferred from the information above?* *If the statements above are true, then which of the following must also be true?* *Which one of the following conclusions can be validly drawn from the passage above?* *Which one of the following conclusions is best supported by the passage above?*	• Read carefully, paying close attention to qualifying language, and then go to the answer choices. • Once there, eliminate any answer choices that are not directly supported by evidence in the passage. • Look for relevance and extreme language to eliminate answer choices. • Use the contrapositive if there are "if...then" statements contained in the passage and in the answer choices.

Question Type	Sample Question Phrasings	Act
Reasoning	*The argument proceeds by...* *Leah responds to Kevin by doing which one of the following?* *The method the activist uses to object to the developer's argument is to...* *Dr. Jacobs does which of the following?*	• Read the arguments carefully and then describe what is happening in your own words, focusing on the author's conclusion and premises. • Take this description and rigorously apply it to all the answer choices. • Once you're at the answer choices, use the technique of comparing the actions described in the answer choices against those that actually occur in the arguments. • Eliminate anything that didn't appear in the argument.
Flaw	*Which of the following indicates a flaw in the author's reasoning?* *A criticism of the arguments would most likely emphasize that it...* *The reasoning in the argument is most vulnerable to criticism on the grounds that the argument...* *The argument above relies on which of the following questionable techniques?*	• Break down the argument into its parts; the flaw is usually related to an assumption. • State in your own words what the problem with the argument is. • With each answer, try to match the actions described in the answer choices with those of the argument itself. Look for the choice that has the same problem you found. • Eliminate the answers that don't match; look for the answer that addresses the assumption.

Question Type	Sample Question Phrasings	Act
Principle Match	*The reasoning above most closely conforms to which of the following principles?* *Which one of the following examples conforms most closely to the principle given in the argument above?*	• Make sure you know in which direction the argument flows. Are you being asked to find a principle that conforms to a situation, or a situation that conforms to a principle? • Once you're sure, look for an answer that most closely matches the general principle underlying the argument.
Parallel-the-Reasoning	*Which one of the following is most similar in reasoning to the argument above?* *The flawed pattern of reasoning exhibited by the arguments above is most similar to that in which of the following?*	• Parallel-the-Reasoning questions will contain either flawed or valid reasoning, and the question will tip you off. • Try to diagram the arguments and then diagram each of the answer choices, comparing each one to the diagram you came up with for the argument itself. • If the argument is flawed, be careful not to choose an answer that fixes it. • Save Parallel-the-Reasoning questions for LAST.

APPLY WHAT YOU'VE LEARNED

Now it's time to put everything you've learned in this chapter to work on the following 13 arguments. The goal of this drill is to see how well you've mastered the four steps and how accurately you can work, not to see how fast you can get through these arguments.

If you want, you can measure the time it takes you to do all 13 questions. By measure, we mean set your timer to count up, and then turn it away so that you can't see the clock as you work on the questions. Put the timer in a drawer or in another room if necessary. When you're done, stop the clock and note how long it took you to complete them and then see how accurate you were. You should be learning to balance speed and accuracy throughout your preparation for the LSAT, but when in doubt, slow down and work for accuracy.

Arguments Practice Drill

Answers can be found in Chapter 8.

1. Most plants have developed chemical defenses against parasites. The average plant contains about 40 natural pesticides—chemical compounds toxic to bacteria, fungi, and other parasites. Humans ingest these natural pesticides without harm every day. Therefore, the additional threat posed by synthetic pesticides sprayed on crop plants by humans is minimal.

   Each of the following, if true, weakens the argument EXCEPT:

   (A) Humans have been consuming natural plant pesticides for millennia and have had time to adapt to them.

   (B) The concentrations of natural pesticides in plants are typically much lower than the concentrations of synthetic pesticides in sprayed crop plants.

   (C) Natural plant pesticides are typically less potent than synthetic pesticides, whose toxicity is highly concentrated.

   (D) Natural plant pesticides generally serve only as defenses against specific parasites, whereas synthetic pesticides are often harmful to a wide variety of organisms.

   (E) The synthetic pesticides sprayed on crop plants by humans usually have chemical structures similar to those of the natural pesticides produced by the plants.

2. Public health expert: Until recently people believed that applications of biochemical research would eventually achieve complete victory over the microorganisms that cause human disease. However, current medical research shows that those microorganisms reproduce so rapidly that medicines developed for killing one variety will only spur the evolution of other varieties that are immune to those medicines. The most rational public health strategy, therefore, would place much more emphasis than at present on fully informing people about the transmission of diseases caused by microorganisms, with a view to minimizing the incidence of such diseases.

   Of the following, which one most accurately expresses the conclusion drawn by the public health expert?

   (A) A medicine that kills one variety of disease-causing microorganism can cause the evolution of a drug-resistant variety.

   (B) A patient who contracts a disease caused by microorganisms cannot be effectively cured by present methods.

   (C) There is good reason to make a particular change to public health policy.

   (D) No one who is fully informed about the diseases caused by microorganisms will ever fall victim to those diseases.

   (E) Some previous approaches to public health policy ignored the fact that disease-causing microorganisms reproduce at a rapid rate.

3. A typical gasoline-powered lawn mower emits about as much air-polluting material per hour of use as does an automobile. Collectively, such mowers contribute significantly to summer air pollution. Since electric mowers emit no air pollutants, people can help reduce air pollution by choosing electric mowers over gasoline ones whenever feasible.

Which one of the following, if true, provides the most support for the argument?

(A) Lawns help to clean the air, replacing pollutants with oxygen.

(B) Electric lawn mowers are more expensive to purchase and maintain than are gasoline mowers.

(C) Producing the power to run an electric mower for an hour causes less air pollution than does running an automobile for an hour.

(D) Most manufacturers of gasoline lawn mowers are trying to redesign their mowers to reduce the emission of air pollutants.

(E) Lawn mowers are used for fewer hours per year than are automobiles.

4. Columnist: The relief from the drudgery of physical labor that much modern technology affords its users renders them dependent on this technology, and, more importantly, on the elaborate energy systems required to run it. This leads to a loss of self-sufficiency. Clearly, then, in addition to undermining life's charm, much modern technology diminishes the overall well-being of its users.

Which one of the following is an assumption required by the columnist's argument?

(A) Physical labor is essential to a fulfilling life.

(B) Self-sufficiency contributes to a person's well-being.

(C) People are not free if they must depend on anything other than their own capacities.

(D) Anything causing a loss in life's charm is unjustifiable unless this loss is compensated by some gain.

(E) Technology inherently limits the well-being of its users.

5. Columnist: If you received an unsigned letter, you would likely have some doubts about the truth of its contents. But news stories often include statements from anonymous sources, and these are usually quoted with the utmost respect. It makes sense to be skeptical of these sources, for, as in the case of the writer of an unsigned letter, their anonymity makes it possible for them to plant inaccurate or slanted statements without ever having to answer for them.

The columnist's argument proceeds by

(A) pointing out that a certain attitude would presumably be adopted in one situation, in order to support the claim that a similar attitude would be justified in an analogous situation

(B) drawing an analogy between an attitude commonly adopted in one situation and a different attitude commonly adopted in another situation, and establishing that the latter attitude is better justified than the former

(C) inferring that an attitude would be justified in all situations of a given type on the grounds that this attitude is justified in a hypothetical situation of that type

(D) calling into question a certain type of evidence by drawing an analogy between that evidence and other evidence that the argument shows is usually false

(E) calling into question the motives of those presenting certain information, and concluding for this reason that the information is likely to be false

6. It is highly likely that Claudette is a classical pianist. Like most classical pianists, Claudette recognizes many of Clara Schumann's works. The vast majority of people who are not classical pianists do not. In fact, many people who are not classical pianists have not even heard of Clara Schumann.

The reasoning in the argument above is flawed in that it

(A) ignores the possibility that Claudette is more familiar with the works of other composers of music for piano

(B) presumes, without providing justification, that people who have not heard of Clara Schumann do not recognize her works

(C) presumes, without providing justification, that classical pianists cannot also play other musical instruments

(D) relies for its plausibility on the vagueness of the term "classical"

(E) ignores the possibility that the majority of people who recognize many of Clara Schumann's works are not classical pianists

7. All the evidence so far gathered fits both Dr. Grippen's theory and Professor Heissmann's. However, the predictions that these theories make about the result of the planned experiment cannot both be true. Therefore, the result of this experiment will confirm one of these theories at the expense of the other.

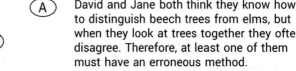

The argument above exhibits an erroneous pattern of reasoning most similar to that exhibited by which one of the following?

(A) David and Jane both think they know how to distinguish beech trees from elms, but when they look at trees together they often disagree. Therefore, at least one of them must have an erroneous method.

(B) Although David thinks the tree they saw was a beech, Jane thinks it was an elm. Jane's description of the tree's features is consistent with her opinion, so this description must be inconsistent with David's view.

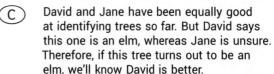

(C) David and Jane have been equally good at identifying trees so far. But David says this one is an elm, whereas Jane is unsure. Therefore, if this tree turns out to be an elm, we'll know David is better.

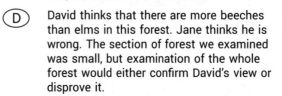

(D) David thinks that there are more beeches than elms in this forest. Jane thinks he is wrong. The section of forest we examined was small, but examination of the whole forest would either confirm David's view or disprove it.

(E) David thinks this tree is a beech. Jane thinks it is an elm. Maria, unlike David or Jane, is expert at tree identification, so when Maria gives her opinion, it will verify either David's or Jane's opinion.

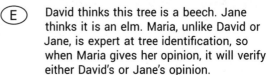

8. It is unlikely that the world will ever be free of disease. Most diseases are caused by very prolific microorganisms whose response to the pressures medicines exert on them is predictable: they quickly evolve immunities to those medicines while maintaining their power to infect and even kill humans.

Which one of the following most accurately describes the role played in the argument by the claim that it is unlikely that the world will ever be free of disease?

(A) It is a conclusion that is claimed to follow from the premise that microorganisms are too numerous for medicines to eliminate entirely.

(B) It is a conclusion for which a description of the responses of microorganisms to the medicines designed to cure the diseases they cause is offered as support.

(C) It is a premise offered in support of the claim that most disease-causing microorganisms are able to evolve immunities to medicines while retaining their ability to infect humans.

(D) It is a generalization used to predict the response of microorganisms to the medicines humans use to kill them.

(E) It is a conclusion that is claimed to follow from the premise that most microorganisms are immune to medicines designed to kill them.

9. Philosopher: The rational pursuit of happiness is quite different from always doing what one most strongly desires to do. This is because the rational pursuit of happiness must include consideration of longterm consequences, whereas our desires are usually focused on the short term. Moreover, desires are sometimes compulsions, and while ordinary desires result in at least momentary happiness when their goals are attained, compulsions strongly drive a person to pursue goals that offer no happiness even when reached.

If all of the philosopher's statements are true, each of the following could be true EXCEPT:

(A) The majority of people do not have compulsions.

(B) Attaining the goal of any desire results in momentary happiness.

(C) Most people do not pursue happiness rationally.

(D) Most people want more than their own personal happiness.

(E) All actions have long-term consequences.

10. Before their larvae hatch, each parental pair of *Nicrophorus* beetles buries the carcass of a small vertebrate nearby. For several days after the larvae hatch, both beetles feed their voracious larvae from the carcass, which is entirely consumed within a week. Since both parents help with feeding, larvae should benefit from both parents' presence; however, removing one parent before the hatching results in larvae that grow both larger and heavier than they otherwise would be.

Which one of the following, if true, best helps to explain why removing one parent resulted in larger, heavier larvae?

(A) Two beetles can find and bury a larger carcass than can a single beetle.

(B) Both parents use the carcass as their own food supply for as long as they stay with the larvae.

(C) Beetle parents usually take turns feeding their larvae, so that there is always one provider available and one at rest.

(D) After a week, the larvae are capable of finding other sources of food and feeding themselves.

(E) Two parents can defend the carcass from attack by other insects better than a single parent can.

11. For many centuries it was believed that only classical Euclidean geometry could provide a correct way of mathematically representing the universe. Nevertheless, scientists have come to believe that a representation of the universe employing non-Euclidean geometry is much more useful in developing certain areas of scientific theory. In fact, such a representation underlies the cosmological theory that is now most widely accepted by scientists as accurate.

Which one of the following is most strongly supported by the statements above?

(A) Scientists who use Euclidean geometry are likely to believe that progress in mathematical theory results in progress in natural science.

(B) Scientists generally do not now believe that classical Euclidean geometry is uniquely capable of giving a correct mathematical representation of the universe.

(C) Non-Euclidean geometry is a more complete way of representing the universe than is Euclidean geometry.

(D) An accurate scientific theory cannot be developed without the discovery of a uniquely correct way of mathematically representing the universe.

(E) The usefulness of a mathematical theory is now considered by scientists to be more important than its mathematical correctness.

12. Experts hired to testify in court need to know how to make convincing presentations. Such experts are evaluated by juries in terms of their ability to present the steps by which they arrived at their conclusions clearly and confidently. As a result, some less expert authorities who are skilled at producing convincing testimony are asked to testify rather than highly knowledgeable but less persuasive experts.

Which one of the following most closely conforms to the principle illustrated by the passage above?

(A) Successful politicians are not always the ones who best understand how to help their country. Some lack insight into important political issues but are highly skilled at conducting an election campaign.

(B) Trial lawyers often use the techniques employed by actors to influence the emotions of jurors. Many lawyers have studied drama expressly for the purpose of improving their courtroom skills.

(C) The opera singer with the best voice is the appropriate choice even for minor roles, despite the fact that an audience may be more affected by a singer with greater dramatic ability but a lesser voice.

(D) It is often best to try to train children with gentle reinforcement of desired behavior, rather than by simply telling them what to do and what not to do. This results in children who behave because they want to, not because they feel compelled.

(E) Job applicants are usually hired because their skills and training best meet a recognized set of qualifications. Only rarely is a prospective employer convinced to tailor a position to suit the skills of a particular applicant.

13. Last month OCF, Inc., announced what it described as a unique new product: an adjustable computer workstation. Three days later ErgoTech unveiled an almost identical product. The two companies claim that the similarities are coincidental and occurred because the designers independently reached the same solution to the same problem. The similarities are too fundamental to be mere coincidence, however. The two products not only look alike, but they also work alike. Both are oddly shaped with identically placed control panels with the same types of controls. Both allow the same types of adjustments and the same types of optional enhancements.

The main point of the argument is that

(A) the two products have many characteristics in common

(B) ErgoTech must have copied the design of its new product from OCF's design

(C) the similarities between the two products are not coincidental

(D) product designers sometimes reach the same solution to a given problem without consulting each other

(E) new products that at first appear to be unique are sometimes simply variations of other products

Summary

○ Arguments make up half of the questions on the LSAT. You must work hard to improve in this section if you want to reach your potential on test day.

○ Always understand the question task before you read the argument. Some questions require you to find the conclusion and the premises; others require a different analysis. Knowing the question types and what makes the credited response correct for that question type will help you get through the section with speed and accuracy.

○ Start thinking about your pacing plan. Know how many arguments you will attempt on test day.

○ As you practice, look for similarities among arguments. You'll find that many arguments follow recognizable patterns; understanding these patterns will help you analyze the argument, eliminate wrong answers, and select the credited response.

Chapter 3
Games

Of all the sections on the LSAT, Analytical Reasoning is the section that initially seems the most intimidating, but we have some good news for you: it's the section where solid technique and plenty of practice pay off the most. If you learn the techniques in this chapter and apply them consistently as you practice, you'll see that these questions follow set patterns, and that all they require is a consistent, careful approach. In fact, you may eventually come to find these questions a little bit—dare we say it?—fun. Don't worry, though; we won't tell your friends.

WHAT IS A GAME?

The folks who write the test call this section the "Analytical Reasoning" section, but really the questions are just puzzles. As a result, we call it the "Games" section. You are presented with the basic format and structure of the game in the *setup*, an initial paragraph that also provides the *elements* or game pieces. Following the setup will be a number of conditions, or *clues*, which put restrictions on how the elements can be manipulated and sometimes give you valuable information about the overall structure of the game as well. Finally, you will have a number of questions, each of which may introduce new restrictions or even occasionally change or replace one of the original clues. Ultimately, the questions will ask you to determine the relationships between these elements. Each question is independent of the others, although work completed for one question may help in eliminating answer choices on another question. Don't worry if all this is overwhelming: we're going to explain how to crack it step by step.

WHAT DOES THIS SECTION TEST?

Games test how well you can organize information, understand spatial relationships, and make deductions from those relationships when presented with limitations on the arrangements allowed by the rules. They also reward you for being able to extract this information efficiently. According to the test-writers, games are designed to predict your ability to perform the kind of detailed analyses required of law students. Obviously, this is patently ridiculous: you won't do any of these in law schools, and you certainly won't do any of these when you become a lawyer. What this section really tests is how well you answer the Games questions under strict time pressure.

Games test your organization skills and your ability to efficiently extract information from incomplete data.

THE SECTION ITSELF

The Games section is made up of four games. Each game includes five to seven questions. The section normally has 22 to 24 questions.

Before we begin, take a moment to read the instructions to this section.

> Directions: Each set of questions in this section is based on a scenario with a set of conditions. The questions are to be answered on the basis of what can be logically inferred from the scenario and conditions. For each question, choose the response that most accurately and completely answers the question.

These are the directions that will appear on your LSAT. As usual on the LSAT, the official directions are of little help. Review them now for your peace of mind: they will not change, so don't waste time reading them in the test room.

The good news is that with some rigorous practice diagramming games, you can radically improve your LSAT score. Many students have walked into The Princeton Review classes getting only a few Games questions right, but they walk out scoring 75 percent or higher on this section! You can do the same, as long as you follow our step-by-step process and practice, practice, practice.

Your mantra on this section is: *I will be systematic in every game I do.*

Systematic: having, showing, or involving a system, method, or plan.

GLOBAL STRATEGIES

The following is a list of general strategies that you should use when you are working the Games section. Many of these strategies can be applied to each section of the test, so make sure that you take them to heart.

Slow and Steady Wins the Race

More than any other type of question on the LSAT, Games questions require a methodical approach. Trying to rush through the section to make sure you'll finish every question will not help your score. You will achieve the highest level of accuracy by using an approach that increases efficiency—not necessarily pace—without sacrificing your ability to be accurate. If you find you can't finish a Games section in the allotted time, don't fret: very few test-takers can. Through consistent practice, you will be able to move more quickly through the section without having to work so fast that you start to make careless errors.

<u>Strategy #1</u>: *I will focus on accuracy and efficiency to improve my score. I will not rush through the section just to complete every question.*

Survey the Field

Every correct answer on the LSAT is worth an equal number of points. Since time is of the essence on games, spend your time on easier questions. Remember, the LSAT Games and the questions attached to them are not necessarily arranged in order of difficulty. Therefore, you should always try to estimate the difficulty of a game before you work it; if it looks difficult, move on. We'll spend time later outlining specific characteristics that make a game more or less attractive.

<u>Strategy #2</u>: *I will not work the games in the order presented. I will assess the difficulty of games before I begin working on them.*

Just Do Something

Keep working; keep moving forward. Don't ever just stare at a game in search of divine inspiration. The only way to deal with a difficult game is to work through it, not think through it. The bottom line is that if your stylus or pen isn't moving, then you are stalling out on a question. Put your pen to scratch paper. We'll discuss in much more detail how to efficiently use your pen on scratch paper to not only diagram each game but also test out possible answer choices.

Strategy #3: *I will keep my pen moving at all times. If my pen isn't moving, I am doing something wrong.*

Choose an Answer for Every Question

Each question will appear on screen individually. When you're confident you've found the credited response, select your answer and move to the next screen. If you aren't sure of an answer, be sure to flag the question so you can return to answer it later. If you don't think you'll have time to return to the question, POE as many choices as you can and select one from the remaining choices. Flag it so you can return if you have time and move on to the next screen.

Strategy #4: *I will select an answer for every question, and flag questions that I skip for the time being.*

Control the Fear

Nerves are a common factor on a high-stakes test. Panic can easily set in on a Games section when you are faced with a difficult game. It can even creep in when you are halfway through a game. One of the biggest benefits you will get from this book is a thorough knowledge of the Games section. You will have a strategy for each game you face. If you find yourself panicking, take a short break. Put your stylus down, close your eyes, and take three slow breaths. As you do, repeat to yourself that you know what you are doing and that you have prepared for this section. Open your eyes, refocus on the game at hand, and dive back in. Think about similar games in this book. You've got this!

Strategy #5: *I will control my panic by focusing on the game in front of me.*

GAMES: SPECIFIC STRATEGIES

The LSAT states that for the Games section "it may be useful to draw a rough diagram" when working the section. That's like saying it may be useful to peel a banana before eating it. It is possible to eat a banana without peeling it, but it's much more enjoyable to peel it first.

Make It Visual

Games are a visual exercise. Games test your ability to determine how various elements can be arranged in space. Therefore, words don't help you; images do. Your goal will be to translate all the words that you are given in the *setup* and the *clues*, and sometimes in the questions themselves, into visual symbols and draw them on your scratch paper. Once you've done this, you won't need to (or want to) refer to that confusing verbal mess again.

You have plenty of scratch paper so use an entire sheet of paper for each game.

The LSAT writers are banking on the fact that most test-takers will try to organize all this information in their heads in their rush to finish. That's a recipe for disaster. Accuracy is crucial on this section, and the only way to ensure accuracy is to work with the information on the page by translating it and drawing it out.

Be Consistent

There are many ways you can symbolize and diagram the information that is presented to you in a game. We're going to show you what we've found to be the best and most efficient way to diagram and symbolize. If something we show you doesn't work well, design your own system. Whatever method you choose, be consistent with your symbols and your diagram. When the pressure is on, you don't want to misinterpret a symbol you've drawn.

Be Careful

We've already stressed the importance of accuracy over speed, but the point is worth making again. You should be confident and aggressive on games, but there is a fine line between aggressiveness and carelessness; don't put yourself on the wrong side of it. This is the only section of the LSAT in which you can be sure an answer is right. Do the work required to take advantage of that.

Be Flexible

The four games that you will see on the actual LSAT will look slightly different from the games that you will have practiced on in this book. However, all these games were written by the *same* test-writers for the *same* test using the *same* basic guidelines. Once you understand how these games work and can recognize the basic structures the test-writers use to build them, you can see how repetitive the patterns really are. Just stay calm and take a step back to evaluate the information. The details will change, but the basic ingredients won't. Focus on the big picture. Find the similarities to the games that you've already worked.

Games Technique: Practicing on your Own   Below you will find a bullet point list of the most effective ways to practice the games section on your own. Game specific strategies will be found in each lesson.

- Do everything in pen, and don't erase your work.
- Work and write small—all of your work must fit on your scratch paper.
- If a particular clue symbolization (discussed later) isn't working, or is even causing mistakes, stop using it. Try something else.
- Do games over and over. If you had trouble with one, go back to it later, and try it again until you get it.
- Practice games only when you are able to give them your full attention.
- Very important: rework all the games you do (including the games in this chapter) at least once.
- Always keep in mind which types of games you're able to do most quickly. Look for those games and do them first on the real LSAT.

CRACKING THE LSAT GAMES SECTION

This chapter is arranged into a series of five lessons. The lessons will introduce you step by step to concepts that you need to master in order to be successful on the Games section. These concepts are scaffolded, which means that later lessons build upon the strategies and techniques taught in earlier lessons. The games types also get progressively more complex. We strongly recommend that you work the lessons in the order given.

Don't just read the text! Take notes on the various strategies and steps provided. Make sure you have a good understanding of why we are showing you various techniques. Finally, the games in each lesson were chosen specifically to highlight the key teaching points in the lesson. Make sure that you take the time at the end of each lesson to fill out the self-evaluation. Work to mentally link the discussion in the lesson to the example game at the end of each lesson. On the next page, you will find the first lesson. Good luck to you and study hard!

Keep your stylus and pen moving!

LESSON 1: A SYSTEMATIC APPROACH

Just as we did in the Arguments section, we have boiled down the Games section into a step-by-step process. You will follow this systematic approach for every game that you work. Learn these steps, practice them religiously, apply them consistently, and you'll improve your score. In this first lesson, we will walk you step by step through your first game. The game will be mixed with the teaching test. At the end of the lesson, we will publish the game as it would appear on the LSAT. You should try your hand at it a second time without our prompts. Sound good? Then let's dive in!

Step 1: Diagram and Inventory Your first step will be to determine the appropriate diagram for the game by evaluating both the setup and the clues. You will be given enough information to understand the basic structure of the game. Your diagram is described by the setup and will become the fixed game board onto which you will place the *elements*—your game pieces. You will want to make an inventory of the elements next to the diagram, so that you'll have everything in one place and will be able to keep track of it easily. Don't rush through this step, because this is the heart of your process. People often want to start scribbling a diagram as soon as something pops out at them from the setup. Take the time to evaluate the setup thoroughly, and you'll be well equipped for the rest of the process.

Remember!
The elements are the mobile pieces in a game; don't forget to list them in an inventory near your diagram.

Step 2: Symbolize the clues and double-check After you've drawn your diagram, transform the clues into visual symbols. Your symbolizations should be consistent with the diagram and with each other. The goal is to change the clues into visual references that will fit into your diagram. Remember the three Cs of symbolization: keep your symbols *clear, consistent,* and *concise.*

Never forget that correctly symbolizing every clue is the key to improving accuracy and efficiency. The most valuable 30 seconds you can spend on any game is double-checking your symbols to make sure that they perfectly match all the information in the clue. Do not merely reread each clue and glance at your symbol again. If you misread the clue once, you might do it again. Instead, work against the grain when you double-check. Number each of your symbolizations. Then articulate in your own words what each symbol means and carry that back up to the clues you were given. When you find a match, check off that clue. Finally, be sure to go back over the information presented in the setup as well because some games may include restrictions or extra rules that should be treated like clues. Once you're sure everything is all accounted for, you're ready to move on.

Step 3: Make deductions and size up the game Now that you're sure you've got everything properly symbolized, it's time to make any *deductions* that you can from the information that was given by the clues. Look for overlap between the clues and the diagram and among the clues that share the same elements. See if there is anything else that you know for sure. Making deductions is not merely suspecting that something may be true; a deduction is something that you know for a fact. It is something that must always be true or must always be false. Add your deductions to the information you already have. You'll notice

Hint:
Repeated elements often provide the opportunity for deductions. If an element is listed in two or more clues, try to combine information to arrive at a new fact.

that many deductions give you concrete limitations about where elements are restricted—where they can't go—rather than where they must go. Consider each clue individually to see what it says about the placement of elements. Then look for overlap between different clues. Do several clues mention the same element? If so, how do they interact? Do you have any clues that restrict movement? How does that affect the placement of other elements?

While you're looking for these deductions, you'll find that you're also learning how the game is going to work. Keep your eyes open for anything that seems as if it will have a particularly large impact on the outcome of the game. The most restricted places and the most restrictive clues tend to have the greatest impact when you start working the questions. The more you know about how the game will work, the more efficient you'll be at working through the questions.

Step 4: Assess the questions   Not all games questions are on the same level of difficulty. As a result, you should move through the questions from easiest to most challenging. We will show you how to identify these questions in detail as we move through this chapter. For now, familiarize yourself with the terminology and basic indicators for each question type.

First, look for what we call Grab-a-Rule questions. Grab-a-Rule questions do not appear on every game, but they are common. They have historically been the first question of a game. These are questions that give you full arrangements of the elements in every answer, and ask you which one doesn't break any rules. Remember, if the question does not deal with every element and every space on your diagram, it is not a true Grab-a-Rule.

Next, look for Specific questions. These questions will further limit the initial conditions of the game and provide you with more information. They will usually start with the word "if." Specific questions tend to be fairly quick since the question itself constrains some of the vagueness of the game. Once you've done all the Specific questions, you'll have a diagram with several valid permutations—or "plays"—of the game.

The third style of question you should work is the General questions. These questions are typically open-ended and ask what could happen without placing specific restrictions. These questions usually begin with the word "which." By saving these for later, you can often use your prior work from the Specific questions to eliminate bad answer choices.

The final question type that you may see is Complex questions. Complex questions can change the original game by adding, changing, or deleting a rule. They can also ask which answer choice could be substituted for a rule without changing the game. No matter what form they take, complex questions should be saved for last since they function differently from the rest of the questions. These questions can also be very time-consuming for little gain. Never forget that the complex question is worth the same number of points as the Grab-a-Rule. It is always worth considering how much you need to get that one question correct. For most test-takers, the best strategy on these questions is to bubble in your letter of the day and move on to the next game. Remember that you can always come back and work a Complex question if you have time.

There is one last thing to know about the questions. No matter what the question type, the question stem will affect how the credited response is reached. The four question stems are must be true, could be true, could be false, and must be false. The LSAT has a wide variety of phrasing, but every question will ultimately use one of these four stems. Make a habit now of underlining each question stem. This will help you to determine the best approach to the question and the type of answer you'll need.

Step 5: Act   Each question task requires its own strategy. Using the proper strategy leads to saving time on a given question without sacrificing accuracy. Plus, by approaching the questions in an efficient order, you'll find that the work you've done on earlier questions will often help you to find the right answer on a later question.

Step 6: Answer using Process of Elimination   Different question stems require POE to different degrees. Sometimes you'll be able to go straight to the right answer from your deductions, but often you'll need to work questions by finding the four wrong answers. As a last resort, you may need to test answer choices one at a time to find the right one.

READY FOR YOUR FIRST GAME?

Now let's see how the six steps work on a real game. Since this is your first game, let's walk through it together. Focus on how each of the steps is applied and how the game should look step by step. Give yourself as much time as you need to learn the method by the following game (feel free to write out the six steps and have them next to you). Pay no attention to timing on this first game—that will come later. This is the foundation you will rely upon for all future games. The full game is reproduced on page 154 for you to try it again on your own. After this first game, all other games in this book will be provided to you to work first, and we will show you how to crack them later. Let's begin.

Game 1 and its questions
are from PrepTest 45,
Section 3, Questions 1–6.

Cracking Game 1

Step 1: Diagram and inventory   Take a moment to read the setup of the first game. Games can be broken into two rough categories: Ordering and Grouping. Ordering games consist of putting elements in some sort of order, while grouping games put the elements into arbitrary groups. Your first question should always be to ask yourself which type of game you are facing. Which one is this one?

> On one afternoon, Patterson meets individually with each of exactly five clients—Reilly, Sanchez, Tang, Upton, and Yansky—and also goes to the gym by herself for a workout. Patterson's workout and her five meetings each start at either 1:00, 2:00, 3:00, 4:00, 5:00, or 6:00. The following conditions must apply:

What we have here are five meetings and a workout and six time slots in the day. There is a natural order to the time slots, so this is an Ordering game. Use a table in this situation to diagram the game and organize the information. Since you want the thing that doesn't change across the top of your diagram, always make the order the core of your diagram. We will be assigning the different appointments to different time slots. In order to keep track of the various elements, list them off to the side of your diagram.

Also, we have what is called a *one-to-one correspondence* in this game—there are six times (*core*) and five appointments and a workout (*six elements*). The setup specifically tells us that Patterson will meet with each one of these people once, so we have to use all of the elements. One-to-one correspondence isn't just a matter of the number of each, but also whether all are used and not reused. This is a great thing because it will limit the number of possible places to which the elements can be assigned. This answers two questions you'll want to ask at this step for every game you work: (1) "Can I leave out any elements?", and (2) "Can there be any repeats?" If the answer to either of these questions is yes, then the game is more complicated. Since this is an Ordering game with a 1:1 correspondence, this is among the most straightforward games you will see on the LSAT. This is the type of game you would want to work first on the test.

Take a look at our diagram for this game.

Tip!
Make sure your diagram
is large enough to be use-
able but small enough that
you won't have to redraw
the game.

RSTUYW	1:00	2:00	3:00	4:00	5:00	6:00

Step 2: Symbolize the clues and double-check
Now that we've drawn a diagram, it's important that we symbolize the clues so that they fit into our diagram. We want to get rid of the words from the clue and transform each into a visual puzzle piece that fits neatly into the diagram we've drawn. As you symbolize, remember the three Cs: *clear, consistent,* and *concise.* Also, make sure to number the clues as you work.

Draw exact symbols for the information given to you. Remember the three C's for symbols: *clear, concise,* and *consistent.*

> Patterson meets with Sanchez at some time before her workout.

Take a moment to think about the logic of this clue. Her meeting with Sanchez occurs at some point in the day before her workout. It could be immediately before the workout, or Sanchez could be at the beginning of her schedule and the workout at the end. The only event that cannot occur is having her workout before her meeting with Sanchez. This is what we call a range clue. Your symbol needs to show both the order of events and the fact that they can be spread apart. Ellipses are a natural way to show this. Take a look at our symbol below.

(1) S...W

Let's look at clue number 2.

> Patterson meets with Tang at some time after her workout.

(2) W...T

Hopefully you already noticed the similarity from clue number 1. This is another range clue. One other important thing to note is that the workout is mentioned by both clues. For now, merely make a mental note of that information and move on to clue number 3.

> Patterson meets with Yansky either immediately before or immediately after her workout.

There is a very important keyword in this clue that changes it dramatically from the previous two. Think about what the word "immediately" does to the logic of this clue. Unlike the previous ranges, this clue forces Yansky and the workout to always occur together. To symbolize this clue, put the two letters next to each other and put a box around them indicating a fixed block of text. Finally, note that the clue establishes an either/or situation. Be sure to symbolize the clue going in both directions. Interestingly, W is mentioned again.

(3) W Y

The great thing about this piece of information is that it will occupy two of the six possible spaces. Blocks are restrictive clues that limit the possible arrangements and will make your job of answering the questions easier. Look for them when you are reading over the clues and deciding whether to do a particular game.

> Patterson meets with Upton at some time before she meets with Reilly.

(4) U…R

Ideally, you had this one symbolized before you saw our example. Now it is time for the most important stage of the clue symbolization process. Double-check your symbols. Remember to not merely reread each of the clues again. Instead work backward. Force yourself to put the symbols into your own words. Here's an example of the process:

Clue 4: You say "R comes later than U." Check the clue. It matches so you move on.

Clue 3: You say "W and Y are next to each other in either order." Check the clue. It matches, so check it off and move on.

Clue 2: You say "T comes later than W." Note how this is the same phrasing from Clue 4. Check it off.

Clue 1: You say "W comes later than S." Check it off.

We can't emphasize enough how important this step is. A mistake at this stage can be extremely costly. If you have a bad symbolization, the best case scenario is that you invest several minutes but are unable to answer any questions. The worst case scenario is that you get down to a single answer on every question, but that answer is wrong. Whenever you are working a game and cannot get down to a single answer, you should always ask yourself first, "Did I take the time to double-check?" If the answer is no, we can guarantee that you missed a clue.

Step 3: Make deductions and size up the game   By now you should have a list of clues that looks like this:

1.   S…W

2.   W…T

3.   W | Y   (block with arrow indicating W and Y are adjacent in either order)

4.   U…R

Now let's take a look at the clues we've drawn to see what kinds of deductions we might make. First, make a *clue shelf* on your diagram. This should be the first row of your diagram. You will put any clues information and all deductions here. This row is vital to a strong diagram. Once you get these deductions down, make sure to draw a line under it and never write on this line again.

Approach the clues in a systematic manner. Start with what we call "single-clue deductions." Look at clue 1 and ask what must be true or must be false based on this information. Range clues lend themselves to a quick deduction. Since Patterson meets with Sanchez before the workout, you can deduce that Patterson's workout cannot be at 1:00. If it was, then it would be impossible for Patterson to meet with Sanchez. Likewise, the meeting with Sanchez cannot be at 6:00. Look at the diagram below to see how we indicated this.

RSTUYW	1:00	2:00	3:00	4:00	5:00	6:00
Clue Shelf	~W					~S

Take a moment to consider the other two range clues from your clue list. We want to challenge you to try and make the same deduction yourself. Have you done it? Your diagram should now look like this.

RSTUYW	1:00	2:00	3:00	4:00	5:00	6:00
Clue Shelf	~W ~T ~R					~S ~W ~U

If this feels shockingly easy to you, don't be embarrassed. As we said at the beginning of this chapter, you can actually find yourself enjoying games once you unlock their secrets.

Now consider clue 3 individually. Is there anything that must be true or false that you can figure out here? The answer is no. Since W and Y can alternate order, we have no way to know from this clue alone where W and Y will be in our diagram. Not every clue will provide you with a deduction. However, it is vital that you establish the habit now of looking at each clue on its own. Being systematic will build your efficiency by helping you not waste time and will improve your accuracy by ensuring that you don't miss a vital deduction.

Once you have considered each clue separately, it is time to look for what we call "multiple-clue deductions." These are found by looking at the interactions of various clues. One of the fastest ways to find multiple-clue deductions is by seeing if different clues share the same elements. Remember earlier when we noted that W seemed to appear often? Let's see how the different clues can combine into a more powerful deduction. First, stack clue one and two together.

$$S...W$$
$$W...T$$

They can be chained together to make a longer range.

$$S...W...T$$

Now combine this deduction with clue three. W and Y are a block element that must always be together so now you have

This deduction comprises four of the six elements. The location of any one of the elements in this deduction will drive the rest of the game by quickly restricting locations of elements. At this point, you have made the most crucial deductions and could proceed into the game. However, you should note that deductions can build upon one another. As a result, you can actually take this new information even further. Think back to the very first deduction we made. Clue 1 means that W cannot be first, which is already noted on the diagram. Now look at the newest deduction above, and apply the same logic to it. What other element cannot be first? Is there anything that cannot be second? What about third, fourth, fifth, or sixth? If you made all the possible deductions, your diagram should now look like this.

RSTUYW	1:00	2:00	3:00	4:00	5:00	6:00
Clue Shelf	~W ~T ~R ~Y	~T	~T	~S	~S	~S ~W ~U ~Y

Finally, note the large number of elements that cannot be scheduled at 1:00 or at 6:00. In rare cases, such as this one, you can transform these deductions from what cannot be there to what can. Since R, T, W, and Y cannot be first, then only S or U can be first. Likewise, since S, U, W, and Y cannot be last, only R or T can be placed there. Here is the final diagram with all deductions.

RSTUYW	1:00	2:00	3:00	4:00	5:00	6:00
Clue Shelf	S/U	~T	~T	~S	~S	R/T

At this point, we've come up with all the deductions we can and have a pretty good sense of the way this game is going to work. Things will hinge on the placement of elements in the long-range deduction. All the information that we've put in the diagram so far will be true for the whole game, so we'll draw a line under it to separate it off and remind ourselves to pay attention to those limitations as we work each new question. We'll call this row of restrictions that apply to the whole game our *clue shelf.*

Steps 4 and 5: Assess the question and Act As we said earlier, there are basically four types of questions that you will encounter on games—Grab-a-Rule, Specific, General, and Complex.

Grab-a-Rule questions are technically a type of General question, but these should be tackled first because they are quick questions that will help you comprehend the game itself. But be careful—not all games have Grab-a-Rule questions. If you don't see this type of straightforward question, fear not. Alternatively, if you dive into a question and realize halfway through that it is not a Grab-a-Rule, fear not! Regardless, just keep moving and look for the next type of question on the list— Specific questions.

Tip!
Be very careful to not work any questions on your clue shelf. These marks that must be true should not be confused with any information that merely could be true.

Grab-a-Rule questions deal with all the clues and the entire diagram. They have historically been the first question on a game when present and often ask you to find an "acceptable order" or "complete and accurate list." Take a moment now to turn to the full game on page 154. Does this game have a Grab-a-Rule?

Seriously, flip to page 154 and take a look. We'll wait.

Welcome back! Specific questions are the kind you should search out and do after the Grab-a-Rule. You'll be able to identify them because they often start with the word "if" and ask you to find the answer choice that *must be true, must be false, could be true,* or *could be false* in a specific situation. These questions give you an extra piece of information that will further limit the possibilities on your diagram. The more concrete the information given by a Specific question, the easier the question is. Again turn to page 154 and find the Specific questions. Which one has the more concrete information?

Once you have completely worked the Specific questions, it's time to tackle the General questions. These usually begin with the word "which" and differ from Specific questions in that they don't give you any extra limiting information. That's why we don't answer them first. If you save these until after you've done the Specific questions, however, you'll find that you will be able to eliminate many answer choices simply by referring back to the work that you've already done on the other questions. How's that for efficiency?

Turn to page 154 and look at each of the General questions. Pay attention to the variability of each one. Do you already have the answer to any of them?

Finally, there are the aptly named Complex questions. Sometimes these will ask what new rule, if substituted for one of the existing clues, would have the same effect. Other times they might start with either "if" or "which" but will have a complicated task like figuring out which of the answer choices, if it were true, would completely determine the outcome of the game. These questions are often among the most difficult and most labor intensive. You'll see later why you should do them last, if that's not clear already. For now, relax: there are no complex questions on your first game.

Step 6: Answer using Process of Elimination You won't always have to work with the answer choices one at a time. The beauty of a systematic approach is that you can often deduce the answer and go straight to it. This is the most efficient approach.

But when you can't do that, POE is the way to go. You'll have to use different methods in different situations, but the point is that it's often faster to find four wrong answers than it is to find the right answer.

Let's apply the approach to the questions in order. Start with the Grab-a-Rule.

1. Which one of the following could be an acceptable schedule of Patterson's workout and meetings, in order from 1:00 to 6:00?

    (A) Yansky, workout, Upton, Reilly, Sanchez, Tang   (A)

    (B) Upton, Tang, Sanchez, Yansky, workout, Reilly   (B)

    (C) Upton, Reilly, Sanchez, workout, Tang, Yansky   (C)

    (D) Sanchez, Yansky, workout, Reilly, Tang, Upton   (D)

    (E) Sanchez, Upton, workout, Yansky, Tang, Reilly   (E)

Here's How to Crack It

We call this type a Grab-a-Rule question because all you have to do is apply each rule—or clue—to the answer choices and eliminate any choice that violates it. It gives you five complete lists and asks you to pick the one that follows the rules. These tend to be straightforward, quick questions that will give you valuable insight into how a game works (if you missed anything during the deductions step). Usually one rule will eliminate one answer choice. While it is possible that a single rule can eliminate multiple answers, it is rare.

Our first clue tells us that W is after S; that eliminates (A), since it has W before S.

Our second clue tells us that T is after W; that eliminates (B), since it has T before W.

Our third clue tells us that W and Y must be immediately next to one another; that eliminates (C), since it has W and Y separated by T.

Our fourth clue tells us that R is after U; that eliminates (D), since it has R before U.

Choice (E) is the only one left; it must be the answer.

Note: Your process here is to take the clues and apply them to the choices, not the other way around. Taking each choice and applying it to each of the clues is very cumbersome and could lead to careless errors. Trust us.

Now, let's tackle the Specific questions.

5. If Patterson meets with Tang at 4:00, then which one of the following must be true?

(A) Patterson meets with Reilly at 5:00.

(B) Patterson meets with Upton at 5:00.

(C) Patterson meets with Yansky at 2:00.

(D) Patterson meets with Yansky at 3:00.

(E) Patterson's workout is at 2:00.

(A) (B) (C) (D) (E)

Here's How to Crack It

Of the two specific questions, you should work this one first since it provides very concrete information about when Tang's meeting is. First, underline the question stem. This question is asking what *must be true.* For every single specific question, you should create a new row on the diagram, and start with the new information from the question on the diagram. Next, determine what other restrictions will allow you to fill in more information by looking for any overlap with your clues. Continue to work on your diagram until you can't fill in any more information. If you find yourself in a situation where slots have been limited to only two options, it's worth filling them in. If there are more than two options, don't bother writing them down, or it will get messy fast.

RSTUYW	1:00	2:00	3:00	4:00	5:00	6:00
Clue Shelf	W T R Y S/U	T	T	S	S	S W U Y R/T
⑤	S	W/Y	W/Y	T	U	R

Putting T at 4:00 leaves only three time slots earlier than T. Based on our deductions, these must be filled with S...W/Y...Y/W. Since the order of W and Y cannot be determined, write both elements into each of slots 2:00 and 3:00. Fill that into the diagram. Our only remaining elements are U and R, which must be in that order, so fill those into the diagram. As you can see from the diagram, the locations of S, U, and R are fixed by T being at 4:00. W and Y can alternate. Since we are looking for what must be true, the credited response will deal with one of the fixed elements. Now, let's head to the answer choices and see if we can find an answer. We can—the answer is (B).

———————————◯———————————

On to the next Specific question.

———————————◯———————————

4. If Patterson meets with Sanchez the hour before she meets with Yansky, then each of the following could be true EXCEPT:

(A) Patterson meets with Reilly at 2:00.   (A̶)

(B) Patterson meets with Yansky at 3:00.   (B̶)

(C) Patterson meets with Tang at 4:00.   (C̶)

(D) Patterson meets with Yansky at 5:00.   (D̶)

(E) Patterson meets with Tang at 6:00.   (E̶)

Here's How to Crack It

Wait! If you ever try something in a game that doesn't work, just draw a line through incorrect information and create a new row. Even bad plays add to your knowledge of how the game works. Specific questions will help you with POE when you get to the General questions. Start another row of information and make sure to write the question number next to it just in case you have to come back to it.

This question is more challenging for several reasons. First, it provides relational information rather than concrete information. S is immediately before Y, but we don't know where in the diagram this goes. Second, the question stem is *could be true EXCEPT*. With EXCEPT/LEAST/NOT question stems, it is helpful to write down what you will POE and what you are looking for. We want to eliminate any answer that could be true, so we are looking to choose the one choice that must be false.

The best way to beat this problem is to apply one of your global strategies: "Keep your pen moving."

According to the question, S is before Y and since S is before Y, W must come immediately after Y according to clue 3. Add this new information to your diagram, and then add to it any information you know.

Since we deduced that S or U must be first, begin by placing the SYW block in slots 1, 2, and 3, respectively. Now put T, U, and R in valid positions. Then check the answer choices.

RSTUYW	1:00	2:00	3:00	4:00	5:00	6:00
Clue Shelf	~~W~~ ~~T~~ ~~R~~ ~~Y~~ S/U	~~T~~	~~T~~	~~S~~	~~S~~	~~S~~ ~~W~~ ~~U~~ ~~Y~~ R/T
⑤	S	W/Y	W/Y	T	U	R
④	S	Y	W	T	U	R

Remember, if we have shown an answer choice could be true, then we need to eliminate that answer choice. Choice (C) matches our diagram, so eliminate it. Don't fret that we got rid of only one answer choice. Keep that pen moving! Try shifting SYW over to slots 2, 3, and 4.

RSTUYW	1:00	2:00	3:00	4:00	5:00	6:00
Clue Shelf	~~W~~ ~~T~~ ~~R~~ ~~Y~~ S/U	~~T~~	~~T~~	~~S~~	~~S~~	~~S~~ ~~W~~ ~~U~~ ~~Y~~ R/T
⑤	S	W/Y	W/Y	T	U	R
④	S U	Y S	W Y	T W	U R/T	R R/T

Note that this play leaves only two time slots available at the end of the day. We know from our deductions that either S or U is first. Since S is second, put U first. This leaves T and R, which can alternate positions. Now, go back to the answer choices. Our diagram matches both (B) and (E), so eliminate these. Repeat the process one last time by moving the SYW block over one more starting at 3. If SWY is placed in 3, 4, and 5, then T must be in 6 and U must be in 1, forcing R to be in 2.

RSTUYW	1:00	2:00	3:00	4:00	5:00	6:00
Clue Shelf	~~W~~ ~~T~~ ~~R~~ ~~Y~~ S/U	~~T~~	~~T~~	~~S~~	~~S~~	~~S~~ ~~W~~ ~~U~~ ~~Y~~ R/T
⑤	S	W/Y	W/Y	T	U	R
④	S U U	Y S R	W Y S	T W Y	U R/T W	R R/T T

This play matches (A), which can now be eliminated. The only remaining answer is (D).

———————◯———————

At this point, you may be feeling frustrated. You are probably thinking that you just did a lot of work for one question. However, don't lose sight of the end game. Each of these different plays provided you with valuable information about the game that will help you on the General questions. Speaking of which, let's move on.

———————◯———————

2. How many of the clients are there, any one of whom could meet with Patterson at 1:00?

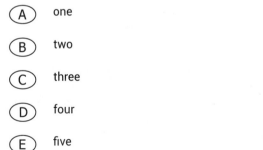

 (A)   one

 (B)   two

 (C)   three

 (D)   four

 (E)   five

Here's How to Crack It

This question hopefully demonstrates to you the necessity of making deductions. From our deductions, we know that only two people can be first. This is further supported by our valid plays from questions 4 and 5. Choose (B) and move on.

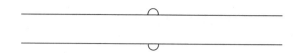

3. Patterson CANNOT meet with Upton at which one of the following times?

   (A) 1:00

   (B) 2:00

   (C) 3:00

   (D) 4:00

   (E) 5:00

   Ⓐ Ⓑ Ⓒ Ⓓ Ⓔ

Here's How to Crack It

Just like the previous question, this question asks for a deduction you could have made. Specifically, this question asks you to identify a time that U cannot be scheduled. For questions like this, always refer to your diagram, checking deductions and previous work from Specific questions and compare them to the answers. We know that U cannot meet at 6:00; however, this is not an answer choice! Since the question is asking for when U cannot be scheduled, we can eliminate any answer that lists a valid time slot for U. Look at your prior work from the specific questions. We know from the work we did on question 5 that U can meet Patterson at 5:00, so eliminate (E). From the work from question 4, U can meet with Patterson at 1:00, so eliminate (A).

Once you've exhausted your prior work, you have no choice but to test each of the remaining answers. When you test answer choices, make sure that you have a clear idea of what you are going to eliminate. In this question, we can eliminate any time slot that is valid for U to use. It is an arbitrary choice, so let's just start with (B). Try to make this answer true.

Putting U at 2:00 forces S to be at 1:00. Now, make sure the rest of the elements can be placed. Work until either you are finished or are sure that there is no way to continue. The play above is one example of a valid play. Your play may look different. The trick is to play out the game and glance at your symbols as you do so to see if you have violated any of the clues.

RSTUYW	1:00	2:00	3:00	4:00	5:00	6:00
Clue Shelf	W̶ T̶ R̶ Y̶ S/U	T̶	T̶	S̶	S̶	S̶ W̶ U̶ Y̶ R/T
(5)	S	W/Y	W/Y	T	U	R
(4)	S U U	Y S R	W Y S	T W Y	U R/T W	R R/T T
(3B)	S	U	R	W/Y	W/Y	T

Since U can meet Patterson at 2:00, eliminate (B).

Now try putting U at 3:00 to check (C).

This forces S to be first based on our deductions. Next, place the WY block since it requires two spaces. Our two remaining spaces have to be T and R. However, neither of these can be placed in time 2:00.

RSTUYW	1:00	2:00	3:00	4:00	5:00	6:00
Clue Shelf	W̶ T̶ R̶ Y̶ S/U	T̶	T̶	S̶	S̶	S̶ W̶ U̶ Y̶ R/T
(5)	S	W/Y	W/Y	T	U	R
(4)	S U U	Y S R	W Y S	T W Y	U R/T W	R R/T T
(3B)	S	U	R	W/Y	W/Y	T
(3C)	S̶		U̶	W/Y̶	W/Y̶	

From this, it is clear that U *cannot* meet at 3:00. This matches the question, so select (C). Finally, make sure that you cross out the attempt to put U at 3:00 so that this invalid play doesn't get mixed with your prior work.

Before we move on to the last General questions, we want you to note the relationship between General *must be true* and *must be false* questions. These questions ask about possible deductions that can be made. As you study for the test and practice making deductions, look at these General questions when you review your work. Ask yourself, "Did I make this deduction?" If the answer is "no," ask yourself why not. Finally, work backward from the correct answer and see if you can make the deduction on your own. This is a powerful method for building your deductive reasoning skills. Now, let's finish this game out.

———————————○———————————

6. Which one of the following could be the order of Patterson's meetings, from earliest to latest?

(A) Upton, Yansky, Sanchez, Reilly, Tang   Ⓐ

(B) Upton, Reilly, Sanchez, Tang, Yansky   Ⓑ

(C) Sanchez, Yansky, Reilly, Tang, Upton   Ⓒ

(D) Sanchez, Upton, Tang, Yansky, Reilly   Ⓓ

(E) Sanchez, Upton, Reilly, Yansky, Tang   Ⓔ

Here's How to Crack It

This question can be very overwhelming. We asked you earlier why this was not a Grab-a-Rule. Hopefully, you noticed that the lack of the element W prevents this question from being a Grab-a-Rule. It also means that three of the four rules do not apply directly to the problem. However, for all General questions, check your deductions first. Just be very careful when you do so since this question does not include all the possible spaces. From our deductions U or S must always be first. This is true of all five answers. Our deductions also show that either R or T must be last. Both (B) and (C) have R and T in the middle of the appointments. This violates the deduction, so eliminate them. Now focus on the long chain deduction which says that S...WY...T. Choice (A) has Y before S so eliminate it. Choice (D) has Y after T so eliminate it. The answer is (E).

———————————○———————————

To summarize, here's the step-by-step approach to all games.

Prepare the Game
- Step 1: Diagram and inventory
- Step 2: Symbolize the clues and double-check
- Step 3: Make deductions and size up the game

Work the Questions
- Step 4: Assess the question
- Step 5: Act
- Step 6: Use Process of Elimination

Now that we've walked you through the process, turn the page and play the game on your own. Feel free to refer to notes on the steps, and don't worry about time. Once you've completed the game a second time, come back to these pages and assess how closely you were able to reproduce the approach on your own.

GAME 1

On one afternoon, Patterson meets individually with each of exactly five clients—Reilly, Sanchez, Tang, Upton, and Yansky—and also goes to the gym by herself for a workout. Patterson's workout and her five meetings each start at either 1:00, 2:00, 3:00, 4:00, 5:00, or 6:00. The following conditions must apply:

  Patterson meets with Sanchez at some time before her workout.
  Patterson meets with Tang at some time after her workout.
  Patterson meets with Yansky either immediately before or immediately after her workout.
  Patterson meets with Upton at some time before she meets with Reilly.

1. Which one of the following could be an acceptable schedule of Patterson's workout and meetings, in order from 1:00 to 6:00?

   (A) Yansky, workout, Upton, Reilly, Sanchez, Tang (A)

   (B) Upton, Tang, Sanchez, Yansky, workout, Reilly (B)

   (C) Upton, Reilly, Sanchez, workout, Tang, Yansky (C)

   (D) Sanchez, Yansky, workout, Reilly, Tang, Upton (D)

   (E) Sanchez, Upton, workout, Yansky, Tang, Reilly (E)

2. How many of the clients are there, any one of whom could meet with Patterson at 1:00?

   (A) one (A)

   (B) two (B)

   (C) three (C)

   (D) four (D)

   (E) five (E)

3. Patterson CANNOT meet with Upton at which one of the following times?

   (A) 1:00 (A)

   (B) 2:00 (B)

   (C) 3:00 (C)

   (D) 4:00 (D)

   (E) 5:00 (E)

4. If Patterson meets with Sanchez the hour before she meets with Yansky, then each of the following could be true EXCEPT:

   (A) Patterson meets with Reilly at 2:00. (A)

   (B) Patterson meets with Yansky at 3:00. (B)

   (C) Patterson meets with Tang at 4:00. (C)

   (D) Patterson meets with Yansky at 5:00. (D)

   (E) Patterson meets with Tang at 6:00. (E)

5. If Patterson meets with Tang at 4:00, then which one of the following must be true?

(A) Patterson meets with Reilly at 5:00. (A)

(B) Patterson meets with Upton at 5:00. (B)

(C) Patterson meets with Yansky at 2:00. (C)

(D) Patterson meets with Yansky at 3:00. (D)

(E) Patterson's workout is at 2:00. (E)

6. Which one of the following could be the order of Patterson's meetings, from earliest to latest?

(A) Upton, Yansky, Sanchez, Reilly, Tang (A)

(B) Upton, Reilly, Sanchez, Tang, Yansky (B)

(C) Sanchez, Yansky, Reilly, Tang, Upton (C)

(D) Sanchez, Upton, Tang, Yansky, Reilly (D)

(E) Sanchez, Upton, Reilly, Yansky, Tang (E)

Tip!
If most of the questions are on the second page of a game, start drawing the diagram on the second page so your workspace is more compact.

Cracking Game 1

Games Technique: Self Analysis There's an old axiom that says we learn best from our mistakes. This axiom holds true on the Games section. A key strategy is to fill out a self-analysis of the game. Figure out what you did well and how to replicate your success. Also, focus on where and how you messed up. Try to identify the failed approaches that you used and figure out ways to avoid these mistakes in the future.

Every successful self-analysis will include a few things. It will include data on the basic approach, the question types, and the number right and wrong. Next, a good self-analysis should also distinguish between when you get something correct and when you got something right but got lucky. For wrong answers, you should distinguish between careless mistakes and don't know hows. You are reading this book to help you with the know-how. Careless mistakes are something only you can control. Something we tell all of our classroom students is that getting an answer wrong because you don't know how to work it is fine. Getting an answer wrong that you know how to work, but just mess up, is a lost point. Remember, only you can prevent test errors!

Below you will find a sample self-analysis. You are encouraged to use this one or develop one that fits your study style.

Steps 1–3 Assessment

Diagram and elements: I got this correct without issues.

Symbolize and double-check: I got burned here. The clues seemed too easy. I sort of double-checked but really just reread each of the clues. I ended up reading the second clue wrong twice in a row. Next time, I will force myself to double-check by looking at the symbol I made and then going back to the clue.

Deductions: These were tough. I missed two from the explanation. However, I didn't waste too much time and after finding the clue I got wrong, I was still able to get most questions correct. Next time I will specifically look for deductions from clues that share the same element.

Steps 4–6 Assessment

Question 1: Grab-a-Rule. I was stuck between two answers that were both "correct." I ended up triple-checking my clues and found an error in my symbols. I got this right in the end. I know I can do that again.

Question 2: General question; saved for later; got it right but guessed; had some deductions, but not all. I used prior work and deductions to eliminate (A), (D), and (E). Got stuck after that. Next time, I will get my pen moving and diagramming to see if a third element would work.

Question 3: General question; did it last; got it wrong; I honestly had no idea where to start on this one. It wasn't on my deduction list and I wasn't able to eliminate anything from my prior work! I understand the explanation, but I'm not sure I can do that on my own yet. I will play this game again in a few days to see if I can get it right then.

Question 4: Specific question, did it last of the specifics (3rd I think); got it wrong. I forgot about the except. I eliminated (A) and (B), but then chose (C) since it worked. Next time, I will write out next to the question what I am going to POE.

Question 5: Specific question; did it right after the Grab-a-Rule; got it right and I know why. I can do this question again on a different game with full confidence.

Question 6: General question; I did it differently from the explanation but got it right. My way was pretty time-consuming. I'm not sure if I can get the same style of question right on a different game. I'm going to hit this question again when I replay the game.

On the next page, you will find a place for you to perform your own self-analysis of Game 1.

Self-Assessment

Steps 1–3 Assessment

Steps 4–6 Assessment

LESSON 2: GOOD SYMBOLIZATION AND DEDUCTIONS

Good symbolization is a major step toward getting all the questions in a particular game correct. Success with symbolization comes from familiarity and practice. There are a number of common types of clues that you'll see repeatedly on the LSAT; once you become familiar with them, most of the process becomes mechanical. While you're practicing your symbolization, keep in mind the three Cs: *clear, consistent,* and *concise*.

Clear: Your symbols should make quick and apparent sense. If you find yourself having to interpret a clue as you use it in the game, your symbol isn't working.

Consistent: As we mentioned above, you should start to recognize distinct types of LSAT clues that you'll symbolize in the same manner each time they show up in a game. But you should also be sure that your clues are consistent with one another within a game and that they are consistent with the way that you drew your diagram. In other words, everything should fit together.

Concise: Keep symbols as short and simple as possible. Part of the reason for having them is to eliminate the wasted energy and time of reading those long-winded, confusing clues each time you refer to them in working the questions.

While the language of a clue can make it challenging to interpret, the LSAT has produced clues that match recurring patterns. For the ease of categorization, we have named these clues patterns. Common clues on the LSAT include *range, block and antiblock, concrete and placeholders, element,* and *conditionals*. Conditional clues require special focus and we will cover them in a later lesson. Let's take a look at good symbols for these other common types of clues.

Range

Range clues are a category of clues exclusive to Ordering games. Range clues establish some sort of spatial relationship between two or more elements. Several of the clues from the Patterson game in Lesson 1 were range clues. Range clues are most easily symbolized with ellipses (though dashes may also be used). Below, we have some examples of range clues. Practice symbolizing each first, and then read the cracking explanation.

Anna sits to the east of Bob and to the west of Carol.

This clue is giving you two pieces of information about A. It is always best to consolidate these pieces of information into one symbol, but be careful! Make sure you are consistent throughout the game about which way is east and which way is west—under time pressure, these basic pieces of knowledge can get twisted around.

> **Tip!**
> One useful thing to do on Ordering games is to label the directions above the first and last position. For example, if an Ordering game deals with directions, write "west" above column 1 and "east" above the final column.

"To the east" on a game would mean to the right, so the first thing to do would put A to the right of B. Then, the clue states that A is west of C. This would mean that A is to the left of C. Your final clue should look similar to this.

$$B...A...C$$

The ellipses indicate that the distance between B and A is unknown. There might be one or more elements in between them or they could end up right next to each other. For example, B could be first and A could be second, or B could be second and A could be fifth. You can think of the ellipses as a rubber band; sometimes the elements will be pulled apart from one another and one or more other elements will be placed in between them.

Let's consider another example.

In a five-story building, John lives on a higher floor than Walter.

A clue's symbol makes sense only in the context of a diagram. So for our next example, we're going to draw a rough diagram similar to what you would have already constructed in an actual game. After looking at the diagram, try symbolizing this clue on your own.

Remember one of our Cs: *consistent*. We want our symbol to look like what happens in our diagram. At the same time, we don't want to create a different symbol for every possible situation the LSAT throws at us. We want our symbol system to be *concise* as well. This is another range clue; therefore, we will still use ellipses. However, we also want our symbol to look like our diagram, so the clue should be vertical too. Take a look at our symbol.

$$\begin{array}{c} J \\ \vdots \\ W \end{array}$$

Range clues can also take more complex forms. Consider the following:

A comes before both B and C.

Of course, you could break this clue into two distinct pieces and symbolize each half of the clue individually. However, one of our three Cs is *concise*. The more information we can pack into a single clue, the more powerful it is. Be careful about making assumptions though. Below you will find a bad symbolization. Take a moment to think about the symbol compared to the clue. Why is this example wrong?

A...B...C   (Remember this is wrong!!)

We're hoping that you spotted an assumption that we made. According to the clue, A is before both B and C, which is supported by the symbol. However, what we don't know is the relationship between B and C. It is possible that C could be before B without violating this clue. As a result, we need our symbol to show that the relationship between B and C is unknown. Your final clue should look similar to this.

Let's look at one final example of a more complex range clue. As above, try to symbolize it yourself without making any assumptions.

X does not follow Y.

You may have been tempted to switch this clue back to front to read "X is before Y." Be very careful if you do this! Technically, that is a deduction and not a clue symbolization. Depending on the structure of the ordering game, it is possible that switching the clue back to front would include some assumptions. We recommend symbolizing the clue as literally as possible. After you move into the deduction stage, you can consider whether switching the clue back to front is supported by the diagram. Your final symbolization should look like the following.

Block and Antiblock Clues

The next category of clues is closely related to range clues, with one major difference. Consider the following example.

In the alphabet, A comes immediately before B.

Similar to range clues, the relative position of the two elements is fixed. A is first, B comes later. The key difference is the idea of "immediately." There is an additional constraint in this type of clue that removes the ambiguity inherent in range clues. These two letters must appear in this order and next to each other each time. Since this clue forms a block of two or more elements, we have dubbed it a block clue. Symbolize this clue by placing the elements in the proper order and putting a block around them. Make sure to draw a line between the two elements to show that they appear in different columns (block clues can also place two elements in the same category). The symbol should look similar to this.

Block clues are among the most useful clues in any game because they use up more spaces with fixed information. Even if the block is reversible, like the WY clue in Game 1, you still know that two spaces must be filled at the same time. If you have a game with multiple block clues, it is useful to take a minute to consider how the blocks must interact with one another. Sometimes, multiple block clues will limit a game to only two or three possible solutions. Dare we say, block party anyone?

Now that you are done groaning, let's look at a few more examples.

> The three boys all sit in consecutive seats, with one girl immediately before them and one girl immediately after.

This clue gives you several pieces of information. First, there are exactly three boys. Second, there are at least two girls. Third, the three boys all sit together. Fourth, one girls sits on either end of the line of boys. Let's put it all together.

Notice that we didn't write "G3BG." Instead, we wrote out three separate Bs. The same goes for symbolizing the elements when you know how many of each type you have. If a clue tells you that you have five engines, for example, write "EEEEE" and not "5E." And if later you are given further characteristics about the boys and girls, such as what color hats they might be wearing, you will be able to note these characteristics as another layer below the first symbol. There will be more on this method later in this lesson.

Think about the building example above. Below is a variant of that clue. Remember to be *consistent:* we want our symbol to look like what happens in the diagram.

> In a five story building, J lives two floors above W.

As with the earlier range clue, this clue should be vertical too. But be careful here—if J lives two floors above W, there is only one floor that actually separates them. Take a look at our symbol.

As you can see, the wording is meant to lead you astray: there is a big difference between "J lives two floors above W" and "there are two floors between J and W." If you weren't vigilant and had inserted an extra floor, your game would have swiftly degenerated into confusion.

Tip!
If you are ever playing a game and a specific question is impossible to play due to the clues, double-check your clues. It is likely you missed something.

As you read and attempt to symbolize the next clue, take a moment to think about its similarity and differences to the other clues in this section. Ask yourself why it was included here.

> The two philosophers never sit together.

This is very similar to a clue that you will see in the game at the end of this section. This clue doesn't give us information about how two elements *must* be positioned with relation to each other, but rather how they *cannot* be. Here we know that there are two Ps and that these two Ps can never be together. This is a basic *antiblock.*

If the game ever gives us the placement of one of our philosophers, we know now that the other philosopher can't go immediately to the right or left of the first one. We also know that there are exactly two philosophers from the concrete language used in the clue. If we weren't sure how many philosophers there were in the game, we would want to be sure to note that fact in addition to our antiblock clue.

Concrete Clues

Concrete clues are exactly what they sound like. Any clue that gives you specific, concrete information is a concrete clue. The best way to symbolize these is directly on the diagram. Consider the following.

> E is the fifth letter of the alphabet.

If your diagram consists of seven places, you would place E under the fifth column on the clue shelf of your diagram. It is also useful to write "on diagram" next to the number for this clue on your clue list.

1	2	3	4	5	6	7
				E		

For the rest of the example clues in this section, we have provided a sample diagram. Practice symbolizing each one on your own before reading the explanation.

Either M or N is chosen first.

1	2	3	4	5	6	7

While this clue is less specific than the previous one, we still know that there are only two possibilities for the first column. Use a slash to indicate "or" and put both letters in column one on your clue shelf.

1	2	3	4	5	6	7
M/N						

O is either second, third, or fourth.

1	2	3	4	5	6	7

This clue is a bit more complex. The clue limits O to one of three possible rows out of seven. However, there is still a lot of flexibility here. One way to efficiently symbolize this is with a spider diagram. Place the O above the diagram and draw three arrows from the O to each of the spots 2, 3, and 4.

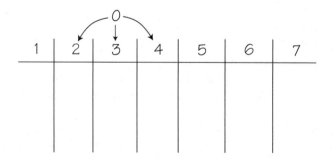

The first letter is always the same as the last letter.

Believe it or not, this is still a concrete clue. You might be feeling a bit out of your element here (since none are mentioned). However, this clue provides specific information about two positions on the diagram. Once another clue or question places an element in either position, the other position is automatically filled. The easiest way to symbolize this clue is with an equals sign.

$$1 = 7$$

Notice that we didn't draw an arrow from column 1 to column 7. Since clues must be *consistent*, we don't want to confuse the use of arrows in the spider-like diagram with arrows for this type of clue.

B is neither first nor last.

Just like antiblocks are related to block clues, concrete clues can also be negative. Simply mark this element on your clue shelf and draw a line through it to indicate that elements cannot belong there.

Placeholders are a type of concrete clue specific to Grouping games. We will be covering those in more detail in the next lesson.

Element Clues

Some clues can address the elements in the game by adding repeating elements or limiting how often a specific element can occur. Clues can even divide elements into distinct categories. These need to be symbolized correctly. Consider the following.

A, B, and C are saxophonists; D, E, and F are percussionists.

In this case, we are given elements that fall into two categories: saxophonists and percussionists. We must have a way to keep these straight as we work the game. Probably the simplest way to accomplish this is by symbolizing one group with uppercase letters and one with lowercase letters. We'll end up with the following symbols.

$$S: A\ B\ C$$
$$p: d\ e\ f$$

There are games that have more than two types of elements, or elements that can have more than one characteristic associated with them. In these cases, you should use subscripts to distinguish the elements. For instance, if we had those same saxophonists and percussionists, but we were also told that A and f were leads and C and e were backups, we would need some way to keep all of this straight. Furthermore, we might have to assign these elements to either the marching band or the orchestra, if these are the groups available in the game. We would need to make sure that we could tell what characteristics each element had so that we could assign them accordingly. Here's how we would symbolize the leads (L) and backups (B).

$$S: A_L\ B\ C_B$$
$$p: d\ e_B\ f_L$$

You'll have to make an effort to keep your diagram neat, but now you'll be able to work with the elements effectively.

In addition to clues organizing the elements into categories, clues can also expand or limit the total number of elements you have. These affect the distribution of elements. Let's look at an example.

There is at least one fire drill per week.

How would you do this one? This doesn't give us very concrete information because we still don't know exactly how many fire drills there will be each week. But it is an important piece of information because we know for sure that we have to include a fire drill in each valid arrangement for the game. It's a pretty simple piece of information, so our symbol will also be pretty simple. Don't succumb to the urge to just keep it in your head; yes, it's simple, but no, that doesn't give you license to skip the visualization. Here's a good way to symbolize it.

$$F^{1+}$$

We used the plus sign to indicate *at least*, which will remind us that we can have more than one of these, according to the rules. A corollary clue type is one that tells you that an element will be used *at most* a certain number of times; in that case we would use a minus sign as the superscript.

Here's a summary of how we symbolized each clue type.

Clue	Symbol	Clue Pattern
Anna sits to the east of Bob and to the west of Carol.	B...A...C	Range Clue
In the alphabet, A comes immediately before B.	[A|B]	Block Clue
The two philosophers never sit together.	[P̸|P̸]	Antiblock Clue
Either M or N is chosen first.	1 2 3 4 / M/N	Concrete Clue
A, B, and C are saxophonists; D, E, and F are percussionists.	S: A B C p: d e f	Element (inventory) Clue
There is at least one fire drill per week.	F¹⁺	Element (distribution) Clue

Games Technique: When Pictures Fail

Ideally, you will symbolize every clue. Some clues, however, have no clear and concise visual equivalent, especially negative clues that do not refer to any specific element. For example, consider the following.

No more than three books of any given subject are put on the shelf.
Players cannot score more than three points in the first round.

A visualization of these statements would end up being obtuse and potentially confusing, ruining the point of symbolizations in the first place. We need another method. Remember that we want to keep all clue information in one place and not have to refer to the written information provided. The key is crib notes. Jot down the essence of the clue in a few words among the rest of your clues. That way you can't forget about it and you won't have to wade through the original, confusing clue. Here's our examples for the two clues above.

Max 3/subject
Round 1: max 3 points

Games Technique: Making Deductions

Even though we've worked through only a single game, you should already be realizing how important it is to make deductions before you start to work the questions. Think of them as unwritten clues. You can't make good deductions by briefly glancing at your diagram and clues while hurrying to get to the questions. You have to look carefully at the diagram and your symbols. Some people think that making deductions is the result of some kind of epiphany—that you either see them or you don't. Actually, finding deductions is the result of a purely mechanical process. Once you understand the process and have had some time to practice it on a number of different games, you'll be able to ferret out those critical extra pieces of information that will save you valuable time down the road. Here's an overview of the process.

- Start with each clue individually. Check the fit of your clues into your diagram. Sometimes combined clues can get very large, and they may fit into your diagram in only one or two ways. Even if a clue isn't particularly large, you should still be able to get some information this way: for a range clue, often you can find places where the elements involved can't go; for a block clue, you will sometimes find that the number of places it can actually fit is very restricted. Think about the clue from Game 1 about Sanchez and the workout. S was before W so W could never be first.

- Look for elements, or for areas of your diagram, that are mentioned in more than one clue. The more times an element or location is mentioned in the clues, the more likely you can combine the clues into some powerful deductions. Sometimes, particularly in Ordering games, you'll be able to combine more than one range clue or block into a single symbol and that provides you with new information. We saw this with the large deduction we were able to make with S… W/Y…T in the first game.

- Look for sweeping or powerful clues. These are clues that affect many elements and many areas of your diagram. Such clues are fairly rare, but when they're present, pay close attention to them. They often work like super-antiblocks—clues that tell you whole elements types can't appear next to one another in your diagram. Because they apply so broadly, they're often the source of fruitful deductions.

- Look for the ways that your deductions interact with new rules and the remaining elements. Deductions can often build off one another. It is often helpful to make a round of deductions, and then run through the clues a second time to see if you can make any new deductions. We saw this in the first game. We first noted that W, T, and R couldn't be first. Once we made the large chain deduction, we were able to deduce that Y couldn't be first. Finally, since there were only six elements and the first space couldn't have four of them, we were able to deduce that only S/U could be first!

- Deductions that start with *if* are bad; deductions that start with *either* are good. In other words, you don't want to find yourself following lines of reasoning like this: "Well, if F goes there, then that means G has to go here, and then…." Those deductions are rarely, if ever, useful. Remember that you are looking for things you can write down that are true all the time. The good twin of this kind of deduction is the one that goes something like this: "Either F is here, or else F is there; there are no other choices." That deduction, because it's so well defined and concrete, is going to be extremely useful.

Finally, it's important to keep deductions in perspective. Remember that the reason you're looking for them is to make your life *easier*, not harder. Deductions save you time by giving you more information to use on every question, but you give that advantage back if you spend a long time starting unproductively at a game hoping to find a deduction.

When you're looking for links, go through the following checklist:

- ✔ I have looked at each clue individually for deductions.
- ✔ I have looked at combinations of clues that share the same element.
- ✔ I have looked at combinations of clues that mention the same location in the diagram.
- ✔ I have compared my deductions against the remaining elements.
- ✔ I have not found any deductions for the last 30 seconds.

Once you've moved through the list in this order, head decisively to the questions. It's okay if you don't find any deductions, or if you find just one or two small ones; games don't always have big deductions. And realize that it's not the end of the world if you're working a game that does have big deductions and you somehow miss them. The first few questions will take a little longer, but they'll still be workable, and you can learn about the game as you go. Sometimes the only way to find big deductions on a game is to stumble across them, and the only way to do that is to actually get into the game and start working with it. As long as you keep moving forward, you'll be all right. If you sit and stare, you'll get yourself in trouble.

Finally, you should always take several minutes to self-assess your progress after playing a game. One of your self-assessment questions should be about deductions. Did you make all the deductions possible? Were there any you noticed during the game? How can you notice them sooner? You should also look at all the General *must be true* and *must be false* questions. The correct answer to each of these is technically a deduction that you could have made. Sometimes the answer to these questions will rely on a complex interaction of several clues, and you shouldn't feel bad about missing them. At other times, the credited response will be something you could have made by combining two clues. If this is the case, figure out why you didn't see it and then commit to noticing that kind of deduction in the future.

The first two games in this chapter use some of the most common deductions found on the LSAT. Make sure you pay close attention to them as you work through the next game and review your work. The better you get at pattern recognition, the better you will do on the games section. To help you with this, you'll find a discussion below about making deductions and an exercise to help you practice.

Range and Block Clue Deductions   Range and block clues lend themselves to some quick deductions. You can approach these very quickly. Think back to the game in Lesson 1. The first clue was symbolized as S...W. We were able to deduce from this that W could not be at 1:00 and S could not be at 6:00. The same logic is true of block clues. If A always immediately precedes B, then B cannot be first and A cannot be last. One note of warning with block clues though: be careful with reversible blocks such as the WY block clue in Game 1. No deduction can be made with that clue alone since either W or Y could be first. On the next page we have recreated some of the clues from this section and placed them next to an example diagram. Do your best to best to mark any deduction you find and then read the explanations.

Concrete Clue Deductions   Concrete clues provide highly specific information. Specific information is concise and keeps your diagram neat. Consider the final clue above. While we could deduce that if B is neither first nor last, then it must be somewhere in positions two through six, that deduction is not super helpful. The same is true of the first example. If E is fifth and presuming that elements can be placed only once, then logically it cannot be placed elsewhere. However, you don't want to clutter up your diagram with information about where E cannot go if you already know where it could be. As a result, count your blessings when you have a concrete clue, but do not waste time finding single clue deductions with this type of clue. Instead, look at how concrete clues interact with other clues.

DEDUCTION EXERCISE

1. B ... A ... C

1	2	3	4	5	6	7

2. J
    ⋮
    W

3.

1	2	3	4	5	6	7

4. Y ̷ ... X

1	2	3	4	5	6	7

5. Y ̷ ... X

1	2	3	4
--	--	--	--

6. | G | B | B | B | G |

1	2	3	4	5	6	7

7.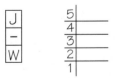

8. | P̷ | P |

1	2	3	4	5	6	7

Cracking Deduction Exercise—Answers and Explanations

1. Since C is last in the range, it cannot be first. Likewise, B cannot be last. However, with longer ranges, more can be deduced. C follows not one but two elements. Therefore, C cannot be second either. Likewise, A follows B so it cannot be first. You can also apply the same logic to the end of the diagram. B cannot be second to last and A cannot be last. Your deductions should look like this.

1	2	3	4	5	6	7
A̶C̶	C̶				B̶	B̶ A̶

2. This deduction was hopefully straightforward for you. The one twist to this deduction is that the diagram runs horizontally instead of vertically. However, if you followed our advice to make the clue match the diagram, you will not have had any problems. W cannot live on the top floor and J cannot live on the ground floor.

5	W̶
4	
3	
2	
1	J̶

3. This next one was a bit more nuanced. You have to be careful since you don't know the order of B and C. Neither one can be first, but either can be second. On the end of the ordering diagram, things are a bit more straightforward. Since A must be before two other elements, A cannot be last or second to last.

1	2	3	4	5	6	7
B̶C̶					A̶	A̶

4. To show you the dangers of confusing symbolization with deductions, we've included two possible diagrams for this one. The first diagram was a simple ordering game with one element per category. As a result, swapping the clue is a valid deduction. Since only one element can be in each location, X cannot be last and Y cannot be first.

1	2	3	4	5	6	7
Y̶						X̶

5. The next diagram for this clue allows two elements to belong in each space. It may have been tempting to make the same deduction as above. However, X and Y could occur in the same space without violating the clue. Remember that the clue only restricts Y coming before X. As a result, Y could follow X or be placed in the same space as X. Therefore, you cannot make a deduction using this clue on this diagram. Your diagram should be blank.

1	2	3	4
_ _	_ _	_ _	_ _

6. The fact that there are exactly three boys means that boys will never be first or last in this diagram.

1	2	3	4	5	6	7
~B						~B

7. With this deduction, remember to take into account not only the order of the two elements but also the fixed distance between them. Since J is two floors above W, he cannot be on the first or second floors. Likewise, since J is two floors above W, W cannot be on the top or the second highest floor.

5	W̶
4	W̶
3	
2	J̶
1	J̶

8. Antiblock clues are very useful. However, their utility only becomes evident once the placement of other elements is known. As a result, there are no single clue deductions that can be made with antiblocks. Your diagram should be blank.

1	2	3	4	5	6	7

MULTICATEGORY ELEMENTS AND 2D GAMES

As we showed in the discussion about clue symbolization, some elements can be placed into more than one category. We showed you that the best way to deal with this issue in the elements was to use upper- and lowercase letters. However, good symbolization is only half of what you need to master every game. You also need a solid, functional diagram that helps you organize the elements efficiently and accurately. Whenever you have elements that need to be tracked in more than one way, you have what we call a 2-dimensional or 2D game. 2D games, by definition, are more complex than 1D games simply because there is more information to note in the diagram. Additionally, the LSAT question writers will have more leeway in how they phrase the questions.

Think about the first game we did. What if Patterson was meeting with lawyers and accountants? In addition to tracking the order of her meetings, we would also need to track what type of job each person had. The question writers could then ask questions such as "if Patterson's first meeting is with a lawyer, which of the following could be a valid time for her workout?" Ouch! As you can see, these types of games are a bit rougher than 1D games.

The trick to mastering these games is to separate your diagram into two rows and label each row with a relevant category. To practice this, we'll walk you through Step 1 of Game 2. Once we've done this, turn the page and work Game 2 on your own.

Game 2

On each of exactly seven consecutive days (day 1 through day 7), a pet shop features exactly one of three breeds of kitten—Himalayan, Manx, Siamese—and exactly one of three breeds of puppy—Greyhound, Newfoundland, Rottweiler. The following conditions must apply:

> Greyhounds are featured on day 1.
> No breed is featured on any two consecutive days.
> Any breed featured on day 1 is not featured on day 7.
> Himalayans are featured on exactly three days, but not on day 1.
> Rottweilers are not featured on day 7, nor on any day that features Himalayans.

Game 2 and its questions are from PrepTest 32, Section 3, Questions 19–24.

Step 1: Diagram and Inventory First, ask yourself what are you doing to the elements. We are told that the pet shop will feature the animals on consecutive days. Therefore, this is an Ordering game and the numbers one through seven should form the core of your diagram. Next, note that there are now two categories of pets: kittens and puppies. Using the same method as described above, use uppercase letters for one group and lower case letters for the other.

$$K: H\ M\ S$$
$$p: g\ n\ r$$

Finally, the setup specifically notes that the pet shop will feature exactly one kitten…and exactly one puppy. Thus, we need to create a separate row on the diagram to represent this. Your final diagram should look like this.

Now that we have provided the diagram for Game 2 and discussed multiple ways to categorize and symbolize clues, turn the page and work Game 2 on your own. As with Game 1, don't worry about timing as much as focusing on how to use the basic approach with more complex games. Finally, a hint: remember that the point of symbolization is to provide you with visual puzzle pieces that drop directly into the diagram. Do your best to symbolize each clue in a way that matches the diagram.

GAME 2

On each of exactly seven consecutive days (day 1 through day 7), a pet shop features exactly one of three breeds of kitten—Himalayan, Manx, Siamese—and exactly one of three breeds of puppy—Greyhound, Newfoundland, Rottweiler. The following conditions must apply:

Greyhounds are featured on day 1.
No breed is featured on any two consecutive days.
Any breed featured on day 1 is not featured on day 7.
Himalayans are featured on exactly three days, but not on day 1.
Rottweilers are not featured on day 7, nor on any day that features Himalayans.

1. Which one of the following could be the order in which the breeds of kitten are featured in the pet shop, from day 1 through day 7 ?

(A) Himalayan, Manx, Siamese, Himalayan, Manx, Himalayan, Siamese

(B) Manx, Himalayan, Siamese, Himalayan, Manx, Himalayan, Manx

(C) Manx, Himalayan, Manx, Himalayan, Siamese, Manx, Siamese

(D) Siamese, Himalayan, Manx, Himalayan, Siamese, Siamese, Himalayan

(E) Siamese, Himalayan, Siamese, Himalayan, Manx, Siamese, Himalayan

2. If Himalayans are not featured on day 2, which one of the following could be true?

(A) Manx are featured on day 3.

(B) Siamese are featured on day 4.

(C) Rottweilers are featured on day 5.

(D) Himalayans are featured on day 6.

(E) Greyhounds are featured on day 7.

3. Which one of the following could be true?

(A) Greyhounds and Siamese are both featured on day 2.

(B) Greyhounds and Himalayans are both featured on day 7.

(C) Rottweilers and Himalayans are both featured on day 4.

(D) Rottweilers and Manx are both featured on day 5.

(E) Newfoundlands and Manx are both featured on day 6.

4. If Himalayans are not featured on day 7, then which one of the following pairs of days CANNOT feature both the same breed of kitten and the same breed of puppy?

(A) day 1 and day 3

(B) day 2 and day 6

(C) day 3 and day 5

(D) day 4 and day 6

(E) day 5 and day 7

5. Which one of the following could be true?

(A) There are exactly four breeds that are each featured on three days.

(B) Greyhounds are featured on every day that Himalayans are.

(C) Himalayans are featured on every day that Greyhounds are.

(D) Himalayans are featured on every day that Rottweilers are not.

(E) Rottweilers are featured on every day that Himalayans are not.

(A) (B) (C) (D) (E)

6. If Himalayans are not featured on day 7, which one of the following could be true?

(A) Greyhounds are featured on days 3 and 5.

(B) Newfoundlands are featured on day 3.

(C) Rottweilers are featured on day 6.

(D) Rottweilers are featured only on day 3.

(E) Rottweilers are featured on exactly three days.

(A) (B) (C) (D) (E)

Self-Assessment

Steps 1–3 Assessment

Steps 4–6 Assessment

Cracking Game 2

Step 1: Diagram and Inventory
We took care of this step in the lesson component.

Step 2: Symbolize the Clues and Double-check
The rules in this game are a little different from the ones we saw in the first game. Take another look at the first clue, "Greyhounds are featured on day 1." This is a concrete clue that tells us an exact location for greyhounds. Notice that it does not say that greyhounds can occur only on day 1. Symbolize this clue by putting it directly on the diagram.

 diagram
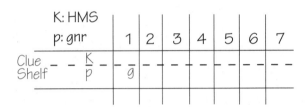

The next clue should seem very familiar. It states that "no breed is featured on any two consecutive days." This is an antiblock clue. Notice that this clue applies to all six elements. While you could create six versions of this clue, one for each element, it would not be very *concise*. Here, the most concise way to symbolize this clue is to write the word "same" twice inside the antiblock.

② |same|same|

Alternatively, you could choose a letter like "X" to represent a generic element. While this would work for many games, we do not recommend this as a strategy since some LSAT games use X as an element. Using an X, therefore, would not be *clear* every time.

The next clue provides information about days 1 and 7. The clue restricts the two spaces to being different from one another. This is a concrete clue since it gives us some solid information. The minute an element is placed on day 1, it cannot be on day 7, and vice-versa. Symbolize this clue by demonstrating that the two days cannot be the same as one another.

③ 1 ≠ 7

This next clue is very complex, but it also provides quite a bit of useful information. First, note that the clue provides the exact number of Himalayan kittens. This is an element clue. Second, notice that the clue gives some concrete information about where H cannot go. The best way to handle this clue is to be *consistent*. Begin with the second half. Mark an H̶ on your diagram on day 1. Next, write "HHH exactly" with your other clues. The final symbolization should look like the following.

④ HHH exactly
and diagram

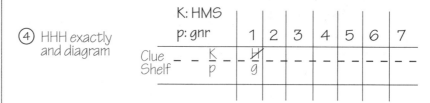

The final clue also provides quite a bit of information that is impossible to symbolize as a single concise clue. Therefore, just as in the previous clue, break this clue into two pieces. The first half of the clue is concrete information. Mark this on your diagram. The second half of the clue is an antiblock. Remember that all of your symbolizations should fit neatly onto your diagram. Since we have a diagram with two rows, one of kittens and one of puppies, make sure that this antiblock is vertical.

⑤ diagram and

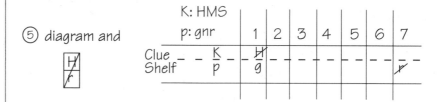

Make sure to double-check those clues, and we're on to the deductions.

Step 3: Make Deductions and Size Up the Game

By now, you should have a list of clues that looks like this. Some of these will actually be on your diagram, but we placed them here to give you the concise list.

1. diagram

2. same̶ s̶ame

3. 1 ≠ 7

4. HHH exactly and diagram

5. diagram and H̶/r̶

As discussed in the lesson, with concrete clues, it is best to skip ahead directly to multiclue deductions. Notice how clue 2 overlaps clue 1. Since g is on day 1 and since breeds cannot be shown consecutively, then g cannot be on day 2. Mark this on your diagram.

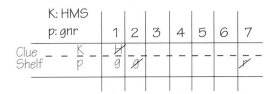

Next, note how the first clue, which is on day 1, also overlaps with clue 3. Since g is on day 1, then g cannot be on day 7. Mark this on your diagram.

The next thing to notice is that there are only 3 possible breeds of dogs to be shown. Day 7 now states that neither r nor g can be on day 7. Therefore, n must be the puppy breed shown. Specific *must be true* information is always better than *must be false* information. Mark n on the diagram.

Deductions can build on one another. Antiblocks are some of the most powerful clues possible in an LSAT game. Go back to clue 2. Now that we know that n is shown on day 7, we can deduce that n cannot be shown on day 6! Mark this on the diagram.

Finally, look at clue 4. This clue states that H is featured exactly 3 times. Clue 2 states that the same breed cannot be featured consecutively. As a result, there will be at least one space after each of the first two Hs. Be careful here. Do not assume that there must be exactly one space between each. There is enough space on the diagram to have a double gap between either the first and second H or the second and third H. The final deduction should look like this.

$$\boxed{H}\boxed{-}...\boxed{H}\boxed{-}...H$$

Remember that part of the deduction stage is assessing the game. Which element or clue will have the greatest impact on the game? Since the H will take up so much room on the diagram and since it cannot be placed with r, the H will drive this game. Make every effort to place the three Hs first as you work through the game.

Steps 4 and 5: Assess the Question and Act
See a Grab-a-Rule question? Possibly? Try it first, even if you are not sure.

Step 6: Answer Using Process of Elimination

1. Which one of the following could be the order in which the breeds of kitten are featured in the pet shop, from day 1 through day 7 ?

   (A) Himalayan, Manx, Siamese, Himalayan, Manx, Himalayan, Siamese

   (B) Manx, Himalayan, Siamese, Himalayan, Manx, Himalayan, Manx

   (C) Manx, Himalayan, Manx, Himalayan, Siamese, Manx, Siamese

   (D) Siamese, Himalayan, Manx, Himalayan, Siamese, Siamese, Himalayan

   (E) Siamese, Himalayan, Siamese, Himalayan, Manx, Siamese, Himalayan

Tip!
2D games will often feature a question that appears to be a Grab-a-Rule, but isn't. If you aren't sure, go ahead and try it. Best case scenario: it is one. If you get stuck, don't panic. Just move on to the Specific questions and come back to this one.

Here's How to Crack It
Remember to grab rules one by one.

Rule one deals with puppies, so it doesn't help.
Rule two says no consecutive breeds, so there goes (D).
Rule three says 1 ≠ 7, so we can say goodbye to (B).
Rule four says "exactly three" Hs, so (C) is gone.
Rule four also states, H is not on day 1, so (A) is also out.

Choice (E) is the only one left, so it must be the answer.

Time to move on to the Specific questions. Let's look at question 2.

⎯⎯⎯⎯⎯⎯⎯⎯⎯◠⎯⎯⎯⎯⎯⎯⎯⎯⎯

2. If Himalayans are not featured on day 2, which one of the following could be true?

(A) Manx are featured on day 3.   Ⓐ

(B) Siamese are featured on day 4.   Ⓑ

(C) Rottweilers are featured on day 5.   Ⓒ

(D) Himalayans are featured on day 6.   Ⓓ

(E) Greyhounds are featured on day 7.   Ⓔ

Here's How to Crack It

First, note the question stem is *could be true*. This means that we can eliminate any answer choice that must be false. As with all Specific questions, first put the new information in the diagram and then deduce what else happens with that information. Note that now H cannot be first or second. Our deduction with H proved that both the first and second H must have at least one space following it. Therefore, there is just enough room left on the diagram to place all three Hs. Your diagram should now look like the following.

			1	2	3	4	5	6	7
K: HMS										
p: gnr										
Clue Shelf	– –	K̶ – p	H̶ g	∅	– –	– –	– –	– –	H̶	n(r̶g̶)
②	– –	K̶ – p	H̶ g	H̶	H	– –	H	– –	H n	–

Next, clue 5 prevents r from being with H, so note on the diagram that r cannot be on day 3 or 5. Nothing else seems to be forced, so move on to the answer choices. Let's eliminate any answer choice that must be false.

Choice (A) must be false since H is on day 3. Choice (B) seems fine. Choice (C) is false since H is on day 5. Choice (D) is false since H is on days 3, 5, and 7. Finally, (E) is false based on our deductions. Choice (B) is the only one remaining, so it must be the answer.

⎯⎯⎯⎯⎯⎯⎯⎯⎯◠⎯⎯⎯⎯⎯⎯⎯⎯⎯

Now you can move on to the Specific question number 6.

6. If Himalayans are not featured on day 7, which one of the following could be true?

(A) Greyhounds are featured on days 3 and 5.

(B) Newfoundlands are featured on day 3.

(C) Rottweilers are featured on day 6.

(D) Rottweilers are featured only on day 3.

(E) Rottweilers are featured on exactly three days.

(A) (B) (C) (D) (E)

Here's How to Crack It

This question tells us that H cannot be last. Since H is the most restrictive element, let's place the three Hs and see what else happens with the diagram. Next, carry down deductions from the clue shelf and make new ones. Day 2 cannot be g and now it cannot be r either. Thus, day 2 must be n and day 3 cannot be n. Likewise, day 6 cannot be n and now it cannot be r either; thus, day 6 must be g and day 5 cannot be g. Finally, r cannot be on day 4. Now, dive into the answers. Just like with question 2, we are looking for a *could be true* answer, so eliminate everything that *must be false.*

Choice (A) has g on days 3 and 5. We deduced that g cannot be on day 5, so eliminate (A). Choice (B) has n on day 3, but we know that day 3 cannot be g, so eliminate (B). Choice (C) has r on day 6, but that would pair r with H, so get rid of (C). Choice (D) seems possible, so hold onto it for now. Choice (E) has r on exactly three days. However, we have no r on days 1, 2, 4, 6, and 7. Therefore, it is impossible for there to be three r. Eliminate (E). The answer is (D).

Let's move on to the final Specific question, number 4.

4. If Himalayans are not featured on day 7, then which one of the following pairs of days CANNOT feature both the same breed of kitten and the same breed of puppy?

(A) day 1 and day 3

(B) day 2 and day 6

(C) day 3 and day 5

(D) day 4 and day 6

(E) day 5 and day 7

Ⓐ
Ⓑ
Ⓒ
Ⓓ
Ⓔ

Here's How to Crack It

This question is pretty nice since it is asking us for roughly the same distribution as the previous one. One thing to note: the question asks what day CANNOT feature the same pairs. Make a note that we will POE any answer that could be a pair of days that feature the same breeds. Set up your diagram from the previous problem on a new line.

See any more deductions? No? If the correct answer does not jump out at you, it is always better to "get your pen moving" when you don't see anything more. In other words, stop trying to work this one out in your head. Since we can eliminate any answer choice that could be true, let's just start trying answer choices. The first one that forces us to break a rule is the correct answer. Choice (A) says days 1 and 3. We already know that g is on day 1, so put g on day 3. Next, pick a kitten for days 1 and 3. It cannot be H, so let's arbitrarily try M. The g on day 3 means that day 4 must be n. We have to have at least one r, so put that on day 5. Finally, fill out the kittens for days 5 and 7. We have used M and H already, so let's put S on each of those days.

K: HMS
p: gmr

			1	2	3	4	5	6	7
Clue Shelf	– –	K̶/p	H̶/g	ø̶	–	–	–	–	H̶	n(r̶ø̶)
②	– –	K/p	H̶/g	H̶	H		H		H	H/n
⑥	– –	K/p	H̶/g	H/ø̶n	H/r̶	H	ø̶	H̶/g/r̶	H/n	H̶/n
④	– –	K/p	H̶/g	H/n		H		H/g	H̶/n	
④A	– –	K/p	H̶M/g	H/n	M/g	H/n	S/r	H/g	H̶S/n	

We were able to completely fill in the diagram without violating any rules, so let's eliminate (A). Now try (B). We know from the question that H is on both day 2 and day 6. However, we also deduced that g must be on day 6 and n must be on day 2. Therefore, it is impossible for those two days to be exactly the same. Doing so would force us to break one or more rules. Since these two days CANNOT be the same, this is the answer. Select (B) and move on to the General questions.

K: HMS
p: gnr

			1	2	3	4	5	6	7
Clue Shelf	– –	K̶/p	H̶/g	ø̶	–	–	–	–	H̶	n(r̶ø̶)
②	– –	K/p	H̶/g	H̶	H		H		H	H/n
⑥	– –	K/p	H̶/g	H/ø̶n	H/r̶	H	ø̶	H̶/g/r̶	H/n	H̶/n
④	– –	K/p	H̶/g	H/n		H		H/g	H̶/n	
④A	– –	K/p	H̶M/g	H/n	M/g	H/n	S/r	H/g	H̶S/n	
④B	– –	K/p	H̶/g	(H/n)	–	H	–	(H/g)	H̶/n	

Let's look at question 3.

———————————○———————————

3. Which one of the following could be true?

(A) Greyhounds and Siamese are both featured on day 2. (A)

(B) Greyhounds and Himalayans are both featured on day 7. (B)

(C) Rottweilers and Himalayans are both featured on day 4. (C)

(D) Rottweilers and Manx are both featured on day 5. (D)

(E) Newfoundlands and Manx are both featured on day 6. (E)

Here's How to Crack It

Since this question asks for what could be true, focus on your deductions and eliminate any answer choice that *must be false*.

Choice (A) puts g on day 2. We know that is false from our deductions. Eliminate it.

Choice (B) puts g on day 7. We deduced that n is on day 7. Get rid of (B).

Choice (C) has r and H together on day 4. This violates clue 5. Eliminate it!

Choice (D) has r and M on day 5. This appears plausible. Let's hold on to it.

Choice (E) has n and M on day 6. We know from deductions that n cannot be on day 6. Get rid of (E). The only remaining answer is (D). There is no reason to play it since it is the only one remaining.

———————————○———————————

If this question felt like a Grab-a-Rule, that is a good thing. However, the only reason we were able to answer this question so efficiently is that we took the time to make some awesome deductions. Never skip the making deductions step. If you do, you will be forced to try each answer choice until one works. This is a tedious process that will always take longer than the 2–3 minutes you spend finding and marking deductions.

One question to go! Onwards to question 5.

5. Which one of the following could be true?

(A) There are exactly four breeds that are each featured on three days.

(B) Greyhounds are featured on every day that Himalayans are.

(C) Himalayans are featured on every day that Greyhounds are.

(D) Himalayans are featured on every day that Rottweilers are not.

(E) Rottweilers are featured on every day that Himalayans are not.

Here's How to Crack It

This question follows the same logic as the previous one. Let's use our deductions to eliminate any impossible answer choices. If we get stuck, we can always play the remaining choices. Take a look at the answer choices. See anything that can be eliminated? Confused? These answer choices are very hard to parse. Rather than digging through each one, figuring it out, and then thinking about whether it is possible, let's just start trying answers. Since the question asks what *could be true*, the first answer choice that works is the credited response.

Start with (A). This answer choice means that four different breeds of pets will each appear on three different days. We already know from the rules that this is true of H, so really we are looking for whether this can be true of three other breeds. Begin by placing H in the diagram in a valid position. To be as quick and efficient as possible, put H on days 3, 5, and 7. Since H is with n on day 7, put n on days 3 and 5 as well. Now we need another puppy to be on three different days. Since there is already a g on day 1, put g on days 4 and 6. Next, put r on day 2. Finally, see if you can place either S or M with g every time. M can go on days 1, 4, and 6. S can go on day 2.

		1	2	3	4	5	6	7
K: HMS **p: gnr**								
Clue Shelf	- - K̶/p	H̶/g	∅	-	-	-	H̶ n(r̶∅)	
②	- - K/p	H̶/g	H̶	H		H		H/n
⑥	- - K/p	H̶/g	H̶/∅/H	H/∅	H	∅	H/H̶/g	H̶/n
④	- - K/p	H̶/g	H/n		H		H/g	H̶/n
④A	- - K/p	H̶M/g	H/n	M/g	H/n	S/r	H/g	H̶S/n
④B	- - K/p	H̶/g	(H/n)	-	H	-	(H/g)	/n
⑤A	- - K/p	H̶M/g	S/r	H/n	M/g	H/n	M/g	H/n

No rules have been broken, so (A) is the answer. Please note that this is not the only valid way to make four sets of three animals. You may have made a valid play with a slightly different distribution.

While you would finish here with this game and move on to the next when taking the actual test, we want to take a brief moment to discuss (B) and (C) or (D) and (E). Many students want to wrongly remove these answers since they appear similar. The LSAT will never provide freebies by having two game answer choices say blatantly the same thing. While these answer choices use similar phrasing, the differences are very important. Choice (B) means that on every day with an H there will also be a g. However, g can occur on its own isolation without violating the answer choice. Choice (C) is the same situation in reverse. Choice (C) means that on everyday which has a g, there must also be an H. Hs can occur without gs in this answer choice. The same logic applies to (D) and (E). Again, the moral of the story is never eliminate a games answer just because it appears to be the same as another answer.

LESSON 3: POE, BASIC CONDITIONALS, AND GROUP GAMES

In the previous game, we saw a variety of different question phrasings. In the end, though, it turns out that all of the variations of must/could, true/false, and EXCEPT/NOT require only two POE strategies. Understanding what the questions actually mean can show you why.

If a question asks what could be true, there needs to be only one situation when the right answer can happen. What, then, do we know about the other four choices? Well, if the right answer can happen, then the four wrong answers can't. That is, the wrong answers on a Could Be True question are things that must be false.

Think about a Must Be False question now. What do we know about the other choices? Well, since the right answer is something that can never happen, the wrong answers are things that can. It shouldn't surprise you, then, that the wrong answers on a Must Be False question are things that could be true.

What happens when we add an EXCEPT or a NOT to one of these questions? These words, on the LSAT, can be interpreted as meaning "find four." So when a questions asks you "...each of the following could be true EXCEPT," what they're asking you to find is four choices that could be true; the remaining one is the answer you want to pick. What do we know about this choice? That's right: it must be false.

What we're seeing here is that Could Be True/Must Be False form a pair. Adding an EXCEPT or a NOT just changes one to the other.

Now think about an answer choice that must be true. This means it has to be true all the time, no matter what. When the right answer must be true, what we know is that the other four don't have to be true all the time—that is, they could be false. Not surprisingly, Could Be False questions turn out to be the flipside of this; on a Could Be False question, the other four answers must be true. And as before, adding EXCEPT or a NOT turns one of these types of questions into the other.

POE Guide: Knowing Right from Wrong with "Could" and "Must"

Could Be True/Must Be False

POE strategy: Try to make the choice true; make an example.

For *could be true* and *must be false* EXCEPT
 If you can make the choice true, pick it.
 If you can't, eliminate it.
For *must be false* and *could be true* EXCEPT
 If you can make the choice true, eliminate it.
 If you can't, pick it.

Must Be True/Could Be False

POE strategy: Try to make the choice false; make a counterexample.

For *must be true* and *could be false* EXCEPT
 If you can make the choice false, eliminate it.
 If you can't, pick it.
For *could be false* and *must be true* EXCEPT
 If you can make the choice false, pick it.
 If you can't, eliminate it.

So hopefully we've demonstrated that the four major question types can logically be reduced into two complementary pairs. We have even more good news for you though. Each pair of questions has a POE strategy that works for both, but you have to be careful to keep your eye on the ball. It's easy to forget what you're doing in the midst of actually doing it. It's also extremely important to understand that the only way you can be sure something happens all the time—or that it can never happen—is to deduce that fact. When you generate an example, you're looking at what could happen, not what must happen.

The upshot of all this is best summarized in the gray box. If you put these ideas in your own words and use them assiduously whenever you work games, they will become more intuitive, but you'll have to focus and work carefully for some of the more complicated variations.

Games Technique: Smart POE

Now that you have a better understanding of the logic behind each question stem and how to test remaining answer choices, we want to walk you through the most accurate and efficient way to use POE. As we have demonstrated in the two previous games, having a good set of deductions can simplify a game and improve speed. The other major factor in how quickly you're able to work games is having a smart approach to the questions, and especially to the answer choices.

For many questions, it's hard to know in advance what method will turn out to be the fastest, and there are often several methods to choose from. But there are some methods that are more time-efficient than are others on average. Here, in rough order of decreasing speed, are the strongest POE techniques for Games.

Deductions   When you work a game, you should always look for deductions. When you work a Specific question, the first thing you should do is represent the new information given and deduce everything you can from it. Why? Because deductions give you the best chance of getting to the answer quickly. Of course you must be efficient when you're making deductions—don't just stare; keep your pen moving—but the deductions you find will always be your best ammunition. In many cases, your deductions will allow you to find the correct answer directly, and in many others they will allow you to eliminate four wrong answers, which is just as good. If they don't, a good set of deductions will usually eliminate a few answer choices and help you narrow the field significantly.

Prior Work   As we described earlier, a big benefit of working Specific questions on the first pass through the game is that, when you get to the General questions, you already have a set of examples and counterexamples handy. Often you can use the information to find the answer to a General question without having any real idea why it's the answer. This is not only a satisfying feeling, but a very time-efficient practice. The one caution about using prior work is that, generally, you cannot use information from one Specific question to help you answer another. There are certain special circumstances where this can be made to work, but it should be done with extreme care. On General questions, however, this is an extremely powerful technique. A final note about prior work: be careful about the question stem and the POE approach. Prior work provides *examples* of valid plays. Therefore, they show Could Be True and Could Be False possibilities. They should be used as POE tools rather than proof on Must Be questions.

Grabbing Rules   When the answer choices contain a lot of information, often you can narrow the field significantly by eliminating blatant rule violations. In a pure Grab-a-Rule question, in which the answer choices are all complete listings, this is the only technique you need in order to find the answer. Even in less extreme circumstances—in which the answer choices are partial lists, or even in many Specific questions—you'll be able to find choices that contain outright violations of the rules. Spotting them may be a matter of going through your clue list only once and looking for these violations in the remaining choices.

Testing the Answer Choices   This is the most time-consuming method of POE and therefore should be saved as a last resort. For many of the questions, if you have invested a good amount of time into your deductions, you can find the correct answer. On General questions, you can also look at previous work to eliminate wrong answer choices. Unfortunately, every once in a while you will encounter a question where, even after applying these three techniques above, you still have more than one answer choice left. In these cases, you need to know what kind of answer you want. This was covered earlier and is summarized in the gray box just to the left here, but you also need a method for making choices true or false.

If an answer choice could be true, that just means that if you plugged it into the diagram, it wouldn't force you to break any rules. So when all else fails on Could Be True or Must Be False questions, you can always Plug In the Answers.

Having a consistent method is particularly helpful when you get stuck on a Must Be True question, since most of these are answered by deductions (on General questions) or by deducing from the information in the question (on Specific questions).

When an answer choice must be true, that means that it could never be false. If you can find one instance—any instance—for which the answer choice isn't true, it's an answer choice that could be false. So, if you get stuck on a *Must Be True* question, you can make up any scenario, and chances are that several of the answers won't be true in that scenario: those are answers that could be false. If one scenario won't eliminate all four that could be false, rearrange your scenario to see what else you can get rid of. It usually takes only two or three valid scenarios to get rid of all wrong answers.

For *Could Be True* and *Must Be False* questions:

- Find the answer or answers that must be false by Plugging In the Answers and deducing.
- If the answer must be false, it will force you to break a rule.

For *Must Be True* and *Could Be False* questions:

- Find the answers that *Could Be False* by making up any possible scenario you want, within the constraints of the question.
- If an answer is false in that scenario, it must be false.
- On a *Must Be True* question, you may have to make up a new scenario or two to eliminate the remaining answers.

Let's see how well you've comprehended the importance of POE. Below you will find a short multiple-choice quiz that will assess how you should approach various types of questions.

POE QUIZ

1. A question stem asks, "if A is on day 2, which of the following must be true?" You don't have the answer in your deductions. What do you do on your diagram?

    (A) Choose the first answer that works.
    (B) Eliminate answer choices that work as stated.
    (C) Eliminate answers that can work in positions other than those stated.
    (D) Ignore the question stem and trust your luck.

2. A question asks "Which of the following answers could be true?" How do you check the answers?

    (A) Choose the first answer that works.
    (B) Eliminate answer choices that work as stated.
    (C) Eliminate answer choices that work in multiple positions.
    (D) Ignore the question stem and trust your luck.

3. A question stem asks "...each of the following could be true EXCEPT...." What do you do?

    (A) Choose the first answer that works.
    (B) Eliminate answer choices that work as stated.
    (C) Eliminate answer choices that do not work.
    (D) Ignore the question stem and trust your luck.

4. A question stem asks "which must be false...." You are not able to answer it using your deductions. How do you test each answer choice?

    (A) You don't. That's too time-consuming.
    (B) You plug each answer into your diagram as written. The one that works is correct.
    (C) You plug each answer into your diagram as written. Eliminate the ones that work.
    (D) You plug each answer into a different location in your diagram. If it works, eliminate it.

5. A question asks "which of the following could be false." What do you do?

(A) Find and select the answer that must be true…duh!
(B) Eliminate any answer that must be true.
(C) Eliminate any answer that could be true (but doesn't have to be).
(D) Give up on this test and become a doctor instead.

Cracking the POE Quiz

Ok, let's see how you did.

Question 1 asks about Must Be True answers. Remember, the only way to prove a Must Be True/False answer is through deductions. If you don't have deductions, you need to resort to testing each answer choice. The correlate to a Must Be True answer is a Could Be False. In order to test each answer choice, you must falsify it and see if it is still possible to have a valid play of the game. If the answer choice works in a position other than that stated in the answer, then that choice could be false. The answer to question 1 is (C).

Question 2 asks about Could Be True answers. You would first eliminate any answers you knew to be false from your deductions. If you have to test answers on your diagram, these are straightforward. Since only one choice can be correct, the first one that works in a valid diagram is the answer and you would choose it. The answer to question 2 is (A).

Question 3 asks about could be true EXCEPT. Remember that EXCEPT/NOT transform the question into its opposite. In reality, this question is asking for which answer choice must be false. You should find and eliminate the four "Could Be True" answers. Therefore, if an answer choice works as stated, it should be eliminated. The answer to question 3 is (B).

Question 4 asks about Must Be False answers. Wrong answers could be true. If you do not have the answers as a deduction, you have to test them. Plug in the answer choices directly as written into the diagram. If they work, then they could be true, so eliminate them. The answer to question 4 is (C).

Question 5 asks about Could Be False answers. These are among the most challenging of all question types. First, using your deductions you need to eliminate any answer choice that you have deduced must be true. If you have to test any remaining answer choices, you need to plug in an answer choice in a different location or manner than what is stated. If it still produces a valid diagram, then that is the answer choice. If you are unable to get the answer choice to work in a different way than what is stated, you would eliminate that answer as a Must Be True. The answer to question 5 is (B).

Games Technique: Group Games

So far, the games we've seen have asked us to put things in order to arrange them in space. The clues often provide information about the location of elements relative to one another. The next basic game task is *grouping*. Grouping games are often fairly easy to identify from the setup: putting people on committees, assigning commuters to cars, picking players for teams, and so on. Sometimes they can be more difficult to recognize, but in those cases, you can get help from the clues. In a Grouping game, the clues most often talk about elements that have to go together, or those that can't go together.

There is an important difference between Group games and Ordering game block symbols. You'll note that when we symbolized block and antiblock clues with Ordering games, the elements were separated by a vertical line. This vertical line indicated that the elements were located in different columns. With Grouping games, the vast majority of block and antiblock clues deal with situations within a single column. As a result, you should not include a line between elements. Here's an example.

A and B always work together.

A and B are always together, so place them in a block. Also, since order is not an issue here, you don't need an arrow indicating that BA is also valid. A single symbol stands for both. The symbol for the above clue should look like the following.

A key thing to keep track of in Grouping games is how many elements each group contains. These are called *placeholders*. Group games are often driven by placeholders. Sometimes the setup will specify exactly how many placeholders belong in each group. The setup will use language such as "exactly three people will be in each location." These are the easier variant of Grouping games.

Placeholders can by symbolized very easily. Simply put the correct number of lines in each group. We could symbolize the statement above in a three-category game by placing three lines under each column.

$$1 \mid 2 \mid 3$$
$$-- \mid -- \mid --$$

Hint:
A grouping game asks you to put the elements into collections of some sort; Grouping games usually include clues that can easily be translated as blocks or antiblocks.

A more challenging variety will not specify exactly how many elements belong in each group. In this instance, focus on placeholder deductions. By focusing on the block and antiblock clues provided by the game, you can often figure out whether a category must have a placeholder. Consider the following situation. A job has three categories and is diagrammed below. Note how basic this diagram appears since we do not know exactly how many places go in each category.

category 1	category 2	category 3

We also have three clues. Clue 1 states that "A cannot work with B." Clue 2 states "A cannot work with C," and clue 3 states "B cannot work with C." These should all be symbolized as antiblocks.

Take a moment to think about the logic here. Since A cannot work with either B or C, once A is placed into one of the three categories, then B and C must go into the other two. However, since B cannot be with C, these two elements must also be split up. No matter what, this situation forces at least one element to be placed into each category. This is symbolized below.

category 1	category 2	category 3
—	—	—

There are several other methods for making placeholder deductions. We will discuss these in the next lesson.

Games Technique: Basic Conditional Statements

In addition to blocks and antiblocks, Group games often employ the use of conditional clues. We have already seen how important conditional clues are on the Arguments section. Not surprisingly, they are also extremely important to the Games section of the LSAT. These are also the most frequently misinterpreted and misunderstood clues; everyone who takes the LSAT should exercise extra care when working with them.

We have previously introduced the arrow as a symbol for conditional clues on the arguments. If you haven't read the arguments chapter yet, we recommend turning to page 167 in this book and reading the discussion there to help you better understand conditionals in games. We will use the same symbolization here. Suppose we're symbolizing the following clue.

If X is on floor 3, then Y is on floor 5.

When using the arrow diagram, the "if" statement always goes to the left of the arrow. The "then" statement goes to the right of the arrow. When conditional statements indicate a specific position for the elements, as in the clue above, it is best to use subscripts. Therefore, the clue should be symbolized like this.

$$X_3 \rightarrow Y_5$$

Whenever we're given a conditional clue, we should also *immediately* represent its contrapositive. The way to make a contrapositive statement is to flip and negate the statement. We exchange the order of the statements, and then we add a negation sign. We often use the tilde (~) to indicate negation on conditional clues. The contrapositive of the clue symbolized looks as follows.

$$\sim Y_5 \rightarrow \sim X_3$$

By making the contrapositive (through flipping and negating), you are technically making a deduction. However, do not wait until the deduction stage to do so. Let's practice a few more.

If X is on floor 3, then Y is not on floor 5.

Note the slight change in language. Y is now not located on the fifth floor. Don't panic, simply add this into the symbolization.

$$X_3 \rightarrow \sim Y_5$$

The contrapositive is still made by flipping and negating the conditional. The only difference here is that a negative of a negative becomes a positive.

$$Y_5 \rightarrow \sim X_3$$

Here's a trickier one.

W is on floor 4 if Z is on floor 2.

Remember that the order of the sentence does not affect the order of the conditional. The "if" statement *always* goes to the left of the arrow. It doesn't matter if the "if" condition occurs in the second half of the sentence. Therefore, this clue should be symbolized like the following. We also immediately did the contrapositive.

$$Z_2 \rightarrow W_4$$

$$\sim W_4 \rightarrow \sim Z_2$$

To check out which law schools are "Toughest to Get Into," take a look at your online student tools. If you haven't registered yet, go to PrincetonReview.com/prep.

One last note about symbolizing conditional statements: make sure that your arrows align! Conditional clues are inherently confusing. Having the arrows aligned removes some of the confusion associated with these clues by forcing them into some semblance of an order. The other pragmatic reason for aligning the arrows will be revealed as we discuss the logic of conditionals below.

It's important to understand what we can conclude—and, just as important, what we can't conclude—from a pair of conditional statements. Generally speaking, we use an arrow to symbolize these clues because we can draw conclusions only in one direction. It's best to think of using these clues as a two-stage process. First, we examine the statement on the left-hand side of the arrow. If it doesn't match the diagram, then the rule doesn't apply! There's nothing more we can do; the rule might as well not exist. If that statement does match the diagram or question, then the rule applies, and we can move on to stage two. Follow the arrow to the right-hand side, which shows the conclusion we're allowed to draw.

Here's a summary of the process using the first conditional statement.

If X is on floor 3, then Y is on floor 5.

$$X_3 \rightarrow Y_5$$

$$\sim Y_5 \rightarrow \sim X_3$$

If we know...	...then we can conclude.
X is on three	Y is on 5
Y is not on 5	X cannot be on three
X is not on 3	nothing!
Y is on 5	nothing!

Here are some possible valid arrangements that can be made from this clue.

Floor 1	Floor 2	Floor 3	Floor 4	Floor 5
		X		Y
Y	X			
X				Y*
	X		Y	

The only arrangement that the rule forbids is when X is on floor 3 and Y is **not** on 5!

The arrangement marked with the * above is usually the one that gives test-takers trouble; for this reason you'll often encounter it. Note that we can conclude nothing if Y is on 5. You cannot move against the arrow. Similarly, we can conclude nothing if X is not on 3. This rule has nothing to say about the layout of the diagram unless X is on 3.

Interpreting your symbols correctly is a big part of being able to work with conditional clues. You must be very careful to follow the symbol, rather than relying on what you think "should" be true. If you have aligned your arrows, there is an easy, mechanical way to interpret the clues:

Aligned arrows → easy way (see what we did there?)

Use your hand to cover the right side of the arrows. Then, looking only at the left side, ask yourself, "does clue 1 apply?" If the left side doesn't apply, ignore that rule. If the left side applies, remove your hand and check to see that the right side of the arrow clue is also followed. Continue the process for each conditional.

Conditional statements are such an important part of the Games section that we will address them in much more detail in the next lesson. For now, you have the necessary tools to tackle your first Group game. Remember to first determine the core of the diagram and the elements. This can sometimes be challenging in a Group game. If you need help, glance at the clues and questions to see what is moving around. These will be your game pieces or elements. Remember with group game blocks and antiblocks, you are now dealing with what must be together (or can never be together) *within* a single column rather than between columns. As a result, your block symbols should not insert a line between the elements.

Go ahead and dive into Game 3.

GAME 3

Game 3 and its questions are from PrepTest 44, Section 3, Questions 7–12.

During a certain week, an animal shelter places exactly six dogs—a greyhound, a husky, a keeshond, a Labrador retriever, a poodle, and a schnauzer—with new owners. Two are placed on Monday, two on Tuesday, and the remaining two on Wednesday, consistent with the following conditions:

  The Labrador retriever is placed on the same day as the poodle.
  The greyhound is not placed on the same day as the husky.
  If the keeshond is placed on Monday, the greyhound is placed on Tuesday.
  If the schnauzer is placed on Wednesday, the husky is placed on Tuesday.

1. Which one of the following could be a complete and accurate matching of dogs to the days on which they are placed?

(A) Monday: greyhound, Labrador retriever
Tuesday: husky, poodle
Wednesday: keeshond, schnauzer

(B) Monday: greyhound, keeshond
Tuesday: Labrador retriever, poodle
Wednesday: husky, schnauzer

(C) Monday: keeshond, schnauzer
Tuesday: greyhound, husky
Wednesday: Labrador retriever, poodle

(D) Monday: Labrador retriever, poodle
Tuesday: greyhound, keeshond
Wednesday: husky, schnauzer

(E) Monday: Labrador retriever, poodle
Tuesday: husky, keeshond
Wednesday: greyhound, schnauzer

2. Which one of the following must be true?

(A) The keeshond is not placed on the same day as the greyhound.

(B) The keeshond is not placed on the same day as the schnauzer.

(C) The schnauzer is not placed on the same day as the husky.

(D) The greyhound is placed on the same day as the schnauzer.

(E) The husky is placed on the same day as the keeshond.

3. If the poodle is placed on Tuesday, then which one of the following could be true?

(A) The greyhound is placed on Monday.

(B) The keeshond is placed on Monday.

(C) The Labrador retriever is placed on Monday.

(D) The husky is placed on Tuesday.

(E) The schnauzer is placed on Wednesday.

4. If the greyhound is placed on the same day as the keeshond, then which one of the following must be true?

(A) The husky is placed on Monday.

(B) The Labrador retriever is placed on Monday.

(C) The keeshond is placed on Tuesday.

(D) The poodle is not placed on Wednesday.

(E) The schnauzer is not placed on Wednesday.

5. If the husky is placed the day before the schnauzer, then which one of the following CANNOT be true?

(A) The husky is placed on Monday.

(B) The keeshond is placed on Monday.

(C) The greyhound is placed on Tuesday.

(D) The poodle is placed on Tuesday.

(E) The poodle is placed on Wednesday.

(A) (B) (C) (D) (E)

6. If the greyhound is placed the day before the poodle, then which one of the following CANNOT be placed on Tuesday?

(A) the husky

(B) the keeshond

(C) the Labrador retriever

(D) the poodle

(E) the schnauzer

(A) (B) (C) (D) (E)

Self-Assessment

Steps 1–3 Assessment

Steps 4–6 Assessment

Cracking Game 3

Step 1: Diagram and Inventory

We have a total of six dogs that need to be placed over a span of three days. Our diagram will consist of three columns labeled M, T, and W. Additionally, the setup tells us that exactly two dogs are placed each day. As a result, add two place-holder lines under each column. From the phrase "exactly six dogs," we know that we'll need to use all the elements and that we can't have any repeats. Finally, all of our elements belong to the same category (dogs), so simply write them above the diagram.

GHKLPS	M	T	W
Clue Shelf	– –	– –	– –

Step 2: Symbolize the Clues and Double-check

We've got several clues that should feel familiar from the first two games, and some new conditional clues discussed in the lesson. You should be comfortable by now with how the blocks and antiblocks work. The first two clues should be symbolized as follows.

1. $\boxed{LP}$

2. $\boxed{G\!\!\!/\!\!H}$

The next two clues are conditional statements. However, if you followed the lesson, you should have had little trouble symbolizing these. The elements should be the primary focus of the symbol, and the categories should be noted using subscripts. The "if" statement should be to the left of the arrow. You should have immediately done the contrapositive for each clue and made sure your arrows aligned. Here are clues 3 and 4.

3. $K_M \rightarrow G_T$
    $\sim G_T \rightarrow \sim K_M$

4. $S_W \rightarrow H_T$
    $\sim H_T \rightarrow \sim S_W$

We are able to symbolize all the information, but since these clues are new, it may not seem very useful at this point. Don't forget to double-check before moving on to the next step.

Step 3: Make Deductions and Size up the Game

Now let's see if we can come up with any deductions. We'll use our standard methods because we have some new clue types. Remember that you have technically already made two powerful deductions when you diagrammed the contrapositives. As long as you did this step, you have enough information to work the game. However, let's dig a little deeper and see what else we can learn about the game. We should also pay special attention to the distribution to see if we can narrow down the possible ways that the elements can be arranged.

Let's begin with clue 1. By itself, it doesn't give us too much information. However, it is important to note that this block will completely fill up one of the three days. This clue appears to be very limiting.

Now look at clue 2. This clue says that G and H cannot be together. Again, by itself it doesn't seem to provide much information.

For clues 3 and 4, the single clue deduction is the contrapositive. Make sure you have both flipped and negated the original statement and move on to multiclue deductions.

Consider how the block of clue 1 will interact with the antiblock of clue 2. The block will fill up one full day, and the antiblock will force G and H into the two separate remaining days. The two remaining spaces will be taken up by K and S. The important thing to note here is that K and S cannot be together as a result of the combination of clues 1 and 2. Note this near your clue list or on your clue shelf.

GHKLPS	M	T	W
Clue Shelf K̶S̶	— —	— —	— —

Next, notice how the elements G and H from clue 2 overlap with clues 3 and 4. Let's see if we can figure anything out from this. If clue 3 applies, then G is on Tuesday. However, clue 2 tells us that therefore H cannot be on Tuesday. This is the contrapositive of clue 4. If H is not on Tuesday, then S cannot be on Wednesday. To be more concise, if K is on Monday, then S is not on Wednesday.

With conditional clues, it is often possible to make several long chains such as this. However, remember that deductions that begin with "if" should generally be avoided. Now that we have brought your attention to the relationship between each of these clues, we recommend that you stop here. There are several more chains that you can make using "if…then" statements. However, these will clutter your diagram with possibilities, not certainties. It is best at this point to know that you have sized up the game adequately and move on to the questions.

Steps 4 and 5: Assess the Questions and Act

See a Grab-a-Rule? Dive into it first. However, be very careful when checking the
conditional rules. Your final clue list should look similar to the following one.

1. $\boxed{LP}$

2. $\boxed{\cancel{KS}}$

3. $K_M \rightarrow G_T$
    $\sim GT \rightarrow \sim KM$

4. $S_W \rightarrow H_T$
    $\sim H_T \rightarrow \sim S_W$

Deduction $\boxed{\cancel{GH}}$

Step 6: Use Process of Elimination

1. Which one of the following could be a complete and accurate
    matching of dogs to the days on which they are placed?

(A) Monday: greyhound, Labrador retriever
     Tuesday: husky, poodle
     Wednesday: keeshond, schnauzer   Ⓐ

(B) Monday: greyhound, keeshond
     Tuesday: Labrador retriever, poodle
     Wednesday: husky, schnauzer   Ⓑ

(C) Monday: keeshond, schnauzer
     Tuesday: greyhound, husky
     Wednesday: Labrador retriever, poodle   Ⓒ

(D) Monday: Labrador retriever, poodle
     Tuesday: greyhound, keeshond
     Wednesday: husky, schnauzer   Ⓓ

(E) Monday: Labrador retriever, poodle
     Tuesday: husky, keeshond
     Wednesday: greyhound, schnauzer   Ⓔ

Here's How to Crack It

Start with the first clue. L and P must be together, so eliminate (A).

Move on to the second clue. G and H cannot be together, so eliminate (C).

Now, go on to clue 3. Remember, clue 3 applies only if the left side matches the answer choice. In (B), K is on Monday, but G is not on Tuesday. Eliminate (B). This rule does not apply to (D) and (E), so move on to clue 4.

Clue 4 says if S is on Wednesday, then H is on Tuesday. In (D), S is on Wednesday, but so is H. Eliminate (D).

Choice (E) is the only remaining choice. Lock it in and move on to the Specific questions.

———————⚬———————

Question 3 provides the most specific information so let's start with that one.

———————⚬———————

3. If the poodle is placed on Tuesday, then which one of the following could be true?

(A) The greyhound is placed on Monday.   Ⓐ

(B) The keeshond is placed on Monday.   Ⓑ

(C) The Labrador retriever is placed on Monday.   C̶

(D) The husky is placed on Tuesday.   D̶

(E) The schnauzer is placed on Wednesday.   Ⓔ

Here's How to Crack It

First, begin by placing P and L on Tuesday. Next, check your other rules. Tuesday is completely full, so use the contrapositive of clue 3. G cannot be on Tuesday, so K cannot be on Monday. Therefore, place K on Wednesday. Clue 4 says if H is not on Tuesday, then S cannot be on Wednesday. Thus, S must be on Monday. We are left with G and H. The only rule that applies now is clue 2. However, we have only one space left in each available day. It doesn't matter which one is which, so indicate both possibilities on your diagram. Your final play should look like this.

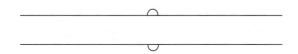

We are looking for what could be true. Choice (A) is supported by our diagram; G can, in fact, be on Monday. Lock this answer in and move on.

———————————————○———————————————

———————————————○———————————————

4. If the greyhound is placed on the same day as the keeshond, then which one of the following must be true?

<table>
<tr><td>(A)</td><td>The husky is placed on Monday.</td><td></td></tr>
<tr><td>(B)</td><td>The Labrador retriever is placed on Monday.</td><td>(B)</td></tr>
<tr><td>(C)</td><td>The keeshond is placed on Tuesday.</td><td></td></tr>
<tr><td>(D)</td><td>The poodle is not placed on Wednesday.</td><td></td></tr>
<tr><td>(E)</td><td>The schnauzer is not placed on Wednesday.</td><td>(E)</td></tr>
</table>

Here's How to Crack It

This question creates a block of GK but doesn't specify a location. As a result, get your pen moving and place the GK block on the diagram quickly. Start by placing GK on Monday and start applying the clues. Clue 3 says that if K is on Monday then G is on Tuesday. Our placement violated that rule. Draw a line through this play and try again.

Put GK on Tuesday. Clue 4 says that since H is not on Tuesday, S cannot be on Wednesday. Put S on Monday, which forces LP to Wednesday and H to Monday. Now, approach the answer choices. This question asks for which answer must be true, so you want to eliminate any answer that you have proven can be false with your play.

GHKLPS	M	T	W
Clue Shelf [KS]	– –	– –	– –
③	S̲ $^{G/}$H	P L	K̲ $^{G/}$H
④	K̲ G̲		
	S̲ H̲	K̲ G̲	L̲ P̲

Choice (A) is true, so ignore it. Choice (B) does not have to be true, so eliminate it. Choice (C) is true, so ignore it. Choices (D) and (E) are also true, so ignore them. It's time to try another possibility. The only place we haven't tried is Wednesday. Put GK on Wednesday, LP on Monday, and SH on Tuesday.

GHKLPS	M	T	W
Clue Shelf [KS]	– –	– –	– –
③	S̲ $^{G/}$H	P L	K̲ $^{G/}$H
④	K̲ G̲		
	S̲ H̲	K̲ G̲	L̲ P̲
	L̲ P̲	S̲ H̲	K̲ G̲

Again, use POE to eliminate any answer that you have proven could be false. H is on Tuesday, so eliminate (A); K is on Wednesday, so eliminate (C), and P is on Monday, so eliminate (D). The only remaining answer is (E).

Let's move on to question 5.

5. If the husky is placed the day before the schnauzer, then which one of the following CANNOT be true?

(A) The husky is placed on Monday.

(B) The keeshond is placed on Monday.

(C) The greyhound is placed on Tuesday.

(D) The poodle is placed on Tuesday.

(E) The poodle is placed on Wednesday.

Here's How to Crack It

If this question (and the next) sounded more like an Ordering game question, you are correct! Even though this is primarily a Grouping game, there is a natural order to the days of the week, which allows the test-writers to slip in different question styles. The important thing here is to be flexible. The next thing you want to do *before* diagramming the new information is to reformulate the question stem. As discussed in this lesson, the words EXCEPT and NOT create the question stem's opposite. Change "CANNOT be true" to "must be false." Now, get that pen moving! K is before S, so let's just put K on Monday and S on Tuesday. This forces LP to be on Wednesday. Since K is on Monday, clue 3 applies, so put G on Tuesday and H in the final spot on Monday.

GHKLPS	M	T	W
Clue Shelf K̶S̶	– –	– –	– –
③	S̲ G̲/H	P̲ L̲	K̲ G̲/H
④	K̲ G̲	– –	– –
	S̲ H̲	K̲ G̲	L̲ P̲
	L̲ P̲	S̲ H̲	K̲ G̲
⑤	K̲ H̲	S̲ G̲	L̲ P̲

We are looking for the answer that *must be false*, so eliminate any answer choice that your diagram proves could be true. Our play has proven that (A), (B), (C), and (E) can all be true. Since (D) is the only remaining answer, lock it in and move on to the final Specific question.

6. If the greyhound is placed the day before the poodle, then which one of the following CANNOT be placed on Tuesday?

(A) the husky

(B) the keeshond

(C) the Labrador retriever

(D) the poodle

(E) the schnauzer

(A)
(B)
(C)
(D)
(E)

Here's How to Crack It

Start by figuring out the question stem. This one is a little more nuanced than the previous one, so it doesn't lend itself to a quick rewrite. Instead, focus on what you are looking for and what you will eliminate. We are looking for the single answer choice that can never be on Tuesday. Therefore, we want to eliminate any element that can be on Tuesday. As with the previous problem, do not waste precious test time thinking about all the different ways this can work. Pick up your pen and commit something to paper.

Begin by placing G on Monday and P on Tuesday. Now, apply the other rules. L must also be on Tuesday. K cannot be on Monday, so K goes on Wednesday. S must then be on Monday and H is on Wednesday.

GHKLPS	M	T	W
Clue Shelf K̶S̶	— —	— —	— —
③	S G/H	P L	K G/H
④	K G	— —	— —
	S H	K G	L P
	L P	S H	K G
⑤	K H	S G	L P
⑥	G S	P L	K H

We have shown that both L and P can be placed on Tuesday, so eliminate (C) and (D). Next, try putting G on Tuesday and P on Wednesday. L must also be on Wednesday. H must be on Monday. Stop here for a moment and read the conditional clues very carefully! Neither clue 3 nor clue 4 applies since K is not on Monday and S is not on Wednesday. Therefore, K and S are interchangeable. Mark this on your diagram.

GHKLPS	M	T	W
Clue Shelf K̶S̶	– –	– –	– –
③	S ᴳ/ₕ	P L	K ᴳ/ₕ
④	K̶ G̶		
	S H	K G	L P
	L P	S H	K G
⑤	K H	S G	L P
⑥	G S	P L	K H
	H ᴷ/ₛ	G ᴷ/ₛ	P L

This play proves that both K and S can be on Tuesday when G is on the day before P. Eliminate (B) and (E). Since (A) is the only remaining answer choice, lock it in. The important take away from this question is *not* that your order or play exactly matches ours. The important thing is that you were aware of what you needed from the correct answer and what you were looking to eliminate. Also, it is important that you kept your pen moving, eliminating what you could, and repeating the process until you were down to a single answer choice.

Now, onward to the final question.

───────────────── ○ ─────────────────

2.   Which one of the following must be true?

   (A)   The keeshond is not placed on the same day as the greyhound.   (A)

   (B)   The keeshond is not placed on the same day as the schnauzer.   (B)

   (C)   The schnauzer is not placed on the same day as the husky.   (C)

   (D)   The greyhound is placed on the same day as the schnauzer.   (D)

   (E)   The husky is placed on the same day as the keeshond.   (E)

Here's How to Crack It

This question asks us which of the following must be true. From our deductions, we noted that K and S can never be together. Lock in (B).

On the actual exam, you would now move on to the next game. Before we do, however, we want to emphasize the POE approach discussed in the chapter. We went straight to deductions and happily, our question was answered. However, what would you do if you didn't have the KS antiblock deduction?

You would, of course, want to look at prior work. It is crucial to remember that prior work shows possibilities, not certainties. Therefore, for this question, prior work can be a POE tool. This is a Must Be True question, so any answer that shows a Could Be False possibility can be eliminated.

Choice (A) is disproven by our play from question 4 (incidentally, it is also disproven by the question stem of question 4). Choice (B) is not disproven by our diagram, so move on. Choice (C) is disproven by our first valid play from question 4, so it is gone. Choice (D) is disproven by our play for question 5. Choice (E) is also disproven by our play from question 5. Thus, even using this method, (B) is quickly shown to be the only remaining answer choice.

───────────────── ○ ─────────────────

LESSON 4: IN-DEPTH CONDITIONALS AND IN/OUT GAMES

The games in Lesson 1 and 2 were Ordering games. Lesson 3 consisted of a Grouping game. These two kinds of tasks are very important and are often seen in LSAT games, but they aren't the only games tasks around. The task here is to pick some, but not all, of the elements. Those selected will be "In" the collection; those not selected will be "Out." As a result, we have ingeniously dubbed these "In/Out games." In fact, any game that hinges upon elements being grouped into one of two possibilities is an In/Out game. If items are selected/not selected, carried/not carried, chosen/not chosen, then you need to use an In/Out setup. It might be helpful to think of In/Out games as a very special two-column Grouping game.

In games with an In/Out task, it is just as important to keep track of the Out elements as it is to keep track of the ones that are In. Remember that we always want to have a place in our diagram to put all the elements in a game.

In Lesson 3, we saw one way in which conditionals can appear in Grouping games. Not surprisingly, they are vital to In/Out games. You could say that the majority of In/Out games are driven by conditional statements. Let's take a look again at an In/Out conditional clue.

If X is chosen, then Y is not chosen.

As indicated above, the central task on an In/Out game is to decide which elements are chosen and which are not. As we'll see in a moment, we diagram these by having two columns—one marked "In," and the other marked "Out"—to keep track of our elements. When we see clues like the previous one, we use a little shorthand, since they're so common. To show that an elements is In, we leave it alone. To show that it's Out, we negate it with a tilde (~) or a slash (/). Thus, the clue above would have a symbol that looks like this.

$$X \rightarrow \sim Y$$

Its associated contrapositive would be

$$Y \rightarrow \sim X$$

Just as with Grouping games in general, pay attention to what you can conclude and what you can't conclude from conditional clues.

Here's a summary of the process.

If we know...	...then we can conclude
X is In	Y is Out
Y is In	X is Out
X is Out	nothing
Y is Out	nothing

Possible arrangement that satisfy the rule include

IN	OUT
X	Y
Y	X
	XY*

The only arrangement precluded by the clue is

IN	OUT
XY	

The arrangement marked with the * above is usually the one that gives test-takers the most trouble; for this reason, expect to encounter it often. Note that we can conclude nothing from this rule if we know that X is Out; similarly, we can conclude nothing if Y is Out. Thus, the rule doesn't apply when X or Y is Out. Just like with Group games, a mechanical way to determine whether clues apply is to cover the right side of the arrow with your hand. If something from the diagram matches the left side of the arrow, then that rule applies. Otherwise, ignore the rule and move on to check the next one.

In the Arguments chapter, we discussed how conditionals can be viewed as either sufficient or necessary factors (see page 77 for a full discussion). Another way to conceptualize conditionals is dependent versus independent. Focus again on our example conditional.

$$X \rightarrow \sim Y$$

$$Y \rightarrow \sim X$$

Based on the discussion above, ~Y is independent. It can occur on its own without any knowledge of where X is located. The same is true of ~X. This is why both Y and X can be Out. The right side of the arrow is the independent factor. The left side of the arrow, thus, is the dependent factor. It depends upon the requirement being followed. In other words, the moment that X is In, you can depend upon Y also being Out.

For In/Out games, the independent factor is the more important one. The LSAT test-writers enjoy crafting trap answers that hinge upon common misunderstandings of Independent factors. Consider the following conditional/contrapositive pair for the clue "if X is chosen, then so is Y."

$$X \rightarrow Y$$

$$\sim Y \rightarrow \sim X$$

At first glance, many students *wrongly* assume that this clue means that X and Y must always be together. This is not the case. Apply the discussion about Independent factors to this clue. The right side of the clue is independent. Therefore, the right side can occur without the left side happening. Thus, one valid permutation that satisfies this rule is

IN	OUT
Y	X

If you are having trouble following this logic, apply the mechanical approach to checking conditionals clues. Cover the right side of the arrows, and ask yourself if the rule applies. Based on this one clue, we have no knowledge of what occurs when Y is In or when X is Out.

Games Technique: If...Then and Its Relatives

We showed you in Lesson 3 how to diagram basic "if...then" statements. The "if" always occurs on the left side of the arrow, while the "then" statement is always to the right of the arrow. However, these are not the only ways the LSAT will structure conditional statements. There are two other major conditional phrases that you need to be on the lookout for.

The first of these is the word "only" (or "only when" or "only if"). The word "only" establishes a requirement. Thus, whatever condition follows the word "only" should be placed to the right side of the arrow.

> X will be In only if Y is Out.

The diagram for this is as follows:

$$X \rightarrow \sim Y$$

If your head is spinning with all this logic, fret not intrepid tester! There is a fast way to ensure that you diagram the conditional correctly every time. Simply find the word only and draw the conditional arrow directly on top of it.

> X will be In only if Y is out.

As you can see, the statement practically diagrams itself. One final note: just as with "if...then" statements, the order of the sentence does not affect the diagram. The same statement could have been written as follows:

> Only if Y is Out will X be in.

Use the same method by drawing the arrow over the "only if" phrase. Since the arrow points to ~Y, that must be placed on the right side of the diagram.

> Only if Y is Out will X be in.

Here's your rule of thumb: draw an arrow pointing to the right through the word "only." The thing on the point of the arrow should also be on the point of the arrow in your diagram. Be careful with these; it's easy to reverse them by mistake.

The next major word that the LSAT uses to create conditional statements is the word "unless." This one is a little harder for most people to wrap their heads around. However, consider the two sides to every conditional statement as described in the Arguments chapter. The left side is sufficient—it provides enough information to know that something else has or will occur. The right side is necessary—it provides some sort of requirement or rule that must be met. Now, try to apply that logic to the following statement.

> X will not be In unless Y is Out.

It can be a little confusing, but thinking in terms of requirements, Y Out is the requirement for X In. Therefore, this can be diagrammed as follows:

$$X \rightarrow \sim Y$$

If this is confusing, don't worry. Just like the word "only," there is a fast way to figure out the diagram for these statements. Take the word "unless," and replace it with "if not."

> if not
> X will not be In ~~unless~~ Y is Out.

Now, diagram the statement mechanically.

$$\sim (\sim Y) \rightarrow \sim X$$

Remember that two "not" become yes, so simplified we have

$$Y \rightarrow \sim X$$

Now take the contrapositive.

$$X \rightarrow \sim Y$$

We ultimately end up with the same result. The rule of thumb here is to cross out "unless" and write "if not," and then symbolize the clue as you would any "if... then" statement. The word "unless" is the most frequently misinterpreted clue on LSAT games; be extremely careful with these.

Tip!
While understanding the logic of conditionals is vital to mastering games, begin mechanically. Use the rules of thumb described here to play each game. Focus on understanding the logic during your self-analysis stage.

Games Technique: Conditionals with "And" or "Or"

On the LSAT, the word "and" means just what you think it does. "Or," on the other hand, means one or the other, or both. In other words, "A or B is chosen" could mean A, or B, or AB are chosen. Take a look at the following clue:

> If F is chosen, then G or H must also be chosen.

What does this mean? Well, whenever F is In, we know that at least one of G or H is In, and possibly both of them are. The only possibility this clue excludes is having both G and H Out.

How do we symbolize this? Since "and" and "or" appear so often on the test, we simply incorporate these words into our symbols.

$$F \rightarrow G \text{ or } H$$

Since the symbol implies both G and H as a possibility, we don't need to include anything else.

As always, we need to draw a symbol for the contrapositive of the clue. In order to elucidate the logic behind "and/or" statements, let's take a trip back to primary school. If you remember, the colors red and blue are both required to make purple. If you see that I have made purple, you know that I have mixed red and blue. This can be symbolized by writing

$$\text{Purple} \rightarrow \text{Red and Blue}$$

Now imagine that I tell you that I cannot make purple today. What must be true? It is possible that I lack both red and blue, but that's a bit extreme. Only missing one of the required colors would prevent me from being able to make purple. Therefore, when I write the contrapositive, I need to falsify only one half of the requirement to falsify the sufficient factor.

$$\sim\text{Red or} \sim \text{Blue} \rightarrow \sim\text{Purple}$$

Remember the rationale behind the contrapositive: we look for a case when the thing on the left-hand side must also be untrue. Apply this logic to the original example. What does it mean for "G or H" to be untrue? Well, the only way we can be sure that neither G nor H is In would be to have both of them Out. Put it another way, the contrary of the statement G is In or H is In (or both) is "G is Out and H is Out." Negating our "or" statement turns it into an "and" statement. Thus, the contrapositive here is as follows:

$$\sim G \text{ and } \sim H \rightarrow \sim F$$

This is how we negate the "or" statement. Not surprisingly, negating an "and" statement changes it into—you guessed it—an "or." After all if we flip and negate the symbol we've drawn above, we should be back to our original symbol. In order to do that, we would turn the statement "not G and not H" into the statement "G or H."

Remember that when you're working with a statement involving "and" or "or," you have to negate every part of the statement. When you negate "and," it becomes "or"; when you negate "or," it becomes "and."

One last note of caution: be careful with the phrase "neither...nor." Many students mistakenly think that "nor" is the same as "or" since they sound alike. In reality, "neither A nor B" means "not A and not B." Consider the following phrase.

> If neither Harry nor Sally is at the party, then John will not be at the party.

This phrase literally means if not Harry *and* not Sally, then not John. Therefore, it should be symbolized as

$$\sim\!H \text{ and } \sim\!S \rightarrow \sim\!J$$
$$J \rightarrow H \text{ or } S$$

Do not make the mistake of thinking that because "or" and "nor" look alike, they must mean the same thing.

DIAGRAMMING CONDITIONALS DRILL

In order to practice diagramming conditionals, we've created a little quiz for you to practice these crucial skills and concepts. Make sure you translate each one carefully and generate the contrapositives before you move on.

1. If Jack attends, Mark must attend.

2. Ann will work only if Kate works.

3. Bob cannot work unless Gary is working.

4. Sid will attend the party only if Nancy attends.

5. If Will goes to the party, Cam won't go.

6. If Harry is invited, both Charles and Linda must be invited.

7. John will not speak unless neither Bill nor Harry speaks.

8. Doug will drive unless either May or Sue drives.

Cracking the Diagramming Conditionals Drill

We have placed each of these in table form, so that you have a quick reference guide for your notes as you study.

Clue	Symbol	Contrapositive
If Jack attends, Mark must attend.	J → M	~M → ~J
Ann will work only if Kate works.	A → K	~K → ~A
Bob cannot work ~~unless~~ (if not) Gary is working.	~G → ~B	B → G
Sid will attend the party only if Nancy attends.	S → N	~N → ~S
If Will goes to the party, Cam won't go.	W → ~C	C → ~W
If Harry is invited, both Charles and Linda must be invited.	H → C and L	~C or ~L → ~H
John will not speak ~~unless~~ (if not) neither Bill nor Harry speaks.	B or H → ~J	J → ~B and ~H*
Doug will drive ~~unless~~ (if not) either May or Sue drives.	~M and ~S → D	~D → M or S*

The two marked with an * deserve additional explanation. "Unless" statements with "and" or "or" can be incredibly challenging to diagram. Remember that when you negate, you have to negate the entire side. A more expanded diagram of John, Bill, and Harry is below.

$$\sim(\sim B \text{ and } \sim H) \rightarrow \sim J$$

The double negatives become positives and the "and" becomes an "or." Thus, the final diagram of

$$B \text{ or } H \rightarrow \sim J$$

The last one is even trickier, but follows the same process by expanding out the diagram even more.

$$\sim (M \text{ or } S) \rightarrow D$$

The negative applies to both M and S and the "or" becomes an "and." Thus, the final diagram of

$$\sim M \text{ and } \sim S \rightarrow D$$

Games Technique: Placeholder Deductions

While In/Out games often have tons of conditionals, as we have already discussed, creating conditional chains can be time-consuming, tedious, and distracting. Often, it is best to stick with the original conditionals and leave your clue list relatively uncluttered. You should, however, make some deductions that are rather sophisticated but are useful on In/Out games. These are called *placeholder deductions*.

Consider the original example in this section. If X is selected, Y is not selected. We summarized this clue by noting that one of them could be In, or they could both be Out. The only situation that could not occur is both X and Y being In at the same time (see the table on page 213 if you need to refresh your memory). In essence, this conditional statement creates an antiblock in the In column. At any given time, one of the two elements, X or Y, must be Out. This means that the Out column will always have at least one element in it. This deduction can be symbolized as follows.

$$\boxed{XY}\; \text{In} \qquad \Big| \qquad \text{Out}$$
$$\qquad\qquad\qquad\qquad \underline{X/Y}$$

Note that on this diagram we have provided both the antiblock and the placeholder deduction. On an actual game, you need to focus on getting only the placeholder deduction. Let's consider another example.

> If A is not selected, then B is.

Start by symbolizing this clue and finding the contrapositive.

$$\sim\!A \rightarrow B$$

$$\sim\!B \rightarrow A$$

Now, take some time to consider the different possibilities here. Remember that the right side of the arrow is independent. Both B and A can be selected individually. However, if A is Out, then B must be In, and vice versa. What is the only possibility that cannot occur? Hopefully, you said that they cannot both be Out. Again, we have an antiblock created, this time in the Out column. As a result, there will be a placeholder in the In column.

$$\text{In} \qquad \Big| \qquad \text{Out} \quad \boxed{AB}$$
$$\underline{A/B}$$

As with the earlier section on "unless" and "only" statements, there is a shortcut that can be taken. On a side note, isn't it curious that some of the most confusing logic clues on the Games section all have shortcuts? Let's look at our original conditional statement and deduction.

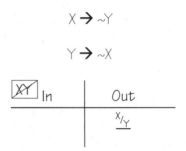

Take a look at the right side of the arrows in the conditional/contrapositive pair. Do you see how both elements share the same sign (both are Out)? This is what is called *paired independent factors*. When you have paired independent factors from a single conditional statement, you can immediately make the placeholder in the column indicated by the sign. Here, the paired factors are Out, so put the placeholder in the Out column, and then simply fill in the either/or situation with the elements from the clue: here, X or Y.

The same shortcut applies to the second example.

$$\sim\!A \rightarrow B$$

$$\sim\!B \rightarrow A$$

A and B on the right side of the arrows form paired independent factors. They are In, so the placeholder goes In and is filled with A/B.

Understanding both the logic and mechanics of paired independent factors is important for finding all the placeholder deductions without creating false deductions. For example, consider the following situation. Before reading the explanation, take a few minutes to determine why a placeholder deduction cannot be made.

$$A \rightarrow B$$

$$\sim\!B \rightarrow \sim\!A$$

The short answer to the question above is that the independent factors are not paired, but why is this crucial? As we have told you repeatedly, the right side can occur independently of the left. The table below shows you the different valid permutations.

IN	OUT
AB	
	AB
B	A

As you can see, we cannot determine from this single clue whether one of the two elements is always forced into either the In or Out column.

There can also be variations in placeholder deductions. Placeholders, for example, can deal with more than two clues. The same principles apply, nonetheless. Here's an example.

If A or B is selected, then C and D are not.

First, diagram the conditional and the contrapositive.

$$A \text{ or } B \rightarrow \sim C \text{ and } \sim D$$

$$C \text{ or } D \rightarrow \sim A \text{ and } \sim B$$

Note the paired independent factors. Each possibility includes an "and" situation, but this is not as frightening as it initially appears. Either a CD block or an AB block will always be Out. This means that you have already determined that there is a minimum of two elements Out every time. The placeholder deduction would appear as follows:

Another, more challenging, variant could be like this.

If neither A nor B are selected, then C or D is.

The diagram would appear as follows:

$$\sim A \text{ and } \sim B \rightarrow C \text{ or } D$$

$$\sim C \text{ and } \sim D \rightarrow A \text{ or } B$$

We still see the paired independent factors, but this time they include an "or" situation. This is more complicated. Basically, either C or D -OR- A or B will always be in. This is highly unspecific, and arguably the usefulness of the deduction is limited. However, we would still be able to note that in any play of the game, there is at least one element always In. This is useful since many In/Out games ask about the minimum or maximum numbers of elements that can be in one of the columns. The deduction would look like the following:

In	Out
$^A/_B$ / $^C/_D$	

Paired independent factors do not have to perfectly align with all elements in the clue in order for a placeholder deduction to be made. Look at the following item.

If A is selected, then B is also but C is not.

$$A \rightarrow B \text{ and } \sim C$$

$$\sim B \text{ or } C \rightarrow \sim A$$

This one is daunting. However, paired independent factors would suggest that either A or C is always Out. Should we actually put a placeholder there? Let's look at a table to be sure.

IN	OUT
A B	C
	B C A
C	A B
C B	A
B	C A
~~A B C~~	
~~A C~~	~~B~~
~~A~~	~~B C~~

This is a complex clue, so there are multiple possible permutations that do not violate the rule. Every single valid permutation has either A or C, or both, Out. Therefore, we can safely make a placeholder for A/C in the Out column.

In	Out
	$^A/_C$

Do not worry about breaking apart a whole clue to make the deduction. You will still have the original clue symbolized in your clue list and you should be referencing it every time you play the game. The deduction helps us narrow the number of possible elements that can be located in either column.

On the next page is a drill for finding placeholder deductions. Assume that all clues pertain to In/Out games. Not every question will have a valid deduction. If that is the case, write "none" on the diagram.

PLACEHOLDER DEDUCTION DRILL

		In	Out
1.	If A is out, then B is in.		
2.	If C is today, then D is tomorrow.		
3.	E and F cannot both be chosen.		
4.	G or H is chosen only if J is not.		
5.	If K or L, then M and N.		
6.	If O is Out, then so is P.		
7.	Unless Quinn is chosen, Rachel will be chosen.		
8.	S and T will occur only when U or V doesn't.		
9.	Will and Xavier always speak on different days.		
10.	If Y, then not Z.		

Cracking the Placeholder Deduction Drill

Each question has been placed in a table to help you study.

Statement	Diagram	Deduction
If A is out, then B is in.	$\sim A \rightarrow B$ $\sim B \rightarrow A$	**In** │ **Out** — $\underline{A/B}$ under In
If C is today, then D is tomorrow.	$C \rightarrow \sim D$ $D \rightarrow \sim C$	**In** │ **Out** — $\underline{C/D}$ under Out
E and F cannot both be chosen.	$\boxed{EF}$ **In** │ **Out**	$\boxed{EF}$ **In** │ **Out** — $\underline{E/F}$ under Out
G or H is chosen only if J is not.	$G \text{ or } H \rightarrow \sim J$ $J \rightarrow \sim G \text{ and } \sim H$	**In** │ **Out** — $\underline{J/\boxed{GH}}$ under Out
If K or L, then M and N.	$K \text{ or } L \rightarrow M \text{ and } N$ $\sim M \text{ or } \sim N \rightarrow \sim K \text{ and } \sim L$	none
If O is out, then so is P.	$\sim O \rightarrow \sim P$ $P \rightarrow O$	none
~~Unless~~ (if not) Q is chosen, R will be chosen.	$\sim Q \rightarrow R$ $\sim R \rightarrow Q$	**In** │ **Out** — $\underline{Q/R}$ under In
S and T will occur only when U or V doesn't.	$S \text{ and } T \rightarrow \sim U \text{ or } \sim V$ $U \text{ and } V \rightarrow \sim S \text{ or } \sim T$	**In** │ **Out** — $\underline{U/V \big/ S/T}$ under Out
Will and Xavier always speak on different days.	$\boxed{WX}$	$\boxed{WX}$ **In** │ **Out** $\boxed{WX}$ — $\underline{W/X}$ under In and $\underline{W/X}$ under Out
If Y then not Z.	$Y \rightarrow \sim Z$ $Z \rightarrow \sim Y$	**In** │ **Out** — $\underline{Y/Z}$ under Out

Now that you have been introduced to detailed conditional clues, placeholder deductions, and their relationship to In/Out games, it is time to try your hand at one.

GAME 4
Game 4 and its questions are from PrepTest 36, Section 4, Questions 1–6.

A fruit stand carries at least one kind of the following kinds of fruit: figs, kiwis, oranges, pears, tangerines, and watermelons. The stand does not carry any other kind of fruit. The selection of fruits the stand carries is consistent with the following conditions:

> If the stand carries kiwis, then it does not carry pears.
> If the stand does not carry tangerines, then it carries kiwis.
> If the stand carries oranges, then it carries both pears and watermelons.
> If the stand carries watermelons, then it carries figs or tangerines or both.

1. Which one of the following could be a complete and accurate list of the kinds of fruit the stand carries?

  (A) oranges, pears   Ⓐ
  (B) pears, tangerines   Ⓑ
  (C) oranges, pears, watermelons   Ⓒ
  (D) oranges, tangerines, watermelons   Ⓓ
  (E) kiwis, oranges, pears, watermelons   Ⓔ

2. Which one of the following could be the only kind of fruit the stand carries?

  (A) figs   Ⓐ
  (B) oranges   Ⓑ
  (C) pears   Ⓒ
  (D) tangerines   Ⓓ
  (E) watermelons   Ⓔ

3. Which one of the following CANNOT be a complete and accurate list of the kinds of fruit the stand carries?

  (A) kiwis, tangerines   Ⓐ
  (B) tangerines, watermelons   Ⓑ
  (C) figs, kiwis, watermelons   Ⓒ
  (D) oranges, pears, tangerines, watermelons   Ⓓ
  (E) figs, kiwis, oranges, pears, watermelons   Ⓔ

4. If the stand carries no watermelons, then which one of the following must be true?

  (A) The stand carries kiwis.   Ⓐ
  (B) The stand carries at least two kinds of fruit.   Ⓑ
  (C) The stand carries at most three kinds of fruit.   Ⓒ
  (D) The stand carries neither oranges nor pears.   Ⓓ
  (E) The stand carries neither oranges nor kiwis.   Ⓔ

5. If the stand carries watermelons, then which one of the following must be false?

(A) The stand does not carry figs.

(B) The stand does not carry tangerines.

(C) The stand does not carry pears.

(D) The stand carries pears but not oranges.

(E) The stand carries pears but not tangerines.

(A) (B) (C) (D) (E)

6. If the condition that if the fruit stand does not carry tangerines then it does carry kiwis is suspended, and all other conditions remain in effect, then which one of the following CANNOT be a complete and accurate list of the kinds of fruit the stand carries?

(A) pears

(B) figs, pears

(C) oranges, pears, watermelons

(D) figs, pears, watermelons

(E) figs, oranges, pears, watermelons

(A) (B) (C) (D) (E)

Self-Assessment

Steps 1–3 Assessment

Steps 4–6 Assessment

Cracking Game 4

Step 1: Diagram and Inventory

This is a fairly standard 1D In/Out game. The fruit stand will either carry a fruit, or it won't. The elements are the six different types of fruit, which all fall into a single category. Set up a two-column diagram where Carries is In and Not Carries is Out. If you need to, go ahead and put both labels on your columns.

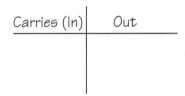

As you can see, the diagram is fairly straightforward. The only thing that we don't know is how many of each type of fruit must be In or Out. Therefore, we will have to rely on making placeholder deductions.

Step 2: Symbolize the Clues and Double-check

All of the clues are conditional statements. Remember that every time you have a conditional clue, you also should deduce the contrapositive. Symbolize the contrapositive as soon as you've symbolized the clue. Here are the four clues.

1. {
          K → ~P
          P → ~K

2. {
          ~T → K
          ~K → T

3. {
          O → P and W
      ~P or ~W → ~O

4. {
          W → F or T
     ~F and ~T → ~W

It's crucial to double-check carefully when you're symbolizing conditional clues, and check your contrapositives closely as well. Forgetting even one negation or an and/or switch can cause a great deal of mischief. If your symbols don't match the ones above, be sure to go back and review this lesson on symbolizing conditional clues.

Step 3: Make Deductions and Size Up the Game

For In/Out games, always begin by looking for placeholder deductions. The key with these, as described in the lesson, is to find clues that create antiblocks in one of the columns. The placeholder will then go in the other column. The shortcut is to find single clues that have paired independent factors. Begin with clue 1. The independent factors ~P and ~K are paired because both are out. This clue creates an antiblock in the In column. Both P and K cannot be In at the same time. Therefore, the placeholder clue should be in the Out column.

Carries (In)	Out
	P/K

Clue 2 has the same pattern. K and T are paired independent factors since they are both In. Therefore, the placeholder should be placed in the In column for these two elements.

Carries (In)	Out
K/T	P/K

Clues 3 and 4 do not have paired independent factors, so no placeholder deductions can be made. At this point, you would look at multi-clue deductions, but you have a decision to make. Take a look at the first, second, and third clues. The third clue tells us that if O is In, then so are P and W; the contrapositive of the first clue says that if P is In, then K is Out; and, finally, the second clue tells us that if K is Out, then P is In. In a case like this, it's possible to combine the clues together into a single "chain" leading from O to P to ~K to T. Similarly, this chain has a contrapositive—~T to K to ~P to ~O.

This is only one example of several such chains that can be made on this game, which is why you have a choice to make. In the end, by writing out the chain, you're primarily reproducing information you already have, but you do benefit by having it all in one place. The disadvantage of making these chain deductions is twofold. First, they can be time-consuming to find and write out; second, they clutter your page and make it more difficult to find information when you're working questions.

We recommend looking for placeholder deductions and moving on. The choice, however, is up to you. Some students benefit from spending a little bit more time focusing on the conditionals since doing so helps them size up the game better. A majority of students, though, spend too much time chaining them—time that could be better spent working through the questions. A good rule of thumb is that chain deductions are most useful on games that include a small number of relatively straightforward conditional clues. If there are a large number of conditionals, or if the conditionals strike you as complicated, it's usually best to keep your clue list as uncluttered as possible.

Steps 4–6: Assess the Question, Act, and Answer Using POE

As always, begin by determining whether there is a Grab-a-Rule question.

You probably went straight to question 1. This is understandable since it uses the phrase "complete and accurate list." However, if you noticed that the list focused only on the In column and skipped it, that is also understandable. On In/Out games, a question like this being a true Grab-a-Rule is hit or miss—sometimes it is and at other times, we need information about the Out column in order to finish it out. If you are ever unsure, dive into the question. Worst case scenario, you can't get down to a single answer. If that occurs, mark the question number, work the Specific questions, and then come back and finish this one. The good news is that this question is in fact a Grab-a-Rule!

---

1. Which one of the following could be a complete and accurate list of the kinds of fruit the stand carries?

   (A) oranges, pears   (Ⓐ)

   (B) pears, tangerines   (Ⓑ)

   (C) oranges, pears, watermelons   (C̶)

   (D) oranges, tangerines, watermelons   (D̶)

   (E) kiwis, oranges, pears, watermelons   (Ⓔ)

Here's How to Crack It

Remember when assessing conditional clues to only look at the left side (sufficient factor) of the arrow to determine whether a clue is applicable.

Clue 1 says "if K…." Choices (A), (B), (C), and (D) do not have K so they must be skipped—the rule simply doesn't apply. Choice (E) does, so now check the full rule. P is also listed which violates rule 1, so eliminate it.

Clue 2 deals with if "~T…." While you might be able to use this rule, we recommend skipping it. Remember, the whole point of a Grab-a-Rule question is to apply the rules without deep thoughts or diagramming. All of the answers are In; therefore, clue 2 does not apply.

Clue 3 says "if O…." Check (A). W is missing so eliminate it. The rule doesn't apply to (B). Check (C), which is valid. Check (D), which is missing P, so eliminate it. Now look at clue 4. The rule doesn't apply to (B), so skip it. The rule applies to (C), so check it. Choice (C) has neither F nor T; therefore, eliminate it. You are down to (B), so that must be the correct answer.

Now move on to the Specific questions. Let's look at question 4.

---

4. If the stand carries no watermelons, then which one of the following must be true?

(A) The stand carries kiwis.

(B) The stand carries at least two kinds of fruit.

(C) The stand carries at most three kinds of fruit.

(D) The stand carries neither oranges nor pears.

(E) The stand carries neither oranges nor kiwis.

(A)

(B)

(C)

(D)

(E)

Here's How to Crack It

In/Out games can be frustrating to many students because of the flexibility of the elements and the general confusion caused by conditional clues. Control this by getting your pen moving (we told you at the beginning of the lesson that this should be your mantra. If you're not sick of hearing us say this, then you're not moving your pen enough)!

Begin by symbolizing the new information, bringing down your deductions, and applying your clues. W is Out, so O must also be Out according to clue 3. Next, carry down your placeholder. You know that in addition to W and O, either P/K must be Out and T/K must be In. F has no rules at all that apply in this case.

FKOPTW	Carries (In)	Out
Clue Shelf	$^K/_T$ ___	$^P/_K$ ___
④	$^K/_T$ ___	$^P/_K$ ___ WO

This is a Must Be True question. We have gone as far as the rules will take us, so let's see if we already have the answer choice in our diagram. Choice (A) could be false based on our placeholder, so eliminate it. We know from our In placeholder that that stand always has at least one piece of fruit. If you're not sure if the stand carries at least two, hold on to this one. Never eliminate an answer choice on a Must Be True if you aren't 100% sure it's wrong. Choice (C) says that the stand carries at most 3 kinds of fruit. This also seems plausible since we have six fruits, 3 of which must be Out. Again, if you're not positive, let's leave this one for now. We know that O must be Out, but our placeholder shows us that either P or K can be Out. Neither of these elements is forced, so both (D) and (E) can be false. Get rid of them. We are now down to at least two versus at most 3. Be very careful when you falsify these answer choices. If you are able to put two fruit In the stand and four Out, both these answer choices would still be valid. If you *can't* put three fruit Out, then (C) is gone. If you can put *only one* fruit In and the other five Out, then (B) is eliminated.

Let's try to break (B). We know that K or T must be In. We also know that P or K must be Out. Since K is the overlap, let's make that the only element in. Quickly write the other five elements in the Out column and then check your rules (this is more efficient).

FKOPTW	Carries (In)	Out
Clue Shelf	K/T —	P/K —
④	K/T —	P/K — WO
④Ⓑ	K	PWOTF

This doesn't break any rules. Therefore, the stand does not have to carry "at least two" kinds of fruit. Eliminate (B); (C) is the right answer.

Let's keep going.

5. If the stand carries watermelons, then which one of the following must be false?

  (A) The stand does not carry figs.   Ⓐ

  (B) The stand does not carry tangerines.   Ⓑ

  (C) The stand does not carry pears.   Ⓒ

  (D) The stand carries pears but not oranges.   Ⓓ

  (E) The stand carries pears but not tangerines.   Ⓔ

Here's How to Crack It

Begin by placing W in the In column and deducing any new information that must be true based on the question. Since W is In either F/T must be In. Now carry down your deductions. We have at least one fruit Out and at least two In. Be careful here! Since the element T is in both placeholders we can be sure only one more element will be In.

FKOPTW	Carries (In)	Out
Clue Shelf	$K/_T$ ___	$P/_K$ ___
④	$K/_T$ ___	$P/_K$ ___ WO
④B	K	PWOTF
⑤	W $F/_T$ ___	$P/_K$ ___

Again, check the answers quickly to see if we have identified any answer choice that must be false. If nothing jumps out at you, eliminate what you can based upon rules and deductions. Next, it is time to stop thinking and start diagramming. Apply clue 4 first, but pick one of the two elements. Let's place F In and T Out. This forces K into our In placeholder, in turn forcing P into the Out placeholder. Our last element, O, is also forced out due to clue 3. Now eliminate any answer choice that we have proven could be true. On our diagram, T, P, and O can all be Out. Eliminate (B) and (C).

FKOPTW	Carries (In)	Out
Clue Shelf	$K/_T$ ___	$P/_K$ ___
④	$K/_T$ ___	$P/_K$ ___ WO
④B	K	PWOTF
⑤	W $F/_T$ ___	$P/_K$ ___
⑤	WFK	PTO

Now, try a different approach. W is in from the question, but this time, put T In with F Out. Next, let's try focusing on our independent factors, since challenging questions often test your understanding of these. Notice in clue 3 that P and W In and ~O are independent. Let's diagram that, so put P in with W and O out. This forces K out to fill our placeholder.

FKOPTW	Carries (In)	Out
Clue Shelf	K/T	P/K
④	K/T	P/K WO
④ⓑ	K	PWOTF
⑤	W F/T	P/K
⑤	WFK	PTO
⑤	WTP	KFO

Go back to the questions and continue using POE on any answer choice that could be true. F is Out, so eliminate (A). P is In while O is Out, so eliminate (D). Choice (E) is the only choice remaining, so select it.

Notice that (D) specifically tests your understanding of independent and dependent factors. When you are dealing with In/Out questions and have many answer choices to eliminate, proactively look for independent factors that confuse many students and apply those to your diagram. You'll be pleased with how often this gets rid of tricky answers!

At this point, we are done with Specific questions and should move on to General questions. Now, some of you may be saying, "wait a moment…question 6 begins with *If* as well!" Remember, all that glitters is not gold. Way back in the first lesson, we described four types of questions. The fourth type was Complex questions. These are any questions that alter rules. Question 6 says "If the condition… is suspended…." This question eliminates a rule and is thus a Complex question. It should be tackled last!

2. Which one of the following could be the only kind of fruit the stand carries?

(A) figs

(B) oranges

(C) pears

(D) tangerines

(E) watermelons

Ⓐ Ⓑ Ⓒ Ⓓ Ⓔ

Here's How to Crack It

This question asks which of the following answers could be the only fruit In. Remember to look at your deductions. We have a placeholder that tells us that either K or T must always be In. Therefore, one of these two fruits must be the answer. Eliminate any answer choice that is not K or T. The answer is (D).

3. Which one of the following CANNOT be a complete and accurate list of the kinds of fruit the stand carries?

(A) kiwis, tangerines

(B) tangerines, watermelons

(C) figs, kiwis, watermelons

(D) oranges, pears, tangerines, watermelons

(E) figs, kiwis, oranges, pears, watermelons

Ⓐ Ⓑ Ⓒ Ⓓ Ⓔ

Here's How to Crack It

This question asks us which of the five answers is the only one that is invalid. In other words, it is either incomplete or breaks a rule. Begin by looking at your deductions. Start with the In column. We know that either T or K must be In. Check the answers. Unfortunately, they all include either T or K or both. Next, look at the Out column. We know that either P or K or both must be Out. Since each of the answers is a "complete and accurate list," we can assume that any fruit not on the list is Out. In (A), P is Out; both are Out in (B); P is Out in (C); K is Out in (D); but both are In in (E). Therefore, this violates a rule and cannot be an accurate list. Choice (E) is the credited response, so select it.

If you struggle with In/Out games, there is an alternative approach to these complete list questions. Simply write out the answer choice exactly as stated. Then place every remaining element Out. Finally, check the rules and apply POE as needed for the question stem. This can be time-consuming, so use this as a last resort. However, it is good practice for understanding In/Out game logic.

Now, onward to our final question. The difficulty of complex questions can vary widely. The most challenging of these ask which answer choice would have the same effect on a game as one of the rules. In general, the more the complex question changes your deductions, the harder it is.

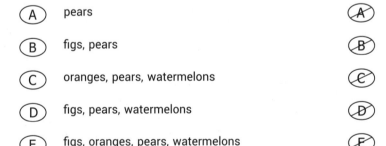

6. If the condition that if the fruit stand does not carry tangerines then it does carry kiwis is suspended, and all other conditions remain in effect, then which one of the following CANNOT be a complete and accurate list of the kinds of fruit the stand carries?

    (A) pears   (A)

    (B) figs, pears   (B)

    (C) oranges, pears, watermelons   (C)

    (D) figs, pears, watermelons   (D)

    (E) figs, oranges, pears, watermelons   (E)

This question eliminates clue 2. As a result, our placeholder in the In column must also be removed. Therefore, the only deduction we have is the P/K placeholder in the Out column. Since this clue is removed, there are no additional deductions to be made.

FKOPTW	Carries (In)	Out
Clue Shelf	K/T —	P/K —
④	K/T —	P/K — WO
④B	K	PWOTF
⑤	W F/T —	P/K —
⑤	WFK	PTO
⑤	WTP	KFO
Clue Shelf ⑥		P/K —

The fastest way to check the answer on complex questions is to find new deductions; however, none are forthcoming. This question also asks for an answer choice that is either incomplete or violates a rule in some way. If you are struggling with these, just plug them into your diagram! Questions that use the phrase "complete and accurate" can be diagrammed with speed. We'll show you how quick this can be. Start with (A). If P is the complete list of fruit, then F, K, O, T, and W must be Out.

FKOPTW	Carries (In)	Out
Clue Shelf	K/T —	P/K —
④	K/T —	P/K — WO
④B	K	PWOTF
⑤	W F/T —	P/K —
⑤	WFK	PTO
⑤	WTP	KFO
Clue Shelf ⑥		P/K —
⑥A	P	FKOTW

Remember that clue 2 no longer applies. Rules 1, 3, and 4 are not violated, so get rid of (A). Now, repeat the process with (B). F and P make the complete list, so put K, O, T, and W out and check the rules.

FKOPTW	Carries (In)	Out
Clue Shelf	$^K/_T$ ——	$^P/_K$ ——
④	$^K/_T$ ——	$^P/_K$ —— WO
④B	K	PWOTF
⑤	W $^F/_T$ ——	$^P/_K$ ——
⑤	WFK	PTO
⑤	WTP	KFO
Clue Shelf ⑥		$^P/_K$ ——
⑥A	P	FKOTW
⑥B	PK	KOTW

No rules are violated, so (B) is Out. Once more with (C)! O, P, and W are In, so F, K, and T are Out. However, this violates clue 4. Therefore, this cannot be a complete list. Choice (C) is correct.

FKOPTW	Carries (In)	Out
Clue Shelf	$^K/_T$ ——	$^P/_K$ ——
④	$^K/_T$ ——	$^P/_K$ —— WO
④B	K	PWOTF
⑤	W $^F/_T$ ——	$^P/_K$ ——
⑤	WFK	PTO
⑤	WTP	KFO
Clue Shelf ⑥		$^P/_K$ ——
⑥A	P	FKOTW
⑥B	PK	KOTW
⑥C	~~OPW~~	~~FKT~~

This concludes the In/Out game. At this point, you have now been introduced to, and worked through, all the major game types. You have also been exposed to in-depth discussions of POE, deductions, clue symbolization, and the approach. The next lesson will discuss how the LSAT will often take these basic game patterns and twist them into more complex forms. As you dive into the next lesson, keep in mind that you should be building upon the basics.

LESSON 5: TWISTS, TURNS, AND GAME RANKING

This is it! Believe it or not, there are only a few more things you need to focus on as you advance toward a mastery of the Games section. You have been shown the basic approach to games and used it on four different examples. You have been introduced to all the major games patterns: Ordering, Grouping, and In/Out. You have also seen and studied POE skills, clue symbolizations, and deductions. You have seen some level of complexity by playing a 2D Ordering game. This lesson will focus on the twists that the LSAT test-writers can introduce into these game patterns.

In order to master the LSAT, or any standardized exam for that matter, you need to develop and hone two complementary skills. These two skills appear contrary at first, but they really do work well together. The two skills are consistency and flexibility.

The reason that many students struggle with the LSAT is that they approach each question as unique. As we have hopefully demonstrated through the previous lessons in this chapter, the LSAT Games section is anything but unique. The games and the questions are highly patterned. If you focus on the logic behind the methods we teach, you will notice that at its core, we have been teaching you to approach every single game and every single question the same way. The specifics of the approach, such as diagramming or POE, can adapt based on the question type; however, the general approach is always true.

This is undoubtedly a challenging test. The test-writers are highly skilled at taking these familiar patterns and masking them in order to make them harder. This is where flexibility comes in. Now that you have made significant strides toward mastering the general techniques, you will want to build in the flexibility needed to adapt the approach to any situation the LSAT throws at you. This lesson will discuss various ways in which games can be changed from the patterns discussed previously. Make sure you take the time both to study the possible changes and to focus on how the solutions we provide are similar to the major game types that you know.

Games Technique: Draw the Right Diagram

A common variation of games is arranging elements spatially. Any setup that provides a specific arrangement of the slots for the elements could be a spatial setup. Let's look at an example.

> Eight vegetables—asparagus, broccoli, carrots, eggplant, green beans, kale, legumes, and spinach—are being placed around a circular buffet table.

This seems quite different from the earlier examples that we have investigated here. However, if this was a straight table, these vegetables would be placed in some sort of *order*. In other words, this is an Ordering game. The difference with this one and earlier Ordering games is that this is circular. The simplest way to deal with any spatial arrangement is to draw a template instead of a grid diagram. For the example above, we would draw four intersecting lines and would place our elements at the ends of each line. This would allow us to see what is next to each dish and which dishes were directly across the buffet from each other.

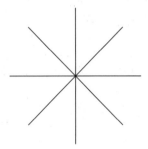

We'll fill in the first template with all the concrete information we have and any deductions we come up with, effectively like a clue shelf. For each question we work, we'll draw a new diagram, carry over our deductions, and enter the new information from the question. You might think that redrawing the diagram for each question will be too time-consuming, but if you keep it simple, you can create one quickly and then have a concrete space in which to work through the question.

Occasionally, the LSAT folks will surprise you with their generosity and will actually tell you how to draw the diagram. By all means, use their description. Copy it as many times as you need to, but draw it more simply if necessary.

Games Technique: 2D and 3D Games

As we discussed on Game 2, Ordering games can have a second dimension added to them that ups their difficulty level. On that game, we separated the game into two rows on our diagram that allowed us to keep track of the puppies and kittens separately.

It will probably come as no surprise to you, but every major game type can have 2D variants. For example, our grouping game had two dogs being placed with new owners on subsequent days. What if, in addition to the different types of dogs, the games told us that the owners lived in either an apartment building or a house? What types of new clues would the game give you? How would this twist affect the questions and answers? What about the difficulty level of the game?

Likewise, our In/Out game had us placing fruit in a stand. A 2D variant could ask us to categorize the fruit as either $1 or $2 per item. The same questions could be asked of this variation. What would this twist do to the game?

Finally, consider the 2D Ordering game about kittens and puppies. What if the game also stipulated that at least once each week, a breed of pet would be placed on sale? How would this information affect the game?

You need to adapt your diagram to cope with all the information in the setup and clues. Remember that the entire point of diagramming is to make your life simple by organizing and managing the games information. Many 2D games are fairly straightforward twists. They can be dealt with by adding a second row to the diagram, adding subscripts to the elements (if the new information is pre-assigned), or by adding notes underneath the placeholders of Grouping and Ordering games. Other information can be more challenging. In the example above about putting at least one pet type on sale, you would need to come up with some method of symbolizing the sale. For example, you could note on your clue shelf that a circled element would be on sale. Then if a question stipulated that H were on sale Tuesday, you would put H on Tuesday with a circle around it and apply your rules accordingly.

The bottom line is that whenever the LSAT test-writers throw a curveball at you, do not focus on the differences. Instead, focus on the similarities with games that you are already know. Then adapt your diagram so that it will help you keep track of all the new, twisted information.

Games Technique: Question and Deduction Driven Games

As we have said in earlier lessons, not every game has deductions. In some games, the number of deductions you can make is severely limited. These games we have nicknamed Question Driven games. Question Driven games typically have only one (or even zero) deductions that can be made. They also typically have a majority of Specific questions. These games have to be played over and over again. The trick with this type of game is to not panic when no deductions are forthcoming. Hold to the systematic approach that we have shown you. Be prepared to play several answer choices on the first couple of questions that you work in order to get down to a single answer. This can be challenging since you have only a finite amount of time, but if you keep moving, you will eventually start to see patterns emerging. You will also quickly generate a large amount of work that will help you on later questions.

On the other end of the spectrum are Deduction Driven games. If you begin a game and notice that there are very few (sometimes only 1) Specific questions and the rest are General, then take a few extra minutes to note deductions. These games almost always have some very large deductions that limit the game to only one or two possible distributions. Other things to look for on games like this are several large block clues, several connected range clues, or some sort of spatial distribution that prevents the game from being too flexible. The strategy here is to invest extra time finding deductions so that you don't have to check individual answers on those General questions.

Games Technique: Twisted Conditionals

Based on the fact that we have already discussed conditional statements in two previous lessons, it should come as no surprise that conditionals can be even more complex than what we have looked at. Sometimes conditional clues can be masked with abstract language. Conditional clues can be linked with other clue types, such as block or range clues. Finally, conditionals can include extra language that makes them challenging to diagram. Let's look at a few examples. The first should be familiar to you since it was from the game we played in Lesson 2. Let's look again at question 5 from that game.

5. Which one of the following could be true?

(A) There are exactly four breeds that are each featured on three days.

(B) Greyhounds are featured on every day that Himalayans are.

(C) Himalayans are featured on every day that Greyhounds are.

(D) Himalayans are featured on every day that Rottweilers are not.

(E) Rottweilers are featured on every day that Himalayans are not.

(B) H → G
(C) G → H
(D) ~R → H
(E) ~H → R

This time, let's focus on parsing the language of the answer choices. Let's start with (B). This answer says that G is featured every time that H is. Many students wrongly conclude this means that G and H are always together. However, think in terms of sufficient and necessary factors. Which pet location provides sufficient information to know the other, the G or the H? It is the H. Therefore, this answer choice is actually stating H → G. G is independent, so it can occur on other days, but it will always be with an H. Let's look at (C) now. Now that you know these are conditionals, you can see how these answer choices are distinct. This answer has H as the independent and should be diagrammed as G → H. These answers in reality are conditional statements that are twisted by using different language than the easy-to-parse if…then phrasing. Why don't you try your hand at diagramming the statements in (D) and (E) before moving on.

Conditional statements can also include aspects of block or range clues. Consider the following examples.

> If A is first, then B is sometime before C.

This clue is clearly a conditional statement. However, it also reads like a range clue. Start by diagramming it as normal with the "if" statement on the left side. Then take the mechanical contrapositive.

$$A_1 \rightarrow B...C$$
$$\cancel{B...C} \rightarrow \sim A_1$$

Once you've done this, you can determine based on the game and diagram whether it is valid to make additional deductions, such as C...B.

Conditionals can also include block clues.

> Every A also has a B.

Words like "all" and "every" are all-inclusive and therefore are sufficient to know what comes next. Therefore, they go on the left side of the arrow. They can be diagrammed as follows.

$$\boxed{A \rightarrow AB}$$

The contrapositive of this statement is a little tricky. A mechanical version would read "if I don't have an A and B block, then I don't have A." However, let's think about this in a little more detail. Any block clue can also be read as A and B together. When you negate, "and" becomes "or," so a less mechanical contrapositive would be if ~A or ~B → ~A. Logically, if you don't have A, then you don't have A (duh!). Therefore, the true contrapositive of this statement is simply

$$\sim B \rightarrow \sim A$$

Finally, conditional statements can include strange phrasings that combine parts of other conditional statements. Consider the phrase "if, but only if...." For example, a clue could read

> A is on committee 1 if, but only if, B is also on committee 1.

Each statement separately would be pretty easy to diagram. "A is on committee 1 if B is also on committee 1" or "A is on committee 1 only if B is on committee 1." By combining these two phrases into a single statement, the LSAT is telling you that each element is both a sufficient and necessary factor. You can either diagram this as two separate clues, or you can treat them as a single clue with an arrow moving both directions.

$$A \rightarrow B$$
$$\sim A \rightarrow \sim B$$

Finally, consider the following example of a highly complex conditional statement.

> If Stone evaluates a proposal, then Uqbar does not also
> evaluate that proposal, unless Stone evaluates proposal K.

The first half of this clue seems to be another straightforward conditional statement. The second half introduces a twist. There, the "unless…" phrase lets you know that this rule does not apply when S is evaluating K, but it does apply on all other proposals.

APPLY WHAT YOU'VE LEARNED

Now it's time to put everything you've learned in this section about twisted games into practice on the next game. We're not going to tell you anything more about this game. Your job is to identify the similarities between this game and previous ones that you've worked. Then identify how the twisted information affects the game and how you should adapt your diagram. Do your best on this one. We don't recommend timing yourself, as this will likely be a challenging game for you.

After this game and the self-evaluation worksheet, you will find one more technique on how to determine the best order of games to work. Good luck!

GAME 5

Game 5 and its questions are from PrepTest 32, Section 3, Questions 1–6.

Of the eight students—George, Helen, Irving, Kyle, Lenore, Nina, Olivia, and Robert—in a seminar, exactly six will give individual oral reports during three consecutive days—Monday, Tuesday, and Wednesday. Exactly two reports will be given each day—one in the morning and one in the afternoon—according to the following conditions:

   Tuesday is the only day on which George can give a report.
   Neither Olivia nor Robert can give an afternoon report.
   If Nina gives a report, then on the next day Helen and Irving must both give reports, unless Nina's report is given on Wednesday.

1. Which one of the following could be the schedule of students' reports?

(A) Mon. morning: Helen; Mon. afternoon: Robert
Tues. morning: Olivia; Tues. afternoon: Irving
Wed. morning: Lenore; Wed. afternoon: Kyle

(B) Mon. morning: Irving; Mon. afternoon: Olivia
Tues. morning: Helen; Tues. afternoon: Kyle
Wed. morning: Nina; Wed. afternoon: Lenore

(C) Mon. morning: Lenore; Mon. afternoon: Helen
Tues. morning: George; Tues. afternoon: Kyle
Wed. morning: Robert; Wed. afternoon: Irving

(D) Mon. morning: Nina; Mon. afternoon: Helen
Tues. morning: Robert; Tues. afternoon: Irving
Wed. morning: Olivia; Wed. afternoon: Lenore

(E) Mon. morning: Olivia; Mon. afternoon: Nina
Tues. morning: Irving; Tues. afternoon: Helen
Wed. morning: Kyle; Wed. afternoon: George

2. If Kyle and Lenore do not give reports, then the morning reports on Monday, Tuesday, and Wednesday, respectively, could be given by

(A) Helen, George, and Nina

(B) Irving, Robert, and Helen

(C) Nina, Helen, and Olivia

(D) Olivia, Robert, and Irving

(E) Robert, George, and Helen

3. Which one of the following is a pair of students who, if they give reports on the same day as each other, must give reports on Wednesday?

(A) George and Lenore

(B) Helen and Nina

(C) Irving and Robert

(D) Kyle and Nina

(E) Olivia and Kyle

4. If George, Nina, and Robert give reports and they do so on different days from one another, which one of the following could be true?

(A) Helen gives a report on Wednesday.

(B) Nina gives a report on Monday.

(C) Nina gives a report on Tuesday.

(D) Olivia gives a report on Monday.

(E) Robert gives a report on Wednesday.

5. If Kyle gives the afternoon report on Tuesday, and Helen gives the afternoon report on Wednesday, which one of the following could be the list of the students who give the morning reports on Monday, Tuesday, and Wednesday, respectively?

(A) Irving, Lenore, and Nina

(B) Lenore, George, and Irving

(C) Nina, Irving, and Lenore

(D) Robert, George, and Irving

(E) Robert, Irving, and Lenore

6. If Helen, Kyle, and Lenore, not necessarily in that order, give the three morning reports, which one of the following must be true?

(A) Helen gives a report on Monday.

(B) Irving gives a report on Monday.

(C) Irving gives a report on Wednesday.

(D) Kyle gives a report on Tuesday.

(E) Kyle gives a report on Wednesday.

Self-Assessment

Steps 1–3 Assessment

Steps 4–6 Assessment

Cracking Game 5

Step 1: Diagram and Inventory

As we warned, this game was going to have a few twists to it. Hopefully, though, you noticed that this seems most similar to a 2D Ordering game. There are three consecutive days (which have a natural order). Two people will be giving a report each day—once in the A.M. and once in the P.M.—making the second dimension that we need to keep track of. The first twist to this game is that we have eight people, but only six speakers. Therefore, we also need to add an "Out" column to keep track of those who will not be speaking at all. Your diagram should look as follows.

Step 2: Symbolize the Clues and Double-check

Whenever there is a twist to the game, you must be extra careful when you symbolize the clues. Focus on the wording of each clue and look for markers like "must" or "may" that indicate rigidity or flexibility in the clue. Let's look at the first clue. This clue says that G can give a report only on Tuesday. Notice that the clue does *not* say that G must speak only Tuesday. The clue merely implies that *if* G is giving a report, then that report must be on Tuesday. Therefore, G can either be on Tuesday or Out. This is a concrete clue and can be drawn above the diagram.

The next clue is a fairly straightforward concrete clue providing negative information. This can also be symbolized on the diagram. However, since it deals with the second dimension, it should go to the side of the diagram.

The final clue is the second major twist to the game. It is a twisted conditional. The clue first provides sufficient information that if N speaks, then both H and I speak the next day. What we don't know is which speaks in the morning or the afternoon. However, let's start by diagramming the conditional.

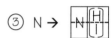

Note that we wanted to include as much information as possible. Therefore, on the left, we put N → since that is sufficient information. The right side is more challenging. However, the clue forms a block. We put N straddling the line between A.M. and P.M. to indicate either, and then put H and I in the next column. The final piece of information we included was to put a set of parentheses around H and I indicating that they could be in either position. This looks pretty good, but now we need to consider the second half of the clue. This clue says that the rule applies unless N is on Wednesday. Remember that if a clue is hard/impossible to symbolize, then use crib notes. Let's just add the phrase "except W" to our symbol to indicate that this rule doesn't apply when N = W.

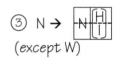

(except W)

Finally, with super complex conditionals, it may be more confusing and time-consuming to do the contrapositive. As a result, we will skip this step. It is hard to determine when to skip the contrapositive. In general, this shouldn't be done. However, if you can't simply flip and negate the sides, and looking at the clue doesn't help you see how to do it, then skip it.

Step 3: Make Deductions and Size Up the Game
As discussed in an earlier lesson, concrete clues can be used to make deductions, but it is usually not worth the time to do so. For example, if G can only be On T or Out, then G cannot be on M or W. But this is already suggested by our symbolization. Likewise, if neither O nor R can be in the P.M., then they are either in the A.M. or Out. Again, this information is included in the symbol. Finally, with the conditional clue, we already discussed why we shouldn't take the contrapositive, which is the primary deduction for conditionals. None of the elements are mentioned in more than one clue either. If you are really unsure about missing something, you can always glance at the questions. Notice that of the six questions, five of them are Specific. As discussed in the lesson, this indicates a question-driven game with few deductions.

One thing that can be deduced is the interaction between clues 1 and 3. Clue three completely fills up a day. Therefore, if N = M, then G must be Out. This can symbolized as follows.

$$N_m \rightarrow G_{out}$$

$$G \rightarrow \sim N_m$$

Even though this isn't a specific deduction and starts with an "if," it is still pretty powerful since only two elements can be Out. Despite a lack of specific deductions, sizing up the game is always beneficial. There are several limiting elements here. Specifically, N is the most powerful element in the game since its location on either M or T fills up half the diagram. Likewise, O, R, and G, if placed, are going to limit the location of various elements. We know nothing about elements L and K, so these will be the most flexible of the elements.

Steps 4–6: Assess the Question, Act, and Use Process of Elimination

Question 1 appears to be a Grab-a-Rule, so let's dive into that one.

——————○——————

1. Which one of the following could be the schedule of students' reports?

   (A) Mon. morning: Helen; Mon. afternoon: Robert
       Tues. morning: Olivia; Tues. afternoon: Irving
       Wed. morning: Lenore; Wed. afternoon: Kyle

   (B) Mon. morning: Irving; Mon. afternoon: Olivia
       Tues. morning: Helen; Tues. afternoon: Kyle
       Wed. morning: Nina; Wed. afternoon: Lenore

   (C) Mon. morning: Lenore; Mon. afternoon: Helen
       Tues. morning: George; Tues. afternoon: Kyle
       Wed. morning: Robert; Wed. afternoon: Irving

   (D) Mon. morning: Nina; Mon. afternoon: Helen
       Tues. morning: Robert; Tues. afternoon: Irving
       Wed. morning: Olivia; Wed. afternoon: Lenore

   (E) Mon. morning: Olivia; Mon. afternoon: Nina
       Tues. morning: Irving; Tues. afternoon: Helen
       Wed. morning: Kyle; Wed. afternoon: George

Here's How to Crack It

Begin with rule 1. Choice (E) has G on W, so eliminate it.

Rule 2 discusses R and O. Choice (A) has R in the P.M., so eliminate it. Choice (B) has O in the P.M., so get rid of that one as well.

Finally, look at rule 3. Remember with conditionals to look only at the left side. Choice (C) doesn't have an N so the rule doesn't apply. Choice (D) has N on M, but H is also on M, so eliminate (D). The answer is (C).

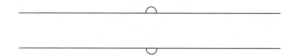

2. If Kyle and Lenore do not give reports, then the morning reports on Monday, Tuesday, and Wednesday, respectively, could be given by

(A) Helen, George, and Nina   (A)

(B) Irving, Robert, and Helen   (B)

(C) Nina, Helen, and Olivia   (C)

(D) Olivia, Robert, and Irving   (D)

(E) Robert, George, and Helen   (E)

Here's How to Crack It

This question tells us the two elements that are Out, so we know that everyone else must be In. Begin by diagramming the new information. Now consider the remaining elements and what we learned when we sized up the game. O and R are highly restrictive and both are In. Furthermore, they must both be placed in the A.M. At this point, you can go straight to the answer choices and POE. Since O and R must be in the A.M., the correct answer must include both of these. Eliminating any answer that doesn't include O and R gets rid of (A), (B), (C), and (E). Therefore, the correct answer must be (D).

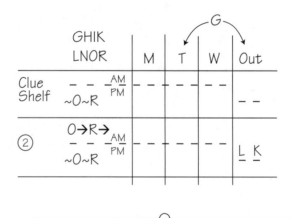

Let's do another. Not all Specific questions have the same difficulty. Choose ones that provide highly specific information. Let's look at question 5.

5. If Kyle gives the afternoon report on Tuesday, and Helen gives the afternoon report on Wednesday, which one of the following could be the list of the students who give the morning reports on Monday, Tuesday, and Wednesday, respectively?

(A) Irving, Lenore, and Nina

(B) Lenore, George, and Irving

(C) Nina, Irving, and Lenore

(D) Robert, George, and Irving

(E) Robert, Irving, and Lenore

Here's How to Crack It

Begin by drawing a new row on your diagram and put in the new information. We know that since H is on W, the only possible locations for N are fairly limited. Let's try N on T. This forces I on W. Since T is now full, G is Out. Either O or R must be M A.M., so L is M P.M.

Now check your answers for the possibility of O/R…N…I. This combination is not there, so let's try again. Let's try N being on W A.M. There's only one answer choice with N in the A.M., so let's just try plugging in (A).

That didn't work because there was nowhere to put O, R, and G, so we know N must be Out for the credited response. Let's eliminate any answer choice that includes N, so (A) and (C) are gone. Since only one other element is Out with N, then either O or R (or both) is In during the A.M. Let's eliminate any answer choice that doesn't include either O or R. Choice (B) is also gone. We are now down to either (D) or (E). Rather than thinking about this further, let's plug in another answer and see if it works. Try out (D). Put R, G, and I in the A.M. in that order. O must be Out with N, so L is on M in the P.M. This diagram works, so (D) is the answer.

Let's keep going.

6. If Helen, Kyle, and Lenore, not necessarily in that order, give the three morning reports, which one of the following must be true?

(A) Helen gives a report on Monday.

(B) Irving gives a report on Monday.

(C) Irving gives a report on Wednesday.

(D) Kyle gives a report on Tuesday.

(E) Kyle gives a report on Wednesday.

Here's How to Crack It

As with all Specific problems, begin with a new row. However, this one is a bit challenging to diagram. We know that H, K, and L are in the A.M., but we don't know their order. The three elements completely fill up the three A.M. slots, though. This forces O and R to be Out. Therefore, G must be In on T in the P.M. N must also be In. Remember clue 3 is highly restrictive, and we deduced that if G was on T, then N couldn't be on M. Our A.M. slots are filled, so N must be W P.M. Our final element is I, who must be on M P.M. We still don't know the location of H, K, and L, so leave these off the diagram.

GHIK LNOR		M	T	W	Out
Clue Shelf	- - $\frac{AM}{PM}$ ~O~R	-	-	-	- -
②	O→R→ - - $\frac{AM}{PM}$ ~O~R	-	-	-	L K
⑤	- - $\frac{AM}{PM}$	O/R / L	N / K	I / H	G O/R
⑤A	$\frac{AM}{PM}$	I / O/R	L / K	N / H	
⑤D	- - $\frac{AM}{PM}$	R / L	G / K	I / H	N O
⑥	- - $\frac{AM}{PM}$	_ / I	_ / G	_ / N	O R

(G with arrows from T to W above the columns)

We are looking for the single answer that must be true. Choice (B) must be true, so lock it in and move on.

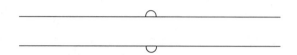

4. If George, Nina, and Robert give reports and they do so on different days from one another, which one of the following could be true?

(A) Helen gives a report on Wednesday.   (A̶)

(B) Nina gives a report on Monday.   (B̶)

(C) Nina gives a report on Tuesday.   (C̶)

(D) Olivia gives a report on Monday.   (D̶)

(E) Robert gives a report on Wednesday.   (E̶)

Here's How to Crack It

Begin by putting the most restricted information on the new row in your diagram. Since G is In, put G on T. It's not clear when on T, so let's arbitrarily put G in the A.M. Since G is In, N cannot be on Monday. Therefore, R is on M A.M., and N is sometime on W. At this point, use POE to get rid of any answer choice that must be false.

	GHIK LNOR	M	T	W	Out
Clue Shelf	− − AM/PM ~O~R	−	−	−	− −
②	O→R→ AM/PM − − ~O~R	−	−	−	L K
⑤	− − AM/PM	O/R L	N K	I H	G O/R
⑤A	AM/PM	I O/R	L K	N H	
⑤D	− − AM/PM	R L	G K	I H	N O
⑥	− − AM/PM	I	G	N	O R
④	− − AM/PM	R	G	(N) (N)	

We don't know anything about H, so skip (A). N must be on W, so eliminate (B) and (C). O cannot go on Monday since O must be in the A.M. but R is already there; get rid of (D). Finally, R must be on M, so eliminate (E). The answer is (A).

Let's move on to the final question. Question 3 is a bit twisted, just like other aspects of this game. This appears to be a General question, but also includes the phrase "if they give reports on the same day...." If you aren't sure how to approach a question like this, treat it as a General question.

3. Which one of the following is a pair of students who, if they give reports on the same day as each other, must give reports on Wednesday?

(A) George and Lenore   (A)

(B) Helen and Nina   (B)

(C) Irving and Robert   (C)

(D) Kyle and Nina   (D)

(E) Olivia and Kyle   (E)

Here's How to Crack It

Let's treat this like a General question since it is a bit twisted. Our deduction doesn't really apply since we are looking only at W. First, let's use our rules and some prior work to eliminate answers. G can be only on T, so get rid of (A). We know from question 4 that H and N could be together on W, so let's hold on to this one (you don't want to lock in an answer on a Must Be True question unless you are positive that it will always occur). We see from the flexibility in question 4 that I and R could pair together on Monday. Since they are paired on a day other than Wednesday, eliminate (C). From our first play in question 5 we saw that K and N could be paired together on T, so get rid of (D). We don't have any prior work that helps us with (E), so skip that one. We will have to play one of these remaining answer choices. Since this is a Must Be True question, we want to try to see if an answer could be false. Let's look at (B). If we put H and N on M or T, then rule 3 will apply. Since H is with N, there is no way to pair N with H on a day other than W. This must be true, so choose (B).

Now that we have wrapped up five games, we want to provide you with one last technique that will aid you in moving through the games sections with a maximum of accuracy and efficiency.

Games Technique: Ranking and Ordering Your Games

To be successful in a Games section, it is important to be able to predict the relative difficulty of the games before you get started. How can you tell? There are several things to look for after you've read through the setup and clues.

Start with the relationship between the elements and the places to which they'll be assigned. In an Ordering game, you want a one-to-one correspondence between elements and slots. In a Grouping game, by definition, there will be more than one element in each group. In this case, you want to know if there is a set number of elements per group. If there are multiple distributions, the game is more complicated than if everything is determined at the outset. Pure In/Out games usually do not have big deductions, but if they have several complex conditional clues, they may be more time-consuming.

Next, you'll want to ask two important questions: can we leave out any elements? Can any elements be repeated? If the answer to either or both of those questions is yes, the game will be more complicated. Remember that whenever elements can be left out, you should add an "Out" column so that you have a place to put them.

Historically, the LSAT Games section has had two easier games and two harder games. Ideally, you want to identify and work the two easier games first. Approaching the games in a "workable" order is the most powerful tool you have for doing well on this section. Even if you're working all four games, it still makes sense to leave the one that looks worst for last. The easiest and quickest way to order your section is to read the setup and the clues for each of the first two games only. Don't work with your pen; just evaluate each to see whether you know how to diagram them and whether the clues look familiar and straightforward, or intricate and complicated. You should be able to tell how many twists (if any) the test-writers have put into each game.

You'll probably find that you have a preference for one of the games over the other. If you do, dive into the one you prefer. In the rare case in which both games look awful, you can navigate to the other two games, but you don't want to spend a ton of time previewing. Get to work as soon as possible.

Once you've finished the first game, evaluate the next two games. At this point, decide which of the three remaining games you'd rather work next. You may decide to go back to one of the first ones you saw, but usually you'll find that one of the second pair looks pretty approachable. It might even be easier than the first one you worked. Now that you're warmed up, you should be able to tear through it with confidence.

No matter how many games you see, there may be some that initially look innocuous but turn out to be harder than you expect. Don't let these make you anxious though. With a bit of experience, you should have no trouble identifying a tricky game.

There are things you can look for that may suggest difficulty: uncertainty about the diagram is a big one. Still, you may have a diagram solidly in mind and encounter problems once you begin working the questions. If this happens to you on the LSAT, don't panic—and, especially, don't abandon ship! Many games start slowly, but if you keep going, you will realize that not all of the questions are equally tough. Remember that there is always more you can do, even if it's just generating an example to eliminate that next answer choice. Games become better only when you work with them one step at a time and remain calm! Don't just stare, and don't give up.

Selecting games is important, but don't feel like something's gone wrong if the first game you work doesn't seem that easy once you're into it. No one is 100 percent reliable at predicting a game's difficulty. If the first one you work takes you a little while, chances are that there are one or two other games on the section that will take you less time. Remain calm, keep working, and look for an easy game to do next so you can make up time.

TECHNIQUE DRILL: RANKING AND ORDERING GAMES

Take a moment to flip back through the manual and rank the games that you worked in Lessons 2–5. We will provide a few lines for you to justify your response. After you have done so, we will provide you with our recommendation for the order you should work these games in had they all appeared on a single LSAT section. Ultimately, ranking and ordering games is subject to personal biases and interests. However, there are usually clear now games (super easy) and clear later games. You can find Game 2 on pages 176–177, Game 3 on pages 200–201, Game 4 on pages 228–229, and Game 5 on pages 248–249.

First Game (circle one):   Lesson 2   Lesson 3   Lesson 4   Lesson 5

Why?: _____

_____

_____

Second Game (circle one):   Lesson 2   Lesson 3   Lesson 4   Lesson 5

Why?: _____

_____

_____

Third Game (circle one):   Lesson 2   Lesson 3   Lesson 4   Lesson 5

Why?: _____

_____

_____

Fourth Game (circle one):   Lesson 2   Lesson 3   Lesson 4   Lesson 5

Why?: _____

_____

_____

Cracking the Ranking Drill

This is our order. Yours may have been different from ours in some small ways. As long as you have clear justifications for your choices and you are consciously thinking about your order, you should be fine.

First game: Lesson 3. This is a very straightforward 1D Grouping game. It also has some ordering elements bringing it into familiar territory. The clues are standard block, antiblock, and conditionals.

Second game: Lesson 2. This is a 2D Ordering game and elements repeat making it more challenging than the 1D Grouping game. In spite of this, as long as you keep track of the different dimensions, this game is not that challenging. The clues are pretty clear and easy to diagram.

Third game: Lesson 4. Many students strongly dislike In/Out games because they struggle with conditional statements. However, if you understand (or even enjoy) conditionals, this may have been earlier in your ranking. However, we put this game here because it is a 1D In/Out game. Among In/Out games, this one is easier than most. There are only a small number of elements. The clues are mostly standard, non-confusing conditionals. As long as you understand how conditional statements work, a game similar to this one should pose few problems on the actual exam.

Fourth game: Lesson 5. This shouldn't be a surprise to any of you. Just as lesson 3 was a clear winner for easiest game, this is a clear "winner" for hardest game. The complexity of the diagram, the extra elements, the 2D nature of the game, and the twisted conditional all combine to make this game quite challenging. Even if you are pacing at the 4 game pace on the test, save a game like this one for last on the exam.

PUTTING IT ALL TOGETHER

That's it for your five-lesson foray into the LSAT Games section. It is time to combine what you have learned and try your hand at four games in a row. Before you begin this section, we recommend reviewing your notes, the process, and the techniques from each lesson. Make sure that you understand the approach for all games and question types. Take the time to work the games in the most efficient order possible. In the answer key, we will provide a ranking for these games as well as the way to crack it. Don't flip to the answers until you have worked all four games.

If you want, you can measure the time it takes you to do each game. By measure, we mean set your timer to count up, and then turn it away so that you can't see the clock as you work on the game. Put the timer in a drawer or in another room if necessary. When you're done, stop the clock and note how long it took you to complete the game and then see how accurate you were. This will help you figure out approximately how long it takes you to do a game accurately, and by extension, how many games you can reasonably expect to get through on a given section.

Games Practice Drill

Answers can be found in Chapter 8.

GAME 1

This Game and its questions are from PrepTest 44, Section 3, Game 3, Questions 13–17.

<u>Questions 1–5</u>

A tour group plans to visit exactly five archaeological sites. Each site was discovered by exactly one of the following archaeologists—Ferrara, Gallagher, Oliphant—and each dates from the eighth, ninth, or tenth century (a.d.). The tour must satisfy the following conditions:

    The site visited second dates from the ninth century.
    Neither the site visited fourth nor the site visited fifth was discovered by Oliphant.
    Exactly one of the sites was discovered by Gallagher, and it dates from the tenth century.
    If a site dates from the eighth century, it was discovered by Oliphant.
    The site visited third dates from a more recent century than does either the site visited first or that visited fourth.

1. Which one of the following could be an accurate list of the discoverers of the five sites, listed in the order in which the sites are visited?

  (A) Oliphant, Oliphant, Gallagher, Oliphant, Ferrara

  (B) Gallagher, Oliphant, Ferrara, Ferrara, Ferrara

  (C) Oliphant, Gallagher, Oliphant, Ferrara, Ferrara

  (D) Oliphant, Oliphant, Gallagher, Ferrara, Gallagher

  (E) Ferrara, Oliphant, Gallagher, Ferrara, Ferrara

2. If exactly one of the five sites the tour group visits dates from the tenth century, then which one of the following CANNOT be a site that was discovered by Ferrara?

  (A) the site visited first

  (B) the site visited second

  (C) the site visited third

  (D) the site visited fourth

  (E) the site visited fifth

3. Which one of the following could be a site that dates from the eighth century?

  (A) the site visited first

  (B) the site visited second

  (C) the site visited third

  (D) the site visited fourth

  (E) the site visited fifth

4. Which one of the following is a complete and accurate list of the sites each of which CANNOT be the site discovered by Gallagher?

(A) third, fourth, fifth

(B) second, third, fourth

(C) first, fourth, fifth

(D) first, second, fifth

(E) first, second, fourth

(A) (B) (C) (D) (E)

5. The tour group could visit at most how many sites that were discovered by Ferrara?

(A) one

(B) two

(C) three

(D) four

(E) five

(A) (B) (C) (D) (E)

GAME 2

This Game and its questions are from PrepTest 45, Section 3, Game 2, Questions 7–12.

Questions 6–11

Exactly six people—Lulu, Nam, Ofelia, Pachai, Santiago, and Tyrone—are the only contestants in a chess tournament. The tournament consists of four games, played one after the other. Exactly two people play in each game, and each person plays in at least one game. The following conditions must apply:

Tyrone does not play in the first or third game.
Lulu plays in the last game.
Nam plays in only one game and it is not against Pachai.
Santiago plays in exactly two games, one just before and one just after the only game that Ofelia plays in.

6. Which one of the following could be an accurate list of the contestants who play in each of the four games?

(A) first game: Pachai, Santiago; second game: Ofelia, Tyrone; third game: Pachai, Santiago; fourth game: Lulu, Nam   (A)

(B) first game: Lulu, Nam; second game: Pachai, Santiago; third game: Ofelia, Tyrone; fourth game: Lulu, Santiago   (B)

(C) first game: Pachai, Santiago; second game: Lulu, Tyrone; third game: Nam, Ofelia; fourth game: Lulu, Nam   (C)

(D) first game: Nam, Santiago; second game: Nam, Ofelia; third game: Pachai, Santiago; fourth game: Lulu, Tyrone   (D)

(E) first game: Lulu, Nam; second game: Santiago, Tyrone; third game: Lulu, Ofelia; fourth game: Pachai, Santiago   (E)

7. Which one of the following contestants could play in two consecutive games?

(A) Lulu   (A)

(B) Nam   (B)

(C) Ofelia   (C)

(D) Santiago   (D)

(E) Tyrone   (E)

8. If Tyrone plays in the fourth game, then which one of the following could be true?

(A) Nam plays in the second game.   (A)

(B) Ofelia plays in the third game.   (B)

(C) Santiago plays in the second game.   (C)

(D) Nam plays a game against Lulu.   (D)

(E) Pachai plays a game against Lulu.   (E)

9. Which one of the following could be true?

(A) Pachai plays against Lulu in the first game.   (A)

(B) Pachai plays against Nam in the second game.   (B)

(C) Santiago plays against Ofelia in the second game.   (C)

(D) Pachai plays against Lulu in the third game.   (D)

(E) Nam plays against Santiago in the fourth game.   (E)

10. Which one of the following is a complete and accurate list of the contestants who CANNOT play against Tyrone in any game?

(A) Lulu, Pachai

(B) Nam, Ofelia

(C) Nam, Pachai

(D) Nam, Santiago

(E) Ofelia, Pachai

Ⓐ Ⓑ Ⓒ Ⓓ Ⓔ

11. If Ofelia plays in the third game, which one of the following must be true?

(A) Lulu plays in the third game.

(B) Nam plays in the third game.

(C) Pachai plays in the first game.

(D) Pachai plays in the third game.

(E) Tyrone plays in the second game.

Ⓐ Ⓑ Ⓒ Ⓓ Ⓔ

GAME 3

This Game and its questions are from PrepTest 44, Section 3, Game 1, Questions 1–6.

Questions 12–17

In the course of one month Garibaldi has exactly seven different meetings. Each of her meetings is with exactly one of five foreign dignitaries: Fuentes, Matsuba, Rhee, Soleimani, or Tbahi. The following constraints govern Garibaldi's meetings:

She has exactly three meetings with Fuentes, and exactly one with each of the other dignitaries.

She does not have any meetings in a row with Fuentes.

Her meeting with Soleimani is the very next one after her meeting with Tbahi.

Neither the first nor last of her meetings is with Matsuba.

12. Which one of the following could be the sequence of the meetings Garibaldi has with the dignitaries?

(A) Fuentes, Rhee, Tbahi, Soleimani, Fuentes, Matsuba, Rhee

(B) Fuentes, Tbahi, Soleimani, Matsuba, Fuentes, Fuentes, Rhee

(C) Fuentes, Rhee, Fuentes, Matsuba, Fuentes, Tbahi, Soleimani

(D) Fuentes, Tbahi, Matsuba, Fuentes, Soleimani, Rhee, Fuentes

(E) Fuentes, Tbahi, Soleimani, Fuentes, Rhee, Fuentes, Matsuba

13. If Garibaldi's last meeting is with Rhee, then which one of the following could be true?

(A) Garibaldi's second meeting is with Soleimani.

(B) Garibaldi's third meeting is with Matsuba.

(C) Garibaldi's fourth meeting is with Soleimani.

(D) Garibaldi's fifth meeting is with Matsuba.

(E) Garibaldi's sixth meeting is with Soleimani.

14. If Garibaldi's second meeting is with Fuentes, then which one of the following is a complete and accurate list of the dignitaries with any one of whom Garibaldi's fourth meeting could be?

(A) Fuentes, Soleimani, Rhee

(B) Matsuba, Rhee, Tbahi

(C) Matsuba, Soleimani

(D) Rhee, Tbahi

(E) Fuentes, Soleimani

15. If Garibaldi's meeting with Rhee is the very next one after Garibaldi's meeting with Soleimani, then which one of the following must be true?

(A) Garibaldi's third meeting is with Fuentes.

(B) Garibaldi's fourth meeting is with Rhee.

(C) Garibaldi's fifth meeting is with Fuentes.

(D) Garibaldi's sixth meeting is with Rhee.

(E) Garibaldi's seventh meeting is with Fuentes.

16. If Garibaldi's first meeting is with Tbahi, then Garibaldi's meeting with Rhee could be the

(A) second meeting

(B) third meeting

(C) fifth meeting

(D) sixth meeting

(E) seventh meeting

Ⓐ

Ⓑ

Ⓒ

Ⓓ

Ⓔ

17. If Garibaldi's meeting with Matsuba is the very next meeting after Garibaldi's meeting with Rhee, then with which one of the following dignitaries must Garibaldi's fourth meeting be?

(A) Fuentes

(B) Matsuba

(C) Rhee

(D) Soleimani

(E) Tbahi

Ⓐ

Ⓑ

Ⓒ

Ⓓ

Ⓔ

GAME 4

This Game and its questions are from PrepTest 45, Section 3, Game 4, Questions 18–22.

Questions 18–22

The Export Alliance consists of exactly three nations: Nation X, Nation Y, and Nation Z. Each nation in the Alliance exports exactly two of the following five crops: oranges, rice, soybeans, tea, and wheat. Each of these crops is exported by at least one of the nations in the Alliance. The following conditions hold:

> None of the nations exports both wheat and oranges.
> Nation X exports soybeans if, but only if, Nation Y does also.
> If Nation Y exports rice, then Nations X and Z both export tea.
> Nation Y does not export any crop that Nation Z exports.

18. Which one of the following could be an accurate list, for each of the nations, of the crops it exports?

   (A) Nation X: oranges, rice; Nation Y: oranges, tea; Nation Z: soybeans, wheat

   (B) Nation X: oranges, tea; Nation Y: oranges, rice; Nation Z: soybeans, wheat

   (C) Nation X: oranges, wheat; Nation Y: oranges, tea; Nation Z: rice, soybeans

   (D) Nation X: rice, wheat; Nation Y: oranges, tea; Nation Z: oranges, soybeans

   (E) Nation X: soybeans, rice; Nation Y: oranges, tea; Nation Z: soybeans, wheat

19. If Nation X exports soybeans and tea, then which one of the following could be true?

   (A) Nation Y exports oranges.

   (B) Nation Y exports rice.

   (C) Nation Y exports tea.

   (D) Nation Z exports soybeans.

   (E) Nation Z exports tea.

20. If Nation Z exports tea and wheat, then which one of the following must be true?

   (A) Nation X exports oranges.

   (B) Nation X exports tea.

   (C) Nation X exports wheat.

   (D) Nation Y exports rice.

   (E) Nation Y exports soybeans.

21. It CANNOT be the case that both Nation X and Nation Z export which one of the following crops?

   (A) oranges

   (B) rice

   (C) soybeans

   (D) tea

   (E) wheat

22. Which one of the following pairs CANNOT be the two crops that Nation Y exports?

(A)   oranges and rice   (A̶)

(B)   oranges and soybeans   (B̶)

(C)   rice and tea   (C̶)

(D)   rice and wheat   (D̶)

(E)   soybeans and wheat   (E̶)

Game 1 Self-Assessment

Steps 1–3 Assessment

Steps 4–6 Assessment

Game 2 Self-Assessment

Steps 1–3 Assessment

Steps 4–6 Assessment

Game 3 Self-Assessment

Steps 1–3 Assessment

Steps 4–6 Assessment

Game 4 Self-Assessment

Steps 1–3 Assessment

Steps 4–6 Assessment

Summary

Here's a list of the major ideas and strategies for the Games section.

- ○ Pacing and Selection
  - • If you're getting fewer than 12 questions right on the Games section, focus on two games; if you're getting fewer than 18 questions right, focus on three games.
  - • Look for games with familiar clues, a one-to-one correspondence, and concrete questions; avoid games with difficult diagrams, vague clues, and Complex questions.

- ○ Step 1: Diagram and Inventory
  - • The elements are the mobile pieces in a game; don't forget to list them in an inventory near your diagram.
  - • When elements come with two types of fixed characteristics, use uppercase and lowercase letters to distinguish them; if uppercase and lowercase are not appropriate, use subscripts.
  - • Always keep track of the rules for using elements: can they be used more than once? Do all of them have to be used?
  - • To diagram the game, look for what stays the same. If it isn't clear what stays the same, be sure to inspect the clues for ideas.
  - • If the game asks you to put the elements in order, the ordered collection (days of the week, times, positions from right to left) will usually serve as the core of your diagram.
  - • If an Ordering game asks you to put more than one thing at each time/position, stack your boxes into tiers or use a chart.
  - • If a game asks you to arrange elements spatially, draw a picture of the space and use that as your diagram. Keep your pictures small so you don't have to erase.
  - • A Grouping game asks you to put the elements into collections of some sort; Grouping games usually include clues that can be easily translated as blocks or antiblocks.
  - • An In/Out game asks you to choose some of the elements but not others; these are similar to Grouping games, but the "Out" column may not obey the same rules as the "In" column.
  - • Hybrid games may combine two or more of the tasks described; construct the diagram for a hybrid game by fusing together the diagrams appropriate for each task. If one task is more important than another, make that one the core of your diagram.

o   Step 2: Symbolize the Clues and Double-Check
  •   Remember the three Cs: *clear, concise,* and *consistent.* Symbols should be visual (if possible), easily understood, and should match your diagram.
  •   Range clues talk about the order in which elements must appear, but they don't indicate a fixed amount of space that must appear between the elements.
  •   Block clues indicate a fixed relationship. In Ordering games, they show the precise position of elements relative to one another; in other games, they indicate elements that must appear in the same area of the diagram.
  •   Antiblock clues are the opposite of blocks; they show elements that can't appear together.
  •   Conditional clues tell you what happens if a particular condition is met; we symbolize them with arrows because they can be read only from left to right. DON'T GO AGAINST THE ARROW.
  •   The contrapositive of a conditional clue is formed by flipping the order of the statements around the arrow and negating each one; this is the only certain deduction that can be made from a conditional clue. When you symbolize a conditional clue, symbolize its contrapositive right away.
  •   Conditional clues most often include the words "if," "only," or "unless." Each of these must be translated into symbols in slightly different ways; make sure you know these methods.
  •   Wherever possible, symbolize clues directly on or above your diagram.
  •   Double-check by going against the grain: look at each clue, express its meaning in your own words, and look for a listed clue that means the same thing; once you find it, check the clue off in the original list. Before you move on, make sure all of the clues are checked.

o   Step 3: Make Deductions and Size Up the Game
  •   Deductions improve efficiency by saving you time on the questions; look for them, but don't get bogged down.
  •   Repeated elements often provide the opportunity for deductions: if an element is mentioned in two or more clues, try to combine the information to arrive at a new fact.
  •   Combine clues, when possible, into a single symbol. This is particularly useful on Ordering games.
  •   Large clues, such as blocks or range clues containing multiple elements, are often a good source of deductions. There may be only a few ways you can fit a large clue into your diagram.

- General clues—clues that pertain to many elements and to many places in the diagram—often yield deductions when they are applied to specific items of information within the diagram.
- When a clue mentions numbers—the number of elements in a group, for example, or the number of times an element can be used—be on the lookout for distribution deductions. You may have to try several possibilities to learn that only certain distributions are possible.
- Before you move to the questions, ask yourself "What's the most restricted part of this game? What's the least restricted? What's likely to be the most useful clue?"

○ Step 4: Assess the Question
- A Grab-a-Rule question has answer choices that are complete listings of where the elements go. If a game has this type of question, it will appear first; you should work it first.
- A Specific question adds information to the rules initially given for the game; this new rule applies only to that question. Work Specific questions on your first pass through the game, except for those you identify as Complex.
- A General question asks you to deal with the game as-is, without offering further information. Work these on your second pass through the game.
- A Complex question has a vague, open-ended, or difficult task. Work through these on your second pass through the game.

○ Step 5: Act
- On a Specific question, follow this process: symbolize the new information; often this can be done right in a new line of your diagram. Then deduce everything you can from it. In many cases, this will get you directly to the answer. If it doesn't, then you should begin POE.
- If a General question asks you about something in your initial deductions, you may be able to answer it right away. Most often, you'll have to use POE.

o   Step 6: Using POE
  •   For a Grab-a-Rule question, begin by eliminating anything that obviously doesn't fit your de-
     ductions. Then take one rule at a time, scanning the answer choices and eliminating those that
     don't follow the rule. When there's only one left, pick it and move on.
  •   For General questions, use your prior work to find examples and counterexamples to help you
     with POE. This can save you a great deal of time and effort.
  •   For Could Be True and Must Be False questions, try to make the choice you're working on true.
  •   For Must Be True and Could Be False questions, try to make the choice you're working on false.
  •   Remember that the goal on all games questions is to find either the one right answer or the four
     wrong answers, but not both. Your goal is to work carefully and accurately. Trust your work.

Chapter 4
Reading Comprehension

The Reading Comprehension section, as you might suspect, consists of long, fairly complex passages, each accompanied by a series of questions about that passage. The passages span quite a range in subject matter, but typically there's one from each of the following areas: arts/humanities, social sciences, natural sciences, and law. You do not need any prior knowledge of any of these areas to be able to answer the questions.

In this chapter, we will walk through the basics of taking apart Reading Comprehension passages and answering each type of Reading Comprehension question, with a special focus on the skills and techniques specific to the newer comparative question types.

WHAT IS READING COMPREHENSION?

"Reading Comprehension" sounds pretty straightforward, doesn't it? But, this is the LSAT, so it isn't quite as simple as it may seem. One way in which the test-writers make the section more challenging is how they construct the passage texts. Most of the time, the LSAT writers will take material from a book or journal and then adapt it to make it suitable for testing purposes. What does "adapt" mean? Because you're not supposed to need outside information to be able to understand the passage, the test-writers must remove any material that would require a deeper understanding of the subject beyond the limits of the passage. On one hand, this is a great advantage. Everything you need to know in order to answer the questions is right there in the passage. On the other hand, when they make these edits, much of the transitional material that made the original text more readable is taken out as well. What you're left with is often a pretty dense passage, chock full of details, with choppy or sometimes even nonexistent transitions from one subject to the next.

What's on This Section?

The Reading Comprehension section contains four passages (three single passages and one set of dual passages). Each passage has five to eight questions attached to it, for a total of 26 to 28 questions. The passages are typically between 55 and 65 lines long.

Before we begin, take a moment to read the instructions to this section.

> Directions: Each set of questions in this section is based on a single passage or a pair of passages. The questions are to be answered on the basis of what is **stated** or **implied** in the passage or pair of passages. For some questions, more than one of the choices could conceivably answer the question. However, you are to choose the **best** answer; that is, choose the response that most accurately and completely answers the question.

These are the directions that will appear on your LSAT. As usual on the LSAT, the official directions provide very little help. Review them now. They will not change. Don't waste time reading them in the test room.

What Does This Section Test?

Reading Comprehension tests your ability to not only find details scattered throughout the passage, but also to answer questions about the logic of the author's argument, or to apply new information given in the questions to what is already presented in the passage. And, because of the intense time pressure of the section, it also tests your ability to manage these tasks in the most efficient way possible.

Why Is This Section on the LSAT?

Reading Comprehension is on the LSAT to test your ability to read carefully and manage large amounts of information in a short period of time. This section also tests your ability to answer questions about a passage without bringing in any information from outside the passage.

READING COMPREHENSION: SECTION-WIDE STRATEGIES

First, let's go through the general strategies that will allow you to take control of the section as a whole. In the following portions of the chapter, we'll break down your step-by-step strategies for attacking each passage in the section.

It's Your Section: Prioritize

Choose Your Passages

The people who write this test are not your friends. Therefore, they may not give you the easiest passage first or the hardest passage last. Fortunately, you don't have to work the passages in the order that they appear. It is important to take a few seconds to assess the difficulty level of a passage before you dive in. Quickly read the first few sentences to get a sense of how tough the passage text will be, and glance over the questions. Abstract, theoretical language and ideas will make a passage hard to understand, while concrete and descriptive passages will be much easier to follow. Long question stems and answer choices, as well as questions that ask you to apply new information to the passage, will usually be much more challenging than short and straightforward questions. Don't overreact to unfamiliar topics; remember that all the information you need to answer the questions will be included right there in the passage text. Given that you're planning to apply to law school, a passage on some law-related theme might be of greater interest, but if it is written in a very abstract manner or about complicated legal theories, that doesn't necessarily mean that it will be easier to read and understand. Likewise, a science passage might not be familiar territory, but the language and ideas may be very direct and the questions themselves could be quite straightforward.

> **Here's What to Look for When You're Evaluating the Difficulty Level of a Passage**
>
> - Level of language and ideas: Passages that have clear, straightforward language and that have concrete, descriptive content will be easier to work than those that have abstract language and ideas.
> - Sentence structure: Long, convoluted sentences don't bode well. Nor do long paragraphs, which probably contain multiple themes which will take some effort to separate from each other. Short, declarative sentences and shorter paragraphs will probably be easier to comprehend.
> - Questions and answer choices: Scan the questions. Do you notice a lot of Reasoning questions? How long are the question stems and answer choices? Passages with long questions and lots of Reasoning questions will probably be more difficult to attack.

Some students also think that the number of questions a passage has should determine if and when they should attempt it. But if a really difficult passage has more questions, that doesn't mean that it will be any easier to get those questions right. In fact, you may end up sacrificing a lot of your time struggling through those questions, getting a high percentage of them wrong, causing you to miss out on an easier passage where you may be able to get all of those easier questions correct.

However, if two passages appear to be of equal difficulty, feel free to go for the one with more questions. All in all, if a passage looks especially formidable, nobody says that you have to do it now, or at all. Leave the hardest passage for last, or randomly guess on it and spend your time getting the other questions right.

Control Your Own Question Ordering

Just as you have control over which passages you do and when you do them, there is no need to complete the questions in the same order in which the test-writers happen to give them to you. Does the third question look especially formidable? Move past it and come back once you've worked the others on that passage. Are you having a horrible time deciding between two answer choices? Pick the one that looked right to you the first time, move on, and come back to that question one more time before going on to the next passage. You'd be amazed what a few minutes away from a question that's giving you trouble can do to clear your head. However, don't get bogged down on one question, reading it over and over. If you are really stuck, take your best shot and move on.

Your mantra: *I will remember that I am in control of the section. If a passage or question seems likely to be especially difficult, I will move past it. If a question frustrates me, I will work on a different one and return to it later with a fresh perspective. If I am still stuck, I will pick the most likely choice and move on.*

Take Control of the Passage: Read Actively

Reading Comprehension is probably the section of the test that feels the most familiar; you have been reading things and answering questions about those things for most of your life. However, doing well on LSAT Reading Comprehension requires reading in a way that is different from how you handle material for school, work, personal enjoyment, or even for other standardized tests. Too many test-takers read the passage the first time through like a text book, scrutinizing every word and trying to remember all of the details. This approach uses up too much of your limited time. You gain points by correctly answering the questions, not by memorizing the passage. Going back to the passage to find details once you know that you need them to answer a question or to make a tough decision between two answer choices isn't wasted time; it's what Reading Comprehension is all about.

However, you do need to have a basic understanding of the author's argument in the passage in order to effectively address the questions. This involves knowing where key ideas are located, understanding the logical structure of the passage, and defining the purpose of the passage as a whole. Each passage has several big ideas, which will be illustrated or expanded upon. As you read, actively separate the core ideas, or claims, from the evidence used to support those claims. Focus your energy on identifying and understanding the claims, and leave the details for later (if and when they become necessary for answering the questions). The passage isn't going anywhere; if a question asks you for a detail that you skimmed over, you can always go back to find it. If you feel yourself getting bogged down, don't read troublesome text multiple times. Instead, push forward and keep an eye out for something else that helps you understand the content or purpose of that confusing part of the passage. Most fundamentally, as you read you should think about how the major claims relate to each other and how they finally add up to the main point and purpose, or bottom line, of the entire passage.

Many people find it useful to quickly preview the questions before reading the passage. This can help you decide which parts of the passage to read more carefully, and which sections you can skim through more quickly.

Your mantra: *I will get through the passage efficiently, concentrating on the big ideas and logical structure, leaving the details for later.*

Select an Answer on Every Question

Each question will appear on screen individually. When you're confident you've found the credited response, select your answer and move to the next screen. If you aren't sure of an answer, be sure to flag the question so you can return to answer it later. If you don't think you'll have time to return to the question, POE as many choices as you can and select one from the remaining choices. Flag it so you can return if you have time and move on to the next screen.

Your mantra: *I will select an answer for every question and flag questions that I skip for the time being.*

Breathe

After you've completed each passage, take three deep breaths. You've cleared your mind, and you're ready to push on to the next passage.

Your mantra: *I will take time after each passage I complete to take some deep breaths.*

Here Are Your Reading Comprehension Mantras

I will remember that I am in control of the section. If a passage or question is difficult, I will move past it to work on a different one. I'll come back later with a fresh perspective. If I am still stuck, I will pick the most likely choice and move on.

I will get through the passage efficiently, concentrating on the big ideas and logical structure, leaving the details for later.

I will select an answer for every question and flag questions that I skip for the time being.

I will take time after each passage I complete to take some deep breaths.

Pro Tip
Previewing the questions before working the passage is an optional step, but it works very well for many students. See the section on "Refining Your Skills" for some more guidance.

READING COMPREHENSION: A STEP-BY-STEP PROCESS

The next several sections of this chapter will give you a four-step process for attacking each Reading Comprehension passage. First, let's run through an overview of the steps, and then we will break down each step in detail, with guided practice so that you can see what each part of the process looks like in practice.

Step 1: Prepare the Passage

Here are the basics of preparing a passage:

A. Preview the questions, looking for lead words that tell you what parts of the passage will be especially relevant.
B. Work the passage efficiently, focusing on the main claims made by the author.
C. Annotate the passage, highlighting key words that relate to the question topics or that provide clues to the structure and tone of the author's argument, and making brief notes on scratch paper.
D. Define the Bottom Line of the passage as a whole: the main point, purpose, and tone of the text.

Step 2: Assess the Question

Translate exactly what each question is asking you to do with or to the passage.

Step 3: Act

Just as some games questions require you to make new deductions before you attack the answers, or some arguments questions are best answered by first identifying or analyzing certain aspects of the paragraph, most reading comprehension questions are most accurately and efficiently attacked by doing some work with the passage text before looking at a single answer choice.

Step 4: Answer

Use a combination of your understanding of the question and of the relevant part or parts of the passage to use Process of Elimination on the answer choices.

This probably all sounds a bit abstract so far, so now let's break down each step in more concrete and practical terms.

Step 1: Prepare the Passage

Why?

You would never attempt the questions on an LSAT game without setting up the game, or try to answer an Arguments question without analyzing the argument first. The same applies to a Reading Comprehension passage. In your first read-through of the passage, you are laying the groundwork for the process of answering the questions. If you have little or no understanding of the passage text before you begin attacking the questions, your efficiency and accuracy will suffer. However, if you plod through the passage text, paying close attention to every single word, trying to understand and memorize every minor statement, you will be overwhelmed by the mass of information, not get what you really need out of the text, and take too much time away from the crucial process of actually answering the questions. Your goal is to spend 3–5 minutes on your first reading of the passage. Much more than that, and you won't have time to do the work you need to do while answering the questions.

Too many students fail to work on and refine their skills in working the passage and keep making the same kinds of mistakes on the questions without realizing that those mistakes track back to problems with how they worked the passage in the first place. Remember—yes, this is essentially an open-book test in that all the information you need is there in the passage. But, you wouldn't go into an open-book test in a class without having a good sense of how your materials and notes are organized and where you will be able to find the relevant information you need to answer the questions.

How: Principles of Active Reading

Find the Main Point of Each Paragraph   As you read through each paragraph for the first time, focus on separating out the major claims made by the author from the evidence used to support those claims. It is those main claims that will tell you what the author is trying to communicate in each paragraph and through the passage as a whole. Much of the supportive evidence will be unnecessary for answering the questions, but if you need it, when you have read the passage actively and with focus, you will know where to find it.

Authors use words purposefully to help you to understand what they are writing. Yes, the LSAC writers often edit passage texts to make them difficult to follow and understand, but they leave in a lot of clues as well. Use those clues to your advantage, and you will give yourself an excellent foundation for attacking the questions.

Let's take a look at a sample paragraph.

> The classic defining work of social choice theory is Ken Arrow's careful investigation of voting through a series of thought experiments. The result—Arrow's Impossibility Theorem—indicated that no method of conducting a majority decision vote can be guaranteed to conform to the basic requirements of democracy. A simple example illustrates Arrow's idea: For an electorate of three voters—1, 2, and 3—there are three candidates—A, B, and C. Voter 1 prefers A to B, and B to C; voter 2 prefers B to C and C to A; voter 3 prefers C to A and A to B. In such an electorate, a runoff between A and B declares A the winner; a runoff between B and C is won by B, and a runoff between A and C is won by C. Therefore, whichever candidate wins, that candidate is actually less preferable to the electorate than the candidate that was not involved in the runoff.

What is really important here, in terms of getting a basic understanding of the author's main point in this paragraph? (And, was that example really so simple?) The main claims are (1) that Arrow's work is central to social choice theory, and (2) that he suggested that this method of voting elects a candidate that no one actually prefers, and (3) that Arrow believes this is non-democratic. So, what wording tells you what to pay attention to, and what to move through more quickly on your first reading of the passage? The first sentence gives you your first clue: "The classic defining work of social choice theory." Right there, the author is telling you: "This is important, pay attention!" The second sentence tells you what the result of Arrows investigation was, which is why his work was so important. But then the author says: "A simple example...," which alerts you to the fact that what follows will just be further illustration of what you already know: that Arrow believes that "no method of conducting a majority decision vote can be guaranteed to conform to the basic requirements of democracy." So, skim thorough all those complicated details—if a question asks you about the mechanics of the whole thing, you know exactly where to find them. Notice one more key word: "Therefore." This conclusion indicator tells you "slow down again, here comes something else important." And, this is the final main claim in the passage; it tells you why Arrow believes that the results are undemocratic—the winner of the election is not the one preferred by the electorate.

So, what is the author's main point in this paragraph? "Arrow's work suggesting the non-democratic nature of majority-decision voting is central to social choice theory." That's really all you need to get out of this paragraph before you move on to the next.

Fit the Pieces Together and Find the Bottom Line   So, you now know what this paragraph is all about, but what about the passage as a whole? Do you know at this point that the main point of this paragraph is the central point of the entire passage? Of course not; you have to see what the author says next, and how it relates to what you just read.

Imagine that the next paragraph begins, "However, recent research has called the basic premises of Social Choice Theory into question." That word "However" and what follows tells you that now the passage may be going in a very different direction. As you read that next chunk of passage, then, go through the same process of finding the main claims and tracking the argument the author is making. Pay especially close attention to any words or phrases that indicate the author's attitude or opinion. From the first paragraph, you know that the author thinks Arrow's thought experiment was "careful," and that those who believe in Social Choice Theory agree with Arrow's results. Does that guarantee that the author agrees as well? Certainly not, and the beginning of this next paragraph indicates that the author may be about to describe some flaws in Arrows work or ideas. If you keep tracking those main claims through the passage, you will know what the author's central point and purpose is; that is, the Bottom Line of the passage as a whole. That will give you an excellent basis on which to answer a variety of questions quickly and accurately, and as well to easily identify and avoid trap answers that misrepresent what the author has in fact claimed.

There are certain passage purposes that commonly appear on the LSAT, and being familiar with them can help you fit the pieces together as you read. So, as you read each paragraph and define the Bottom line, ask yourself if the author is doing one of the following.

Telling a Story   These are the passages that sound least like arguments; the author is often simply relating a series of events with a neutral tone. The passage may, for example, describe the development of an artistic style, or the process involved in a scientific discovery, or the progression of a political movement. However, these passages are still made up of "moving parts," each of which performs a particular function. Pay close attention to words that indicate a transition between one event or issue and another. When you are answering the questions, look out for wrong answers that misrepresent the sequence of events or that attribute an inappropriate tone to the author.

Comparing or Contrasting   These passages often compare and/or contrast different theories or points of view. What distinguishes them from passages that defend, advocate, or criticize, is that the authors themselves do not take sides. In your annotation and analysis, pay close attention to the transitions between one side and the other, and to the differences or similarities described. When answering the questions, use your prep work to help you eliminate answers that describe the wrong position or side, or that mistake a similarity for a difference, or vice versa.

Defending or Advocating   In these passages, the author will express a definitive point of view, either defending an idea or policy against its detractors, or making a recommendation about a particular point of view or course of action. As you work the passage, pay close attention to words that indicate the strength of the author's argument and make sure to carefully distinguish the author's position from any opposing positions that might be described. As you answer the questions, use this work to eliminate wrong answers that inaccurately describe the author's tone (often by making it stronger or more extreme) or that confuse the author's point of view with an opposing position.

Criticizing   *Criticize* passages do just that; they say bad things about an idea, policy, or action. What distinguishes them from *Defend/Advocate* passages is that the author does not suggest or recommend an alternative. As you read and annotate the passage, pay close attention to exactly what is being criticized, and how strong the argument is (for example, is the author denouncing something, or rather just pointing out certain drawbacks). As you answer the questions, use your understanding of this logic to eliminate choices that describe supposed author recommendations that the author did not in fact make, answers that mix up what is and is not criticized, and choices that are inappropriate to the strength of the argument in the passage.

Highlight

A big part of active reading involves what your brain is doing as you read—mentally taking control over the material by focusing on what is important and avoiding getting caught up in the quicksand of potentially irrelevant or unnecessary details. Another part of active reading is using your stylus and pen to support your brain—mark up the passage in a way that helps you both to keep your focus and to find information you may need later as you answer the questions. There are two key forms of annotation you should be using:

The highlight and underline tools on the tablet are most helpful on Reading Comprehension. Be sure to practice using these tools consistently!

- making concise notes indicating the main point of each paragraph and the Bottom Line of the passage as a whole on scratch paper
- highlighting or underlining logically important words and phrases

Let's take each of these and break them down further.

1. Notes

We have already talked about how to find the main points and identify the Bottom Line. It is a little too easy, however, to passively read through a passage and think "Yeah, got it" and only realize when you are done with the passage, or trying to answer the questions, that you really didn't "get it" after all, and all you have in your brain are a bunch of disconnected words and ideas. So, make yourself write down at least a few words for each paragraph and for the Bottom Line. And a few words is enough; you are not outlining every little thing that happened in each paragraph, but simply putting those central ideas into a short sentence or phrase. Even if you never look at those notes again, they will have served their main purpose of making you define those core ideas. However, if you are having trouble finding information later on as you answer the questions, those notes will come in very handy, as you can use them to figure out where that information may be hiding.

2. Symbols

There are a few things that deserve extra emphasis: indications of the author's attitude or opinion, any topic sentences or thesis statements that express the main point of a paragraph or of the passage as a whole (keeping in mind that not every paragraph or passage will have one), and, if you are previewing the questions, locations of question topics. Pick a single color of highlighter to mark opinions, thesis statements, or questions topics. If you have previewed the questions, highlight a relevant word or two when you find those topics in the passage. Don't jump out of the passage and answer the question before reading the rest of the passage; by highlighting them, you make them easy to find once to do get to that question, however.

3. Underline text

Use the underline tool to mark text within the passage. Underlining should be limited to things that you have good reason to think are logically important to the author's central points. Here are the key things to underline and why.

A. **Conclusion indicators**
   Words like "therefore," "thus," "hence," or "in conclusion" tell you "this is what all that stuff I was just telling you leads up to." That is, what follows conclusion indicators tend to be major claims that are important for the main points and Bottom Line.

B. **Attitude indicators**
   Tracking and identifying the author's tone is crucial to understanding the author's real position (and to avoiding wrong answers that misrepresent it). Many passages are neutral in tone; the author is simply describing or analyzing something without offering any positive or negative judgment. But, if you see words like "unfortunately" or "sadly" or "thankfully" or "brilliantly," or any other word or phrase that indicates similar ideas, they deserve your close attention.

C. **Changes in direction**
   Difficult passages often have twists and turns, and the questions on these passages will very purposefully test if you have been able to track them accurately. So, if you see words like "however," "but," "on the other hand," "yet," or "in contrast," underline them and think carefully about how what came before that word or phrase logically relates to what comes after, and how it connects to the author's argument as a whole.

4. **Continuations**
   Often authors will make a series of connected points, and to answer the questions, you need to see that they are in fact connected and how. So, when you see words like "furthermore," "additionally," or "moreover," underline them and think about what larger point or claim all those segments of the author's argument relate to. And, when you are going back to the passage to find that part of the argument, use your annotations to make sure that you are taking into account all of the relevant parts of the author's argument.

5. **Lists or sequence indicators**

Often when answering the questions, it is important to know what came first, or last, or sooner, or later. Or, you may need to find a particular item on a list. Underline words like "first, "next," before," and "after" to help yourself answer those questions quickly and accurately.

6. **Example or support indicators**

We already discussed that examples and other kinds of support for larger claims are not particularly important to pay attention to the first time through a passage. But underlining words like "for example" or "because" or "since" has two functions. First, it reassures you that you can in fact find those details later on if you need them (and so helps you move through them more quickly in the moment) and second, it actually helps you find them later if you need them for the questions.

PUTTING IT ALL TOGETHER

So, let's see how it works in practice. Work the passage on the following page as we have just discussed: define the main points and the Bottom Line and make thoughtful and concise annotations. Then turn the page and compare your work to the marked-up passage. That passage will not only have sample annotations, but also explanations of how you ideally should have read through the passage: what questions you should ask yourself as you read, and what deserves more or less attention in the text.

One of the most prolific authors of all time, Isaac Asimov was influential both in science fiction and in the popularization of science during the twentieth century, but he is also justly famous for the scope of his interests. Although the common claim that Asimov is the only author to have written a book in every category of the Dewey decimal system is untrue, its spirit provides an accurate picture of the man: a dedicated humanist who lauded the far-reaching power of reason. His most famous work, the *Foundation* trilogy, can be read as an illustration of Asimov's belief in reason and science, but even while he expressed that belief, science itself was calling it into question.

Foundation describes a time in which a vast empire spanning the galaxy is on the verge of collapse. Its inevitable doom is a consequence not of its size, but of the shortsightedness of its leaders. In this environment, a scientist named Hari Seldon devises an all-encompassing plan to help human civilization recover from the trauma of the empire's coming collapse. Using mathematics, Seldon is able to predict the future course of history for thousands of years, and he takes steps that are geared toward guiding that future in a beneficial direction. The trope of the benevolent and paternalistic scientist shaping existence from behind the scenes, present in much of Asimov's fiction, is never more explicit than in the *Foundation* series, which describes with an epic sweep the course and progress of the Seldon Plan.

As naïve and, perhaps, self-serving as the conceit of *Foundation* may seem to contemporary readers, it retains to some degree its ability to comfort by offering an antidote to the complex and unpredictable nature of experience. Science in Asimov's time was, in popular conceptions, engaged in just this pursuit: discerning immutable laws that operate beneath a surface appearance of contingency, inexplicability, and change. But even while Asimov wrote, science itself was changing. In physics, the study of matter at the subatomic level showed that indeterminacy was not a transitory difficulty to be overcome, but an essential physical principle. In biology, the sense of evolution as a steady progress toward better-adapted forms was being disturbed by proof of a past large-scale evolution taking place in brief explosions of frantic change. At the time of Asimov's death, even mathematics was gaining popular notice for its interest in chaos and inexplicability. Usually summarized in terms of the so-called "butterfly effect," chaos theory showed that perfect prediction could take place only on the basis of perfect information, which was by nature impossible to obtain. Science had dispensed with the very assumptions that motivated Asimov's idealization of it in the Seldon Plan. Indeed, it was possible to see chaos at work in *Foundation* itself: As sequels multiplied and began to be tied into narrative threads from Asimov's other novels, the urge to weave one grand narrative spawned myriad internal inconsistencies that were never resolved.

One of the most prolific authors of all time, Isaac Asimov was influential both in science fiction and in the popularization of science during the twentieth century, but he is also justly famous for the scope of his interests. Although the common claim that Asimov is the only author to have written a book in every category of the Dewey decimal system is untrue, its spirit provides an accurate picture of the man: a dedicated humanist who lauded the far-reaching power of reason. His most famous work, the *Foundation* trilogy, can be read as an illustration of Asimov's belief in reason and science, but even while he expressed that belief, science itself was calling it into question.

Foundation describes a time in which a vast empire spanning the galaxy is on the verge of collapse. Its inevitable doom is a consequence not of its size, but of the shortsightedness of its leaders. In this environment, a scientist named Hari Seldon devises an all-encompassing plan to help human civilization recover from the trauma of the empire's coming collapse. Using mathematics, Seldon is able to predict the future course of history for thousands of years, and he takes steps that are geared toward guiding that future in a beneficial direction. The trope of the benevolent and paternalistic scientist shaping existence from behind the scenes, present in much of Asimov's fiction, is never more explicit than in the *Foundation* series, which describes with an epic sweep the course and progress of the Seldon Plan.

Possible attitude toward IA

Disagreement with common claim

Back to positive

Key change in direction, and introduction of new theme

Description—Don't get bogged down in these details. Keep focus on purpose of author.

Question: "So is the passage likely to be all about the greatness of Asimov's work?"

Answer: "No—there is some inconsistency between Asimov's beliefs and the reality of science."

Main Point: *"IA's work expressed a belief about science and reason that may not be true."*

Question: "Why is the author giving me all of these details about IA's work and themes?"

Answer: "Given the end of P. 1, it's likely that the author will tell me later that they are unrealistic."

Main Point: *"Theme of IA's work—scientists can help save society."*

As <u>naïve and, perhaps, self-serving</u> as the conceit of *Foundation* may seem to contemporary readers, it retains to some degree its <u>ability to comfort</u> by offering an antidote to the complex and unpredictable nature of experience. <u>Science in Asimov's time was, in popular conceptions,</u> engaged in just this pursuit: discerning immutable laws that operate beneath a surface appearance of contingency, inexplicability, and change. But even while Asimov wrote, <u>science itself was changing</u>. In physics, the study of matter at the subatomic level showed that indeterminacy was not a transitory difficulty to be overcome, but an essential physical principle. In biology, the sense of evolution as a steady progress toward better-adapted forms was being disturbed by proof of a past large-scale evolution taking place in brief explosions of frantic change. At the time of Asimov's death, even mathematics was gaining popular notice for its interest in chaos and inexplicability. Usually summarized in terms of the so-called "butterfly effect," chaos theory showed that perfect prediction could take place only on the basis of perfect information, which was by nature impossible to obtain. Science had dispensed with the very assumptions that motivated Asimov's idealization of it in the Seldon Plan. <u>Indeed</u>, it was possible to see chaos at work in *Foundation* itself: As sequels multiplied and began to be tied into narrative threads from Asimov's other novels, <u>the urge to weave one grand narrative spawned myriad internal inconsistencies that were never resolved.</u>

Mildly negative wording, but then back to some positive

Crucial change in direction, and back to theme of end of P. 1

Thesis statement for paragraph

Examples of major claim just made—keep focus on purpose and how this relates to previous paragraphs, not details themselves

Thesis paragraph

Negative about an aspect of IA's work

Question: "So, what does the author really think about Asimov's work and relationship to science?"

Answer: "Science was evolving toward recognition of lack of control, which Asimov himself may have been realizing."

Main Point: *Changes in science in IA's time undermined assumptions of his work.*

Bottom Line of passage: *IA's main work expressed belief that science could be controlled for the good, but new scientific ideas in his own time cast doubt on that assumption.*

Steps 2 and 3: Assess and Act

Once you have prepared the passage, you are ready to assess the questions. Read each question **word for word** to understand exactly what that question is asking you to do. The LSAT writers are quite skilled at finding complicated ways to phrase what could have been a very straightforward question. Always take a moment to paraphrase the question before you take the next step.

Think of the question as setting out a task for you to accomplish. Identifying the question task allows you to define what the correct answer needs to do, and what you need to do with or to the passage in order to find that correct answer as efficiently as possible.

If you can't identify the exact question type in the moment, don't panic; paraphrase the question and define for yourself what that question is asking you to do. However, most LSAT questions fall neatly into particular categories, and those categories are easy to learn and then apply. So, it is worth some work and time on your part to learn the types, keep the type and its logic clearly in mind as you are attacking the question, and then evaluate after having completed a passage or practice test if you did in fact correctly identify, translate, and address the question (and how you might have been able to do it even better).

Different types of questions require different kinds of actions on your part before you begin to evaluate the answer choices. So, it makes sense to talk about Assess and Act together for each of the question types.

LSAT Reading Comprehension questions fall into four basic categories. Here are those four categories, the question subtypes that fall under each, and the essential process to go through for each question type before you have read a single answer choice.

Big Picture Questions

Assess   These questions require you to take the passage (or, in some cases for a Comparative Reading passage, both passages) as a whole into account.

There are three subtypes of Big Picture Questions.

- Main Point

    These questions are often worded as follows:

    Which of the following most accurately expresses the main point of the passage?

    Which title best describes the contents of the passage?

- Primary Purpose

These questions are usually phrased as follows:

The primary purpose of the passage is to

In the passage, the author is primarily concerned with doing which of the following?

- Overall Attitude

These questions may be phrased as follows:

Which of the following most accurately describes the author's attitude in the passage?

The author's opinion regarding the ideas described in the passage can best be described as

> Purpose and Attitude questions may also ask you about the author's purpose in, or opinion about, a more specific or limited part of the passage rather than about the passage as a whole. Make sure that you define the relevant scope of the question as part of translating the question task.

Act Think about the work you did to Prepare the passage. What was your last step of that part of the process? You defined the Bottom Line, based on the author's central point and overall purpose and attitude. Therefore, in most cases you will not need to go back to the passage before you start evaluating the answer choices. However, you may well need to refer back to the text at some point before you make a final choice, especially if you are stuck between two answers. Remember that even on a Big Picture question, one word can be enough to invalidate an answer choice.

Extract Questions

Assess Extract questions are asking you to find and select the answer choice that is best supported by the information in (and only in) some particular part or parts of the passage.

There are two subtypes of Extract questions.

- Fact

These questions are often worded as follows:

According to the passage

The author states that

Which of the following is mentioned in the passage?

- Inference

These questions are phrased as some variation of the following:

It can most reasonably be inferred from the passage that

Which of the following is implied/suggested/assumed?

Which of the following conclusions is best supported by the passage?

With which of the following would the author be most likely to agree?

Which of the following can be most reasonably concluded from the passage?

As it is used in the passage, X refers most specifically to

Which of the following does the author appear to value most?

Act   The answers to *Extract: Fact* questions will tend to be close paraphrases of something stated in the passage. *Extract: Inference* questions will sometimes require you to do a bit more work; the correct answer will be directly supported by one or more statements in the passage, but may not be stated outright in the text.

However, the approach to any *Extract* question is the same. Don't rely only on your memory! Use the passage actively, and whenever possible, before you look at a single answer choice. The test-writers will give you plenty of wrong answers that "sound good" but that have something wrong with them that you will catch only if you go back and see exactly what the author actually said. If the question stem gives you lead words or directs you to a specific location in the passage, go back to the passage first and read at least five lines above and below that reference. Be sure to reread all of the relevant information. If the author's discussion of that topic begins earlier or continues longer (including situations in which the topic is discussed in more than one section of the passage), you will need to read more than those 10 or 11 lines. Once you have read and paraphrased the passage information, generate an answer in your own words (based on what the passage says), defining what the correct answer needs to do. Regardless of the exact form of the question, here is where previewing the questions and annotation really pays off; if you have already highlighted or underlined the relevant words in the passage, your task becomes much easier. Also, use your annotations that indicated key transitional points and claims equally actively. For example, if you have read five lines below, but the next sentence begins with a word like "however," keep reading. What comes after that shift is highly likely to be relevant to the question and to the correct answer.

Structure Questions

Assess   There are two subtypes of Structure questions.

*   Organization

    Structure Organization questions ask you to describe the passage as a whole, piece by piece. These questions may be phrased as follows:

    Which one of the following most accurately states the organization of the passage?

- Function

  Structure Function questions ask you to describe WHY the author made a particular statement or included a particular paragraph. That is, they are testing to see if you understood the logical function or purpose of some part of the larger whole of the author's argument. These questions will be phrased with some variation of the following:

  The primary function of the second paragraph is to

  The main function of the reference to X is to

  The author mentions X in order to

Act   For both versions of *Structure* questions, go back to the passage and use your annotation actively. Words like *therefore, for example, in contrast,* and so on tell you a lot about the purpose and function of that part of the passage.

Structure: Organization questions require you to describe the passage as a whole. They differ from *Big Picture* questions in that the correct choice will describe the logical structure of the passage step by step, rather than summarizing the content of the passage in a single statement. To answer these questions, break down each choice into pieces and check each piece against the passage. Here is where your preparation of the passage in defining the main point of each paragraph in succession will be especially useful, as the correct answer will follow the same progression.

Structure: Function questions have a more narrow focus. Because they ask you to define why the author included a particular paragraph or made a specific claim, go back to that part of the passage first. If it asks for the purpose of a paragraph, use your definition of the main point of that chunk, but also think about how it fits into the author's overall argument in the passage. If it asks for the purpose of a specific claim, go back to that part of the passage, read above and below the claim (just like you would for an Extract question), and paraphrase the claim being made. However, you have to take one more step before going to the answer choices: think not just about WHAT the author said but also WHY the author said it. That requires defining how that claim or statement relates to the rest of the paragraph and potentially to the passage as a whole.

Occasionally, Application questions will give you the new information in the question stem rather than in the answer choices. In that case, define the theme of the new information and how it relates to the relevant part of the passage before evaluating the answer choices.

Application

Assess   Most Application questions involve using new information, that is, information that is not already provided in the passage, and applying it to what the author of the passage has already argued or stated. The majority of Application questions will fit into one of two subtypes:

- Strengthen/Weaken

  Strengthen questions may be phrased as follows, with the "X" in the sample question referring to a particular claim made in the passage:

  Which of the following would most clearly support the author's contention that "X"?

  The author's reasoning in support of her claim that "X" is justified would be most strengthened if which of the following were true?

  Conversely, a Weaken question may be phrased something like this:

  Which of the following, if true, would most undermine the author's claim that "X"?

Whether or not the question explicitly tells you to take the answer choices as true or valid, do so. That is, the question is not asking you to figure out what is already true based on the passage. Rather, it is asking you to **assume each answer choice to be a true statement**, figure out how each would or would not apply or relate to the passage, and to find the one that either **most** strengthens or **most** weakens the cited claim or argument made by the author. These are the only LSAT Reading Comprehension questions that will ask you to essentially change (for better or worse) the logic of the author's argument, so it is especially crucial to understand the question task before taking your next steps.

- Analogy

  Analogy questions may be phrased something like this:

  Which of the following is most similar it its approach to the author's approach as it is described in the passage?

  Which of the following is most analogous to the situation described in the second paragraph?

  Which of the following describes a relationship that is most logically similar to the relationship between X and Y described in the passage?

Analogy questions are similar to Strengthen/Weaken questions in that they give you new information in the answer choices. However, they are very different in that they ask you not to make the author's argument better or worse, but rather to define the logic (not the topic or content) of the author's argument, and to find the answer choice that is most similar in its theme or logic.

Act Even though Application questions involve working with new information, this does not mean that you should go right to the choices without going back to the passage first. Nor does it mean that the correct answer will go beyond the scope of the passage. Any credited response (unless it is an Except question) still has to be directly relevant to an issue raised in the passage. Therefore, it is still crucial to go back to the passage, find and paraphrase the relevant claim or relationship, and define for yourself what the correct answer needs to look like. For a Strengthen/Weaken question, that means knowing ahead of time what issue and direction (with or against the passage) the correct answer needs to include. For an Analogy question, that means defining what theme or logical relationship the correct answer needs to describe or portray.

Step 4: Answer

Basics

As you evaluate the answer choices for each question, here are some essentials to keep in mind.

1.   Always read each choice word for word the first time. This is no time to waste all of the good work you have done up to this point by skimming through the answers and making snap decisions based on what "sounds good" or "sounds bad." The test-writers will often write wrong answers in attractive ways, trying to distract you from the credited response. If you read the choices carelessly, you will fall for many of these traps.

2.   Read all five choices before making a final decision. You are looking for the best answer, not the first one that sounds good.

3.   Use Process of Elimination aggressively. Look for what is wrong with each choice, keeping in mind that one small part of the choice that doesn't match the passage and/or the question task means the whole choice is bad.

4.   Use the passage and your own answer actively (especially when the nature of the question has made it possible to generate an answer in your own words first). Correct answers on LSAT Reading Comprehension questions almost always have solid support in the passage. Use that to your advantage, and don't assume that an answer that matches your expectations must be a trap!

Two Cuts

You will often find yourself going through the set of choices twice, eliminating the most obviously wrong choices the first time through, and then coming back to make a final decision between the two or three that you have left.

When you are down to two or three choices, don't panic and guess—this is a normal part of the process. Stay methodical, and go through the following final steps:

1. Reread the question stem, and make sure that you have correctly identified the question task.
2. Compare the remaining choices to each other, and identify relevant differences. That may be enough to alert you to the correct answer.
3. If not, go back to the passage one more time with the question task and the differences between the remaining choices in mind. Remember that you should still be using your main points, your Bottom Line, and your passage annotation actively to make sure that you are (1) going back to the correct section or sections of the text, and (2) correctly understanding what the relevant part of the passage is saying.
4. If you have eliminated four choices but aren't sure exactly why the remaining choice is correct, go ahead and pick it! That is the beauty of POE—if four choices are definitively wrong, you don't have to know exactly why the remaining choice is correct. And, while the correct answer may not exactly match what you were looking for, it will always be the one that has the least wrong with it.
5. If you have good support for one choice, but aren't sure exactly why one or more of the other four is wrong (and you have been through the process outlined above), go ahead and pick that well-supported answer and move on.

Attractive Distractors

These are common types of wrong answers that you will see over and over. The more familiar you are with how the test-writers often write wrong answers, the more quickly and accurately you will identify and eliminate them.

Wrong Part of the Passage   Many of the wrong answer choices do contain content consistent with the passage. The problem is that this information is from a different part of the passage. For instance, if a passage is describing the properties of three different kinds of acids, and an Extract question asks about the properties of the second acid, many of the wrong choices will be properties of the first and third acids. As long as you focus on the information about the second acid only, you'll be able to eliminate any choices that talk about the first and third acids. Or, if a Structure Function question asks about the purpose of a particular statement, there will likely be a wrong answer that is about the purpose of some different statement made in the passage. Keep your focus on the purpose of the statement referenced in the question, and you will easily avoid the trap.

Extreme Language   As we mentioned in the Arguments section, answer choices that make extreme claims or that use absolute wording often go beyond what can be supported by the passage. Because LSAT authors can have some strong opinions from time to time, however, you shouldn't simply eliminate choices with extreme language without checking that language against what was said in the passage. Think of extreme language as a red flag. When you see it, you should automatically look back to the passage to see whether the passage supports such a strong statement. If it doesn't, and the question hasn't asked you to strengthen or weaken the passage, then you can eliminate the answer choice. This is a particularly common trap on Extract and Big Picture questions.

Too Narrow or Too Broad   Main Idea and Primary Purpose questions often have wrong answers that are either too narrow or too broad. Remember that the main idea or primary purpose should encompass the entire passage but not more or less than that. You'll see many wrong answers that either mention something that was contained in only a part of the passage or was accomplished in only a single paragraph, or others that would include not only the main topic of the passage, but also much more beyond that (for instance, the passage discusses dolphins, but the answer choice talks about all marine mammals).

Partially Wrong   This is a popular type of wrong answer on LSAT Reading Comprehension. Your goal is to seek out and eliminate answer choices that contain anything at all that might make them wrong. No matter how good a choice may start out, if you see anything amiss, you have to get rid of the answer. Very often, a single word may be the cause of the problem (for example, use of the word *not* to turn the answer into the opposite of the credited response). In addition, it's possible that the problem with the answer choice may show up late in the choice—the test-writers are hoping to lull test-takers into a false sense of security. For this reason, it is imperative that you read each answer choice thoroughly and carefully all the way to its end. Don't allow the good part of a choice to cause you to overlook or ignore the bad part—part wrong means all wrong no matter how good the good part might be.

Not Supported by the Passage   You must be able to prove your answer with information from the passage. Any answer choice that can't be proven in this way can't be right, even if you know it to be true from outside knowledge of a subject. Don't invent a connection between an answer choice and the passage if you can't find one already present.

PUTTING IT ALL TOGETHER

So, let's see how it works in practice. Work the passage on the following page as we have just discussed: define the main points and the Bottom Line and make thoughtful and concise annotations. Then turn the page and compare your work to the marked-up passage. That passage will have not only sample annotations, but also explanations of how you ideally should have read through the passage: what questions you should ask yourself as you read, and what deserves more or less attention in the text.

This Reading Passage and its questions are from PrepTest 44, Section 1, Questions 1–7.

Questions 1–7 are based on the following passage:

The Canadian Auto Workers' (CAW) Legal Services Plan, designed to give active and retired autoworkers and their families access to totally prepaid or partially reimbursed legal services, has been in operation since late 1985. Plan members have the option of using either the plan's staff lawyers, whose services are fully covered by the cost of membership in the plan, or an outside lawyer. Outside lawyers, in turn, can either sign up with the plan as a "cooperating lawyer" and accept the CAW's fee schedule as payment in full, or they can charge a higher fee and collect the balance from the client. Autoworkers appear to have embraced the notion of prepaid legal services: 45 percent of eligible union members were enrolled in the plan by 1988. Moreover, the idea of prepaid legal services has been spreading in Canada. A department store is even offering a plan to holders of its credit card.

While many plan members seem to be happy to get reduced-cost legal help, many lawyers are concerned about the plan's effect on their profession, especially its impact on prices for legal services. Some point out that even though most lawyers have not joined the plan as cooperating lawyers, legal fees in the cities in which the CAW plan operates have been depressed, in some cases to an unprofitable level. The directors of the plan, however, claim that both clients and lawyers benefit from their arrangement. For while the clients get ready access to reduced-price services, lawyers get professional contact with people who would not otherwise be using legal services, which helps generate even more business for their firms. Experience shows, the directors say, that if people are referred to a firm and receive excellent service, the firm will get three to four other referrals who are not plan subscribers and who would therefore pay the firm's standard rate.

But it is unlikely that increased use of such plans will result in long-term client satisfaction or in a substantial increase in profits for law firms. Since lawyers with established reputations and client bases can benefit little, if at all, from participation, the plans function largely as marketing devices for lawyers who have yet to establish themselves. While many of these lawyers are no doubt very able and conscientious, they will tend to have less expertise and to provide less satisfaction to clients. At the same time, the downward pressure on fees will mean that the full-fee referrals that proponents say will come through plan participation may not make up for a firm's investment in providing services at low plan rates. And since lowered fees provide little incentive for lawyers to devote more than minimal effort to cases, a "volume discount" approach toward the practice of law will mean less time devoted to complex cases and a general lowering of quality for clients.

1. Which one of the following most accurately expresses the main point of the passage?

   (A) In the short term, prepaid legal plans such as the CAW Legal Services Plan appear to be beneficial to both lawyers and clients, but in the long run lawyers will profit at the expense of clients.

   (B) The CAW Legal Services Plan and other similar plans represent a controversial, but probably effective, way of bringing down the cost of legal services to clients and increasing lawyers' clientele.

   (C) The use of prepaid legal plans such as that of the CAW should be rejected in favor of a more equitable means of making legal services more generally affordable.

   (D) In spite of widespread consumer support for legal plans such as that offered by the CAW, lawyers generally criticize such plans, mainly because of their potential financial impact on the legal profession.

   (E) Although they have so far attracted many subscribers, it is doubtful whether the CAW Legal Services Plan and other similar prepaid plans will benefit lawyers and clients in the long run.

2. The primary purpose of the passage is to

   (A) compare and contrast legal plans with the traditional way of paying for legal services

   (B) explain the growing popularity of legal plans

   (C) trace the effect of legal plans on prices of legal services

   (D) caution that increased use of legal plans is potentially harmful to the legal profession and to clients

   (E) advocate reforms to legal plans as presently constituted

3. Which one of the following does the author predict will be a consequence of increased use of legal plans?

   (A) results that are largely at odds with those predicted by lawyers who criticize the plans

   (B) a lowering of the rates such plans charge their members

   (C) forced participation of lawyers who can benefit little from association with the plans

   (D) an eventual increase in profits for lawyers from client usage of the plans

   (E) a reduction in the time lawyers devote to complex cases

4. Which one of the following sequences most accurately and completely corresponds to the presentation of the material in the passage?

(A) a description of a recently implemented set of procedures and policies; a summary of the results of that implementation; a proposal of refinements in those policies and procedures

(B) an evaluation of a recent phenomenon; a comparison of that phenomenon with related past phenomena; an expression of the author's approval of that phenomenon

(C) a presentation of a proposal; a discussion of the prospects for implementing that proposal; a recommendation by the author that the proposal be rejected

(D) a description of an innovation; a report of reasoning against and reasoning favoring that innovation; argumentation by the author concerning that innovation

(E) an explanation of a recent occurrence; an evaluation of the practical value of that occurrence; a presentation of further data regarding that occurrence

5. The passage most strongly suggests that, according to proponents of prepaid legal plans, cooperating lawyers benefit from taking clients at lower fees in which one of the following ways?

(A) Lawyers can expect to gain expertise in a wide variety of legal services by availing themselves of the access to diverse clientele that plan participation affords.

(B) Experienced cooperating lawyers are likely to enjoy the higher profits of long-term, complex cases, for which new lawyers are not suited.

(C) Lower rates of profit will be offset by a higher volume of clients and new business through word-of-mouth recommendations.

(D) Lower fees tend to attract clients away from established, nonparticipating law firms.

(E) With all legal fees moving downward to match the plans' schedules, the profession will respond to market forces.

6. According to the passage, which one of the following is true of CAW Legal Services Plan members?

(A) They can enjoy benefits beyond the use of the plan's staff lawyers.

(B) So far, they generally believe the quality of services they receive from the plan's staff lawyers is as high as that provided by other lawyers.

(C) Most of them consult lawyers only for relatively simple and routine matters.

(D) They must pay a fee above the cost of membership for the services of an outside lawyer.

(E) They do not include only active and retired autoworkers and their families.

7. Which one of the following most accurately represents the primary function of the author's mention of marketing devices in the last paragraph?

(A) It points to an aspect of legal plans that the author believes will be detrimental to the quality of legal services.

(B) It is identified by the author as one of the primary ways in which plan administrators believe themselves to be contributing materially to the legal profession in return for lawyers' participation.

(C) It identifies what the author considers to be one of the few unequivocal benefits that legal plans can provide.

(D) It is reported as part of several arguments that the author attributes to established lawyers who oppose plan participation.

(E) It describes one of the chief burdens of lawyers who have yet to establish themselves and offers an explanation of their advocacy of legal plans.

Explanations and Annotations

The Canadian Auto Workers' (CAW) Legal Services Plan, designed to give active and retired autoworkers and their families access to totally prepaid or partially reimbursed legal services, has been in operation since late 1985. Plan members have the option of using either the plan's staff lawyers, whose services are fully covered by the cost of membership in the plan, or an outside lawyer. Outside lawyers, in turn, can either sign up with the plan as a "cooperating lawyer" and accept the CAW's fee schedule as payment in full, or they can charge a higher fee and collect the balance from the client. Autoworkers appear to have embraced the notion of prepaid legal services: 45 percent of eligible union members were enrolled in the plan by 1988. Moreover, the idea of prepaid legal services has been spreading in Canada. A department store is even offering a plan to holders of its credit card.

Description of CAW plan and popularity

While many plan members seem to be happy to get reduced-cost legal help, many lawyers are concerned about the plan's effect on their profession, especially its impact on prices for legal services. Some point out that even though most lawyers have not joined the plan as cooperating lawyers, legal fees in the cities in which the CAW plan operates have been depressed, in some cases to an unprofitable level. The directors of the plan, however, claim that both clients and lawyers benefit from their arrangement. For while the clients get ready access to reduced-price services, lawyers get professional contact with people who would not otherwise be using legal services, which helps generate even more business for their firms. Experience shows, the directors say, that if people are referred to a firm and receive excellent service, the firm will get three to four other referrals who are not plan subscribers and who would therefore pay the firm's standard rate.

Lawyers worried about lower fees, while directors claim benefit from referrals

But it is unlikely that increased use of such plans will result in long-term client satisfaction or in a substantial increase in profits for law firms. Since lawyers with established reputations and client bases can benefit little, if at all, from participation, the plans function largely as marketing devices for lawyers who have yet to establish themselves. While many of these lawyers are no doubt very able and conscientious, they will tend to have less expertise and to provide less satisfaction to clients. At the same time, the downward pressure on fees will mean that the full-fee referrals that proponents say will come through plan participation may not make up for a firm's investment in providing services at low plan rates. And since lowered fees provide little incentive for lawyers to devote more than minimal effort to cases, a "volume discount" approach toward the practice of law will mean less time devoted to complex cases and a general lowering of quality for clients.

But these plans probably not good for either lawyers or clients

Bottom Line: *Legal Services plans like the CAW's are popular, but likely to negatively impact lawyers' profits and client satisfaction.*

Step 1: Prepare

Paragraph 1 Main Point: Description of CAW plan and its popularity.

This paragraph introduces the CAW plan and goes on to describe who it covers and how it works. You should notice, and mark with your annotation, that there are differences in ways that lawyers can participate and in how fee payment works. But, don't try to memorize all these variations—you know where to find the details if and when you need them later. The end of the paragraph tells you that this kind of plan appears to be popular and that the idea is spreading. Notice, however, that you don't know at this point if the author shares the positive point of view that others have about this type of plan. So far, the author isn't taking sides.

Paragraph 2 Main Point: Lawyers worried about lower fees, while directors claim benefit from referrals.

Notice the word "While" that starts this paragraph off. Already you get a hint that there may be those who are not as happy as others about these plans. (You might also notice that the author says that members "seem to be happy," but doesn't actually say that they are satisfied with the plan. You don't know yet why the author uses this kind of language, but keep it in mind as you read further into the passage.) And yes, the first part of this second paragraph introduces a contrast to the first paragraph: many lawyers think that such plans are already negatively affecting their profits. But now, with a "however," the passage moves back to a different and more positive point of view: the directors of the plans (whom you can identify as proponents of the plan) think lawyers and firms will benefit overall from increased business. Don't worry too much of the details of how; keep your focus on the directors' main claim.

The question to ask yourself at this point is "Do I know yet what the author thinks?" The answer is no. So far you have only contrasting points of view held by other people.

Paragraph 3 Main Point: But these plans are probably not good for either lawyers or clients.

Only now do you get definitive evidence about the author's own point of view. The passage states outright "But it is unlikely that increased use of such plans will result in long-term client satisfaction or in a substantial increase in profits for law firms." The word "Since" that begins the next sentence tells you that here comes the support for that judgment. So, while you do want to note (if you previewed the questions) that the reference to "marketing devices" is made in the context of the author's criticism, don't get too caught up in the explanation in the middle of the paragraph. As long as you get the two key ideas—the author thinks neither lawyers nor clients will get much benefit—you are good to go for the Bottom Line and to start on the questions.

Bottom Line: Legal Services plans like the CAW's are popular, but likely to negatively impact lawyers' profits and client satisfaction.

This is a "Criticize" passage, and in this case (but keep in mind this will not always be the case!) the author essentially expresses the Bottom Line through the main point of the last paragraph.

Steps 2–4: Attacking the Questions

Along with the explanations for each step of attacking each question, we have marked the questions up to show how you might do the same to help yourself to understand the question, evaluate each choice, and track your Process of Elimination.

1. Which one of the following most accurately expresses the main point of the passage?

(A) In the short term, prepaid legal plans such as the CAW Legal Services Plan appear to be beneficial to both lawyers and clients, but in the long run lawyers will profit at the expense of clients.

(B) The CAW Legal Services Plan and other similar plans represent a controversial, but probably effective, way of bringing down the cost of legal services to clients and increasing lawyers' clientele.

(C) The use of prepaid legal plans such as that of the CAW should be rejected in favor of a more equitable means of making legal services more generally affordable.

(D) In spite of widespread consumer support for legal plans such as that offered by the CAW, lawyers generally criticize such plans, mainly because of their potential financial impact on the legal profession.

(E) Although they have so far attracted many subscribers, it is doubtful whether the CAW Legal Services Plan and other similar prepaid plans will benefit lawyers and clients in the long run.

Here's How to Crack It

Step 2: Assess

This is a Big Picture: Main Point question. Therefore, it is asking you what the central point of the entire passage is.

Step 3: Act

Remind yourself of the Bottom Line you already defined: "Legal Services plans like the CAW's are popular, but likely to negatively impact lawyers' profits and client satisfaction."

Step 4: Answer

As you move through the choices, keep reminding yourself of the scope of the passage (the two aspects of the CAW and similar plans) and the negative attitude of the author.

The first part of (A) sounds OK, since it says "appear to be beneficial," but the second part goes wrong. The author indicates that lawyers may in fact not profit in the long run. This choice is half right but half wrong, and it misrepresents the author's attitude and opinion. So, (A) is out.

Choice (B) begins with suspicious wording with "controversial"; while there is debate regarding the value of the plan, the author doesn't go quite this far. However, if you are unsure about whether or not there is enough support for the word "controversial," there is an even more obvious reason to eliminate the choice: it is the opposite of the author's opinion. The author states clearly that he or she believes that such plans will be ineffective, not effective. Choice (B) is out.

Choice (C) may be momentarily tempting, given its negative tone. However, the author never goes so far as to claim such plans should be rejected, and also never indicates that the problem is that they are inequitable or unfair. This choice is both too extreme and out of scope, and should be eliminated.

You may have left (D) in contention the first time through the choices. "Widespread" and "generally" are a bit strong, based on the more moderate wording used by the author in paragraph 1, but at least some lawyers do in fact criticize such plans because of their financial impact on the profession. Let's imagine you left (D) in, and move on for the moment to the last answer.

Choice (E) matches your Bottom Line nicely. Yes, the plans have been popular and attracted subscribers, but no, the author does not think that such plans will benefit either lawyers or clients in the long run. And, if you go back and compare (E) and (D), you will see that (D) mentions only the lawyers' side and issue, leaving out the other key issue which is the potential negative impact on client satisfaction.

This leaves you with a clear decision: Choice (E).

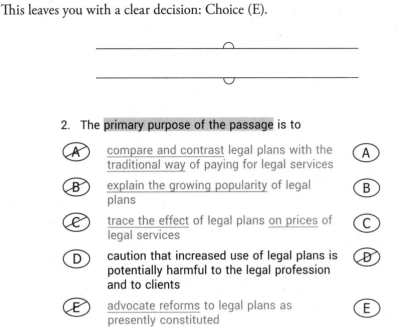

2. The primary purpose of the passage is to

(A) compare and contrast legal plans with the traditional way of paying for legal services   (A)

(B) explain the growing popularity of legal plans   (B)

(C) trace the effect of legal plans on prices of legal services   (C)

(D) caution that increased use of legal plans is potentially harmful to the legal profession and to clients   (D)

(E) advocate reforms to legal plans as presently constituted   (E)

Here's How to Crack It

Step 2: Assess

The wording "primary purpose" makes it clear that this is a Big Picture: Primary Purpose question. So, the task is similar to that in question 1: find the answer that best represents the author's central goal in writing the passage as a whole.

Step 3: Act

Again, remind yourself of the Bottom Line you already defined: "Legal Services plans like the CAW's are popular, but likely to negatively impact lawyers' profits and client satisfaction." So, the purpose of the passage is to tell you that such plans may have these particular drawbacks.

Step 4: Answer

Choice (A) is problematic from the beginning. The author is not comparing and contrasting types of plans, nor is he or she spending much time at all describing how these legal services plans are different from traditional methods of payment. So, (A) is out of scope and out of contention.

Choice (B) may have tempted you for a moment, since the author does indicate in paragraph 1 that such plans are popular. However, does the author spend much time *explaining* that popularity? No. Is the passage as a whole about their popularity? No. Therefore, this choice is too narrow to have any chance of describing the author's primary purpose.

If you are attuned to this very common "too narrow" Attractive Distractor on Big Picture questions, you will have easily eliminated (C) as well. While the author does discuss effects on prices of legal services, he or she also discusses effects on client satisfaction. Therefore, (C) is out for a similar reason as (B) (as well as (D) in question 1).

Choice (D) nicely corresponds to the scope and tone of your Bottom Line. So, let's leave it in for now and consider (E).

Choice (E) is a trap for test-takers who think too far beyond the scope of the passage. Yes, the author indicates problems with legal services plans. However, does he or she take the further step of advocating changes or reforms? No. Remember, we defined the purpose of the passage as to criticize, not to advocate. Even if you are speculating that perhaps the author has this in mind, you can't point to any evidence of this in the passage.

This leaves you with (D) as the best representation of the author's primary purpose.

3. Which one of the following does the author predict will be a consequence of increased use of legal plans?

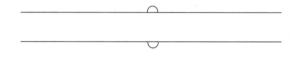

(A) results that are largely at odds with those predicted by lawyers who criticize the plans (A)

(B) a lowering of the rates such plans charge their members (B)

(C) forced participation of lawyers who can benefit little from association with the plans (C)

(D) an eventual increase in profits for lawyers from client usage of the plans (D)

(E) a reduction in the time lawyers devote to complex cases (E)

Here's How to Crack It

Step 2: Assess

This is an Extract: Fact question. It is asking you what the author said will happen as a result of use of such plans.

Step 3: Act

This is the time to go back to the passage before POE. You know from your preparation of the passage that the author made two predictions in the last paragraph. One is that "downward pressure on fees" may hurt law firms' profits, and the other is that clients will receive lower quality service, in part because lawyers will spend less time on complicated cases. Go into the choices, then, with these two possible answers in mind.

Step 4: Answer

Read and paraphrase (A) carefully. It is using convoluted language to try to distract you from the fact that this is the exact opposite of what the author predicted. In paragraph 2, the author describes the fear of some lawyers that legal services plans will depress (and in some cases already have depressed) prices "in some cases to an unprofitable level." In paragraph 3, the author agrees that this may in fact occur. Therefore, the author predicts results that are consistent, not at odds with, these lawyers' prediction.

Choice (B) requires equally careful reading to see what it is really saying. Does the author predict a lowering of the rates *charged by the plans to their members*? No, he or she predicts a lowering of fees paid to lawyers. This wrong answer is a trap set for test-takers who rely only on their memory, and/or who do not read the answer choices word for word.

Choice (C) immediately leaves the scope of the passage. The author never indicates that any lawyer will be forced to participate; paragraph 1 makes it pretty clear that lawyers join or cooperate voluntarily. So, (C) is gone.

Even though this is an Extract: Fact question, using your Bottom Line actively should allow you to eliminate (D) the first time through the answers. A major part of the author's criticism is that legal services plans may decrease, not increase, profits. This choice invalidates itself by contradicting the passage.

So, we are down to (E). Remember to read every choice carefully, even if you have eliminated (A)–(D). But all is good, as (E) is already one of the options you had in mind based on going back to the last paragraph before POE. This leaves you with (E) as the supported credited response.

---

4. Which one of the following sequences most accurately and completely corresponds to the presentation of the material in the passage?

(A) a description of a recently implemented set of procedures and policies; a summary of the results of that implementation; a proposal of refinements in those policies and procedures

(B) an evaluation of a recent phenomenon; a comparison of that phenomenon with related past phenomena; an expression of the author's approval of that phenomenon

(C) a presentation of a proposal; a discussion of the prospects for implementing that proposal; a recommendation by the author that the proposal be rejected

(D) a description of an innovation; a report of reasoning against and reasoning favoring that innovation; argumentation by the author concerning that innovation

(E) an explanation of a recent occurrence; an evaluation of the practical value of that occurrence; a presentation of further data regarding that occurrence

Here's How to Crack It

Step 2: Assess

The wording "sequences most accurately and completely corresponds to the presentation of the material in the passage" tells you that this is a Structure: Organization question. Therefore, it is asking you to find the choice that piece by piece follows and matches the main sections of the passage.

Step 3: Act

If you have prepared the passage well by defining the main point of each paragraph, you can move right into the choices, using that "outline" as your guide.

Step 4: Answer

Work actively to break down the pieces of each choice the first time through the answers; don't just read the whole choice as one big chunk and then ask "does anything sound wrong?" One useful technique is to visually break each answer up with a slash in between each section, making it easier for you to identify and check each individual chunk.

The first part of (A) is suspicious with the word "recently," but don't get stuck at this point trying to decide if 1985 can be called recent or not. Once you move on to the next two chunks of the choice, you can see where it goes definitively wrong. Paragraph 2 of the passage describes the positive and negative points of view regarding the eventual effects of the plan, not a summary of any actual results, and paragraph 3 presents the author's criticism with no proposals for reforms or refinements.

Choice (B) starts off wrong: you defined the purpose of paragraph 1 as describing, not evaluating, the plan. Chunk 2 is wrong as well: there is no comparison with related past phenomena, and chunk 3 seals the deal: the author disapproves, not approves of the plan. Recognizing any one of these three problems would be enough to eliminate the choice.

Choice (C) begins problematically—this is an existing plan, not a proposal. But, if you are unsure about that, there are plenty of other reasons to eliminate (C). Paragraph 2 does not discuss how likely the "proposal" is to be implemented but rather existing positive and negative views of the existing plans, and paragraph 3 expresses the author's criticism, but he or she does not go so far as to say the plans should be rejected.

Choice (D) nicely matches your main points piece by piece and in the correct order: description of the CAW and similar plans (which, since they began in 1984, can reasonably be called an "innovation"), arguments for and against such plans, and finally the author's argument that such plans will likely have two types of negative effects.

Choice (E) begins okay (again, don't get stuck at this point trying to decide if 1985 qualifies as "recent"), but then goes wrong. Paragraph 2 presents contrasting points of view but not the author's evaluation of the practical value of the plans, and there is no actual data presented in paragraph 3.

This leaves you with (D) as the best piece by piece match to the passage presentation.

---

5. The passage most strongly suggests that, according to proponents of prepaid legal plans, cooperating lawyers benefit from taking clients at lower fees in which one of the following ways?

(A) Lawyers can expect to gain expertise in a wide variety of legal services by availing themselves of the access to diverse clientele that plan participation affords.

(B) Experienced cooperating lawyers are likely to enjoy the higher profits of long-term, complex cases, for which new lawyers are not suited.

(C) Lower rates of profit will be offset by a higher volume of clients and new business through word-of-mouth recommendations.

(D) Lower fees tend to attract clients away from established, nonparticipating law firms.

(E) With all legal fees moving downward to match the plans' schedules, the profession will respond to market forces.

Here's How to Crack It

Step 2: Assess

The wording "The passage most strongly suggests" tells you that this is an Extract: Inference question. Translate the rest of the question carefully, however! This question is NOT asking you what the author agrees with, but rather what the *proponents* of prepaid legal plans would think, and the author is definitively NOT a proponent.

Step 3: Act

You know from your passage prep that the paragraph 2 describes the proponents' argument. Going back to that part of the passage, you see that their argument is that cooperating lawyers will come out ahead profit-wise when they get more business out of the deal: "if people are referred to a firm and receive excellent service, the firm will get three or four other referrals who are not plan subscribers and who would therefore pay the firms' standard rate." So, you are looking for something along these lines in a correct answer.

Step 4: Answer

Choice (A) is out of scope and therefore wrong. There is no discussion in the passage of greater diversity of clientele or of gaining greater expertise. The issue is volume and fees, not range of experience. Make sure not to speculate past the boundaries of the passage; even if you think that this could be a result, there is no evidence for it in the passage. If you left (A) in during your first cut through the choices, comparing it with (C) would alert you to what the real issue is in the passage.

Choice (B) may be momentarily attractive because it mentions profits. However, it introduces two comparisons—between experienced and new lawyers, and between fees for complex versus less complex cases—that are not supported. Note the trap; the author talks about inexperienced lawyers and complex cases later on in paragraph 3, but does not indicate any relevance of these issues to arguments made by proponents of the plans.

Choice (C) has the right issue (profiting through referrals and increased volume) and the right positive tone. So, leave it in and move on to (D).

Choice (D), like (A) and (B), brings in an issue that is not addressed in the passage. The author never indicates that proponents of the plans believe that cooperating lawyers will benefit through stealing clients away from other firms.

The trap in (E) is that it is not even clear what "respond to market forces" means. Probably that fees would decrease overall, which is definitely not in line with the proponents' argument, but why take the time to figure that out when you already have a choice that nicely matches what is directly discussed in the passage.

So, eliminate (E), pick (C), and move on!

6. According to the passage, which one of the following is true of CAW Legal Services Plan members?

(A) They can enjoy benefits beyond the use of the services of the plan's staff lawyers. (A)

(B) So far, they generally believe the quality of services they receive from the plan's staff lawyers is as high as that provided by other lawyers. (B)

(C) Most of them consult lawyers only for relatively simple and routine matters. (C)

(D) They must pay a fee above the cost of membership for the services of an outside lawyer. (D)

(E) They do not include only active and retired autoworkers and their families. (E)

Here's How to Crack It

Step 2: Assess

"According to the passage" tells you that this is an Extract: Fact question. So, it is asking you to find the answer that is most directly supported by what is explicitly stated in the passage.

Step 3: Act

Paragraph 1 describes the CAW and who its members are. There are a variety of things in that paragraph that the correct answer might reference. So, it is reasonable, once you have identified the relevant section of the passage, to move into POE and then go back to the passage text as needed.

Step 4: Answer

Choice (A) may not immediately leap out at you, but when you go back to paragraph 1 you see the following: "Plan members have the option of using either the plan's staff lawyers, whose services are fully covered by the cost of membership in the plan, or an outside lawyer." If a plan member uses an outside lawyer, he or she would either pay the same as for a plan lawyer, or a reduced rate (whatever exceeds the plan's fee schedule). This definitely qualifies as a benefit beyond use of the plan's staff lawyers, so leave in (A).

Choice (B) is out of scope and therefore wrong. All you know from the passage is that "Autoworkers appear to have embraced the notion of prepaid legal services...." This tells you nothing about members' perceptions regarding the *quality of services* received from staff lawyers. Make sure not to over-speculate; if quality of service is not mentioned in this context, it cannot be in the correct answer to an Extract: Fact question.

Choice (C) is also out of scope. There is no discussion in the relevant part of the passage of what issues member consult lawyers about. This is a trap based on the last paragraph, where the author says that lawyers in the plan will have little incentive to devote lots of time to complex cases, which is a very different issue.

Choice (D) includes a word that should set off alarms in your POE brain: "must." Do members HAVE to pay additional fees? No, not if a cooperating lawyer "accept[s] the CAW's fee schedule as payment in full." Therefore, this choice is too extreme and should be eliminated.

Choice (E) requires careful, word-for-word reading. The passage states that the CAW plan is "designed to give active and retired autoworkers and their families access" to legal services. Therefore, the word "not" in this choice turns it into the opposite of what the author describes.

So, (E) is out, leaving you with (A) as the directly supported correct answer.

7. Which one of the following most accurately represents the primary function of the author's mention of marketing devices in the last paragraph?

(A) It points to an aspect of legal plans that the author believes will be detrimental to the quality of legal services.

(B) It is identified by the author as one of the primary ways in which plan administrators believe themselves to be contributing materially to the legal profession in return for lawyers' participation.

(C) It identifies what the author considers to be one of the few unequivocal benefits that legal plans can provide.

(D) It is reported as part of several arguments that the author attributes to established lawyers who oppose plan participation.

(E) It describes one of the chief burdens of lawyers who have yet to establish themselves and offers an explanation of their advocacy of legal plans.

Here's How to Crack It

Step 2: Assess

This question asks you for the "primary function" or purpose of a reference in the passage, making it a Structure: Function question. Your task, then, is to figure out WHY the author mentions marketing devices in that part of the passage.

Step 3: Act

You already know from preparing the passage that the third paragraph sets out the author's criticism of prepaid legal plans. Going back to that particular part of the paragraph, you see that the author states that the plans will function mostly as "marketing devices" for inexperienced lawyers, and that these lawyers "will tend to have less expertise and to provide less satisfaction to clients." So, your own answer to this question might be something like: "It is one of the problems with these legal plans."

Step 4: Answer

Choice (A) nicely matches the answer we just generated based on the question task and relevant part of the passage—leave it in!

The problem with (B) is clear if you have already identified the purpose of the reference. It is part of the author's criticism, not part of the proponents' defense of the plans.

Even though this is not a Big Picture question, your articulation of the Bottom Line eliminates (C). The author criticizes these legal plans, and nothing in the passage indicates any real benefit, including this "marketing device." Be careful not to use your own opinion; "marketing device" may sound like a positive thing to many people, but the author has the opposite opinion.

Choice (D) attributes this argument to the wrong people. Yes, there are lawyers who criticize the plans, but the "marketing device" argument is the author's, not these lawyers'. Your tracking of the structure of the passage, including the main points, helps you to eliminate this choice.

Choice (E) has a variety of problems. First, while the author does indicate that new lawyers would need to market themselves, the passage does not go so far as to describe this as "one of the chief burdens" of new lawyers. Even more importantly, the only lawyers' point of view described in the passage is in opposition to, not in support of, the plan; you are not told of any lawyers who are advocating legal plans.

This leaves you with (A) as the credited response.

READING COMPREHENSION: DUAL PASSAGES

LSAC's one Reading Comprehension passages on each test is a comparative reading set comprised of two shorter passages, each with a different treatment of a similar subject. These passages require the same skills as a regular Reading Comprehension passage; in fact, analyzing these passages is very similar to analyzing a single passage with multiple viewpoints. The difference is that the questions will often ask you to compare and contrast the structure, tone, and content of the two passages. Sometimes the questions will ask you to find differences or similarities between the two passages. You may also be asked how the author of one passage would respond to a part of the other author's passage. As you read, keep an eye out for these similarities and differences so you'll be ready to answer the questions. Part of your preparation should be to define not only the main points and Bottom Line of each passage, but also the relationship between the two. And, as you go through Assess, Act, and Answer on the questions, make sure that you carefully determine if the question is asking about only one of the two passages, or if it is asking what information appears in only one or the other or both, or if it is asking about some relationship between the two.

Let's work a comparative reading set together.

This Reading Passage and its questions are from PrepTest 58, Section 2, Questions 21–27.

Passage A

In music, a certain complexity of sounds can be expected to have a positive effect on the listener. A single, pure tone is not that interesting to explore; a measure of intricacy is required to excite human curiosity. Sounds that are too complex or disorganized, however, tend to be overwhelming. We prefer some sort of coherence, a principle that connects the various sounds and makes them comprehensible.

In this respect, music is like human language. Single sounds are in most cases not sufficient to convey meaning in speech, whereas when put together in a sequence they form words and sentences. Likewise, if the tones in music are not perceived to be tied together sequentially or rhythmically—for example, in what is commonly called melody—listeners are less likely to feel any emotional connection or to show appreciation.

Certain music can also have a relaxing effect. The fact that such music tends to be continuous and rhythmical suggests a possible explanation for this effect. In a natural environment, danger tends to be accompanied by sudden, unexpected sounds. Thus, a background of constant noise suggests peaceful conditions; discontinuous sounds demand more attention. Even soft discontinuous sounds that we consciously realize do not signal danger can be disturbing—for example, the erratic dripping of a leaky tap. A continuous sound, particularly one that is judged to be safe, relaxes the brain.

Passage B

There are certain elements within music, such as a change of melodic line or rhythm, that create expectations about the future development of the music. The expectation the listener has about the further course of musical events is a key determinant for the experience of "musical emotions." Music creates expectations that, if not immediately satisfied, create tension. Emotion is experienced in relation to the buildup and release of tension. The more elaborate the buildup of tension, the more intense the emotions that will be experienced. When resolution occurs, relaxation follows.

The interruption of the expected musical course, depending on one's personal involvement, causes the search for an explanation. This results from a "mismatch" between one's musical expectation and the actual course of the music. Negative emotions will be the result of an extreme mismatch between expectations and experience. Positive emotions result if the converse happens.

When we listen to music, we take into account factors such as the complexity and novelty of the music. The degree to which the music

sounds familiar determines whether the music is experienced as pleasurable or uncomfortable. The pleasure experienced is minimal when the music is entirely new to the listener, increases with increasing familiarity, and decreases again when the music is totally known. Musical preference is based on one's desire to maintain a constant level of certain preferable emotions. As such, a trained listener will have a greater preference for complex melodies than will a naive listener, as the threshold for experiencing emotion is higher.

1. Which one of the following concepts is linked to positive musical experiences in both passages?

(A) continuous sound

(B) tension

(C) language

(D) improvisation

(E) complexity

2. The passages most strongly suggest that both are targeting an audience that is interested in which one of the following?

(A) the theoretical underpinnings of how music is composed

(B) the nature of the conceptual difference between music and discontinuous sound

(C) the impact music can have on human emotional states

(D) the most effective techniques for teaching novices to appreciate complex music

(E) the influence music has had on the development of spoken language

3. Which one of the following describes a preference that is most analogous to the preference mentioned in the first paragraph of passage A?

(A) the preference of some people for falling asleep to white noise, such as the sound of an electric fan

(B) the preference of many moviegoers for movies with plots that are clear and easy to follow

(C) the preference of many diners for restaurants that serve large portions

(D) the preference of many young listeners for fast music over slower music

(E) the preference of most children for sweet foods over bitter foods

4. Which one of the following most accurately expresses the main point of passage B?

(A) The type of musical emotion experienced by a listener is determined by the level to which the listener's expectations are satisfied.

(B) Trained listeners are more able to consciously manipulate their own emotional experiences of complex music than are naive listeners.

(C) If the development of a piece of music is greatly at odds with the listener's musical expectations, then the listener will experience negative emotions.

(D) Listeners can learn to appreciate changes in melodic line and other musical complexities.

(E) Music that is experienced by listeners as relaxing usually produces a buildup and release of tension in those listeners.

5. Which one of the following most undermines the explanation provided in passage A for the relaxing effect that some music has on listeners?

(A) The musical traditions of different cultures vary greatly in terms of the complexity of the rhythms they employ.

(B) The rhythmic structure of a language is determined in part by the pattern of stressed syllables in the words and sentences of the language.

(C) Many people find the steady and rhythmic sound of a rocking chair to be very unnerving.

(D) The sudden interruption of the expected development of a melody tends to interfere with listeners' perception of the melody as coherent.

(E) Some of the most admired contemporary composers write music that is notably simpler than is most of the music written in previous centuries.

6. Which one of the following would be most appropriate as a title for each of the passages?

(A) "The Biological Underpinnings of Musical Emotions"

(B) "The Psychology of Listener Response to Music"

(C) "How Music Differs from Other Art Forms"

(D) "Cultural Patterns in Listeners' Responses to Music"

(E) "How Composers Convey Meaning Through Music"

7. It can be inferred that both authors would be likely to agree with which one of the following statements?

(A)   The more complex a piece of music, the more it is likely to be enjoyed by most listeners.

(B)   More knowledgeable listeners tend to prefer music that is discontinuous and unpredictable.

(C)   The capacity of music to elicit strong emotional responses from listeners is the central determinant of its artistic value.

(D)   Music that lacks a predictable course is unlikely to cause a listener to feel relaxed.

(E)   Music that changes from soft to loud is perceived as disturbing and unpleasant by most listeners.

Explanations and Annotations

Step 1: Prepare

As you prepare Comparative Reading passages, in most ways treat them the same as any passage: look for key logical clues, identify the main point of each paragraph, and define the Bottom Line of each passage, including the attitude and purpose of the author in the passage as a whole.

As you read Passage B, already be on the lookout for similarities and differences with Passage A. Keep in mind that while Passage B is not written in direct response to Passage A, there will be some relationship between them, including at least some similarities and at least some differences in content, scope, and/or attitude of the author.

Passage A

Paragraph 1 Main Point: While a simple musical sound is not likely to interest people, a certain complexity of sounds will.

Paragraph 2 Main Point: Just like with language, connection and coherence is important for understanding and appreciation.

Paragraph 3 Main Point: People find continuous sounds relaxing, in music and in general.

Passage A Bottom Line: Level of complexity, coherence, and continuity affect the pleasure of listeners.

Passage B

As you read Passage B, you see that it is very similar in content and purpose to Passage A. Note where similar topics appear and what the author has to say about them, as well as where the author raises topics or issues that did not appear in Passage A.

Paragraph 1 Main Point: In music, expectations create tension, and resolution of tension creates relaxation.

Paragraph 2 Main Point: When expectations match resolution, music can inspire positive emotions, and vice versa.

Paragraph 3 Main Point: Also, the right level of complexity and familiarity makes music pleasurable for different listeners.

Passage B Bottom Line: Resolution of expectations, and complexity and familiarity, factor into the pleasure we find in music.

Relationship between Passages A and B: Both passages outline factors that affect our emotional response to music.

Steps 2–4: Attack the Questions

1. Which one of the following concepts is linked to positive musical experiences in both passages?

   (A) continuous sound   *A only*   (A)

   (B) tension   *B only*   (B)

   (C) language   (C)

   (D) improvisation   (D)

   (E) complexity   (E)

Here's How to Crack It

Step 2: Assess

This is an Extract: Fact question that asks about something that happens in BOTH passages.

Step 3: Act

Given that both passages mention a variety of things that can be linked to positive musical experiences, it is best to go directly to the answer choices first, and then go back to each passage and/or to your own passage prep notes as you evaluate the choices.

Step 4: Answer

Choice (A), "continuous sound," is mentioned only in Passage A. This is a classic trap on a question that asks for something that happens in both passages.

Choice (B) is a similar trap. To the extent that it is linked to positive musical experiences, it is discussed only in Passage B (paragraph 1). Don't spend too much time trying to decide if "tension" is close enough, or if it would need to say "resolution of tension" to answer the question; if it isn't addressed at all in the other passage, it has no chance of being the correct answer.

Choice (C), "language," is addressed at all only in Passage A, and there it is as an analogy to music, not as a source of positive musical experiences. Similarly to (B), however, if you have seen that language is not discussed in Passage B, this is enough to eliminate the choice.

Choice (D), "improvisation," is out of scope; it isn't discussed in either passage. Once you have figured out that it isn't in one of the passages, you can eliminate this choice without hunting through the other passage as well.

Choice (E), "complexity," is discussed in both passages in connection to positive musical experiences. You may well have enough information from preparing the passage, including the main points of each paragraph, to select this answer without going back to the passage text again. If not, you would go back to see that it is discussed in the first sentence of Passage A, and in the last paragraph of Passage B.

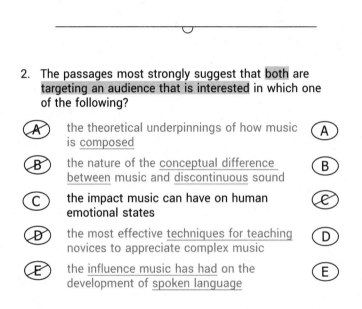

2. The passages most strongly suggest that both are targeting an audience that is interested in which one of the following?

(A) the theoretical underpinnings of how music is composed

(B) the nature of the conceptual difference between music and discontinuous sound

(C) the impact music can have on human emotional states

(D) the most effective techniques for teaching novices to appreciate complex music

(E) the influence music has had on the development of spoken language

Here's How to Crack It

Step 2: Assess

This is an Extract: Inference question. However, in translating the question you would want to notice that it is also very similar to a Big Picture: Primary Purpose question. By asking to whom each author is writing, it is essentially asking about the purpose of both authors.

Step 3: Act

You have already done enough preparation work in Step 1 to have a good answer to this question in mind: both passages are targeting an audience that is interested in the effects music has on the feelings of listeners.

Step 4: Answer

Choice (A) is out of scope for both passages; neither discusses how music is composed. Make sure not to take extra leaps to connect the effect of music to the reason why a piece of music was composed as it was. That connection would have to be made explicitly in both passages for this answer to be correct.

For (B), once you identify that continuous sounds are discussed only in Passage A, this is enough to eliminate the answer choice. Even for Passage A, this doesn't match, however, given that Passage A is not talking about some conceptual *contrast* between music and discontinuous sound.

Choice (C) matches what you would have already defined as the relationship between the two passages: "Both passages outline factors that affect our emotional response to music." So, keep it in!

Choice (D) is beyond the scope of both passages; neither discusses *teaching* music appreciation. The trap is that the end of Passage B mentions trained versus "naive" or novice listeners (although still not in the context of teaching music), and sometimes the last thing you read in a passage stands out in your mind.

Choice (E) is wrong for similar reasons as (D). Language is mentioned only in one passage (Passage A), and even in that passage it is not discussed in the context of how one (music) influences the other (language).

This leaves you with (C) as the straightforwardly supported credited response.

---

3. Which one of the following describes a preference that is most analogous to the preference mentioned in the first paragraph of passage A?

(A) the preference of some people for falling asleep to white noise, such as the sound of an electric fan

(B) the preference of many moviegoers for movies with plots that are clear and easy to follow

(C) the preference of many diners for restaurants that serve large portions

(D) the preference of many young listeners for fast music over slower music

(E) the preference of most children for sweet foods over bitter foods

Here's How to Crack It

Step 2: Assess

This is an Application: Analogy question. In translating it, note two key things. First, it asks only about Passage A. Second, it asks for a preference logically similar to that mentioned in the first paragraph of that passage.

Step 3: Act

Go back to the passage and find the relevant preference: "a certain complexity of sound" that has "some sort of coherence, a principle that connects the various sounds and makes them comprehensible." So, you are looking for a preference, most likely for something other than music (given that this is an Analogy question) that is not too simple, but that is coherent and comprehensible.

Note that you can ignore Passage B for this question, since it asks only about Passage A.

Step 4: Answer

Choice (A) is wrong because it has no complexity to it. White noise, such as the sound of a fan, would be like a "single, pure tone," and the author says that such simple tones are not interesting to listeners.

Choice (B) has the right theme: a plot (which would involve different aspects linked together) that is comprehensible and easy to understand (which has the right type and level of complexity. So, leave it in!

Choice (C) is out of scope. Nothing in Passage A or in this answer choice connects complexity or comprehensibility to size.

Choice (D) is also out of scope. It may be attractive because it mentions music, but remember that Analogy questions have nothing to do with the topic of the passage, only the logic, and choices that have the same topic may in fact be traps. Nothing in the passage connects speed to complexity or comprehensibility.

Choice (E), like (C), is out of scope. There is no evidence in the passage or in the answer choice that sweet foods would be any different than bitter foods in their "comprehensibility" (whatever that might mean in this context) or complexity.

This leaves you with (B) as the best logical match.

4. Which one of the following most accurately expresses the main point of passage B?

(A) The type of musical emotion experienced by a listener is determined by the level to which the listener's expectations are satisfied.

(A)

(B) Trained listeners are more able to consciously manipulate their own emotional experiences of complex music than are naive listeners.

(B)

(C) If the development of a piece of music is greatly at odds with the listener's musical expectations, then the listener will experience negative emotions.

(C)

(D) Listeners can learn to appreciate changes in melodic line and other musical complexities.

(D)

(E) Music that is experienced by listeners as relaxing usually produces a buildup and release of tension in those listeners.

(E)

Here's How to Crack It

Step 2: Assess

This is a Big Picture: Main Point question. Note that it asks for the main point of Passage B, so Passage A is irrelevant to this question.

Step 3: Act

You have already answered this question in your own words when you prepared the passages: resolution of expectations, and complexity and familiarity, factor into the pleasure we find in music. Make sure that you keep the scope of your own answer and of Passage B in mind as you go through POE.

Step 4: Answer

Choice (A) may not perfectly match your own answer; the last paragraph goes a bit beyond expectations of the listener to bring in complexity and novelty (although they are not completely separate issues). But, this choice is definitely close enough to keep in during your first cut through the choices.

Choice (B) is both too narrow and inaccurate. The author discusses trained listeners only in the last paragraph (so, too narrow) and does not talk about how they can consciously manipulate their emotional experience (so, inaccurate). Therefore, (A) is the best match so far.

Choice (C) is very attractive because yes, the author does indicate this to be true in the second paragraph of the passage. But, it is only one theme within the discussion of satisfaction of expectations (for example, it mentions only the negative side). So, (A) is still a better match for the scope of the passage as a whole.

Choice (D) is the same kind of trap as (C): too narrow. You can infer it from the last paragraph, but this is not an Extract: Inference question. It says nothing about a major theme of the passage (resolution of expectations as it relates to emotion), and therefore is significantly more narrow than (A), and so deserves elimination.

Choice (E) is also a "too narrow trap," and is much more narrow in scope than (A). Choice (E) is a major point within the first paragraph of the passage, but compare it with (A), which also includes the main point of the second paragraph of the passage and at least some connection to the final paragraph.

This leaves you with (A) as the best answer, even if you weren't completely satisfied with it when you first read it.

---

5. Which one of the following most undermines the explanation provided in passage A for the relaxing effect that some music has on listeners?

(A) The musical traditions of different cultures vary greatly in terms of the complexity of the rhythms they employ.

(B) The rhythmic structure of a language is determined in part by the pattern of stressed syllables in the words and sentences of the language.

(C) Many people find the steady and rhythmic sound of a rocking chair to be very unnerving.

(D) The sudden interruption of the expected development of a melody tends to interfere with listeners' perception of the melody as coherent.

(E) Some of the most admired contemporary composers write music that is notably simpler than is most of the music written in previous centuries.

Here's How to Crack It

Step 2: Assess

The word "undermines" alerts you that this is an Application: Weaken question. Note also that it references a particular explanation in Passage A. So, you will be looking for an answer that most goes against that explanation (and, Passage B is irrelevant to this question).

Step 3: Act

Go back to Passage A and find the relevant explanation. Use your annotation and main points; the beginning of the third paragraph of that passage says "Certain music can also have a relaxing effect. The fact that such music tends to be continuous and rhythmical suggests a possible explanation for this effect."

Even though you can't predict exactly what new information the correct answer will bring in, you can still come up with a pretty good guideline for what that correct answer needs to indicate: "Continuous and/or rhythmical sounds may not be so relaxing."

Step 4: Answer

Choice (A) is out of scope. Notice that it doesn't tell you a variety of things that it would have to tell you in order to make it a correct answer. For example, it doesn't say that music that is less complex rhythmically is NOT rhythmic or continuous, or, that the people in cultures with more rhythmic music find their music to be LESS relaxing.

Choice (B) is also has no effect on the author's argument. What determines the rhythmic structure of language does not tell you anything about the *effect* of rhythmic sounds on the listener.

Choice (C) is going in the direction we already defined for the question. It describes a "steady and rhythmic sound" that, according to the author's argument, people should find relaxing. However, according to this choice (and remember, you take the choices on Weaken questions as true statements), people instead find it "very unnerving." So, this choice has the right issue and the right direction.

Choice (D) has part of the right issue (continuity) but the wrong direction; this is a classic type of wrong answer on a Weaken question. The answer describes a discontinuity that would interfere with a listener's perception of the melody as coherent. Aside from the fact that the issue of the question is relaxation, not coherence, this choice would be (if anything) consistent with the author's argument. This is the opposite of what you are looking for.

Choice (E), in part in a similar way to (A), introduces an irrelevant comparison. Simplicity is a different issue than continuity and rhythmic nature, and the answer choice does not suggest that this admired "simpler" music is non-rhythmic or non-continuous.

This leaves you with (C) as the answer that goes the furthest to undermine the author's argument.

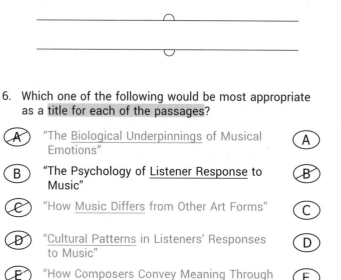

6. Which one of the following would be most appropriate as a title for each of the passages?

   (A) "The Biological Underpinnings of Musical Emotions"

   (B) "The Psychology of Listener Response to Music"

   (C) "How Music Differs from Other Art Forms"

   (D) "Cultural Patterns in Listeners' Responses to Music"

   (E) "How Composers Convey Meaning Through Music"

Here's How to Crack It

Step 2: Assess

This is a Big Picture: Main Point question (if you called it a Big Picture: Primary Purpose question, you were still on the right track). Note that it asks about "each of the passages," so the answer will have to fit with both.

Step 3: Act

Yet again, you have already done the necessary work in your preparation of the passages, with the Bottom Line of each and the relationship between the two.

Our Bottom Line of Passage A is "Level of complexity, coherence, and continuity affect pleasure of listener." Our Bottom Line of Passage B is "Resolution of expectations, and complexity and familiarity, factor into the pleasure we find in music," and the relationship between Passages A and B is "Both passages outline factors that affect our emotional response to music."

The correct answer has to be consistent with these Bottom Lines and this relationship.

Step 4: Answer

Choice (A) is out of scope. Neither passage says anything about biology. Be careful not to read too much into the fact that Passage A mentions language or our brain's reaction to other types of sounds—you can't infer from this that the author is implying any common biological cause. (If you are unsure on that issue, you can still eliminate this choice based on Passage B, which has no such references.) Along the same lines, you can't infer that either author attributes emotional reactions to biological causes.

Choice (B) is consistent with the Bottom Line of each passage and nicely matches our defined relationship between the two. "Pleasure" and "emotion" can definitely be directly connected to "psychology" without any outside knowledge or extra speculation, even if neither author explicitly uses that term.

Choice (C) is out of scope for both passages. Neither compares music to any other art form.

Choice (D) is also out of scope for both Passage A and Passage B. Neither passage talks about different cultures, nor how people in different cultures respond differently.

Choice (E) may be tempting, especially if you haven't defined the Bottom Lines and the relationship between the passages ahead of time. If you have, however, you will quickly see that neither is discussing meaning, but rather, emotional response of the listener.

This leaves you with (B) as the only possible answer.

7. It can be inferred that both authors would be likely to agree with which one of the following statements?

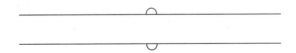

(A) The more complex a piece of music, the more it is likely to be enjoyed by most listeners.   (A)

(B) More knowledgeable listeners tend to prefer music that is discontinuous and unpredictable.   (B)

(C) The capacity of music to elicit strong emotional responses from listeners is the central determinant of its artistic value.   (C)

(D) Music that lacks a predictable course is unlikely to cause a listener to feel relaxed.   (D)

(E) Music that changes from soft to loud is perceived as disturbing and unpleasant by most listeners.   (E)

Here's How to Crack It

Step 2: Assess

This is an Extract: Inference question. Note that it asks about both authors, meaning that it is asking for a statement that is supported by both passages, not just one or the other.

Step 3: Act

Because the question doesn't include any lead words referring to specific passage content, there is no work to be done with the texts before you move into POE.

Step 4: Answer

Notice the strength of language in (A). It indicates a linear relationship between complexity and enjoyment with no upper limit: the higher the complexity, the higher the enjoyment. This directly contradicts the first paragraph of Passage A, in which the author states that "sounds that are too complex or disorganized, however, tend to be overwhelming" and therefore not enjoyable. And, while the author of Passage B does indicate in the last paragraph that trained listeners have a greater tolerance for and enjoyment of complexity, he or she does not go so far as to indicate that there is no upper limit even for these experienced listeners. Therefore, this choice is not supported by either passage.

The easiest way to eliminate (B) is that Passage A never discusses how knowledgeable a listener might be. Furthermore, this choice is too extreme to be supported by the author of Passage B. While the last paragraph indicates that knowledgeable listeners will have a greater preference and enjoyment of discontinuous and unpredictable music than "naive" or new listeners, he or she does not go so far as to say that knowledgeable listeners tend to prefer "discontinuous and unpredictable" music on the whole, but just that they have a "higher threshold" for these qualities.

Choice (C) starts off promisingly, with its reference to the ability of music to elicit emotional responses. However, it goes wrong when it states that this is "the central determinant of its artistic value." The strong wording "central determinant" should be a red flag, and neither author connects emotional response to artistic value of the music. Therefore, this choice is too extreme; if you called it "out of scope," you were also on the right track.

Choice (D) brings in an issue that you already know is discussed in both passages: the emotional effect of music on the listener and what kind of music will or will not be pleasurable. The main point of the last paragraph of Passage A is that "People find continuous sounds relaxing, in music and in general," and the author directly stated in that last paragraph that people associate danger with "sudden, unexpected sounds." So, you can infer that the author of Passage A would agree that unpredictable music will not relax the listener. As for Passage B, the author states at the end of his or her first paragraph that when "resolution occurs, relaxation follows," and then goes on in the next paragraph to state that when what is expected does not occur, negative emotions result. Therefore, you can also infer that the author of Passage B would agree with this choice. Leave it, and move on to (E).

Choice (E) is out of scope. Neither author makes any connection between change from soft to loud and the aspects of music that have an emotional effect on the listener. Be careful not to use outside knowledge or your own opinion to make a connection that is not made by the authors.

This leaves you with (D) as the only statement for which you have any evidence that both authors would accept it as true.

REFINING YOUR SKILLS

Now that you have learned and practiced the basic approach, here are some additional suggestions for further refining your strategy and continuing to improve your performance.

Previewing the Questions

As we mentioned earlier, many test-takers find it useful to preview the questions first, before reading the passage. What does previewing the questions entail? You quickly read through the question stems (not the answer choices), picking out references to passage content. Don't worry about identifying the question types in this stage; that comes later. Knowing what the questions are asking can help you to focus on the important information as you prepare the passage, and to skim over the details that may or may not be important. If there is a reference in the question, go ahead and highlight that text in the passage (but don't jump in and read that section of the passage out of context). As you read the passage, when you come across a topic you recognize from the questions, pay special attention to that section, since you know that you will need it later on. An added benefit of previewing the questions is that having some context when you start to read the passage may well help you to better understand the author's argument the first time through.

Try our four-step strategy—with and without previewing the questions—on two different sets of several passages. If you are not used to previewing, it will feel a bit strange at first. Practice it until you become comfortable with the approach, so that you can know for sure whether or not it is helpful for you. Once you have tried out both ways, choose the method that maximizes your efficiency and your accuracy, and use that approach consistently from then on.

There are a few things to keep in mind when previewing. First, it shouldn't take you more than 20–30 seconds per passage. You are not trying to memorize the questions, but rather to get a sense of what parts of the passage will be most

Preview the Questions
Reading the questions first is an optional part of Step 1. Think of it like watching a preview before going to see a movie. You will already know some of the highlights and plot points, and will be better able to understand the story.

important for answering the questions. Also, don't stop midway through the passage to answer questions, even if you think that you have the relevant information at that point. What the author says later on may affect the answer to that question. Also, for most of the questions it will be necessary to have a good understanding of the main point of the passage. If you stop reading in the middle of the process of preparing the passage, you will likely get distracted and have a harder time understanding the overall logic of the author's argument.

Pacing

Slowing Down

On most tests you have taken in your life, you can't get a good score without completing every question. The LSAT is not that kind of test! Many test-takers will maximize their overall percentage of correct answers on the Reading Comprehension section by randomly guessing on a certain number of questions, and spending their time getting a high percentage of the rest of the questions correct. For many test-takers, that means pacing themselves such that they complete three of the four passages, filling in random guesses for all of the questions on one of the four. As you take more and more practice tests, evaluate your accuracy. If you are getting a high percentage of the questions wrong, and especially if a lot of those questions look fairly easy when you go back over them, that most likely means that you were working too fast and should slow it down, at least at first until your accuracy improves, and perhaps even on the actual LSAT.

Speeding Up

On the other hand, if you are completing two or three passages with a high level of accuracy but can't get to a third or fourth passage, you may be going slower than you need, perhaps by reading the passage text much more carefully than necessary the first time through, or by over-thinking the questions (which can actually also hurt your accuracy). If this is your situation, diagnose where you may be spending more time than necessary. Think about pushing yourself through the passage faster the first time through, not trying to read every word carefully or to understand every little detail. If you are moving through the passage quickly but bogging down in the questions, ask yourself if you are reading the question carefully the first time, getting what you need from the passage, and using that understanding to go through the choices (in more cases) no more than twice. Ask yourself how often you already had the right answer and then unnecessarily "triple checked" it, or even spent more time talking yourself out of it and into a wrong answer. If this is often the case, push yourself through the choices more quickly, trusting your understanding and capacity to make accurate decisions.

Ordering The Questions

Many test-takers find it useful to do the questions in a particular order (within the set of questions attached to a passage). Some find it easier to first do the *Extract* or *Structure* questions that give you some concrete reference to the passage. By going back to the passage to answer these questions, they learn more about the author's argument and have more of a foundation for answering the rest of the set. Other test-takers prefer doing the *Big Picture* questions first, since they have just read the passage and defined the bottom line. Almost everyone does better by leaving the hardest questions within the set for last; these are often the *Application* questions, or any question that is long, convoluted, and hard to translate. Experiment with these different ordering strategies, find the one that works best for you, and use it consistently from that point on.

Self-Evaluation

Diagnosing the causes of your mistakes and refining your strategy based on that evaluation is crucial for continued improvement. Keep a self-evaluation journal or spreadsheet so that you can periodically review it and look for patterns in your own performance. For every question that you miss, or struggle with, ask and answer the following questions:

1. What was wrong with the answer I picked or seriously considered?
2. What attracted me to that wrong answer?
3. What led me to eliminate or just not select the correct answer?
4. What difference could I have seen between those two answers that would have helped me to get the question right, or to get it right faster?
5. What will I do differently in the future?

Also look at questions you got right and passages you did well on, and ask yourself why, and what you can continue to do, and do more consistently, to reach that same high performance level more consistently.

As you can see, there is not one specific characteristic that always makes a passage easier or harder. And, unlike in Games, the nature of the answer choices *can* significantly affect overall difficulty. As you work through the passages in this book and in the real LSATs you've ordered, note your impression of the passage's difficulty on the top of the page before you begin it. Afterward, check that impression against the reality of the passage—was your impression correct? If not, was there something you could have seen by reading the first few sentences and scanning the questions that would have led you to evaluate it more accurately? In this way, you will improve your skill in identifying which passages you should attempt and which you should avoid.

FINAL PASSAGE DRILL

As you do this passage, keep your main focus on strategy and accuracy, not on going as fast as you can. But, do keep track of the amount of time you spend on it so that you can begin to evaluate your pacing. Set a timer to count up but don't look at it while you work (put it in another room if you need to!). Once you are done, note your total time spent and go through the explanations that follow the passage. For every question that you missed, struggled with, or just spent too much time on, answer the self-evaluation questions outlined above.

Reading Comprehension Practice Drill

Answers can be found in Chapter 8.

This Passage and its questions are from PrepTest 44, Section 1, Questions 15–20.

The survival of nerve cells, as well as their performance of some specialized functions, is regulated by chemicals known as neurotrophic factors, which are produced in the bodies of animals, including humans. Rita Levi-Montalcini's discovery in the 1950s of the first of these agents, a hormonelike substance now known as NGF, was a crucial development in the history of biochemistry, which led to Levi-Montalcini sharing the Nobel Prize for medicine in 1986.

In the mid-1940s, Levi-Montalcini had begun by hypothesizing that many of the immature nerve cells produced in the development of an organism are normally programmed to die. In order to confirm this theory, she conducted research that in 1949 found that, when embryos are in the process of forming their nervous systems, they produce many more nerve cells than are finally required, the number that survives eventually adjusting itself to the volume of tissue to be supplied with nerves. A further phase of the experimentation, which led to Levi-Montalcini's identification of the substance that controls this process, began with her observation that the development of nerves in chick embryos could be stimulated by implanting a certain variety of mouse tumor in the embryos. She theorized that a chemical produced by the tumors was responsible for the observed nerve growth. To investigate this hypothesis, she used the then new technique of tissue culture, by which specific types of body cells can be made to grow outside the organism from which they are derived. Within twenty-four hours, her tissue cultures of chick embryo extracts developed dense halos of nerve tissue near the places in the culture where she had added the mouse tumor. Further research identified a specific substance contributed by the mouse tumors that was responsible for the effects Levi-Montalcini had observed: a protein that she named "nerve growth factor" (NGF).

NGF was the first of many cell-growth factors to be found in the bodies of animals. Through Levi-Montalcini's work and other subsequent research, it has been determined that this substance is present in many tissues and biological fluids, and that it is especially concentrated in some organs. In developing organisms, nerve cells apparently receive this growth factor locally from the cells of muscles or other organs to which they will form connections for transmission of nerve impulses, and sometimes from supporting cells intermingled with the nerve tissue. NGF seems to play two roles, serving initially to direct the developing nerve processes toward the correct, specific "target" cells with which they must connect, and later being necessary for the continued survival of those nerve cells. During some periods of their development, the types of nerve cells that are affected by NGF—primarily cells outside the brain and spinal cord—die if the factor is not present or if they encounter anti-NGF antibodies.

1. Which one of the following most accurately expresses the main point of the passage?

   (A) Levi-Montalcini's discovery of neurotrophic factors as a result of research carried out in the 1940s was a major contribution to our understanding of the role of naturally occurring chemicals, especially NGF, in the development of chick embryos.

   (B) Levi-Montalcini's discovery of NGF, a neurotrophic factor that stimulates the development of some types of nerve tissue and whose presence or absence in surrounding cells helps determine whether particular nerve cells will survive, was a pivotal development in biochemistry.

   (C) NGF, which is necessary for the survival and proper functioning of nerve cells, was discovered by Levi-Montalcini in a series of experiments using the technique of tissue culture, which she devised in the 1940s.

   (D) Partly as a result of Levi-Montalcini's research, it has been found that NGF and other neurotrophic factors are produced only by tissues to which nerves are already connected and that the presence of these factors is necessary for the health and proper functioning of nervous systems.

   (E) NGF, a chemical that was discovered by Levi-Montalcini, directs the growth of nerve cells toward the cells with which they must connect and ensures the survival of those nerve cells throughout the life of the organism except when the organism produces anti-NGF antibodies.

2. Based on the passage, the author would be most likely to believe that Levi-Montalcini's discovery of NGF is noteworthy primarily because it

(A) paved the way for more specific knowledge of the processes governing the development of the nervous system

(B) demonstrated that a then new laboratory technique could yield important and unanticipated experimental results

(C) confirmed the hypothesis that many of a developing organism's immature nerve cells are normally programmed to die

(D) indicated that this substance stimulates observable biochemical reactions in the tissues of different species

(E) identified a specific substance, produced by mouse tumors, that can be used to stimulate nerve cell growth

3. The primary function of the third paragraph of the passage in relation to the second paragraph is to

(A) indicate that conclusions referred to in the second paragraph, though essentially correct, require further verification

(B) indicate that conclusions referred to in the second paragraph have been undermined by subsequently obtained evidence

(C) indicate ways in which conclusions referred to in the second paragraph have been further corroborated and refined

(D) describe subsequent discoveries of substances analogous to the substance discussed in the second paragraph

(E) indicate that experimental procedures discussed in the second paragraph have been supplanted by more precise techniques described in the third paragraph

4. Information in the passage most strongly supports which one of the following?

(A) Nerve cells in excess of those that are needed by the organism in which they develop eventually produce anti-NGF antibodies to suppress the effects of NGF.

(B) Nerve cells that grow in the absence of NGF are less numerous than, but qualitatively identical to, those that grow in the presence of NGF.

(C) Few of the nerve cells that connect with target cells toward which NGF directs them are needed by the organism in which they develop.

(D) Some of the nerve cells that grow in the presence of NGF are eventually converted to other types of living tissue by neurotrophic factors.

(E) Some of the nerve cells that grow in an embryo do not connect with any particular target cells.

5. The passage describes a specific experiment that tested which one of the following hypotheses?

(A) A certain kind of mouse tumor produces a chemical that stimulates the growth of nerve cells.

(B) Developing embryos initially grow many more nerve cells than they will eventually require.

(C) In addition to NGF, there are several other important neurotrophic factors regulating cell survival and function.

(D) Certain organs contain NGF in concentrations much higher than in the surrounding tissue.

(E) Certain nerve cells are supplied with NGF by the muscle cells to which they are connected.

6. Which one of the following is most strongly supported by the information in the passage?

(A) Some of the effects that the author describes as occurring in Levi-Montalcini's culture of chick embryo extract were due to neurotrophic factors other than NGF.

(B) Although NGF was the first neurotrophic factor to be identified, some other such factors are now more thoroughly understood.

(C) In her research in the 1940s and 1950s, Levi-Montalcini identified other neurotrophic factors in addition to NGF.

(D) Some neurotrophic factors other than NGF perform functions that are not specifically identified in the passage.

(E) The effects of NGF that Levi-Montalcini noted in her chick embryo experiment are also caused by other neurotrophic factors not discussed in the passage. (E)

Summary

- ○ Here's our step-by-step approach to the Reading Comprehension section:

  Step 1: Prepare

  Step 2: Assess

  Step 3: Act

  Step 4: Answer

- ○ Although you may be more familiar with Reading Comprehension than the other sections of this test, LSAT-style Reading Comprehension brings its own unique challenges and requires a particular strategic approach.

- ○ Proper pacing is the key to a strong performance, and it will come only with a little experimentation and a lot of practice.

- ○ Adjusting your everyday reading habits can also benefit your Reading Comprehension performance. Until you take the test, you should put away the trashy magazines and pick up more challenging reading.

Chapter 5
LSAT Writing

LSAT Writing is a 35-minute ungraded essay with an assigned topic. The LSAT Writing test is administered online separately from the LSAT and must be completed within a calendar year of your LSAT administration. Copies of your essay will be sent to law schools, along with your LSAT score, as part of your official report, so you'll want to do the best you can with the assignment you receive.

Writing Sample
Give this section all the time that an unscored section deserves.

HOW MUCH WILL MY ESSAY AFFECT MY LSAT SCORE?

Not one bit.

Only four sections contribute to your LSAT score: one Games section, two Arguments sections, and one Reading Comprehension section.

If the Writing Sample Is So Unimportant, Why Discuss It?

Just for your own peace of mind. Once you have the other sections of the test under control, look over the rest of this chapter. If you are short on time, you'd be better off practicing Arguments.

There's also the possibility that an admissions officer will accidentally pass his or her eyes over what you have written. If your essay is ungrammatical, riddled with misspellings, off the topic, and wildly disorganized, the admissions officer may think less of you.

Now, we're going to assume that the Writing Sample counts a little bit. You should assume the same thing, but don't lose sleep over it. No one ever got into law school because of the LSAT Writing, and it's doubtful that anyone ever got rejected because of it either. Besides, good writing requires surprisingly few rules, and the rules we'll review will help your writing in general.

WHO WILL READ MY ESSAY?

Possibly no one.

How well or poorly you do on the LSAT Writing will almost certainly not affect your admissions chances.

THEN WHY DO LAW SCHOOLS REQUIRE IT?

Law schools feel guilty about not being interested in anything about you other than your grades and LSAT scores. Knowing that you have spent 35 minutes writing an essay for them makes them feel better about having no interest in reading what you have written.

WILL THE TEST CHANGE?

Always be sure to check the LSAC website at www.lsac.org for any updates to the test.

WHAT ARE THEY LOOKING FOR?

The general directions to the Writing Sample mention that law schools are interested in three things: essay organization, vocabulary, and writing mechanics. Presumably, writing mechanics covers grammar and style.

What They're Really Looking For

Researchers at Educational Testing Service (the folks responsible for the SAT and the GRE, among other tests) once did a study of essay-grading behavior. They wanted to find out what their graders really responded to when they marked papers, and which essay characteristics correlated most strongly with good scores.

The researchers discovered that the most important characteristic, other than "overall organization," is "essay length." Also highly correlated with good essay scores are the number of paragraphs, average sentence length, and average word length. The bottom line? *Students who filled in all the lines, indented frequently, and used big words earned higher scores than students who didn't.*

We will discuss these points in more detail later. Because organization is the most important characteristic, let's start with that.

THE PROMPT
The typical prompt looks something like this:

The program manager of a public television station intends to purchase a documentary program on diabetes and has narrowed the choice down to two programs. Write an argument for purchasing one program over the other, taking into account the following:

- The program manager wants to increase youth awareness of diabetes by engaging a younger audience.

- The program manager wants to air a well-researched and accurate depiction of the challenges of living with diabetes.

"What's Up, Doc?" tells the story of 19-year-old Carlene, a popular rap artist. A physician who worked with Carlene is interviewed, but the documentary focuses primarily on Carlene, her family, and the musicians who work with her. The discussion centers on how Carlene has dealt with her diabetes since it was diagnosed at the age of 14. Carlene explains the innovative and interesting ways she found to integrate the daily monitoring and control of the disease into her very demanding schedule. The program touches on risk factors, warning signs, complications, and self-care skills for managing diabetes. Carlene ends the program by directing a plea to teenagers to learn about the symptoms of diabetes and become more aware of the disease.

"Living with Diabetes" is an investigation of teenagers with diabetes in four different high schools across the country narrated by Andre Smith, a well-known, prizewinning health reporter. Smith interviews a number of students with the disease, along with school administrators and teachers, about the effect of diabetes on the students' lives. He visits local hospitals and counseling centers to interview doctors and psychologists, who outline the various physical and psychological effects of diabetes. The camera also takes viewers to the Diabetes Research Institute's information outreach program, where visitors meet researchers and learn what they are doing to find a cure for the disease. Included in the program are detailed descriptions of treatment options available and their costs, as well as advice about prevention and testing.

Writing Sample prompt from PrepTest 44

What Am I Trying to Do?

You're trying to persuade your reader that one of two given alternatives is better. You cannot *prove* that one side is better; you can only make a case that it is. The test-writers deliberately come up with balanced alternatives so that you can argue for either one of them.

Just choose a side and justify your choice.

Picking Sides

The directions emphasize that neither alternative is "correct." It doesn't matter which side you choose. Pick the alternative that gives you more to work with.

Another way to decide is to compile a little list of the pros and cons on your scratch paper. Then simply pick the alternative whose list of pros is longer. Let's see how you'd do this with the sample topic we've given you.

First, list each alternative (What's Up Doc, Living with Diabetes) as a heading. Underneath each heading draw two columns, one for the pros and one for the cons. Spend the first couple of minutes brainstorming the advantages and disadvantages of each choice. The key to brainstorming is *quantity,* not quality. You can select and discard points later.

Having brainstormed for pros and cons, select the ones you intend to keep and arrange them in order of importance, from *least* to *most* important.

For the purposes of this chapter, let's assume that we intend to give the nod to Living with Diabetes.

Don't Forget the Cons

Some students believe that if you're trying to make a case for something, you should bring up the advantages only. This is wrong.

To persuade readers that Living with Diabetes is the better choice, you must show that you have considered every argument that could be made for What's Up Doc, and found each one unconvincing.

Your argument, in other words, must show that you have weighed the pros and cons of *both* sides. The more forceful the objections you counter, the more compelling your position becomes.

Evaluating the Pros and Cons: the Criteria

As you think of pros and cons for each position, keep in mind the given criteria. Here you have two considerations—appealing to a younger audience or presenting an accurate depiction of the challenges of living with diabetes. You must build

Every LSAT prompt instructs you to make a decision and develop an argument for it. Use the skills you've honed from the Arguments section of the test to help!

your essay around these criteria, so don't ignore them. They give you the structure to follow.

The criteria may not be compatible. If so, weigh the pros and cons in light of this situation. In our example, a documentary featuring a young person living with diabetes might not appeal to a broader audience. You may want to rank the two criteria in terms of importance. Perhaps appealing to larger number of viewers is more important than getting a younger audience. Decide which consideration is more important. If you cannot decide, state so explicitly.

Can I Raise Other Issues?

You *must* weigh the two stated considerations, but nothing prevents you from introducing additional considerations.

You need not raise additional considerations, but if one occurs to you, and you have the time, mention it in passing. If none occurs to you, mention in the conclusion that you have evaluated the two options in view of the two stated considerations only, acknowledging that other considerations may be important.

What's Up Doc Versus Living With Diabetes: Brainstorming the Pros and Cons

Remember, brainstorm first. You can use scratch paper to jot down your ideas before you dive into writing the essay. Next, select the issues you intend to raise. Then, rank the final issues, beginning with the least important.

To organize your brainstorming, use a rough chart like the following one:

	Engages Young Audience	Contains Accurate Research	Other stuff
What's up Doc?	Probable; popular young subject; personal story	Anecdotal information provided; one interview with healthcare professional	Direct plea to teens to learn more about symptoms
Living with Diabetes	Possible; four stories of youth; well-known reporter	Interviews with multiple subjects and healthcare professionals; detailed descriptions of treatment	Advice about prevention and testing

Beginning Your Essay: Restating the Problem

Having brainstormed the pros and cons of each choice in light of the considerations, you are ready to start writing your essay.

Your first paragraph should do little more than state your argument. Try not to use a tedious grade school opening such as, "The purpose of the essay I am about to write is to...."

There are several more interesting ways to introduce an argument. Which one you choose will influence how you organize the rest of your essay. Keep this in mind as you sketch your outline. We'll tell you more about this as we go along.

One possibility for an opening is simply to restate concisely the problem you are to address. Check out the following example:

> The program manager must choose a documentary film about diabetes. The manager wants to engage a young audience while providing accurate and well-researched information about the disease. The two documentaries both have positive and negative aspects that must be weighed in light of the program manager's needs.

This type of introduction sets up the conflict rather than immediately taking a side. The second, third, and fourth paragraphs are then devoted to weighing the specific advantages and disadvantages of each candidate. The author's preference isn't stated explicitly until the final paragraph, although a clear case for one should emerge as the essay progresses.

An essay such as this is really just an organized written version of the mental processes you went through in deciding which documentary to choose. In the first paragraph you say, in effect, "Here are the problems, the choices, and my decision." In the second, third, and fourth paragraphs you say, "Here are the pros and cons I weighed." In the fifth and final paragraph you say, "So you can see why I decided as I did."

Your hope is that the reader, by following your reasoning step by step, will decide the same thing. The great advantage of this kind of organization is that it *does* follow your mental processes. That makes it a natural and relatively easy method.

Beginning Your Essay: Putting Your Cards on the Table

It's also possible to write an essay in which you begin by announcing your decision. You state your preference in the first paragraph, back it up in the middle paragraphs, and then restate your preference with a concluding flourish in the final paragraph.

Here's an example of such an opening paragraph.

> The documentary film "What's up Doc?" shows the daily life of a popular young figure with diabetes which would probably engage a young audience. However, its focus on the life of a single person with the disease may prevent it from providing important information about diabetes. The film "Living with Diabetes" on the other hand would provide the program manager with a documentary about several young subjects that provides important details about diabetes. The program manager should select "Living with Diabetes" because it best suits the needs of the station.

By introducing your argument in this way, you leave yourself with a great deal of latitude for handling the succeeding paragraphs. For example, you might use the second paragraph to discuss both documentaries in light of the first consideration, the third paragraph to discuss both documentaries in light of the second consideration, and the fourth and final paragraph to summarize your argument and restate your preference.

The Body of Your Argument

We've discussed the introductory and concluding paragraphs. Depending on your preference and on the essay topic you actually confront, we recommend three variations for the middle paragraphs.

Variation 1

Paragraph 2:   Both sides in light of the first consideration

Paragraph 3:   Both sides in light of the second consideration

Variation 2

Paragraph 2:   Everything that can be said about What's Up Doc?

Paragraph 3:   Everything that can be said about Living with Diabetes

Variation 3

Paragraph 2:   A sentence or two for What's up Doc?, followed by three or four sentences for Living with Diabetes

Paragraph 3:   A sentence or two for What's up Doc?, followed by three or four sentences for Living with Diabetes

Again, if necessary, you can divide any one of the three middle paragraphs into two paragraphs.

All three variations do the job. Choose a variation you feel comfortable with and memorize it. The less thinking you have to do on the actual exam, the better.

The Princeton Review Thesaurus of Pretty Impressive Words

The following list of words is not meant to be complete, nor is it in any particular order. Synonyms or related concepts are grouped where appropriate.

- example, instance, precedent, paradigm, archetype
- illustrate, demonstrate, highlight, acknowledge, exemplify, embody
- support, endorse, advocate, maintain, contend, espouse, champion
- supporter, proponent, advocate, adherent
- dispute, dismiss, outweigh, rebut, refute
- propose, advance, submit, marshal, adduce
- premise, principle, presumption, assumption, proposition
- advantages, merits, benefits
- inherent, intrinsic, pertinent
- indisputable, incontrovertible, inarguable, unassailable, irrefutable, undeniable, unimpeachable
- unconvincing, inconclusive, dubious, specious
- compelling, cogent, persuasive
- empirical, hypothetical, theoretical

Rules to Write By
1. Write as if you were actually making the recommendation.
2. Write naturally, but don't use abbreviations or contractions.
3. Make sure your position is clear.
4. Write as neatly as possible.
5. Indent your paragraphs.
6. Don't use first person. The assignment is formal enough that it isn't appropriate here. The objective isn't to state what "I think," but to argue in favor of one option or the other. Personal experience is not relevant.

A Note on Diction

Make sure you don't spoil your display of verbal virtuosity by misusing or misspelling these or any other ten-dollar words. Also, get your idioms straight.

A note on a common diction error: if, as in our writing sample, your choice involves only two options, *former* refers to the first and *latter* refers to the second. You cannot use these words to refer to more than two options.

Another common diction error occurs when two or more things are compared. The first option is *better* than the second, but it is not the *best,* which is used when discussing three or more options.

One Final Reminder

Don't forget to use spell-check.

A Sample Essay

A programming manager for a public television station is choosing a documentary film about diabetes and has narrowed the choice to two. "What's Up Doc?" is a documentary about the popular young rap artist living with diabetes and would engage a young audience. "Living with Diabetes" is about diabetes in four high schools and provides details about the disease and its treatments by interviewing students, teachers, and healthcare professionals. With these considerations in mind, the program manager should choose "Living with Diabetes."

"What's Up Doc?" would be extremely engaging for a young audience since it shows the life of a popular rap artist. It would also show some of the ways an individual has managed to cope with the daily challenges caused by the disease as well as point out the importance of testing and early detection. But this documentary would not be thoroughly researched or comprehensive in its coverage of diabetes in youth. By showing the life a single person and relying primarily on her and her family to provide information, this documentary is also unlikely to be completely accurate. While this documentary film would be engaging to a young audience, the cost of greater engagement would be important details and accuracy.

"Living with Diabetes" will also be engaging to a young audience since it focuses on youth as a subject. The popular reporter will also encourage audiences to watch together with families. By looking at diabetes in four different high schools, audiences will get a thorough picture of what daily life is like for a young person with diabetes and his or her family, friends, and teachers. This documentary also interviews multiple healthcare professionals so it is more likely to provide accurate medical information. These professionals also provide helpful information about diabetes prevention and testing. By targeting a young audience and providing comprehensive, accurate information about diabetes this documentary meets the needs of the public television station.

Both documentary films have strengths and weaknesses in regards to the program manager's specific needs. The public television station should choose "Living with Diabetes" for the diabetes documentary because its strengths outweigh its weaknesses.

Summary

- Don't worry about the LSAT Writing test. As long as you spend a little time brainstorming and outlining your essay, this inconsequential section should be no problem.

Chapter 6
Putting It All Together

You've worked through five pretty arduous chapters of *LSAT Premium Prep*. How should you feel? Answer: CONFIDENT! Why? Because you've been given a specific process and approach for each section of the LSAT. You've got a good game plan—and the team with the good game plan usually wins the game. This chapter contains a quick review of your game plan for each section of the exam, as well as some pacing suggestions and tips for the day of the test.

ARGUMENTS

Step 1: Assess the question

Step 2: Analyze the argument

Step 3: Act

Step 4: Answer using Process of Elimination

Pretty simple, right? Well, many people begin to get anxious and they tend to skip Step 3. They want to get right to the answer choices so they can start getting confused and frustrated. However, Step 3 is the most important step in this process. If you come up with your own ideas about what should be the right answer before looking at any of the choices, you'll be misled less often by those appealing but wrong answer choices.

GAMES

Step 1: Diagram and inventory

Step 2: Symbolize the clues and double-check

Step 3: Look for links and size up the game

Step 4: Assess the question

Step 5: Act

Step 6: Answer using Process of Elimination

As in Arguments, many students tend to skip an essential step in the games process. That step is Step 3 (again). Students usually see how necessary it is to draw a diagram and symbolize the clues, but then they get nervous that they've spent so much time drawing and symbolizing that they go straight to the questions. However, looking at the diagram and the symbols you've drawn for 30 seconds before going to the questions will invariably make the game easier—any deductions you make will actually save you time by making you more efficient in answering the questions.

READING COMPREHENSION

Step 1: Prepare

Step 2: Assess

Step 3: Act

Step 4: Answer

Well, here we've once again highlighted Step 3 because it's the most important step and it's the one students tend to skip most often. Again, nervousness about time is the culprit. But as you learned in the Reading Comprehension chapter, pinpointing the correct answer choice becomes much easier when you've already got an idea of what you should be looking for. Don't let the answer choices confuse you—approach the test questions by being ready for them as much as possible.

PACING

The most important principle to keep in mind when you're planning your pacing is balance. Remember that there are two things that determine effective pacing: your speed (the number of questions you attempt) and your accuracy (the chance that, when you attempt a question, you will get it right). Generally, as your speed increases, your accuracy decreases. The challenge is to find the peak pacing strategy for yourself on each section.

The only way to do this effectively is through practice, practice, practice, and analysis, analysis, analysis. Most test-takers do not perform optimally if they charge through at maximum speed. Similarly, dawdling and second-guessing yourself will not get you the most points. You need to adopt a strategy that allows you to slow down in the places you need to, but at the same time keeps you pushing through the questions that come more easily to you so you can devote time where it's needed.

The ideal way to strike this balance differs from section to section and is determined by the different natures of the questions. We have some more specific pacing guidelines for you below, but of course knowing what target you have to hit is different from knowing how it feels to hit that target. To that end, here are some general pacing thoughts on each of the sections of the exam.

Games

Two things about Games are particularly relevant to pacing: first, getting yourself ready to work a game takes a relatively long time; second, Games questions are constructed so that with a solid approach, you can be certain of getting a right answer on any question you attempt.

For this section, you will need to lean heavily toward accuracy. Investing the time needed to make that last decision between two answer choices is unquestionably worth it, even if it seems like a fair amount of work. Take advantage of this section by working for accuracy, and then trusting your work. All you have to do on a Games question is *either* find the one right answer *or* find the four wrong ones, not both. Once you've done this on a question, pick the answer and go.

Try not to change your mind once you've started a game. Otherwise, you're throwing away valuable time. Working a game you've already set up, even if the questions are hard, is typically a better use of your time than working a different game from start to finish. Of course, you want to do everything you can to pick the best games to do, which makes spending a little time on selection eminently worth it.

Arguments

On Arguments, the initial investment for a question is relatively small; and on many Arguments questions, there are things you can do to decide between close answer choices—but only up to a point.

The best approach here is to value speed and accuracy equally. On an easy Arguments question (there are usually many of these toward the beginning of the section), you should be able to proceed through POE and spot one that definitely looks best. In that case, pick it and go.

On a medium Arguments question, you may have two or three answer choices that seem possible. In that case, slow down—look at the conclusion of the argument, review the question if you're uncertain what it's asking you to do, look at the choices carefully, and make close comparisons. Making smart decisions in the down-to-two situation is how you make your money on the Arguments sections.

On difficult Arguments questions (many of these will be near the end of the section), mistrust answers that look extremely attractive. Keep an open mind as you look at the others, and if you're down to two here, follow the same process you use for medium questions. Look for subtle problems. If you can't find them, then go with the choice you thought was right at first and move on. However, if an answer looks too good to be true on a hard question, it probably is.

Pacing
Trust your gut. You know the difference between chipping away at a difficult question and spinning your wheels trying to comprehend what you are reading.

If you begin an Arguments question and it baffles you right away, move on. You can always come back to it, and you haven't lost much if you spend just a little time and then decide to do something else. Similarly, if you've done everything you can in that down-to-two situation and have nothing else to go on, pick the answer you like better and move on. It takes only one or two questions that eat up a lot of time to hurt you on an Arguments section. Be willing to slow down, but don't ever stop.

Reading Comprehension

Speed and efficiency are important on Reading Comprehension. Remember that you don't get points for memorizing the passage; you're reading it to find the answers to the questions. Get through the initial preparation of the passage fairly quickly, without getting bogged down in the details; you can always come back for them later. In this stage, avoid reading parts of the passage over and over; keep moving and come back to difficult sections of the passage only if necessary when answering the questions. However, you *do* need to get a basic understanding of the bottom line of the author's argument. Don't read the passage so quickly that you get little or nothing out of it.

Don't just skim the questions or answer choices in the Assess, Act, and Answer steps; read them carefully, word for word. Always go back to the passage when you are answering the questions. Read for context; don't answer the questions based on only a quick glance at isolated words or phrases from the passage. When you are down to two answer choices, compare them with each other and look for relevant differences. You may need to go back to the passage again at this stage to make a final choice. If you are still stuck, take your best shot, remembering how the test-writers create attractive wrong answers, and continue on. You can come back one more time before you move on to the next passage; sometimes getting a little distance from the question helps you to see what you didn't understand at first. However, don't spend a large percentage of your valuable time on a single question.

Of course, selection is important here, but not nearly as important as it is on Games. Evaluate each passage and the questions very quickly before diving in. If it looks nasty from the outset, then move to another passage; otherwise, start the passage and stick with it.

This is a general chart. Don't worry about being so exact here.

Here's a chart to help you assess your performance on the practice tests.

Pacing Yourself			
If you received...	**Your first goal is...**	**Your intermediate goal is...**	**Your final goal is...**
25–45% correct on Arguments	Work 12–15 Arguments and try to get 10–12 right in 35 minutes	Work 15–18 Arguments and try to get 12–15 right in 35 minutes	Work 18–21 Arguments and try to get 15–18 right in 35 minutes
45–65% correct on Arguments	Work 15–18 Arguments and try to get 12–15 right in 35 minutes	Work 18–21 Arguments and try to get 15–18 right in 35 minutes	Work 21–24 Arguments and try to get 18–21 right in 35 minutes
65–85% correct on Arguments	Work 18–22 Arguments and try to get 15–18 right in 35 minutes	Work 22–24 Arguments and try to get 18–21 right in 35 minutes	Work all the Arguments and try to get 20–23 right in 35 minutes
25–45% correct on Games	Do two Games correctly in 35 minutes	Get through two full Games and halfway through a third one in 35 minutes	Do three Games correctly in 35 minutes
45–65% correct on Games	Get through two full Games and half of a third Game in 35 minutes	Get through three complete Games in 35 minutes, missing only one or two questions	Get through three full Games and half of a fourth Game in 35 minutes
65–85% correct on Games	Do three full Games in 35 minutes	Do three complete Games in 35 minutes and get halfway through the fourth game	Get through the entire section missing only a few questions in 35 minutes
20–35% correct on Reading Comprehension	Do two Reading Comprehension passages in 35 minutes, trying to miss only one question per passage	Do two full Reading Comprehension passages and get halfway through a third passage in 35 minutes	Do three full Reading Comprehension passages in 35 minutes
35–50% correct on Reading Comprehension	Do two full Reading Comprehension passages and get halfway through a third passage in 35 minutes	Do three full Reading Comprehension passages in 35 minutes	Do three full Reading Comprehension passages and get halfway through the fourth passage in 35 minutes
50–80% correct on Reading Comprehension	Do three Reading Comprehension passages in 35 minutes, trying to miss only one question per passage	Do three full Reading Comprehension passages and get halfway through the fourth passage in 35 minutes	Do four full Reading Comprehension passages in 35 minutes

EVALUATING YOUR PERFORMANCE

One of the most important things you can do to continue to improve your score is to analyze the work you do in order to better gauge both the areas in which you're making errors and the amount of time you need to spend on a given question or group of questions to ensure a high level of accuracy. Here we'll discuss several ways to accomplish this.

As we recommended for the practice drills that accompany each of the chapters on Arguments, Games, and Reading Comprehension, it's a good idea to measure how long it takes you to do a game or passage or set of arguments accurately. There's no point rushing to get to questions (and wasting brain power) if you're not going to give yourself the opportunity to get those questions right. Remember, your score is based on how many questions you answer correctly, not on how many questions you actually get to attempt (and of course you're still choosing answers for those you don't attempt). By measuring how long it takes, on average, to work accurately through a game, passage, or group of, say, eight arguments, you can build realistic expectations of how much you'll be able to do on a given timed section. This is important because it can help you set reachable goals for each area of the LSAT—for example, you can't expect to get to all four games if you generally need to spend 15 minutes on just one of them.

To measure your work time, set your timer to count up, not down, and then don't look at it while you're working. Put it face down, in a drawer, or even in another room if necessary. When you've finished working, stop the clock and note the time elapsed. Then check your answers to see how accurate you were. If you missed half or more, you're definitely going too quickly. If, however, you got almost all of them correct, then you can start to think about where you might be able to speed up. Did you linger at an answer choice to convince yourself that it was really right, although you knew the other four choices were unequivocally wrong? Did you try to disprove all the choices in a Games question although you already had the answer in your diagram? As you continue to work questions, you'll eventually find that you hit your optimal speed for each section—if you go any slower, you won't get to the number of questions you know you need to answer to reach your goal, but if you work any faster, your careless errors will increase sharply.

Once you have an idea of how many questions you can reasonably expect to get to, you can start to figure out how you're going to get the score you want. Let's say you're aiming for a 160. You'd need approximately 75 correct answers to achieve that score. (You should use the conversion chart from the most recent LSAT you've ordered when making these estimates.) Perhaps Reading Comprehension is one of your strengths, so you can count on 23 out of 27 questions. Or maybe you average about 18 correct on an Arguments section. That leaves 16 that you'll need to pick up in the Games section. Are you stronger in Games? Then your goal might be 20 from Games and only 21 from Reading Comprehension, with an Arguments goal of 17 per section. Is your goal a 150? That's about 56 questions. How you break that down will be up to you, based on your own strengths and weaknesses.

As with all things on the LSAT, however, it's important not to overanalyze. Not all Games sections are the same (or Arguments or Reading Comprehension, for that matter), which means you shouldn't expect to do the same on every one of them you work. Keep this in mind while you're planning your pacing adjustments and also while you're taking your test. If you came up a little short on Games, don't panic; chances are that you'll be able to pick up the slack on Arguments as long as you give yourself the chance. Setting goals is important, and it's important to have a plan for achieving them, but always be willing to improvise. Focus on what you can control, and take the test as it comes.

Okay, you've figured out how many more questions you need to get right to achieve your goal score. How do you go about fixing your errors? You want to keep track of your progress, preferably in a notebook, on each drill or timed section you do. Analysis is the key to better performance. After each drill or timed section, write down the drill or section number, and for each question you did, note the question number, question type, whether you got it right or wrong, and what happened if you did indeed miss it. After a while, you may begin to see patterns emerge: Maybe you always miss questions that ask what "must be false" because you forget the "false," or you constantly pick answer choices that go beyond the scope of a passage; or you lose focus when tackling EXCEPT questions. Or maybe there's a particular question type you keep misidentifying, or you're not picking the best questions for you to attempt. Whatever the problem is, you have to be able to diagnose it before you can fix it. Keeping track of your progress and reviewing the notes you make about questions you miss will help you further structure your preparation.

ADDITIONAL PRACTICE TIPS

Here are a few final, extra things to think about.

- Try to time your LSAT practice to the time of day you'll be taking the real thing. At the very least, start your practice tests at the same time that the real test will be given. For an afternoon test administration, this means you'll want to concentrate your study time during the afternoon; for all other administrations of the test, you'll want to practice in the morning.
- Although real LSATs from LSAC have only four sections, the actual exam, as you know, has five. It's a really good idea to take an extra section from one of the real LSATs you've ordered and use it as an experimental section when taking full-length practice tests. It will build your stamina, and it will give you a chance to practice with an extra section of each type of question because you never know what question type you could see as an experimental section on test day. Even when doing individual timed sections, try to do a couple of sections back-to-back before checking your answers. Get used to focusing for longer periods of time.

- Don't forget to check out our free online tools at
PrincetonReview.com/prep. You just need to have this book handy
when you log in for the first time.

THE DAY OF THE TEST

There is probably just as much bad advice as good advice dispensed about what to
do on test day. A lot of the good advice is just common sense, but we're going to
give it to you here just in case you're a bit distracted.

Visit Your Test Center Before Test Day

Why worry on test day about the best way to get to the test center? Visit the test
center a few weeks or days before the test so you know exactly where to go on test
day. Better yet, go there with a practice LSAT and try to get into the room where
you're going to take the LSAT. Work the test in that room, if possible, so you're
on familiar ground the day of the test. This will do wonders for your comfort
and confidence. You'll know if the room is hot or cold, what the lighting is like,
whether you'll be working at an individual desk or a long table, and so on. Use the
Boy Scout motto here: be prepared.

Eat and Drink What You Normally Eat and Drink

People have many different ideas about what to eat and drink on the morning
of the test. The most important thing is not to vary dramatically from what you
normally ingest. Don't eat a big, heavy breakfast that will leave you sluggish.
Don't skip breakfast completely. Eat a reasonable meal that will prepare you for a
grueling three-and-a-half-hour test. And don't experiment with caffeine. If you
don't normally have coffee in the morning, don't start on test day. If you do
normally have coffee in the morning, don't skip it on test day. The same advice
applies if you get your caffeine from soda or any other caffeinated beverage.

Take a Snack

Maybe your proctor won't let you munch on anything during the break, but
maybe he or she will. If so, be prepared by taking a bottle of water and a granola
bar or a banana. If you're subtle about it, chances are no one will care one way or
the other. Even if you're not allowed to eat in the testing room, you can always go
outside and fuel up for the second half of the test.

Up-to-date Information:
Check out www.lsac.org
for more information about
specifics: locations, dates,
and restrictions.

Use the Timer

Unlike previous years, the LSAC does not permit the use of digital timers in the testing room, but there is a timer built into the tablet exam. You can turn off the timer if you want to, but we recommend using the timer or an analog watch to track your time. You'll get a digital five-minute warning, so be sure to answer any remaining questions before the time is up.

Take Everything You'll Need

Yes, you will need to present proper identification. You'll also need your registration ticket. Refer to the registration booklet and follow the procedures outlined there. The test administrators will provide you with a stylus, pen, and scratch paper. Don't leave any room for the unexpected.

Get There Nice and Early and Warm Up Your Brain

You're going to be stressed out enough on test day without worrying that you'll be late for the test. Get there nice and early and warm up your brain by working out a game that you've already done and perhaps by running through a few arguments. And don't bother to check the answers; the purpose is warming up, not diagnosis. That way, you'll already be in gear by the time you open up the first section. You want to hit the ground running so you won't be warming up on questions that count toward your score.

Some Stress Is Good; Too Much Stress Is Bad

We know you're going to be stressed the day of the exam, and a little stress is not a bad thing—it will keep you on your toes. But if you tend to get *really* stressed by standardized tests, try a yoga or meditation class, or some other type of relaxation therapy, preferably starting a month before the test. This way, you'll have some techniques to calm you down, taught to you by people who know what they're doing. One Princeton Review student had a dream about test day—she went into the test, and the bubbles were about five feet in diameter. She hadn't even finished bubbling in one bubble before the proctor called time. If you're having dreams like this, relaxation therapy might help.

Wear Layered Clothing

Who knows how cold or how warm the test center will be on test day? Wear your most comfortable layered clothing, so you can put more layers on if you're cold or take layers off if you're hot.

Be Confident and Be Aggressive

Sometimes we'll talk to students after they've taken the LSAT and they'll say, "By the time I got to section 5, I just didn't care anymore. I just filled in whatever." Don't say that; don't think that—section 5 will probably count because the experimental section is usually in the first three sections of the exam. When you open up your test to section 5, keep in mind that it's most likely a real section that will count toward your score. Your goal is to take three deep breaths and to fight your way through that last section, and approach it just as aggressively as you approached the other sections of the exam. It's going to count—don't lose your confidence and your energy here because it's almost over!

Here is another problem students have reported: "I was doing fine until I hit section 3. I didn't know how to do any of the Games, and I couldn't concentrate on the last two sections of the test." Well, guess what? That was probably the experimental section! Don't let a complex or tough section get you down, especially if it's early in the test. Remember that they are using the experimental sections to test new questions—some of them invariably will be a bit strange. And even if it is a section that ultimately counts toward your score, getting stressed out over it will only hurt your performance on that section and potentially on subsequent scored sections as well. Just roll with the punches.

Always Keep Your Stylus Moving

Actively using your stylus will help you to stay engaged. Eliminate all the wrong answer choices; highlight and underline key words in Reading Comprehension and Arguments passages; always diagram and symbolize in Games. By constantly keeping your stylus moving, you'll be keeping your brain moving as well.

If you find that you're losing focus, stop working for a second and regroup. Never waste time working on a question if your mind has gone astray or if you find that you can't focus on the task at hand. The few seconds you invest in a short break will pay off in the long run.

And remember that you can always come back to a question that is giving you grief. Just flag it so that you can find it later if you have time to come back to it. Don't spend too much time on any one question. It will only lead to frustration and lost points.

Your Test Day "Top Ten"
Here are the tips mentioned above in a handy numbered list. Find some room on the fridge.

1. Visit your test center before test day.
2. Eat and drink what you normally eat and drink.
3. Take a snack.
4. Use the timer.
5. Take everything you'll need.
6. Get there nice and early and warm up your brain.
7. Some stress is good; too much stress is bad.
8. Wear layered clothing.
9. Be confident and be aggressive.
10. Always keep your stylus moving.

Good luck on test day!

Summary

- As you practice, your approach will become more intuitive. Until then, be sure to focus on the steps we've outlined so that you have a systematic approach for every section of the test. Most important, do not forget to do a little work before rushing to the answer choices.

- Make sure you are totally prepared for test day. You can't control the questions you will see that day, but you can make sure that you are in the best position to answer those questions.

Chapter 7
Law School Admissions

The process of applying to law school, although simple enough in theory, is viewed by many to be about as painful as a root canal. The best way to avoid the pain is to start early. If you're reading this in December, hoping to get into a law school for the following year, and haven't done anything about it, you're in big trouble. If you've got an LSAT score that you're happy with, you're in less trouble. However, your applications will get to the law schools after the optimum time and the applications themselves, even with the most cursory glance by an admissions officer, may appear rushed. The best way to think about applying is to start early in the year, take care of one thing at a time, and be totally finished by December.

This chapter is mainly a nuts-and-bolts manual on how to apply to law school and when to do it. A checklist, information about Law School Forums, fee waivers, the Credential Assembly Service (CAS), and several admissions calendars, which will show you when you need to take which step, are included.

LSAC, LSAT, CAS

The Law School Admission Council (LSAC), headquartered in Newtown, Pennsylvania, is the governing body that oversees the creation, testing, and administration of the LSAT (Law School Admission Test). The LSAC also runs the Credential Assembly Service (CAS), which provides information (in a standard format) on law school applicants to the schools themselves. All American Bar Association, or ABA-approved, law schools are members of LSAC.

LSAT SCORE DISTRIBUTION

Most test-takers are interested in knowing where their LSAT scores fall within the distribution of all scores. This chart should help you determine how well you did in comparison to fellow test takers over the last few years. Please be aware, however, that percentiles are not fixed values that remain constant over time. Unlike an LSAT score, a percentile rank associated with a given test score may vary slightly depending on the year in which it is reported. This chart is just to give you a roughly accurate idea where you rank compared to those competing for the same spot in law school.

Score	% Below	Score	% Below	Score	% Below	Score	% Below
180	99.9	165	93.2	150	44.9	135	5.3
179	99.9	164	91.4	149	41.0	134	4.4
178	99.9	163	89.7	148	37.0	133	3.5
177	99.8	162	87.3	147	33.4	132	2.9
176	99.7	161	84.9	146	29.6	131	2.3
175	99.6	160	82.2	145	26.4	130	1.9
174	99.5	159	79.1	144	23.3	129	1.5
173	99.3	158	76.5	143	20.2	128	1.2
172	99.0	157	72.6	142	17.7	127	0.9
171	98.5	156	68.7	141	15.2	126	0.7
170	98.1	155	65.7	140	12.9	125	0.6
169	97.5	154	61.5	139	10.9	124	0.5
168	96.7	153	57.3	138	9.2	123	0.4
167	95.7	152	53.2	137	7.8	122	0.3
166	94.6	151	49.1	136	6.5	121	0.3
						120	0.0

WHEN TO APPLY

Consider these application deadlines for fall admission: Yale Law School, on or about February 28; New York University (NYU) Law School, on or about February 15; Loyola University Chicago School of Law, on or about May 1. Although some of this information may make starting the application process in December seem like a viable option, remember that law schools don't wait until they've received every application to start selecting students. In fact, the longer you wait to apply to a school, the worse your chances are of getting into that school. Maybe your chances will go only from 90 percent to 85 percent, but you shouldn't take an unnecessary risk by waiting.

Additionally, some schools have "early admissions decisions" options, so that you may know by December if you've been accepted (for instance, NYU's early admission deadline is on or about November 15). This option is good for a few reasons: it can give you an indication of what your chances are at other schools; it can relieve the stress of waiting until April to see where you're going to school; and if you're put on the waiting list the first time around, you might be accepted a bit later on in the process—i.e., when everyone else is hearing from law schools for the first time. However, not every school has an early admission option, and not every school's option is the same, so check with your prospective institutions' policies before you write any deadlines on your calendar.

> ### Law School Forums
> Law School Forums are an excellent way to talk with representatives and gather information on almost every law school in the country simultaneously. More than 150 schools send admissions officers to these forums, which take place in major cities around the country between February and October. If at all possible, GO. For information about forum dates and locations, check the LSAC website at www.lsac.org.

Let's take a look at the major steps in the application process.

- **Take the LSAT.** All ABA-approved and most non-ABA-approved law schools in the United States and Canada accepts an LSAT score from each applicant. The LSAT is offered multiple times each year. Some schools may accept a GRE score from students who have not taken the LSAT.

- **Register for CAS.** You can register online for the Credential Assembly Service at the same time you register to take the LSAT.

- **Select approximately seven schools.** After you've selected your schools, you'll be able to see which schools want what types of things on their applications—although almost all of them will want three basic things: a personal statement, recommendations, and a résumé. Each applicant should be thinking about putting law schools into three categories: (1) "reach" schools, (2) schools where you've got a good chance of being accepted, and (3) "safety" schools. At a minimum, each applicant should apply to two to three schools in each category. (Most admissions experts will say either 2-2-3 or 2-3-2.) It is not uncommon for those with extremely low grades or low LSAT scores (or both) to apply to 15 or 20 schools.

- **Write your personal statement(s).** It may be that you'll need to write only one personal statement (many schools will ask that your personal statement be about why you want to obtain a law degree), but you may need to write several—which is why you need to select your schools fairly early.

- **Obtain two or three recommendations.** Some schools will ask for two recommendations, at least one of which should be academic (both if you are a recent graduate). Others want more than two recommendations and want at least one of your recommenders to be someone who knows you outside traditional academic circles.

- **Update/create a résumé.** Most law school applications ask that you submit a résumé. Make sure yours is up to date and suitable for submission to an academic institution.
- **Get your academic transcripts sent to CAS.** A minor administrative detail, seemingly, but then again, if you forget to do this, CAS will not send your information to the law schools. CAS helps the law schools by acting as a clearinghouse for information—CAS, not you, sends the law schools your undergraduate and graduate school transcripts, your LSAT score(s), and an undergraduate academic summary.

Those are the major steps in applying to law school. From reading this chapter, you might discover that there are other steps you need to take—such as preparing an addendum to your application, asking for application fee waivers, applying for a special administration of the LSAT, and so on. If you sense that you might need to do anything special, start your application process even earlier than what is recommended. One LSAC sample schedule recommends taking the June LSAT for fall admission the following year. This schedule allows you to focus on the LSAT in the spring and early summer and then start the rest of your application process rolling. That's good advice—as mentioned in the LSAT portion of this book, the LSAT is one of the most important factors in getting into the best law school possible.

The sample schedule also indicates that you should research schools in late July/early August. While you are doing this, go ahead and subscribe to CAS and send your transcript request forms to your undergraduate and any other educational institutions—there's no reason to wait until September to do this (you should pay CAS for seven law school applications, unless you're positive you want to apply to only a few schools). Why do this? Because undergraduate institutions can and will make mistakes and delay the transcript process—even when you go there personally and pay them to provide your records. This is essential if you're applying for early decision at some law schools—the transcript process can be a nightmare.

Finally, you should send your applications to law schools between late September and early November. Naturally, if you bombed the LSAT the first time around, you're still in good shape to take the test again in October. Another good piece of news on that front is that more and more law schools are now just simply taking the highest LSAT score that each applicant has, rather than averaging multiple scores. If you have to take the LSAT again, this is good news—but with proper preparation, you can avoid having to spend too much quality time with the LSAT.

A Simple Checklist

The following is a simple checklist for the major steps of the application process. Each shaded box indicates the recommended month during which you should complete that action.

	Jan.	Feb.	Mar.	Apr.	May	June	July	Aug.	Sept.	Oct.	Nov.	Dec.
Take practice LSAT	▓											
Research LSAT prep companies		▓										
Obtain Registration Information Book*			▓									
Register for June LSAT				▓								
Take LSAT prep course					▓	▓						
Take LSAT						▓						
Register for Credential Assembly Service (CAS)—formerly known as the Law School Data Assembly Service							▓					
Research law schools							▓					
Obtain law school applications								▓				
Get transcripts sent to CAS								▓				
Write personal statement(s)									▓			
Update/create résumé									▓			
Get recommendations									▓			
Send early decision applications										▓		
Finish sending all applications											▓	
Relax												▓

HELPFUL HINTS ON PERSONAL STATEMENTS, RECOMMENDATIONS, RÉSUMÉS, AND ADDENDA

Although your LSAT score is one of the most important factors in the admissions process, you should still present a professional résumé, get excellent recommendations, and hone your personal statement when preparing your law school applications.

Many law schools still employ the "three-pile" system in the application process.

Pile 1 contains applicants with high enough LSAT scores and GPAs to admit them pretty much automatically.

Pile 2 contains applicants who are "borderline"—decent enough LSAT scores and GPAs for that school but not high enough for automatic admission. Admissions officers look at these applications thoroughly to sort out the best candidates.

Pile 3 contains applicants with "substandard" LSAT scores and GPAs for that school. These applicants are usually rejected without much further ado. There are circumstances in which admissions officers will look through pile 3 for any extraordinary applications, but it doesn't happen very often.

What does this mean? Well, if you're lucky, you are in pile 2 (and not pile 3!) for at least one of your "reach" schools. And if you are, there's a good possibility that your application will be thoroughly scrutinized by the admissions committee. Consequently, make sure the following four elements of your application are as strong as you can possibly make them.

Personal Statement

Ideally, your personal statement should be two pages long. Often, law schools will ask you to identify exactly why you want to go to law school and obtain a law degree. "I love *How To Get Away with Murder*" is not the answer to this question. There should be some moment in your life, some experience that you had, or some intellectual slant that you are interested in that is directing you to law school. Identify that reason, write about it, and make it compelling.

Then you should have three or four people read your personal statement and critique it. You should select people whom you respect intellectually, not people who will merely give it a cursory read and tell you it's fine. Also, your personal statement is not the place to make excuses, get on your soapbox, or try your hand at alliterative verse. Make it intelligent, persuasive, short, and powerful—those are the writing and analytical qualities law schools look for.

Recommendations

Most law schools ask for two or three recommendations. Typically, the longer it has been since you've graduated, the tougher it is to obtain academic recommendations. However, if you've kept your papers and if your professors were tenured, chances are you'll still be able to find them and obtain good recommendations—just present your prof of choice with your personal statement and a decent paper you did in his or her course. That way, the recommender has something tangible to work from. And that's the simple secret to great recommendations—if the people you're asking for recommendations don't know anything specific about you, how can the recommendation possibly be compelling? Getting the mayor of your town or a state senator to write a recommendation helps only if you have a personal and professional connection to them in some way. That way, the recommender will be able to present to the admissions committee actual qualities and accomplishments you have demonstrated.

Fee Waivers

Even though the cost of taking the LSAT, subscribing to CAS, paying for LSAT prep materials, and paying application fees will probably be one-hundredth of your total law school outlay, it's still not just a drop in the bucket. The LSAT is $200, CAS is $195 (includes one report sent to a CAS-requiring law school and three letters of recommendation), plus $45 for each additional school you are applying to. And law school applications themselves are typically around $50 each. As a result, LSAC, as well as most law schools, offers a fee waiver program. If you're accepted into the LSAC program, you get two free LSATs per year, one LSAT Writing, one CAS subscription, four CAS law school reports. With proper documentation, you can also waive a good portion of your law school application fees. You can apply for a fee waiver through your LSAC.org account.

If you've been out of school for some time and are having trouble finding academic recommendations, choose people from your workplace, from the community, or from any other area of your life that is important to you. You should respect the people you choose—you should view them as quality individuals who have in some way shaped your life. If they're half as good as you think they are, they will know, at least intuitively, that they in some way were responsible for part of your development or education, and they will then be able to talk intelligently about it. Simply put, these people should know who you are, where you live, what your background is, and what your desires and motivations are—otherwise, your recommendations will not distinguish you from the 10-foot-high pile that's on an admissions committee desk.

Résumés

Résumés are a fairly simple part of your application, but make sure yours is updated and proofed correctly. Errors on your résumé (and, indeed, anywhere on your application) will make you look as if you don't really care too much about going to law school. Just remember that this should be a more academically oriented résumé, because you are applying to an academic institution. Put your academic credentials and experiences first—no matter what they are.

Addenda

If your personal and academic life has run fairly smoothly, you shouldn't need to include any addenda with your application. Addenda are brief explanatory letters written to explain or support a "deficient" portion of your application. Some legitimate addenda topics are academic probation, low/discrepant GPA, low/discrepant LSAT score, arrests/convictions, DUI/DWI suspensions, a leave of absence or other "time gaps," and other similar circumstances.

The addenda are not the place to go off on polemics about standardized testing—if you've taken the LSAT two or three times and simply did not do very well, after spending time preparing with a test prep company or private tutor, merely tell the admissions committee that that's what you've done—you worked as hard as you could to achieve a high score and explored all possibilities to help you achieve that goal. Then let them draw their own conclusions. Additionally, addenda should be brief and balanced—do not go into detailed descriptions of things. Explain the problem and state what you did about it. Simply put, do not whine.

GATHERING INFORMATION AND MAKING DECISIONS

There are some key questions that you should ask before randomly selecting law schools around the country or submitting your application to someone or other's list of the "top ten" law schools and saying, "If I don't get in to one of these schools, I'll go to B-School instead." Here are some questions to think about.

Where Would You Like to Practice Law?

For instance, if you were born and bred in the state of Nebraska, care deeply about it, wish to practice law there, and want to someday be governor, then it might be a better move to go to the University of Nebraska School of Law than, say, the University of Virginia, even though UVA is considered a "top ten" law school. A law school's reputation is usually greater on its home turf than anywhere else (except for Harvard and Yale). Apply to the schools in the geographic area where you wish to practice law. You'll be integrated into the community, you may gain some experience in the region doing clinics during law school, and it should be easier for you to get more interviews and position yourself as someone who already knows, for instance, Nebraska.

What Type of Law Would You Like to Practice?

Law schools *do* have specialties. For instance, if you are very interested in environmental law, it might be better to go to Vermont Law School than to go to NYU. Vermont Law School is one of the most highly regarded schools in the country when it comes to environmental law; so look at what you want to do in addition to where you want to do it.

Can You Get In?

Many people apply to Harvard. Very few get in. Go right ahead and apply, if you wish, but unless you've got killer scores and/or have done some very outstanding things in your life, your chances are, well, *slim*. Apply to a few reach schools, but make sure they are schools you really want to go to.

Did You Like the School When You Went There?

What if you decided to go to Stanford, got in, went to Palo Alto, California, and decided that you hated it? The weather was horrible! The architecture was mundane! There's nothing to do nearby! Well, maybe Stanford wasn't the best example—but you get the point. Go to the school and check it out. Talk to students and faculty. Walk around. *Then* make a decision.

Summary

○   The application process, although detailed, is much easier than taking the extremely stressful LSAT, which in turn will be much easier than your first year of law school—no matter where you go. However, you've still got to want to go to law school. Applying to law school is a demanding process, and if you're not committed to doing it well, it will almost certainly come across in your applications. Be as thorough in preparing your applications as you were in preparing for the LSAT; otherwise you run the risk of turning in applications that are late or contain errors, thereby hurting your chances of getting accepted by the schools to which you really want to go.

○   If all this administrative stuff seems overwhelming (i.e., you're the type of person who dreads filling out a deposit slip), the major test-prep companies have designed law school application courses that force you to think about where you want to go and make sure you've got all your recommendations, résumés, personal statements, addenda, and everything else together.

○   Whatever your level of administrative faculty, the choice of where you want to go to school is yours. You'll probably be paying a lot of money to go, so you should really make sure you go to the place that's best for you. Take the time to research the schools because you'll be paying for law school for a long, long time.

Chapter 8
Drill Answers and Explanations

CHAPTER 2: ARGUMENTS

Answers for Arguments Practice Drill (Pages 121–126)

1. **E** PrepTest 44, Section 2, Question 8

2. **C** PrepTest 45, Section 4, Question 9

3. **C** PrepTest 45, Section 4, Question 7

4. **B** PrepTest 44, Section 2, Question 23

5. **A** PrepTest 45, Section 4, Question 12

6. **E** PrepTest 44, Section 2, Question 21

7. **E** PrepTest 44, Section 2, Question 22

8. **B** PrepTest 44, Section 2, Question 19

9. **B** PrepTest 44, Section 4, Question 18

10. **B** PrepTest 44, Section 2, Question 10

11. **B** PrepTest 44, Section 2, Question 11

12. **A** PrepTest 44, Section 2, Question 12

13. **C** PrepTest 38, Section 1, Question 2

Explanations for Arguments Practice Drill (Pages 121–126)

1. **E**   Weaken Except; Interpret

   The author concludes that synthetic pesticides pose minimal threat to humans. The premise is that plants contain natural pesticides which are not harmful to humans. The author assumes that the effects of natural and synthetic pesticides are comparable. Eliminate answer choices that attack this comparison.

   A. No. This weakens the argument by suggesting a difference between natural and synthetic pesticides. Humans have not had time to adapt to synthetic pesticides as they have to natural pesticides.

   B. No. This weakens the argument by suggesting a difference between natural and synthetic pesticides. If concentrations of synthetic pesticides are higher than those of natural pesticides, the synthetic pesticides could pose a threat.

   C. No. This weakens the argument by suggesting a difference between natural and synthetic pesticides. If synthetic pesticides are more potent, they could pose a threat.

   D. No. This weakens the argument by suggesting a difference between natural and synthetic pesticides. If synthetic pesticides are harmful to a wide variety of organisms, it is possible that they are harmful to humans.

   E. Yes. This strengthens the argument by suggesting that synthetic and natural pesticides are chemically similar.

2. **C**   Main Point; Solve

   The public health expert presents premises in his argument that include reference to recent thoughts that biomedical research would eventually find a way to deal with microorganisms that cause human disease. However, he goes on to state that the development of these microorganisms has been difficult to curb given their ability to reproduce rapidly and evolve in response to medicines designed to kill them. The public health expert concludes that the best public health strategy would place more emphasis on educating citizens about minimizing the transmission of diseases caused by microorganisms and give up hope that research can find a cure for such diseases.

   A. No. This answer paraphrases part of the premises, not the conclusion.

   B. No. This is not stated in the argument.

   C. Yes. This is a great paraphrase of the public health expert's conclusion.

   D. No. This answer is too extreme as well as not an accurate description of the expert's conclusion.

   E. No. This answer paraphrases part of the premises, not the conclusion.

3. **C**   Strengthen; Solve

   The conclusion of the argument is that when it's possible, people should use electric mowers over gasoline mowers to cut down on air pollutants. The author argues his point by presenting several premises. First, most gas mowers put out as much air pollution per hour as does an automobile. Second, gas mowers contribute too much summertime pollution. Finally, electric mowers don't emit any pollutants. The author relies on the assumption that the two types of mowers are comparable in all aspects save the pollution.

   A. No. This answer has nothing to do with the comparison between gas and electric mowers.

   B. No. This could be a reason to not use electric mowers, which weakens the argument.

C. Yes. Since the argument equates the emissions of an automobile and a gas mower, this answer would support the conclusion that an electric mower would indeed create less pollution than a gas mower.

D. No. Even if manufacturers are trying to reduce the emissions of gas mowers, electric mowers still have zero emissions. This doesn't address the comparison between the mowers.

E. No. This answer doesn't address the comparison between gas and electric mowers. Even if mowers are used for less time per year than automobiles, the fact remains that gas mowers still put out as much pollution per hour as automobiles.

4. **B** Necessary Assumption; Interpret

The columnist concludes that modern technology undermines life's charm and diminishes the overall well-being of its users. The premise is that people become dependent on modern technology and on the energy systems required to run it, and they lose self-sufficiency. The author assumes that dependence and lack of self-sufficiency are connected to lack of charm and diminished well-being.

A. No. This is too strong; physical labor does not need to be essential to a fulfilling life.

B. Yes. If self-sufficiency contributes to well-being, the argument's premises are linked to the conclusion.

C. No. This does not specifically link self-sufficiency to well-being.

D. No. This is too broad and general. It does not specifically link self-sufficiency to well-being.

E. No. This goes too far. It's not necessary to assume that technology inherently limits well-being. This choice fails to link self-sufficiency to well-being.

5. **A** Reasoning; Solve

The columnist compares an unsigned letter with an anonymous source used in news stories. The columnist points out that although we would be skeptical about the truth of the contents of an unsigned letter, we many times are not skeptical about the veracity of news reports based on anonymous sources. The columnist goes on to say that such anonymity allows the possibility for these sources to plant inaccurate or slanted statements with no responsibility for such statements.

A. Yes. This answer accurately describes the columnist's comparison of the two different ideas.

B. No. Although there is mention of the analogy used in this argument, this answer choice is half good/ half bad. The argument does not say one attitude is better justified than the other.

C. No. This describes the opposite of what the columnist does in his argument.

D. No. Like (B), this answer is half good/half bad.

E. No. There is no mention of the analogy that the author uses in his reasoning.

6. **E** Flaw; Interpret

The author thinks it highly likely that Claudette is a classical pianist. The premises are that Claudette recognizes many of Clara Schumann's works, as do most classical pianists. In addition, people who are not classical pianists do not recognize Schumann's works and may not have heard of her. The author makes a faulty connection between being a classical pianist and recognizing Schumann's works. It is entirely possible that Claudette is among the people who are not classical pianists but who recognize Schumann's works.

A. No. Claudette's familiarity with other composers is not relevant.

B. No. This does not address the issue of whether a non-pianist can recognize Schumann's works.

C. No. Whether classical pianists can play other instruments is not relevant.

D. No. The definition of "classical" is not relevant.

E. Yes. The majority of people who are not classical pianists don't recognize Schumann's works, which leaves room for the possibility that some non-pianists recognize her works.

7. **E**   Parallel Flaw; Interpret

The author concludes that experimental results will confirm Grippen's or Heissman's theory. The premise states that the evidence fits both theories, but the theories' predictions about the experimental results cannot both be true. The author doesn't consider that perhaps the experiment isn't a good test of the theories or that the experiment might confirm neither theory. The credited response needs to have this structure: two people have conflicting views, and new information will prove one or the other correct.

A. No. The conclusion does not claim that new information will prove either David or Jane correct, so this argument does not match the structure of the original.

B. No. The conclusion does not claim that new information will prove either David or Jane correct, so this argument does not match the structure of the original.

C. No. The conclusion does not claim that new information will prove either David or Jane correct. It refers to determining who is better, so this argument does not match the structure of the original.

D. No. The conclusion does not claim that new information will prove either David or Jane correct, so this argument does not match the structure of the original.

E. Yes. This argument has two conflicting views—David thinks the tree is a beech, and Jane thinks it's an elm. New information (Maria's expert identification) will prove David or Jane correct. This argument contains the same flaw as the original. It fails to consider that Maria could be in error or that her identification might match neither Jane's nor David's.

8. **B**   Reasoning; Interpret

The argument concludes that it is unlikely the world will ever be free of disease. The premise is that most diseases are caused by microorganisms that evolve immunities to medicines designed to combat them. Thus, the claim referred to in the question stem is the conclusion of the argument.

A. No. While the statement is a conclusion, the argument does not claim that microorganisms are too numerous to eliminate.

B. Yes. This choice matches the argument.

C. No. The claim is the conclusion, not a premise.

D. No. The claim is a conclusion, not a prediction of the response of microorganisms to medicines.

E. No. This goes too far. The claim is a conclusion, but the premise does not state that microorganisms are completely immune to medicines.

9. **B**   Inference; Except

Find the answer choice that must be false by eliminating what is true or could be true according to the passage. The passage contains a number of facts: pursuit of happiness ≠ always doing what you desire; pursuit of happiness must include long-term consequences; desires focus on short-term consequences; desires can be compulsions which ≠ happiness.

A. No. You cannot prove this is false from the information given. Though the passage does not discuss the proportion of people who have compulsions, it is possible that the majority do not have them.

B. Yes. This is impossible. The passage states that desires are sometimes compulsions and that satisfying compulsions doesn't bring happiness. Thus, attaining the goals of some desires doesn't result in momentary happiness.

C. No. This could be true because there is no information in the passage about rationality. Nothing in the passage rules this out.

D. No. This could be true because there is no information about what people want besides happiness. Nothing in the passage rules this out.

E. No. This could be true because, again, there is no information in the passage about whether all actions have long-term consequences. Nothing in the passage rules this out.

10. **B** Resolve/Explain

When both parents feed beetle larvae, the larvae should benefit, but larvae grow larger and heavier when only one parent is present. Look for an answer that explains this situation.

A. No. This explains why larvae would fare better with two parents, not one.

B. Yes. If both parents are present and eat the carcass, there is less food for the larvae. This explains why having only one parent present benefits the larvae.

C. No. This explains why larvae would fare better with two parents, not one.

D. No. This is not relevant. The concern is with explaining what happens during the time parents feed the larvae.

E. No. This explains why larvae would fare better with two parents, not one.

11. **B** Inference

People used to believe that only Euclidian geometry provided a correct way of representing the universe, but scientists now believe non-Euclidian geometry is more useful in certain areas, such as cosmological theory.

A. No. This is not supported by the passage.

B. Yes. This fits the passage. Scientists now believe that non-Euclidian geometry is more useful in certain areas, so it's safe to say that they don't believe Euclidean geometry is the only way to go.

C. No. Non-Euclidian geometry is useful in certain areas, but claiming it is more complete is going too far.

D. No. This is far too strong and too broad. The passage does not support the idea that an accurate theory requires a uniquely correct mathematical representation.

E. No. The passage did not distinguish between usefulness and correctness.

12. **A** Principle; Match

The passage concerns the choice of expert witnesses for court cases. The author states that sometimes people who are less expert but better able to give convincing testimony are preferred because their testimony will be better received by juries. Find an answer choice that describes a similar situation.

A. Yes. In this situation, presentation is more important than knowledge. Successful politicians are those who are convincing campaigners, even though they may not know how to help their country.

B. No. Just because this choice talks about trial lawyers doesn't mean the situation is similar. While it deals with persuasiveness of presentation, it does not address level of knowledge.

C. No. This is the opposite of the situation in the passage. It advocates choosing the singer with more skill over the one who is more appealing to the audience.

D. No. This is not at all similar to the situation in the passage. It does not involve choosing someone who gives a better presentation over someone with more knowledge.

E. No. This is not similar to the situation in the passage. It does not involve choosing someone who gives a better presentation over someone with more knowledge.

13. **C** Main Point; Interpret

The author believes that the similarities between the two products are not just a coincidence. The main point is highlighted here by the word "however" in the middle of the paragraph. This indicates where the author's true opinion lies, and therefore his main point.

A. No. This is just a description of a supporting premise for the conclusion.

B. No. This is too strong. It may be true, but the conclusion is that the similarity is not a coincidence, not that one company must have copied the design of the other.

C. Yes. The author believes the similarities are not coincidental.

D. No. This would be the opposite of the main point. Indicating the similarities could be coincidental goes against the author's position that the similarities are too fundamental to be coincidence.

E. No. This is not relevant. Apparent uniqueness versus actual similarity is not the issue in this argument, and this choice does nothing to describe that the products were not a coincidence.

CHAPTER 3: GAMES

Answers for Game 1 (Pages 264–265)

1. **E** PrepTest 44, Section 3, Question 13

2. **C** PrepTest 44, Section 3, Question 14

3. **A** PrepTest 44, Section 3, Question 15

4. **E** PrepTest 44, Section 3, Question 16

5. **D** PrepTest 44, Section 3, Question 17

Explanation for Game 1

Ranking. This game is one of the harder games. While there are several awesome deductions that can be made that make the game fast, if you didn't make them, the large number of general questions will make this game challenging. Hopefully you did this game third or fourth.

Step 1: Diagram and Inventory This is a 2D ordering game, though ordering is a small part of the game. The task in this game is to identify both the discoverer of the site and the century to which it dates. We'll use a standard two-row diagram for this. The numbers 1–5 will go across the top of the diagram indicating the order of sites visited. The top row of the diagram will be the archaeologists, and the bottom row will be the century.

$a = FGO$ $c = 8\,9\,10$	1	2	3	4	5
Clue $\dfrac{a}{c}$ Shelf	– –	– –	– –	– –	– –

Step 2: Symbolize and Double-check the Clues

Clue 1 is a concrete clue and should be placed on the diagram.

$a = FGO$ $c = 8\,9\,10$	1	2	3	4	5
Clue $\dfrac{a}{c}$ Shelf	– –	– 9	– –	– –	– –

Clue 2 is also a concrete clue and should be placed on the diagram.

$a = FGO$ $c = 8\,9\,10$	1	2	3	4	5
Clue $\dfrac{a}{c}$ Shelf	– –	– 9	– –	~O	~O

Clue 3 is a vertical block clue. Also, note that this clue forces the game to have exactly one G.

③ $\boxed{\begin{matrix} G \\ 10 \end{matrix}}$ *exactly once*

Clue 4 is a conditional clue mixed with a block clue. Both the clue and the contrapositive are symbolized below.

④ $8 \rightarrow \boxed{\begin{matrix} O \\ 8 \end{matrix}}$

$\sim O \rightarrow \sim 8$

Clue 5 is a distribution clue that limits the possible elements that can be in each of the mentioned slots. It can be symbolized as follows.

(5) 3rd > 1st or 4th

Be sure to double-check these clues carefully.

Step 3: Make Deductions and Size Up the Game

There are several deductions that can be made in this game. Note the large number of General questions versus Specific questions. When combined with the distribution clue, this suggests that this game is a deduction-driven game.

The most important deductions in this game are made with the discovery years. Since neither the 4th nor 5th site was discovered by O, then they cannot be 8. Next, we know that site 3 must be more recent than sites 1 or 4. We don't know anything about site 1, but we now know that site 4 cannot be 8. Therefore, it must be either 9 or 10. However, site 3 must be more recent than 4, so site 3 must be 10 and site 4 must be 9. Here's what we have marked.

a = FGO c = 8 9 10	1	2	3	4	5
Clue a	—	—	—	~O	~O
Shelf c	~10	9	10	~8̸ 9	~8

Now, looking at the diagram, we can see that if there was an 8th-century site, it must be visited first. Be careful here, though, since there is nothing in the game to mandate that all years will be used!

Next, the fact that there is only 1 G limits the game further. In fact, there are only two possible permutations of the game. The first permutation puts G in the 3rd slot. Since this is the only G, and since O cannot be 4 or 5, then those must be F. Go ahead and commit this to paper and call it distribution 1.

a = FGO c = 8 9 10	1	2	3	4	5
Clue a	—	—	—	~O	~O
Shelf c	~10	9	10	~8̸ 9	~8
Distribution a	—	—	G	F	F
1 c	~10	9	10	9	9/10

Now, let's see if there's another possible place for G. Sites 1, 2, and 4 are not 10th century, so the only other possible place for G is slot 5. If G is here, then slot 4 must still be F, but we don't know which of the two remaining archaeologists found the other sites.

a = FGO c = 8 9 10		1	2	3	4	5
Clue Shelf	a/c	−	_ _ ~10	_ _ 9	_ _ 10	~O _ _ ~8 9	~O _ _ ~8
Distribution 1	a/c	−	_ _ ~10	_ _ 9	G _ 10	F _ 9	F _ 9/10
Distribution 2	a/c	−	_ _ ~10	_ _ 9	_ _ 10	F _ 9	G _ 10

Having these two distributions written down will make working through this game much more expedient.

Steps 4–6: Assess the Question, Act, and Use Process of Elimination Question 1 appears to be a Grab-a-Rule, but it doesn't include the years. Since most of the clues deal with the different years, this must be a General question. Let's move on to the only Specific question.

---

2. If exactly one of the five sites the tour group visits dates from the tenth century, then which one of the following CANNOT be a site that was discovered by Ferrara?

   (A) the site visited first

   (B) the site visited second

   (C) the site visited third

   (D) the site visited fourth

   (E) the site visited fifth

(A) (B) (C) (D) (E)

Here's How to Crack It
Question 2 tells us there is exactly one site from the 10th century. Therefore, we must use distribution 1. Carry this down into the diagram. We know that site 3 was G, and that sites 4 and 5 were F. We are looking for the answer choice that cannot be F, so let's dive straight into the answers. According to our diagram, G must be 3rd; therefore, F cannot have discovered this site. Lock in (C).

$a = FGO$ $c = 8\ 9\ 10$		1	2	3	4	5
Clue Shelf	$\frac{a}{c}$	– / ~10	– / 9	– / 10	~O / ~8 9	~O / ~8
Distribution 1	$\frac{a}{c}$	– / ~10	– / 9	G / 10	F / 9	F / 9/10
Distribution 2	$\frac{a}{c}$	– / ~10	– / 9	– / 10	F / 9	G / 10
②	$\frac{a}{c}$	– / –	– / 9	G / 10	F / 9	F / 9

Now that we have exhausted the Specific question (that was way too fast!), it's time to move on to the General questions.

———————○———————

Let's look at question 3.

———————○———————

3. Which one of the following could be a site that dates from the eighth century?

A the site visited first   Ⓐ

B the site visited second   Ⓑ̶

C the site visited third   Ⓒ̶

D the site visited fourth   Ⓓ̶

E the site visited fifth   Ⓔ̶

Here's How to Crack It

This question asks which site could be dated to the 8th century. Looking at both of our distribution deductions, we can see that the only possibility is the first site. Select (A). Let's move on to the next question.

———————○———————

4. Which one of the following is a complete and accurate list of the sites each of which CANNOT be the site discovered by Gallagher?

(A) third, fourth, fifth   Ⓐ

(B) second, third, fourth   Ⓑ

(C) first, fourth, fifth   Ⓒ

(D) first, second, fifth   Ⓓ

(E) first, second, fourth   Ⓔ

Here's How to Crack It

This question is asking for which sites cannot be discovered by G. Let's begin with our first distribution deduction. We deduced that the third site could be discovered by G. Eliminate any answer choice with third, so (A) and (B) are gone. Now, look at the next distribution. We deduced that G could have discovered the fifth site instead, so now eliminate any remaining answer choices with fifth. Choices (C) and (D) are gone. The only remaining answer choice is (E), so lock it in.

Question 5 is a fairly open-ended *could be* question, so let's go back to the first question.

1. Which one of the following could be an accurate list of the discoverers of the five sites, listed in the order in which the sites are visited?

(A) Oliphant, Oliphant, Gallagher, Oliphant, Ferrara   Ⓐ

(B) Gallagher, Oliphant, Ferrara, Ferrara, Ferrara   Ⓑ

(C) Oliphant, Gallagher, Oliphant, Ferrara, Ferrara   Ⓒ

(D) Oliphant, Oliphant, Gallagher, Ferrara, Gallagher   Ⓓ

(E) Ferrara, Oliphant, Gallagher, Ferrara, Ferrara   Ⓔ

Here's How to Crack It

Remember that this was a General question masquerading as a Grab-a-Rule. However, we have some pretty awesome deductions. Let's use those and our rules to get rid of bad answers. We know that there can be only one G and he can be only on the third or fifth sites. Eliminate (B), (C), and (D). Next, in both of our distributions we deduced that F was fourth. Eliminate (A), so the answer must be (E).

―――――――――――○―――――――――――

Finally, let's look at question 5.

―――――――――――○―――――――――――

5. The tour group could visit at most how many sites that were discovered by Ferrara?

(A) one   Ⓐ

(B) two   Ⓑ

(C) three   Ⓒ

(D) four   Ⓓ

(E) five   Ⓔ

Here's How to Crack It

This question is asking us for the maximum number of Fs possible in the game. Let's look at our distributions. Distribution 1 has two Fs and one G. Therefore, we can eliminate (A) and (E). For questions about the maximum or minimum, use Process of Elimination and work down the list. Let's try four Fs using distribution 1.

$a = FGO$ $c = 8\ 9\ 10$		1	2	3	4	5
Clue Shelf	$\dfrac{a}{c}$	$\dfrac{\_\_}{\sim 10}$	$\dfrac{\_\_}{9}$	$\dfrac{\_\_}{10}$	$\dfrac{\sim O}{\sim 8\ \ 9}$	$\dfrac{\sim O}{\sim 8}$
Distribution 1	$\dfrac{a}{c}$	$\dfrac{\_\_}{\sim 10}$	$\dfrac{\_\_}{9}$	$\dfrac{G}{10}$	$\dfrac{F}{9}$	$\dfrac{F}{9/10}$
Distribution 2	$\dfrac{a}{c}$	$\dfrac{\_\_}{\sim 10}$	$\dfrac{\_\_}{9}$	$\dfrac{\_\_}{10}$	$\dfrac{F}{9}$	$\dfrac{G}{10}$
②	$\dfrac{a}{c}$	$\dfrac{\_\_}{}$	$\dfrac{\_\_}{9}$	$\dfrac{G}{10}$	$\dfrac{F}{9}$	$\dfrac{F}{9}$
⑤	$\dfrac{a}{c}$	$\dfrac{F}{9}$	$\dfrac{F}{9}$	$\dfrac{G}{10}$	$\dfrac{F}{9}$	$\dfrac{F}{9/10}$

The only thing you have to be careful of on a game like this is whether all elements must be used. However, there is no rule in either the setup or the clues that say O must discover a site or that all the researchers discovered at least one site. Therefore, this is a valid play. The answer is (D).

———————————⌒———————————

Answers for Game 2 (pages 266–267)

6. **A** PrepTest 45, Section 3, Question 7

7. **A** PrepTest 45, Section 3, Question 8

8. **A** PrepTest 45, Section 3, Question 9

9. **A** PrepTest 45, Section 3, Question 10

10. **C** PrepTest 45, Section 3, Question 11

11. **E** PrepTest 45, Section 3, Question 12

Explanation for Game 2

Ranking. Between the first and second game, this one is more straightforward. The 2D aspect of the game can be challenging, but all the elements are of the same type. This should be your first game. If you looked at all the games before choosing one, you may have done Game 3 first. Either way, this is one of the easier games and should be done sooner.

Step 1: Diagram and Inventory   This is a 2D ordering game. There are four chess games played in a row with two of the elements matched against one another. Since chess players face each other across the board, we recommend setting this game up as two rows, with each row being one of the two sides of a chessboard. There are six people but eight chess positions; therefore, there will be repeating elements. However, unlike Game 1, we are told that everyone must play at least one game, which limits the repeats to at most two elements. Here's what your final diagram should look like.

LNOPST	1	2	3	4
Clue Shelf	– –	– –	– –	– –

Step 2: Symbolize and Double-check   Clue 1 is a concrete clue and should be marked on the diagram.

LNOPST	🗴 1	2	🗴 3	4
Clue Shelf	– –	– –	– –	– –

Clue 2 is a concrete clue and should be marked on the diagram

LNOPST	1	2	3	4
Clue Shelf	– –	– –	– –	_L_ _

(column headers 1 and 3 are crossed out)

Clue 3 includes two pieces of information. First, N is limited to only one game. This should be crib-noted. The next is an antiblock. N cannot play against P. Make the antiblock vertical to match the diagram.

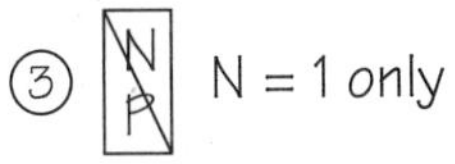

③ [N / P]   N = 1 only

Clue 4 provides quite a bit of information. We are told that S is a repeat but plays exactly 2 games and that O is limited to one game. Finally, we are given a long block since O plays between the two games that S plays. Crib-note the limits on O and S and create the horizontal block with lines in between to indicate different games.

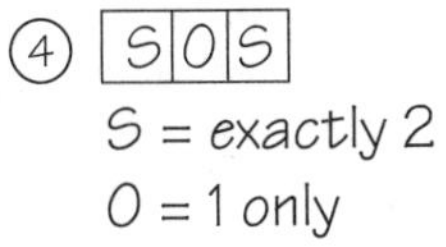

④ [S | O | S]
S = exactly 2
O = 1 only

Be sure to double-check the clues every time!

Step 3: Make Deductions and Size Up the Game

Hopefully, you went immediately to the long horizontal block. This clue uses up three of the four games. We should look for a distribution deduction. Let's place the SOS block in the first, second, and third spaces. L must be in the fourth space.

LNOPST	1	2	3	4
Clue Shelf	– –	– –	– –	_L_ _
Distribution 1	_S_	_O_ (T)	_S_	_L_ (T)

(column headers 1 and 3 are crossed out)

We don't know the location of T. N and P cannot play against each other with this distribution, so that's OK. There are no other deductions to be made, but we have to fill in only four players instead of eight.

Let's try another distribution. Put the SOS block in games two, three, and four. L still must be in game 4, so mark that on the diagram. Since game 4 is full and since everyone must play, T must play game 2. N and P cannot play against one another but each must play, so one of them must be in game 3 and the other in game 1.

LNOPST	~~1~~	2	~~3~~	4
Clue Shelf	– –	– –	– –	L / – –
Distribution 1	_ S _	_ O _ (T)	_ S _	_ L _ (T)
Distribution 2	N/P _	T / S	N/P / O	L / S

This second distribution is pretty restrictive, so you should expect more questions to focus on the first one. Since we have two solid distributions, let's dive into the questions.

Steps 4–6: Assess the Questions, Act, and Use Process of Elimination   Question 6 appears to be a Grab-a-Rule, so let's start there.

6. Which one of the following could be an accurate list of the contestants who play in each of the four games?

(A) first game: Pachai, Santiago; second game: Ofelia, Tyrone; third game: Pachai, Santiago; fourth game: Lulu, Nam

(B) first game: Lulu, Nam; second game: Pachai, Santiago; third game: Ofelia, Tyrone; fourth game: Lulu, Santiago

(C) first game: Pachai, Santiago; second game: Lulu, Tyrone; third game: Nam, Ofelia; fourth game: Lulu, Nam

(D) first game: Nam, Santiago; second game: Nam, Ofelia; third game: Pachai, Santiago; fourth game: Lulu, Tyrone

(E) first game: Lulu, Nam; second game: Santiago, Tyrone; third game: Lulu, Ofelia; fourth game: Pachai, Santiago

Here's How to Crack It

The one thing you have to be cautious of is the format of the answer choices. They tend to blur together, so take your time as you check these.

Choice (B) violates clue 1, so it is eliminated.
Choice (E) violates clue 2, so it is eliminated.
Choice (D) violates clue 3 (N = 1 only), so it is gone.
Choice (C) violates clue 4, so get rid of it too.
Choice (A) is the only one remaining, so it must be the correct answer. Lock it in and move on to the Specific questions.

8. If Tyrone plays in the fourth game, then which one of the following could be true?

   (A) Nam plays in the second game.   ⒜

   (B) Ofelia plays in the third game.   ⒝

   (C) Santiago plays in the second game.   ⒞

   (D) Nam plays a game against Lulu.   ⒟

   (E) Pachai plays a game against Lulu.   ⒠

Here's How to Crack It

This question tells us that T plays in the fourth game. Create a new line on your diagram. We have to use distribution 1, so carry that down as well.

LNOPST	1 (T̸)	2	3 (T̸)	4
Clue Shelf	_ _	_ _	_ _	L _
Distribution 1	_ S _	_ O _ (T)	_ S _	L _ (T)
Distribution 2	_ N/P _	T _ S	N/P _ O	L _ S
⑧	_ S _	_ O _	_ S _	L _ T

We don't have any information about the other three spaces, but let's look at the answer choices. We are asked what could be true, so let's eliminate any answer choice that must be false. Choice (A) could be true based upon our diagram. Hold on to it for now. Choice (B) is false. O can play only one game and she is playing second. Eliminate (B). Choice (C) is also false since S plays first and third, so get rid of it. Choice (D) is false. Based upon our diagram, N can be partnered only against S or O. Choice (E) is false for the same reason. The answer must be (A).

11. If Ofelia plays in the third game, which one of the following must be true?

(A) Lulu plays in the third game.

(B) Nam plays in the third game.

(C) Pachai plays in the first game.

(D) Pachai plays in the third game.

(E) Tyrone plays in the second game.

Ⓐ

Ⓑ

Ⓒ

Ⓓ

Ⓔ

Here's How to Crack It

Since O plays in the third game, we need to use the second distribution. This is good news since this one is much more restrictive! Carry down all the deductions from this distribution and dive into the answer choices.

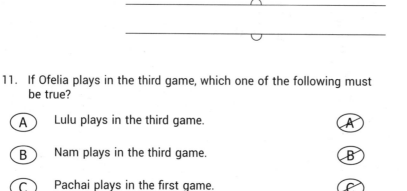

LNOPST	1	2	3	4
Clue Shelf	_ _	_ _	_ _	L _ _
Distribution 1	_ S _	_ O _ (T)	S _	L _ (T)
Distribution 2	N/P _	T _ S	N/P _ O	L _ S
⑧	_ S _	_ O _	S _	L _ T
⑪	_ _ _ N/P	_ S _ T	O _ N/P	S _ L

This question asks for what must be true, so let's see if our diagram matches an answer. N or P could play third, L cannot play third, and we have no information about game 1. However, we have T locked in to game 2 against S. Therefore, (E) must be true. Lock it in and move on.

The General questions on this game may have seemed daunting, but our distribution deductions should make short work of them.

Let's look at question 10.

---

10. Which one of the following is a complete and accurate list of the contestants who CANNOT play against Tyrone in any game?

(A) Lulu, Pachai

(B) Nam, Ofelia

(C) Nam, Pachai

(D) Nam, Santiago

(E) Ofelia, Pachai

(A) ~~(A)~~

(B) ~~(B)~~

(C) ~~(C)~~

(D) ~~(D)~~

(E) ~~(E)~~

Here's How to Crack It

This question asks for a list of people whom T cannot play against. We know from prior work that T can play against S and L, so eliminate any answer choice that includes those elements. Choices (A) and (D) are gone. Now, let's look at our deductions. T has a fixed location in distribution 2, so let's look at distribution 1. In this distribution, T could also play against either O or L (since T can be only in game 2 or 4). Here's an example of one possible play.

LNOPST	↗ 1	2	↗ 3	4
Clue Shelf	_ _	_ _	_ _	_L_
Distribution 1	_S_	_O_ (T)	_S_	_L_ (T)
Distribution 2	_N/P_	_T_ S	_N/P_ O	_L_ S
⑧	_S_	_O_	_S_	_L_ T
⑪	_ _ N/P	_S_ T	_O_ N/P	_S_ L
⑩	_S_ N	_O_ T	_S_ L	_L_ P

Therefore, you can eliminate answers with O in them. Choices (B) and (E) are also gone, leaving you with (C).

---

9. Which one of the following could be true?

(A) Pachai plays against Lulu in the first game.

(B) Pachai plays against Nam in the second game.

(C) Santiago plays against Ofelia in the second game.

(D) Pachai plays against Lulu in the third game.

(E) Nam plays against Santiago in the fourth game.

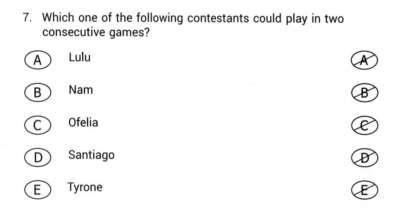

Here's How to Crack It

This question at first glance appears pretty open-ended and thus labor intensive. For questions like this, rely on the POE correlate. Since the answer *could be true*, you can eliminate all the answers which *must be false*. Let's use our two distributions to eliminate anything that must be false.

Choice (A) appears like it could fit into distribution 2, so leave it alone. Choice (B) cannot work in either distribution, so get rid of it. Choice (C) cannot work in either distribution, not to mention that it violates clue 4, so eliminate it. Choice (D) does not work in either distribution, so it too must be false—eliminate it. Choice (E) doesn't work in either distribution and violates clue 2, so it is gone. The only remaining answer is (A).

7. Which one of the following contestants could play in two consecutive games?

(A) Lulu

(B) Nam

(C) Ofelia

(D) Santiago

(E) Tyrone

Here's How to Crack It

This innocuous question is actually among the more challenging of this set, which is why we are explaining it last. The trick with this question is to rely more upon your rules than your deductions to eliminate bad answer choices. Our rules state that O and N play in exactly one game each. Therefore, they cannot play consecutive games. Eliminate (B) and (C). S plays two games, but our rules tell us that his games are separated by O, so eliminate (D). Finally, T cannot play on the odd-numbered games. Therefore, he cannot be consecutive either. Eliminate (E). The only remaining answer choice is (A).

Answers for Game 3 (pages 268–269)

12. **C** PrepTest 44, Section 3, Question 1

13. **D** PrepTest 44, Section 3, Question 2

14. **E** PrepTest 44, Section 3, Question 3

15. **E** PrepTest 44, Section 3, Question 4

16. **D** PrepTest 44, Section 3, Question 5

17. **A** PrepTest 44, Section 3, Question 6

Explanations for Game 3

Ranking. Of the four games, this one is the easiest. You should have done this either first or second.

Step 1: Diagram and Inventory   This is a straightforward 1D ordering game. The seven meetings form the core of the diagram and the five dignitaries are the elements. Since she has more meetings than there are dignitaries, we know that at least one element will be repeating.

FMRST	1	2	3	4	5	6	7
Clue Shelf							

Step 2: Symbolize and Double-check   Clue 1 is an element clue. This clue tells us that that she meets with all of the dignitaries and that F meets with her three times. The best way to symbolize this clue is to go to your clue shelf and add two more Fs to your elements.

FFFMRST	1	2	3	4	5	6	7

Clue 2 is an antiblock clue.

② [F̶F̶]

Clue 3 is a block clue. Be careful about the order of elements as you symbolize it.

③ [T|S]

Clue 4 is a concrete clue and should go on the diagram.

FFFMRST	1	2	3	4	5	6	7
Clue Shelf	M̶						M̶

Be sure to double-check each of these clues!

Step 3: Make Deductions and Size Up the Game   Hopefully from clue 1, you noticed that we now have seven elements for seven spaces. While this isn't a deduction per se, this game suddenly became easier. Clue 2 doesn't give us much information by itself. Clue 3 is a block clue. Since S immediately follows T, we can deduct that S cannot be first, and T cannot be last. Mark this on your diagram.

FFFMRST	1	2	3	4	5	6	7
Clue Shelf	M̶ S̶						M̶ T̶

Now look for multi-clue deductions. The large antiblock and block clue will interact. F has to always be at least one space away from every other F. There also has to be room for the TS block. Consider the following permutation.

FTSF_F

This uses up six of the seven spaces on the diagram. Here's another permutation.

F_F_FTS

This uses up all seven of the spaces in our diagram. There are two important deductions from this. The first is restriction. The elements F, T, and S are the most restrictive in the game. You want these on your diagram first. The other deduction is a little more subtle. Since the minimum space that is needed for these three elements is six spaces, you can deduce that F will be either first or last (or both) every time. Mark this on your diagram.

FFFMRST	1	2	3	4	5	6	7
Clue Shelf	M̶ S̶						M̶ T̶

Steps 4–6: Assess the Question, Act, and Use Process of Elimination

Question 12 appears to be a Grab-a-Rule. Dive into that one first.

12. Which one of the following could be the sequence of the meetings Garibaldi has with the dignitaries?

(A) Fuentes, Rhee, Tbahi, Soleimani, Fuentes, Matsuba, Rhee

(B) Fuentes, Tbahi, Soleimani, Matsuba, Fuentes, Fuentes, Rhee

(C) Fuentes, Rhee, Fuentes, Matsuba, Fuentes, Tbahi, Soleimani

(D) Fuentes, Tbahi, Matsuba, Fuentes, Soleimani, Rhee, Fuentes

(E) Fuentes, Tbahi, Soleimani, Fuentes, Rhee, Fuentes, Matsuba

Here's How to Crack It

Choice (A) violates clue 1, so eliminate it.

Choice (B) violates clue 2, so it is gone.

Choice (D) violates clue 3, so eliminate it.

Choice (E) violates clue 4, so get rid of it.

Choice (C) is the only remaining answer choice, so it must be correct.

Now, move on to the Specific questions. Remember to work the Specific questions that provide you with the most concrete information first. Let's look at question 16.

16 If Garibaldi's first meeting is with Tbahi, then Garibaldi's meeting with Rhee could be the

(A) second meeting

(B) third meeting

(C) fifth meeting

(D) sixth meeting

(E) seventh meeting

(A)

(B)

(C)

(D)

(E)

Here's How to Crack It

Begin by making a new row on the diagram, and place the information from the question. If T is first, then S must be second. Based on our deductions, F must be last. We can then work backward to find the other slots for F. Since F is last, the other two Fs must be in the fifth and third slots. This leaves only two spaces for M and R. These can alternate, so mark that on your diagram.

FFFMRST	1	2	3	4	5	6	7
Clue Shelf	M̷ S̷						M̷ T̷
⑯	T	S	F	M/R	F	M/R	F

The only possibly locations for the meeting with R are either the fourth or sixth meeting. Choice (D) matches this information. Lock it in and move on.

---

13. If Garibaldi's last meeting is with Rhee, then which one of the following could be true?

(A)   Garibaldi's second meeting is with Soleimani.   (A̸)

(B)   Garibaldi's third meeting is with Matsuba.   (B̸)

(C)   Garibaldi's fourth meeting is with Soleimani.   (C̸)

(D)   Garibaldi's fifth meeting is with Matsuba.   (D̸)

(E)   Garibaldi's sixth meeting is with Soleimani.   (E̸)

Here's How to Crack It

On this row of your diagram R should be placed last. Based on our deductions, F must therefore be first. In order for there to be space for the TS block, another F must be sixth. This leaves M, TS, and another F to be placed. This game is fairly constrained, so it is worth diagramming one of the possibilities. Let's arbitrarily put TS in slots second and third, so F must be fourth and M fifth.

FFFMRST	1	2	3	4	5	6	7
Clue Shelf	M̸ S̸						M̸ R̸
⑯	T	S	F	M/R	F	M/R	F
⑬	F	T	S	F	M	F	R

Happily, our diagram matches (D). There is only one other possible permutation for the TS block. Remember with *could be true* questions, if an answer choice matches a valid play on your diagram to lock it in with looking back.

---

14. If Garibaldi's second meeting is with Fuentes, then which one of the following is a complete and accurate list of the dignitaries with any one of whom Garibaldi's fourth meeting could be?

(A) Fuentes, Soleimani, Rhee   (Ⓐ)

(B) Matsuba, Rhee, Tbahi   (Ⓑ)

(C) Matsuba, Soleimani   (C̶)

(D) Rhee, Tbahi   (D̶)

(E) Fuentes, Soleimani   (E̶)

Here's How to Crack It

Go ahead and draw another line on your diagram with F second. Based on our deductions, F must also be last. M, T, S, and F cannot be first anymore. Therefore, R must be first.

FFFMRST	1	2	3	4	5	6	7
Clue Shelf	M̶ S̶						M̶ T̶
⑯	T	S	F	M/R	F	M/R	F
⑬	F	T	S	F	M	F	R
⑭	R	F					F

Since R doesn't repeat, it can never be fourth. Let's eliminate any answer choice with R in it: (A), (B), and (D) are gone. Now, we can apply a bit of test savvy to the remaining choices. Since S is in both answer choices, we can infer that S can be fourth. Therefore, let's put S elsewhere in the diagram. Put S sixth and T fifth. Due to the constraints in our rules, F must be fourth and M third.

FFFMRST	1	2	3	4	5	6	7
Clue Shelf	M̶ S̶						M̶ T̶
⑯	T	S	F	M/R	F	M/R	F
⑬	F	T	S	F	M	F	R
⑭	R	F					F
⑭E	R	F	M	F	T	S	F

We have now proven that F, too, can be fourth. This element must be included in the list. We can eliminate (C), so the answer is (E).

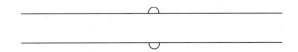

15. If Garibaldi's meeting with Rhee is the very next one after Garibaldi's meeting with Soleimani, then which one of the following must be true?

   (A) Garibaldi's third meeting is with Fuentes.

   (B) Garibaldi's fourth meeting is with Rhee.

   (C) Garibaldi's fifth meeting is with Fuentes.

   (D) Garibaldi's sixth meeting is with Rhee.

   (E) Garibaldi's seventh meeting is with Fuentes.

   Ⓐ Ⓑ ~~Ⓒ~~ ~~Ⓓ~~ Ⓔ

Here's How to Crack It

Question 15 creates a larger block by placing R immediately after S, which we know immediately follows T. The question is a bit challenging though since we don't know where the TSR block goes in the diagram. Put it on the clue shelf next to question 15 for now. We know from our deductions that F must be either first or last, so that's a good place to start. Don't stare at questions like this. Get your stylus moving as quickly as possible. Begin by placing F first and then the TSR block next. This forces F to be fifth and seventh, and M to be sixth.

FFFMRST	1	2	3	4	5	6	7
Clue Shelf	M̶ ∅̶						M̶ T̶
⑯	T	S	F	M/R	F	M/R	F
⑬	F	T	S	F	M	F	R
⑭	R	F					F
⑭E	R	F	M	F	T	S	F
⑮ [TSR]	F	T	S	R	F	M	F

This is a must-be-true question, so let's eliminate every answer choice we proved could be false. On this diagram the third meeting is with S, so eliminate (A). The sixth meeting is with M, so get rid of (D). Now, try another location. Let's begin with F first again, and skip a space to put F third. The TSR block must be in fourth, fifth, and sixth and the final F must be seventh. This means that M has to be second.

FFFMRST	1	2	3	4	5	6	7
Clue Shelf	M̶ ∅̶						M̶ T̶
⑯	T	S	F	M/R	F	M/R	F
⑬	F	T	S	F	M	F	R
⑭	R	F					F
⑭E	R	F	M	F	T	S	F
⑮ [TSR]	F	T	S	R	F	M	F
⑮	F	M	F	T	S	R	F

On this play, the fourth meeting is with T, so get rid of (B). The fifth meeting is S, so (C) is also gone. Choice (E) is the only remaining response.

Now for our final question on this game!

---

17. If Garibaldi's meeting with Matsuba is the very next meeting after Garibaldi's meeting with Rhee, then with which one of the following dignitaries must Garibaldi's fourth meeting be?

(A) Fuentes   (A)

(B) Matsuba   (B)

(C) Rhee   (C)

(D) Soleimani   (D)

(E) Tbahi   (E)

Here's How to Crack It

This question creates a second block. In addition to the TS block that exists in every question, now we have an RM block. We know from our deductions that the antiblock with F and the block clues are going to interact. We also know that F must be first or last. Let's begin with that as a diagram. Place F first. Now, we need to skip two spaces for one of the blocks, so place an F fourth. Next, we need to skip two more spaces, so F is seventh.

FFFMRST	1	2	3	4	5	6	7
Clue Shelf	~~M~~ ~~S~~						~~M~~ ~~T~~
⑯	T	S	F	M/R	F	M/R	F
⑬	F	T	S	F	M	F	R
⑭	R	F					F
⑭E	R	F	M	F	T	S	F
⑮ TSR	F	T	S	R	F	M	F
⑮	F	M	F	T	S	R	F
⑰ RM	F			F			F

(Arrow labeled F spans from column 1 to column 7.)

We don't know which space contains which block, but we should have enough information to answer this Must Be True question. The question asks which element must be fourth. According to the diagram that must be F. Lock in (A).

Answers for Game 4 (Pages 270–271)

18. **A** PrepTest 45, Section 3, Question 18

19. **A** PrepTest 45, Section 3, Question 19

20. **E** PrepTest 45, Section 3, Question 20

21. **C** PrepTest 45, Section 3, Question 21

22. **C** PrepTest 45, Section 3, Question 22

Explanations for Game 4

Ranking. Of the four games, this one is hands down the most complex and should be done last.

Step 1: Diagramming and Inventory   This is a twisted 1D grouping game. The three nations will form the core of your diagram with the crops being the elements. We also have known placeholders so those must be put into the diagram as well. We know from the setup that all elements will be used, but that one must repeat to fill all the spaces. The twist in the game appears in the clues and will be discussed there.

ORSTW	X	Y	Z
Clue Shelf	– –	– –	– –

Step 2: Symbolize and Double-check   Clue 1 is a standard antiblock on Grouping games.

$$ ① \boxed{\text{O\!\!\!/W}} $$

Clue 2 is a twisted conditional. This clue basically says that if X or Y exports S, then so does the other one. "If, but only if" statements can be diagrammed with an arrow going both ways.

$$ S_X \longleftrightarrow S_Y $$

The contrapositive of this statement is simply a negation. If S isn't in one, then it isn't in the other.

$$ \cancel{S}_X \longleftrightarrow \cancel{S}_Y $$

Clue 3 is a standard conditional with "and." Remember that "and" becomes "or" in the contrapositive.

$$ R_Y \rightarrow T_X \text{ and } T_Z $$
$$ {\sim}T_Z \text{ or } {\sim}T_X \rightarrow {\sim}R_Y $$

Clue 4 is also a twisted conditional. This basically tells us that if Z exports something, then Y doesn't.

$$Z \to {\sim}Y$$
$$Y \to {\sim}Z$$

Remember, always double-check your conditionals carefully to ensure that they move in the correct direction.

Step 3: Make Deductions and Size Up the Game

Apart from the contrapositives of the conditional statements above, there aren't many deductions to be found in this game. One important thing to note is that only one element can be repeated. Two of our clues force an element to double—clue 2 and clue 3. While we can't assume that S and T are the only elements that can double, these are fairly restrictive. The one deduction (we're using that term loosely here) that can be made from this restriction is that clue 2 and clue 3 cannot occur simultaneously. If they did, then we'd have to fill four spaces with two elements, not leaving enough room for the rest of the elements to be used at least once.

Steps 4–6: Assess the Question, Act, and Use Process of Elimination

Question 18 appears to be a Grab-a-Rule, so dive into that one.

18. Which one of the following could be an accurate list, for each of the nations, of the crops it exports?

(A) Nation X: oranges, rice; Nation Y: oranges, tea; Nation Z: soybeans, wheat   Ⓐ

(B) Nation X: oranges, tea; Nation Y: oranges, rice; Nation Z: soybeans, wheat   Ⓑ

(C) Nation X: oranges, wheat; Nation Y: oranges, tea; Nation Z: rice, soybeans   Ⓒ

(D) Nation X: rice, wheat; Nation Y: oranges, tea; Nation Z: oranges, soybeans   Ⓓ

(E) Nation X: soybeans, rice; Nation Y: oranges, tea; Nation Z: soybeans, wheat   Ⓔ

Here's How to Crack It

As always with this type of question, focus on a single clue and move through all the answer choices. Stay systematic—even if you think you see one that violates another clue, focus on one clue at a time.

Choice (C) violates clue 1, so eliminate it.
Choice (E) violates clue 2. X has S, but Y doesn't. Get rid of this one.
Choice (B) violates clue 3, so it is gone.
Choice (D) violates clue 4.
Choice (A) is the only one remaining, so select it and move on to the Specific questions.

19. If Nation X exports soybeans and tea, then which one of the following could be true?

(A) Nation Y exports oranges.

(B) Nation Y exports rice.

(C) Nation Y exports tea.

(D) Nation Z exports soybeans.

(E) Nation Z exports tea.

(A) (B) (C) (D) (E)

Here's How to Crack It

Create a new line on the diagram with the new information and then apply your rules. Since S is in X, it must also be exported by Y. Next, S is the only element that doubles, so we cannot have two Ts. Therefore, R must be on Z. O and W are the only elements left. There are no restrictions on which is which, so mark both in your diagram.

ORSTW	X	Y	Z
Clue Shelf	_ _	_ _	_ _
⑲	S T	S $^O/_W$	R $^O/_W$

We are looking for what *could be true*. The only flexibility in the diagram is with O and W, so the credited response will likely be one of those. Choice (A) says that Y has O. We see from our diagram that this could be true. Lock that answer in and move on.

20. If Nation Z exports tea and wheat, then which one of the following must be true?

(A) Nation X exports oranges.

(B) Nation X exports tea.

(C) Nation X exports wheat.

(D) Nation Y exports rice.

(E) Nation Y exports soybeans.

(A̶)

(B̶)

(C̶)

(D̶)

(E̶)

Here's How to Crack It

Begin your new row on the diagram with the new information, and apply your rules. T and W fill up Z leaving O, R, and S to be placed. S has to be in X or Y, so it must be in both. Put S in both X and Y. We can't have R in Y as a result, so R must be in X, leaving O to fill the last slot in Y.

ORSTW	X	Y	Z
Clue Shelf	_ _	_ _	_ _
⑲	S T	S O/w	R O/w
⑳	S R	S O	T W

This is actually a fully constrained diagram. The only answer choice that matches our diagram is (E). Lock it in.

The General questions on this game are pretty daunting. We do not have much prior work to aid us in POE. In situations such as this, mark off what you can and start playing the remaining answer choices. Remember to apply the correct POE approach as you do.

Let's begin with question 22.

22. Which one of the following pairs CANNOT be the two crops that Nation Y exports?

(A) oranges and rice

(B) oranges and soybeans

(C) rice and tea

(D) rice and wheat

(E) soybeans and wheat

(A)

(B)

(C)

(D)

(E)

Here's How to Crack It

First, focus on the question stem. This question asks for the pair that cannot be in Y. We can eliminate any answer choice that can be together in Y. Look at the prior work from questions 19 and 20. We know from each that S can be with O and W in Y. Thus, we can eliminate (B) and (E). We don't have any other prior work to go on, so it is time to plug in the answers. POE rules here tell us that if an answer choice is valid, then we eliminate it. The answer that doesn't work is correct. Let's start with (A).

Put O and R in Y. Clue 3 applies, so T must go in X and Z. T is our repeating element, so S must go in Z. Therefore, W is in X.

ORSTW	X	Y	Z
Clue Shelf	_ _	_ _	_ _
⑲	S T	S O/W	R O/W
⑳	S R	S O	T W
㉒A	T W	O R	T S

This is a valid diagram so eliminate (A). Now try (C).

Put R and T in Y. Clue 3 applies so T must also go in X and Z. You may already see the problem at this point. If not, put S in Z like before. We still have to place both O and W, but we have only one space remaining. Therefore, this play is not valid. Select answer (C).

ORSTW	X	Y	Z
Clue Shelf	– –	– –	– –
⑲	S T	S O/w	R O/w
⑳	S R	S O	T W
22A	T W	O R	T S
~~22C~~	~~T ?~~	~~R T~~	~~T S~~

Be sure to draw a line through the invalid play so that you don't get confused and use bad information.

———————————————◯———————————————

We now have a little more work we can use on question 21.

———————————————◯———————————————

21. It CANNOT be the case that both Nation X and Nation Z export which one of the following crops?

   (A) oranges   (A̶)

   (B) rice   (B̶)

   (C) soybeans   (C̶)

   (D) tea   (D̶)

   (E) wheat   (E̶)

Here's How to Crack It

Question 21 asks for the single element that cannot be in both X and Z. We know from our play of 22 (A) that T can be, so eliminate (D). Unfortunately, nothing else can be eliminated, so let's play this one. Just like the previous diagram, we are looking for the one answer that does not work. We will get rid of the ones that are valid.

Start with (A). Put O in both X and Z. Since O is the repeat, we don't want rule 2 or rule 3 to apply. Put S in Z and R in X. Finally, our two remaining elements, T and W, must go in Y.

ORSTW	X	Y	Z
Clue Shelf	– –	– –	– –
⑲	S T	S ⁰/_w	R ⁰/_w
⑳	S R	S O	T W
㉒A	T W	O R	T S
~~㉒C~~	~~T ?~~	~~R T~~	~~T S~~
㉑A	O R	T W	O S

This doesn't break any rules so eliminate it and move on to (B). This time put R in X and Z. As above, we don't want clue 2 or 3 to kick in, so put S in Z. O and W cannot be together, so T must be in Y and O/W in X and W/O in Y.

ORSTW	X	Y	Z
Clue Shelf	– –	– –	– –
⑲	S T	S ⁰/_w	R ⁰/_w
⑳	S R	S O	T W
㉒A	T W	O R	T S
~~㉒C~~	~~T ?~~	~~R T~~	~~T S~~
㉑A	O R	T W	O S
㉑B	R ⁰/_w	T ⁰/_w	R S

This is a valid play, so eliminate (B). Onward to (C). The good news is that this is our last plug in. If (C) doesn't work, we lock it in. If (C) works, we will eliminate it and select the only remaining answer, (E). Put S in both X and Z. Clue 2 now kicks in, so S must go in Y as well. This is a problem: we have 4 elements that still need placing but only 3 spots for them. This answer choice does not work, so select (C).

ORSTW	X	Y	Z
Clue Shelf	– –	– –	– –
⑲	S T	S $^O/_W$	R $^O/_W$
⑳	S R	S O	T W
22A	T W	O R	T S
22C	T ?	R T	T S
21A	O R	T W	O S
21B	R $^O/_W$	T $^O/_W$	R S
21C	S	S	S

CHAPTER 4: READING COMPREHENSION

Answers for Passage (Pages 339–341)

1. **B** PrepTest 44, Section 1, Question 15

2. **A** PrepTest 44, Section 1, Question 16

3. **C** PrepTest 44, Section 1, Question 17

4. **E** PrepTest 44, Section 1, Question 18

5. **A** PrepTest 44, Section 1, Question 19

6. **D** PrepTest 44, Section 1, Question 20

Explanations

Step 1: Prepare

Note: Science passages on the LSAT (usually one of the four will be on a scientific topic) tend to be especially packed with detail. They also tend to contain information that is less familiar, and even a little scary, to the average LSAT taker. Resist the temptation to actually learn the science in any depth. And, it is especially important to avoid getting caught up in going through the details over and over the first time through the passage until you feel as if you have understood every little thing, or even fully grasped all of the scientific concepts. Science passages will be structured like any other LSAT passage, and the questions will be testing the same kinds of skills (and as always, never testing outside knowledge of the topic). So, prepare it like any other RC passage: look for key conclusions, transitions, and expressions of the author's opinion, define the central theme or purpose of each paragraph and how those paragraphs relate to each other, and articulate the basic Bottom Line of the passage. If a question asks about some small detail, or about a concept you have not yet fully understood, go back to the passage with that specific issue in mind. And remember that POE is still (perhaps even more so) your friend. Often you don't need to fully understand the right answer as long you have good reasons to eliminate the other four.

Paragraph 1 Main Point: Rita Levi-Montalcini's discovery of a substance that regulates nerve cells (NGF) was a key development in biochemistry.

Paragraph 2 Main Point: Her hypotheses and experiments that led to this discovery.

Paragraph 3 Main Point: What she and others since have discovered about how NGF works.

Bottom Line: Rita Levi-Montalcini's discovery of a substance that regulates nerve cells was a crucial development in the history of biochemistry.

Note: In this passage, the Bottom Line is laid out in the first paragraph. The rest of the passage is a lot of detail about what she discovered and how she discovered it. On your first reading, keep your focus on the larger purpose of those second (the "how") and third paragraphs (the "what"), and don't get bogged down in the details.

Steps 2–4: Assess, Act, and Answer

Note: In the explanations for these questions and answer choices, we will put special emphasis on self-evaluation: if you picked or lingered over a wrong answer, why? And, what could you have done to avoid it or eliminate it faster?

1. Which one of the following most accurately expresses the main point of the passage?

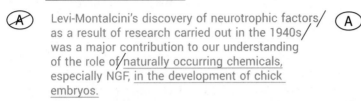

(A) Levi-Montalcini's discovery of neurotrophic factors as a result of research carried out in the 1940s was a major contribution to our understanding of the role of naturally occurring chemicals, especially NGF, in the development of chick embryos.

(B) Levi-Montalcini's discovery of NGF, a neurotrophic factor that stimulates the development of some types of nerve tissue and whose presence or absence in surrounding cells helps determine whether particular nerve cells will survive, was a pivotal development in biochemistry.

(C) NGF, which is necessary for the survival and proper functioning of nerve cells, was discovered by Levi-Montalcini in a series of experiments using the technique of tissue culture, which she devised in the 1940s.

(D) Partly as a result of Levi-Montalcini's research it has been found that NGF and other neurotrophic factors are produced only by tissues to which nerves are already connected and that the presence of these factors is necessary for the health and proper functioning of nervous systems.

(E) NGF, a chemical that was discovered by Levi-Montalcini, directs the growth of nerve cells toward the cells with which they must connect and ensures the survival of those nerve cells throughout the life of the organism except when the organism produces anti-NGF antibodies.

Here's How to Crack It

Step 2: Assess

This is a Big Picture: Main Point question

Step 3: Act

Remind yourself of your Bottom Line: "Rita Levi-Montalcini's discovery of a substance that regulates nerve cells was a crucial development in the history of biochemistry."

Step 4: Answer

Note: Even though this is not a Structure: Organization question, breaking down the answer choices as you would for that question type can help you to (1) understand what each part and the whole of the choice is saying, and (2) look for pieces that have gone wrong.

Choice (A) is basically accurate in each of its pieces, but the emphasis is wrong. Yes, NGF is a naturally occurring chemical, but the importance of her discovery related to neurotrophic and cell-growth factors, not naturally occurring chemicals as a whole. Furthermore, while she experimented on chick embryos (paragraph 2), the value of her research was not primarily in discovering how NGF works in chicks, but how it works in general. You may well have left this answer in contention in your first cut through the choices, but once you compared it to the correct answer, you would see the problem. If you picked this choice, ask yourself some questions such as, did you paraphrase (A) to understand what it was really saying? Did you define the Bottom Line before POE? Did you compare choices to each other once you were down to two or three choices?

Choice (B) accurately represents the passage in each of its parts, has the right focus, and is essentially what we were looking for (along with some extra detail) with our Bottom Line. So, at this point you would leave it in and move on to the next choice.

Choice (C), along with a bit of an accuracy issue (the passage says that she used, but not that she devised the technique of tissue culture) has a similar problem as (A) in its focus. In this case, it says nothing about the fact that L-M's discovery of NGF was "a crucial development in the history of biochemistry" (paragraph 1).

Choice (D) has a variety of focus and accuracy issues as well. Along with the fact that it does not include a mention of the importance of L-M's discovery, it states that NGF is "produced only by tissues to which nerves are already connected," whereas the passage states that "nerve cells apparently receive this growth factor locally from the cells of muscles or other organs *to which they will form* connections…" [emphasis added]. This is the first of the "two roles" mentioned in the last paragraph (and "two roles" would have deserved annotation in your prep of the passage): to "initially…direct the developing nerve processes toward the correct, specific target cells with which they must connect…." If you selected this answer, ask yourself if you not only defined and reminded yourself of the Bottom Line of the passage, but if you broke down the choice and made sure that each piece was accurate.

Choice (E) is a common type of wrong answer on a Big Picture question: all the parts are more or less accurate (although "ensures" is a bit too strong), but it is too narrow in scope to be the main idea. This choice just tells you what NGF does, but nothing about the process or importance of L-M's discovery. If you selected (E), go back now and compare it with (B). That comparison makes it clear that while (E) just mentions that this was L-M's discovery, (B) emphasizes its importance in a historical context, just as the author does.

This leaves you with (B) as the credited response.

2. Based on the passage, the author would be most likely to believe that Levi-Montalcini's discovery of NGF is noteworthy primarily because it

(A) paved the way for more specific knowledge of the processes governing the development of the nervous system

(B) demonstrated that a then new laboratory technique could yield important and unanticipated experimental results

(C) confirmed the hypothesis that many of a developing organism's immature nerve cells are normally programmed to die

(D) indicated that this substance stimulates observable biochemical reactions in the tissues of different species

(E) identified a specific substance, produced by mouse tumors, that can be used to stimulate nerve cell growth

Here's How to Crack It

Step 2: Assess

The wording "Based on the passage, the author would be most likely to believe" tells you that this is an Extract: Inference question. And, in this case, you need to take note of one thing in particular: it is asking about what the *primary* significance of L-M's discovery was.

Step 3: Act

Even though this is an Extract: Inference question, you have already answered it as part of your Bottom Line. That is, L-M's work was so important because of the role it played in "the history of biochemistry." Keeping this firmly in mind will help you to avoid a lot of trap answers.

Step 4: Answer

Choice (A) fits well with our own answer, and it corresponds to what the author said not only in the first paragraph about the history of biochemistry, but also in the last paragraph where the author mentions that "NGF was the first of many cell-growth factors to be found...Through Levi-Montalcini's work and other subsequent research it has been determined that this substance is present in many tissues..." etc. So, you would leave in (A) and move on to the next answer.

Choice (B) is a bit tricky; you might say that this is a true statement based on the passage; tissue culture was in fact a new lab technique, and it did in fact play a role in L-M's important findings. But, does it answer the question? That is, does the author make a big deal out of L-M's use of tissue culture, to the point that it would be the main reason why L-M's work was noteworthy? No, it is just mentioned in passing. If you picked this choice, ask yourself if you read the question carefully, if you noted (and perhaps even annotated) the words "noteworthy primarily because," and if you thought carefully about what the question is really asking before you started in the answer choices.

Choice (C) is even trickier than (B), since not only is it a true statement (see paragraph 1), but it references something that seems much more central to L-M's findings than (B). It would be entirely reasonable to keep this choice in during your first cut through the choices, but you would eventually want to come back, compare it with (A) and your Bottom Line, and see that the place of L-M's discovery of NGF in the history of science is what the author sees as truly important, not just the nature of the discovery itself.

Choice (D) is perhaps a bit easier to eliminate than (C), but still potentially a little attractive given that at least two species (mice and chicks) are mentioned in the passage. But the author never suggests that discovering that NGF acts on or within different species was of primary noteworthiness.

Choice (E) is also attractive because it is absolutely true according to the passage, but this is basically what NGF is, not the reason the author thinks that the discovery of NGF was especially noteworthy. So again, this is the right answer to the wrong question; if you selected (E), ask yourself how carefully you read the question, and if you paraphrased the question task and issue before POE.

Therefore, (A) is the only statement that expresses what the author sees as the true importance of L-M's work.

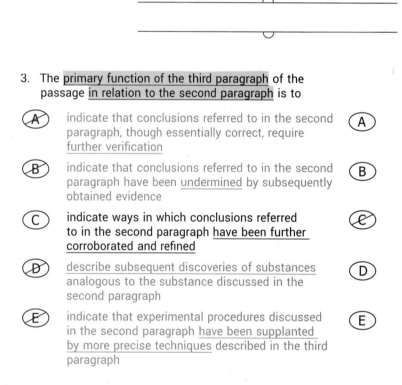

3. The primary function of the third paragraph of the passage in relation to the second paragraph is to

(A) indicate that conclusions referred to in the second paragraph, though essentially correct, require further verification

(B) indicate that conclusions referred to in the second paragraph have been undermined by subsequently obtained evidence

(C) indicate ways in which conclusions referred to in the second paragraph have been further corroborated and refined

(D) describe subsequent discoveries of substances analogous to the substance discussed in the second paragraph

(E) indicate that experimental procedures discussed in the second paragraph have been supplanted by more precise techniques described in the third paragraph

Here's How to Crack It

Step 2: Assess

This is a Structure: Function question, asking specifically about how the second paragraph relates to the third. (Note: The logic of this question is very similar to Comparative Reading passage questions that ask about the relationship between Passage A and Passage B.)

Step 3: Act

Use your existing main points from preparing the passage to answer in your own words first. We defined the main point of paragraph 2 as "Her (L-M's) hypotheses and experiments that led to this discovery (of NGF)," and the main point of paragraph 3 as "What she and others since have discovered about how NGF works." So, a reasonable answer in your own words would be "Paragraph 3 describes the findings regarding NGF of L-M's work and of other subsequent research."

Step 4: Answer

Choice (A) has the wrong tone (as in, a negative tone) and content in describing the relationship between the two paragraphs. The answer choice indicates that the third paragraph discusses ways in which L-M's conclusions described in paragraph 2 were and still are insufficiently supported. However, the third paragraph actually does the opposite; it indicates that L-M's conclusions were correct and were supported by later work.

Choice (B) goes even further in the wrong direction than (A). Paragraph 3 indicates that L-M's conclusions were correct, while this choice indicates that the third paragraph calls them into question. If you selected either (A) or (B), think about if you asked yourself, based on the actual wording of the text, whether the two paragraphs are consistent or inconsistent with each other.

Choice (C) matches what we have already defined as, based on the actual text, the relationship between the two paragraphs. So, you would leave it in and go on to the next answer.

Choice (D) starts off in a promising way, and it may have been the hardest choice to eliminate. The author does in fact talk about subsequent discoveries in paragraph 3, and this choice represents the relationship between the two paragraphs in a more positive light than do (A) or (B). And it isn't necessarily easy to decide if the substances subsequently discovered were in fact "analogous" (as in, other cell growth factors that do similar but not identical things as NGF), or if it would be more accurate to describe them as identical (in that they are all cell-growth factors). So, don't get stuck on this issue—go back to the question and ask again, what is the exact wording and task? Even if (D) did accurately describe part of the content of paragraph 3, is the discovery of other cell-growth factors the *primary* issue? No, that would be too narrow; discovery of other such substances is mentioned only as a part of the larger discussion in the paragraph. Therefore, you can eliminate (D), perhaps only after comparing it with (C), on that basis.

Choice (E) has in part the same problem as (A) and (B): it indicates a negative relationship between the two paragraphs (in that it suggests that the techniques described in paragraph 2 were not as good as later techniques). Also, there is just no evidence in the third paragraph that improved procedures were ever created or used. If you selected this answer, ask yourself if you (1) thoughtfully defined the relationship between the two paragraphs before POE, and (2) if you looked for concrete evidence in the third paragraph to support the statement regarding experimental procedures (or, perhaps instead just assumed that they must have come up with some kind of refinements as they continued to make progress).

This leaves you with (C) as the best match.

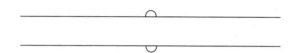

4. Information in the passage most strongly supports which one of the following?

(A) Nerve cells in excess of those that are needed by the organism in which they develop eventually produce anti-NGF antibodies to suppress the effects of NGF.

(B) Nerve cells that grow in the absence of NGF are less numerous than, but qualitatively identical to, those that grow in the presence of NGF.

(C) Few of the nerve cells that connect with target cells toward which NGF directs them are needed by the organism in which they develop.

(D) Some of the nerve cells that grow in the presence of NGF are eventually converted to other types of living tissue by neurotrophic factors.

(E) Some of the nerve cells that grow in an embryo do not connect with any particular target cells.

(A) (B) (C) (D) (E)

Here's How to Crack It

Step 2: Assess

Question that ask you which statement is most strongly supported by the passage are Extract: Inference questions.

Step 3: Act

There are no lead words in the question referring to specific passage content. So, once you have translated the question, you should go directly to the choices, and then back to the passage as needed as you go through POE.

Step 4: Answer

Choice (A) is half right but half wrong; the first part is fine, but the second part goes bad. The passage does not say that excess nerve cells *always themselves produce* antibodies to NGF (in essence, killing themselves off). Rather, the last paragraph states that some nerve cells *may* die if they *encounter* anti-NGF antibodies. If you selected this choice, ask yourself if you read it word for word and made sure that every word was supported by the passage.

Choice (B) introduces a comparison that is not in the passage, and is also too extreme. While the author does indicate that NGF is not always present, and that some nerve cells may grow in the absence of NGF, the text does not indicate (1) how numerous or abundant these nerve cells would be, or (2) if they are qualitatively *identical*.

Choice (C), like (A), requires careful word-for-word reading to see where it goes wrong. The answer states that "Few of the nerve cells *that connect* with target cells" [emphasis added] are needed, whereas the passage suggests that perhaps few of the nerve cells that grow in the first place *are needed to connect*. If you happened to be stuck between (C) and (E), a comparison between the two choices would point out the difference, and that the issue is that not all nerve cells ever eventually connect.

Choice (D) brings in information that is never mentioned in the passage: the conversion of nerve cells to other types of tissue. This choice is out of scope. If you selected it, ask yourself if you perhaps just glanced back at the last paragraph, saw that tissues other than nerve cells are mentioned, and then made up a connection on your own.

Choice (E) takes you back to the second paragraph, where the author introduces L-M's theory that some nerve cells are programmed to die, and her research based in this hypothesis. In the first paragraph, the passage describes L-M's finding that embryos "produce many more nerve cells than are finally required, the number that survives eventually adjusting itself to the volume of tissue to be supplied with nerves." Later, in paragraph 3, the author further describes this in terms of connections between nerve cells and other tissues.

Therefore, (E) is the only one that is fully supported by information in the passage.

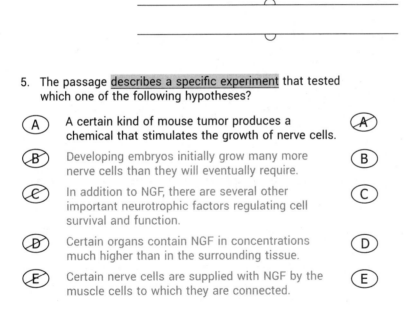

5. The passage describes a specific experiment that tested which one of the following hypotheses?

   (A) A certain kind of mouse tumor produces a chemical that stimulates the growth of nerve cells.

   (B) Developing embryos initially grow many more nerve cells than they will eventually require.

   (C) In addition to NGF, there are several other important neurotrophic factors regulating cell survival and function.

   (D) Certain organs contain NGF in concentrations much higher than in the surrounding tissue.

   (E) Certain nerve cells are supplied with NGF by the muscle cells to which they are connected.

Here's How to Crack It

Step 2: Assess

This is an Extract: Retrieval question. The task is to find a hypothesis in the answer choices that is explicitly described in the passage as being tested by a specific experiment.

Step 3: Act

You may already have an idea based on preparing the passage (especially if you previewed the questions) that the only specific experiment described was in paragraph 2: L-M's work with chick embryos that tested her hypothesis that "a chemical produced by the [mouse] tumors was responsible for the observed growth." If so, you pretty much know what you are looking for in the correct answer. If not, then go back to the passage as you go through POE and see if you can point to (1) the hypothesis, and (2) a specific experiment that was done to test it.

Step 4: Answer

Note: While this question can and should be attacked very straightforwardly, it is possible to get caught up in deciding whether or not a choice is true, or if each really qualifies as a hypothesis, rather than keeping the focus on the question task: finding the one tested by a *specific experiment*. We will see that all of these choices are essentially discussed in the passage, and in fact, it is finding the experiment that is the key and the easiest approach. If you picked a wrong answer, or spent too much time on the question, ask yourself if you (1) identified, and (2) kept your focus on the real and full question task.

Choice (A) is the experiment that you may already have had in mind from the second paragraph. So, keep it and go through the rest of the choices.

Choice (B) may have been the most difficult to eliminate, since the passage does state that L-M did "research" testing something very much like this hypothesis. However, no *specific* experiment is described. If you were unsure what qualifies as a "specific experiment," a comparison between (A) and (B) would lead you to back to (A) as the one tested by a truly specific experiment.

Choice (C) is true according to the beginning of paragraph 3 (although it is not described as a hypothesis), but there is no specific experiment mentioned.

Choice (D) has the same problem as (C). It is suggested (although not described as a hypothesis) in the passage, but there is no specific experiment.

Finally, (E) fails on the same basis as well: true (although not described as a hypothesis), but there is no experiment.

This leaves you with (A) as the only one that actually answers the question being asked.

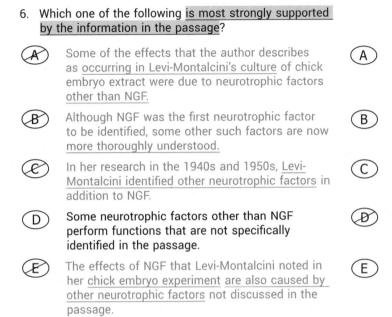

6. Which one of the following is most strongly supported by the information in the passage?

(A) Some of the effects that the author describes as occurring in Levi-Montalcini's culture of chick embryo extract were due to neurotrophic factors other than NGF.

(B) Although NGF was the first neurotrophic factor to be identified, some other such factors are now more thoroughly understood.

(C) In her research in the 1940s and 1950s, Levi-Montalcini identified other neurotrophic factors in addition to NGF.

(D) **Some neurotrophic factors other than NGF perform functions that are not specifically identified in the passage.**

(E) The effects of NGF that Levi-Montalcini noted in her chick embryo experiment are also caused by other neurotrophic factors not discussed in the passage.

Here's How to Crack It

Step 2: Assess

Note that this question is worded much the same as the fourth question on this passage. This is also an Extract: Inference question, with no specific passage reference in the question stem.

Step 3: Act

Since you don't yet know which parts of the passage will be relevant, go directly to POE.

Step 4: Answer

Note: Managing the answer choices on this question is all about (1) careful reading of each choice, and (2) staying within the scope of what is explicitly and directly described in the passage.

Choice (A) is out of scope. You know that L-M identified NGF as a factor in her chick experiments, but there is no evidence that other neurotrophic factors were also involved.

Choice (B) introduces a comparison and a judgment that is not supported by the passage. You do know from the beginning of the third paragraph that NGF was the first neurotrophic factor to be identified, and from the beginning of the passage that other such factors have also been identified, but there is no indication that these other factors are now "more thoroughly understood" than NGF.

Choice (C) has the same problematic word that invalidated (A): "other." You know from the passage only that L-M identified NGF and that other such factors have also been identified; you do not know that L-M *herself* identified other neurotrophic factors.

Choice (D) finds support in the first two sentences of the passage: "The survival of nerve cells, as well as their performance of some specialized functions, is regulated by *chemicals known as neurotrophic factors*, which are produced in the bodies of animals, including humans. Rita Levi-Montalcini's discovery in the 1950s of the *first of these agents*, a hormonelike substance now known as NGF…" [emphasis added]. That tells you that there are neurotrophic factors other than NGF, but the passage never does go on to specifically identify their function.

Choice (E) has the same flaw as (A), (B), and (C): it brings in additional elements that are not discussed in the passage. There is no evidence that the effects of NGF observed by L-M in her experiment are *also* caused by *other* (identified) neurotrophic factors.

This leaves you with (D) as the only answer that is directly and fully supported by the passage.

Notes